T0015254

— CONTENTS —

THE

50 GREATEST
PLAYERS

IN

PITTSBURGH
STEELERS

HISTORY

ROBERT W. COHEN

LYONS
PRESS

Essex, Connecticut

An imprint of Globe Pequot, the trade division of
The Rowman & Littlefield Publishing Group, Inc.
4501 Forbes Blvd., Ste. 200
Lanham, MD 20706
www.rowman.com

Distributed by NATIONAL BOOK NETWORK

Copyright © 2019 Robert W. Cohen

Cover photographs courtesy of the Pittsburgh Steelers

All rights reserved. No part of this book may be reproduced in any form or by any electronic or mechanical means, including information storage and retrieval systems, without written permission from the publisher, except by a reviewer who may quote passages in a review.

British Library Cataloguing in Publication Information available

Library of Congress Cataloging-in-Publication Data

Names: Cohen, Robert W., author.
Title: The 50 greatest players in Pittsburgh Steelers history / Robert W. Cohen.
Description: Guilford, Connecticut : Lyons Press, [2019] | Includes bibliographical references.
Identifiers: LCCN 2019010590 (print) | LCCN 2019013923 (ebook) | ISBN 9781493037940 (e-book) | ISBN 9781493037933 (hardback : alk. paper) | ISBN 9781493037940 (ebk.) | ISBN 9781493071166 (paperback : alk. paper)
Subjects: LCSH: Pittsburgh Steelers (Football team)—History. | Football players—Rating of—United States.
Classification: LCC GV956.P57 (ebook) | LCC GV956.P57 C63 2019 (print) | DDC
796.332/640974886—dc23
LC record available at https://lccn.loc.gov/2019010590

♾™ The paper used in this publication meets the minimum requirements of American National Standard for Information Sciences—Permanence of Paper for Printed Library Materials, ANSI/NISO Z39.48-1992.

ACKNOWLEDGMENTS

I would like to express my gratitude to Karl Roser of the Pittsburgh Steelers, who supplied me with many of the photos included in this book.

I also wish to thank Troy Kinunen of MEARSonlineauctions.com, Kate of RMYAuctions.com, LegendaryAuctions.com, CSU Athletics, PristineAuction.com, SportsMemorabilia.com, George A. Kitrinos, Keith Allison, Michael Rooney, Jeffrey Beall, Douglas A. Smith, Scot Tumlin, and Paula Lively, each of whom generously contributed to the photographic content of this work.

— INTRODUCTION —

THE STEELER LEGACY

Originally founded by Pittsburgh native Arthur J. Rooney, a sports organizer and promoter who made much of his fortune handicapping and placing bets on horse racing, the Pittsburgh Steelers came into existence on July 8, 1933, when the NFL accepted the $2,500 franchise fee Rooney submitted to the league office. Initially dubbed the "Pirates" in deference to Pittsburgh's more established baseball team, the city's NFL representative spent its formative years calling Forbes Field home as it struggled to gain a foothold in the Steel City. Compiling an overall record of just 25-71-6 their first nine years in the league, the Pirates annually finished at, or near, the bottom of the NFL's Eastern Division, where they resided from 1933 to 1949, as Forrest "Jap" Douds (1933), Luby DiMeolo (1934), Joe Bach (1935–1936), Johnny Blood (1937–1939), and Walt Kiesling (1939–1942) all took turns coaching the team. Meanwhile, with America in the depths of the Great Depression, the Pirates proved to be a financial drain on Rooney, who often took his team to such neutral cities as Johnstown and Latrobe in Pennsylvania, Youngstown, Louisville, and New Orleans to avoid competing directly against baseball and college football in Pittsburgh. Nevertheless, Rooney remained determined to make professional football a success in his hometown, with his background in sports promotion eventually paying huge dividends.

Seeking to generate interest in his faltering franchise, Rooney collaborated with the *Pittsburgh Post-Gazette* prior to the start of the 1940 campaign to run a contest dedicated to finding a new name for his team. Subsequently renamed the "Steelers" as a way of paying homage to the city's largest industry of producing steel, the Pittsburgh eleven began competing under its new moniker that year, although the on-field results remained very much the same, with the Steelers finishing just 2-7-2 in 1940.

Growing increasingly frustrated with the lack of success experienced by his ball club, Rooney, who had earlier rejected several offers to relocate or sell the team, finally relented in December 1940 and sold the Steelers to Alexis Thompson, a 26-year-old, New York–based Yale graduate who stood to inherit a fortune in steel. Rooney then immediately invested his windfall in a 50 percent interest in the Philadelphia Eagles, who were owned by his friend, Bert Bell. Rooney, Bell, and Thompson subsequently pooled the rosters of the two squads and essentially conducted a mini-draft that distributed the talent between the teams. However, when Rooney learned that Thompson intended to relocate his club, which would have left his beloved city of Pittsburgh without a football team, he suggested that the two men trade territories, with Rooney's and Bell's Eagles moving to Pittsburgh, where they became the Steelers, and Thompson's newly named Iron Men going to Philadelphia, where they assumed the Eagles moniker. Since all of this occurred during the offseason, the NFL considers the Rooney reign unbroken, with the transaction, which amounted in the end to Bell selling the Eagles and purchasing half-interest in the Steelers, subsequently being termed the "Pennsylvania Polka."

Even with all the machinations, the Steelers continued to struggle on the field in 1941, compiling a record of 1-9-1 that left them last in the NFL's Eastern Division for the second time in four seasons. However, they began to show signs of life in 1942, finishing second in the division with a record of 7-4 following the arrival of "triple-threat" halfback Bill Dudley, who they selected with the first overall pick of that year's NFL Draft. Unfortunately, any momentum the Steelers gained that season proved to be short-lived since the nation's involvement in World War II ended up depleting their roster, forcing them to spend the next two seasons merging with other teams. After merging with the Eagles in 1943 to form a Phil-Pitt "Steagles" squad that posted a record of 5-4-1, the Steelers combined their roster with that of the Chicago Cardinals the following year, with the Card-Pitt "Carpets" compiling a mark of just 2-8. On their own once again in 1945, the Steelers finished 2-8 under new head coach Jim Leonard, who Rooney replaced with former University of Pittsburgh and Brooklyn Dodgers head coach Jock Sutherland at season's end.

With Bill Dudley earning league MVP honors after he returned from the military in 1946, the Steelers fared much better under Sutherland, finishing 5-5-1 in his first year at the helm, before posting a mark of 8-4 that tied them with Philadelphia for first place in the division the following year. However, their season ended abruptly when they lost to the Eagles by a score of 21–0 in a one-game playoff.

After dealing Dudley to the Detroit Lions and losing Sutherland to a brain tumor that took his life during the subsequent offseason, the Steelers entered into an extended period of mediocrity that saw them finish above .500 just five times between 1948 and 1971, a period during which Pitt Stadium gradually replaced Forbes Field as their home venue. Coached at different times by John Michelosen (1948–1951), Joe Bach (1952–1953), Walt Kiesling (1954–1956), Buddy Parker (1957–1964), Mike Nixon (1965), and Bill Austin (1966–1968), the Steelers played their best ball under Parker, compiling an overall mark of 51-43-6 with him at the helm, including a record of 9-5 in 1962 that earned them a second-place finish in the NFL's Eastern Conference. Yet, even as the Steelers continued to toil in mediocrity, several players distinguished themselves while wearing the Black and Gold, with defensive lineman Dale Dodrill, running back John Henry Johnson, defensive back Jack Butler, receivers Elbie Nickel and Buddy Dial, and Hall of Fame defensive tackle Ernie Stautner heading the list.

Things finally began to turn around in Pittsburgh shortly after the Steelers hired Chuck Noll to be their new head coach in 1969 and moved into newly built Three Rivers Stadium one year later. Although the Steelers compiled a losing record in each of their first three seasons under Noll, finishing a league-worst 1-13 his first year at the helm, his exceptional leadership ability, strong attention to detail, and astute player evaluation enabled them to establish a culture of winning before long. After using the fourth overall pick of the 1969 NFL Draft to select future Hall of Fame defensive tackle "Mean" Joe Greene, Noll added fellow Canton-bound stars Terry Bradshaw, Mel Blount, Jack Ham, Franco Harris, Mike Webster, Lynn Swann, John Stallworth, and Jack Lambert in subsequent drafts, turning the Steelers into an NFL powerhouse. After joining the Cleveland Browns, Baltimore Colts, and eight original American Football League teams in the newly formed American Football Conference following the AFL-NFL merger in 1970, the Steelers went on to earn the title "Team of the Decade" by compiling an overall record of 88-27-1 and winning seven AFC Central Division titles, four conference championships, and four Super Bowls between 1972 and 1979. Although the Steelers ended up losing the 1972 AFC championship game to the eventual world champion Miami Dolphins by a score of 21–17, they earned the first playoff victory in franchise history one week earlier by beating the Oakland Raiders on Franco Harris's "Immaculate Reception." The Steelers failed to advance beyond the divisional round of the postseason tournament the following year, but they captured the next two NFL championships, defeating the Minnesota Vikings by a score of 16–6 in Super Bowl IX, before edging out the Dallas Cowboys, 21–17, in Super Bowl X. After coming up short in the playoffs the next two seasons, the Steelers returned to the top of the football world in 1978, outscoring the Cowboys, 35–31, in Super Bowl XIII, before defeating the Los Angeles Rams by a score of 31–19 in Super Bowl XIV.

While the Steelers predicated much of their success on their overpowering "Steel Curtain" defense that included linemen Joe Greene, L. C. Greenwood, Dwight White, and Ernie Holmes, linebackers Jack Lambert and Jack Ham, and defensive backs Mel Blount and Donnie Shell, the Pittsburgh offense also featured several exceptional players, with quarterback Terry Bradshaw, running backs Franco Harris and Rocky Bleier, wide receivers Lynn Swann and John Stallworth, and linemen Mike Webster and Jon Kolb all starring on that side of the ball. The talent and overall level of dominance the Steelers displayed during the 1970s have prompted many football historians to identify the Pittsburgh dynasty of that period as the greatest in NFL history, with the 1975 and 1978 teams often being ranked among the very best of all time. The 1975 club, which featured 11 Pro Bowlers, seven All-Pros, and the NFL Defensive Player of the Year in Blount, finished the regular season with a record of 12-2, outscoring its opponents by a combined margin of 373–162 in the process. Meanwhile, the 1978 squad, which featured 10 Pro Bowlers, five All-Pros, and the league MVP in Bradshaw, compiled a regular-season record of 14-2, outscoring its opponents 356–195 along the way. And, even though the 1976 Steelers suffered a 24–7 defeat at the hands of the Oakland Raiders in the AFC championship game, they recorded five shutouts and held their opponents without a touchdown in eight of their last nine regular-season contests, en route to surrendering a total of only 138 points the entire year.

Unfortunately, the retirements of several key players prevented the Steelers from sustaining the same level of dominance during the 1980s, leading to another period of mediocrity that lasted from 1980 to 1991. Nevertheless, they managed to capture two division titles and advance to the playoffs in four of those 12 seasons before Chuck Noll chose to relinquish his coaching duties following the conclusion of the 1991 campaign. Noll ended his 23-year coaching stint in Pittsburgh with an overall record of 209-156-1 and a bust waiting for him in Canton.

Following Noll's departure, Steelers president Dan Rooney, who also became controlling owner of the team after his father passed away in 1988, named former Kansas City Chiefs defensive coordinator Bill Cowher his replacement. Making an immediate impact upon his arrival in Pittsburgh, the strong-willed and extremely intense Cowher led the Steelers into the playoffs in each of his first six seasons in charge, winning five division titles in the process. However, they ultimately came up short each year, losing in the wild card round of the postseason tournament once, the divisional round twice, the AFC championship game twice, and the Super Bowl once, dropping a 27–17 decision to the Dallas Cowboys in Super Bowl XXX.

Cowher remained head coach in Pittsburgh another nine years, a period during which the Steelers moved into Heinz Field, which opened in 2001. Over the course of those nine seasons, the Steelers captured three more division titles, appeared in three more AFC championship games, and won their fifth Super Bowl, defeating the Seattle Seahawks by a score of 21–10 in Super Bowl XL, just one year after they suffered a disappointing 41–27 loss to the New England Patriots in the conference championship game after compiling a franchise-best 15-1 record during the regular season. Outstanding players to perform for the Steelers under Cowher include linebackers Greg Lloyd, Levon Kirkland, Joey Porter, and James Farrior, defensive backs Carnell Lake and Rod Woodson, running back Jerome Bettis, wide receiver Hines Ward, and offensive linemen Dermontti Dawson and Alan Faneca.

After Cowher handed in his resignation on January 5, 2007, Mike Tomlin assumed the coaching reins in Pittsburgh—a position he has held ever since. After leading the Steelers to a 10-6 record and the AFC North title his first year at the helm, Tomlin directed them to a mark of 12-4, their second straight division title, and their sixth Super Bowl championship in 2008, with the Steelers' 27–23 victory over the Arizona Cardinals in Super Bowl XLIII making them the first team to win the big game that many times. Although the Steelers have failed to capture another NFL championship in the 10 years since, they have continued to perform well under Tomlin, capturing four more division titles, including three of the last five, and making one more Super Bowl appearance, a 31–25 loss to the Green Bay Packers in Super Bowl XLV. Among those who have contributed significantly to the success the Steelers have experienced during Tomlin's coaching tenure are linebacker James Harrison, defensive back Troy Polamalu, quarterback Ben Roethlisberger, running back Le'Veon Bell, and wide receiver Antonio Brown.

Having advanced to the playoffs in 12 of the last 18 seasons, during which time they have won nine division titles, three AFC championships, and two Super Bowls, the Steelers remain one of the NFL's model franchises and most formidable teams. And, with a solid defense and one of the league's most explosive offenses, the Steelers show no signs of falling from the NFL's elite in the foreseeable future. Their next Super Bowl appearance will be their ninth, with their eight conference championships tying them with the Denver Broncos for the second-highest total of any AFC team (the New England Patriots have won 11). The Steelers have also won 23 division titles and six Super Bowls. After posting a winning record in just seven of their first 39 seasons, the Steelers have finished above .500 in 36 of the last

47 campaigns, doing so in each of the last 15 seasons. Featuring a plethora of exceptional performers through the years, the Steelers have inducted 22 players into their Hall of Honor. Meanwhile, 18 members of the Pro Football Hall of Fame spent a significant portion of their careers in Pittsburgh. The Steelers also boast seven NFL Defensive Player of the Year winners and two league MVPs (Bill Dudley in 1946 and Terry Bradshaw in 1978).

FACTORS USED TO DETERMINE RANKINGS

It should come as no surprise that selecting the 50 greatest players ever to perform for a team with the rich history of the Steelers presented quite a challenge. Even after narrowing the field down to a mere 50 men, I still needed to devise a method of ranking the elite players that remained. Certainly, the names of Joe Greene, Franco Harris, Jack Lambert, Jack Ham, Terry Bradshaw, Mel Blount, Rod Woodson, and Ben Roethlisberger would appear at, or near, the top of virtually everyone's list, although the order might vary somewhat from one person to the next. Several other outstanding performers have gained general recognition through the years as being among the greatest players ever to wear a Steelers uniform. Ernie Stautner, Mike Webster, Troy Polamalu, and Hines Ward head the list of other Steeler icons. But, how does one compare players who lined up on opposite sides of the ball with any degree of certainty? Furthermore, how does one differentiate between the pass-rushing and run-stopping skills of players such as Joe Greene and Jack Lambert and the ball-hawking and punt- and kickoff-return abilities of a Rod Woodson? And, on the offensive end, how can a direct correlation be made between the contributions made by Hall of Fame lineman Mike Webster and skill position players such as Terry Bradshaw, John Stallworth, and Jerome Bettis? After initially deciding whom to include on my list, I then needed to determine what criteria I should use to formulate my final rankings.

The first thing I decided to examine was the level of dominance a player attained during his time in Pittsburgh. How often did he lead the NFL in a major statistical category? Did he ever capture league MVP honors? How many times did he earn a trip to the Pro Bowl or a spot on the All-Pro Team?

I also chose to assess each player's statistical accomplishments while wearing a Steelers uniform, reviewing where he ranks among the team's all-time leaders in those categories most pertinent to his position. Of course, even the method of using statistics as a measuring stick has its inherent flaws. Although the level of success a team experiences rushing and passing the ball is impacted greatly by the performance of its offensive line, there really is no way to quantifiably measure the level of play reached by each individual offensive lineman. Conversely, the play of the offensive line affects tremendously the statistics compiled by a team's quarterback and running backs. Furthermore, the NFL did not keep an official record of defensive numbers such as tackles and quarterback sacks until the 1980s (although the Steelers kept their own records prior to that). In addition, when examining the statistics compiled by offensive players, the era during which a quarterback, running back, or wide receiver competed must be factored into the equation.

To illustrate my last point, rule changes instituted by the league office have opened up the game considerably over the course of the last two decades. Quarterbacks are accorded far more protection than ever before, and officials have also been instructed to limit the amount of contact defensive backs are allowed to make with wide receivers. As a result, the game has experienced an offensive explosion, with quarterbacks and receivers posting numbers players from prior generations rarely even approached. That being the case, one must place the numbers Ben Roethlisberger has compiled during his career in their proper context when comparing him to Terry Bradshaw. Similarly, Antonio Brown's huge receiving totals must be viewed in moderation when comparing him to previous Steeler wideouts Lynn Swann and John Stallworth.

Other important factors I needed to consider were the overall contributions a player made to the success of the team, the degree to which he improved the fortunes of the club during his time in Pittsburgh, the manner in which he impacted the team, both on and off the field, and the degree to which he added to the Steeler legacy of winning. While the number of championships and division titles the Steelers won during a player's years with the team certainly factored into the equation, I chose not to deny a top performer his rightful place on the list if his years in Pittsburgh happened to coincide with a lack of overall success by the club. As a result, the names of players such as Jack Butler and Louis Lipps will appear in these rankings.

One other thing I should mention is that I only considered a player's performance as a member of the Steelers when formulating my rankings. That being the case, the names of truly exceptional players such as Bill Dudley and John Henry Johnson, both of whom spent significant portions of their careers playing for other teams, may appear lower on this list than one might expect. Meanwhile, the names of other standout performers such as Jimmy Orr and Eugene "Big Daddy" Lipscomb are nowhere to be found.

Having established the guidelines to be used throughout this book, we are ready to examine the 50 greatest players in Steelers history, starting with number 1 and working our way down to number 50.

JOE GREENE

Although Jack Lambert, whose toothless visage came to represent the great Steeler defenses of the 1970s, proved to be a serious contender for the number one spot in these rankings, he ended up finishing a close second to Joe Greene, whom longtime Steelers linebacker Andy Russell called "the single most important player in the history of our success." Agreeing with Russell's assessment, commentators regularly identify Chuck Noll's selection of Greene in the 1969 NFL Draft as the pivotal moment in franchise history, and with good reason. Prior to Greene's arrival in Pittsburgh, the Steelers had established a long history of losing, posting a winning record in just seven of their first 36 years in the league. However, with Greene's competitiveness, outstanding leadership, and extraordinary playing ability providing much of the impetus, they emerged as perennial contenders before long, winning seven division titles, four AFC championships, and four Super Bowls in his 13 seasons with the team. And, while the Steelers eventually became known as the "team of the seventies," Greene built an individual legacy of greatness that few other NFL players could match. In addition to his 10 Pro Bowl selections, six All-Pro nominations, and 11 All-AFC selections, the big defensive tackle twice earned NFL Defensive Player of the Year honors. Greene also later received the additional distinctions of being named to the NFL's 75th Anniversary Team and the *Sporting News* All-Century Team, receiving a top-15 ranking on both the *Sporting News* and the NFL Network's lists of the 100 Greatest Players in NFL History, being elected to the Pro Football Hall of Fame, and having his #75 officially retired by the Steelers, making him one of just two players to be so honored.

Born in Elgin, Texas, on September 24, 1946, Charles Edward Greene grew up some 55 miles north, in the city of Temple, Texas, where he began his football career at segregated Dunbar High School. Greene, who later became known for his aggressiveness on the playing field, initially proved to be quite the opposite in high school even though, at 6'3" tall and 225

The Steelers' selection of "Mean" Joe Greene in the 1969 NFL Draft proved to be the pivotal moment in franchise history.
Courtesy of the Pittsburgh Steelers

pounds, he towered over his teammates and opponents. In discussing his early years on the gridiron, Greene recalled, "When I started playing, I was very timid. I used to get beat up quite a bit, on and off the field. But something happens when you're out there on the field: You want to win. You're oblivious to everything else. Eventually, my desire to win overcame my fear."

Greene truly came into his own after he accepted an athletic scholarship from North Texas State University (now known as the University of North Texas), where he spent three years starring at defensive tackle for the varsity football team, which he led to an overall record of 23-5-1. Greene, who earned All–Missouri Valley Conference recognition three times and consensus All-America honors in his senior year of 1968, drew praise from North Texas State head coach Rod Rust, who said, "There are two factors behind Joe's success. First, he has the ability to make the big defensive play and turn the tempo of a game around. Second, he has the speed to be an excellent pursuit player." During his time in college, Greene also acquired his famous moniker of "Mean Joe," which derived from the school's nickname, the North Texas State University "Mean Green."

Subsequently selected by the Steelers with the fourth overall pick of the 1969 NFL Draft, Greene became the first of many outstanding selections made by Pittsburgh's new head coach Chuck Noll, whose eye for talent helped build a dynasty in the Steel City. Steeler fans certainly hoped that Greene lived up to the advanced billing he received from one pro scout, who said of him prior to the draft, "He's tough and mean and comes to hit people. He has good killer instincts. He's mobile and hostile." Greene, though, later admitted that he did not like the idea of going to a team that had won a total of just 13 games the previous four seasons, stating, "Oh, my goodness. I did not, did not want to be a Steeler."

After arriving at his first pro training camp, Greene made an immediate impression on his new teammates, dominating the club's offensive linemen in all the one-on-one blocking drills. Continuing to perform well during the regular season, Greene earned NFL Defensive Rookie of the Year honors and the first of his eight consecutive trips to the Pro Bowl, even though the Steelers concluded the 1969 campaign with a franchise-worst record of 1-13. Despite the team's poor showing, the attitude in Pittsburgh began to change, with Greene's fierce competitive spirit and hatred of losing rubbing off on many of his teammates. Playing the game with an edge, Greene served notice to the rest of the league not to trifle with the Steelers, delivering that message on one occasion when he spat in the face of arguably the NFL's most intimidating player, the great Dick Butkus, who merely turned and walked away.

Continuing to live up to his "Mean Joe" moniker the next two seasons as the Steelers gradually emerged from the depths of the NFL, Greene developed a reputation as one of the league's toughest and nastiest players. But, even though Chuck Noll very much appreciated the passion with which Greene played the game, he eventually had to convince him to channel his anger in a more productive way, with Greene later revealing that his coach told him, "It hurts your football team, it's a distraction. You're giving up free extra yardage. If you want to be a championship football team, you can't do those things."

With Greene doing a better job of controlling his emotions and the Steelers subsequently drafting several other extremely talented players who displayed a similar level of intensity and competitiveness, the franchise soon changed its image and developed into the league's dominant team. After posting a mark of 6-8 in 1971, the Steelers won the first division title in franchise history the following year by going 11-3 during the regular season, with Greene earning NFL Defensive Player of the Year honors and being named First-Team All-Pro for the first of three straight times. Two years later, the Steelers won their first Super Bowl, with Greene once again being named the league's top defensive player. Pittsburgh also won the Super Bowl in three of the next five seasons, a period during which Greene established himself as the centerpiece of the team's fabled "Steel Curtain" defense.

Armed with speed, quickness, strength, and determination, the 6'3", 275-pound Greene had the ability to dominate a game almost single-handedly, with running back Dick Hoak saying of his former teammate, "He just took the game over." Greene, who used his strength to manhandle opposing offensive linemen and his quickness to outmaneuver them, also drew praise from Chuck Noll, who noted, "I had never seen anybody block him one-on-one."

In addressing Greene's quickness, legendary head coach Don Shula stated, "He's just a super, super star. It's hard to believe he isn't offside on every play. He makes the other team adjust to him."

Extremely durable, Greene missed only nine games in 13 seasons, beginning his career by appearing in 91 consecutive contests, before sitting out four games in 1975 due to a pinched nerve. Also serving as the Steelers' emotional leader throughout much of his career, Greene spent his final five seasons in Pittsburgh captaining the team's defensive unit, although his leadership extended to the offense as well, with teammates describing him as a huge presence both on and off the field. In speaking of his longtime teammate, Hall of Fame wide receiver Lynn Swann said, "If you were giving less than 100 percent, he let you know one way or the other."

Meanwhile, even though Greene displayed a greater level of self-control as his career progressed, he remained one of the league's most ferocious and intimidating players, instilling fear in his opponents with the intensity of his play. Exhibiting the degree to which he imposed his will on the opposition during a 20–17 loss to the Houston Oilers in 1979, Greene made certain that Oilers quarterback Dan Pastorini did not attempt to add to the Houston lead as he lined up his team near the Pittsburgh goal line for the game's final play. Pointing angrily across the line of scrimmage at Pastorini, Greene warned, "If you come into the end zone, I'll beat the crap out of you! I'm gonna kill you!" After Pastorini responded by taking a knee, Greene laughed and told him, "I knew you weren't going to do it."

Greene, who proved to be equally effective rushing the passer and defending against the run his first several years in the league, lost some of his pass-rushing ability after he sustained his pinched nerve in 1975 and injured his back early the following season. However, he remained a force against the run the rest of his career, performing particularly well in 1978, when he led all Pittsburgh linemen in tackles and recovered five fumbles. Choosing to announce his retirement following the conclusion of the 1981 campaign, Greene ended his career with an unofficial total of 78½ sacks, which represents the second-highest figure in team annals. Greene also ranks among the franchise's all-time leaders with 16 fumble recoveries.

Following his playing days, Greene spent one year serving as a color analyst for CBS's coverage of NFL games, before becoming an assistant coach, first for the Steelers, and, later, for the Miami Dolphins and Arizona Cardinals. After remaining on the sidelines for 16 years, Greene retired from coaching in 2004 and returned to Pittsburgh, where he assumed the role of special assistant for player personnel. Electing to relinquish his post in 2013, Greene retired to his home state of Texas, where he currently resides.

Generally considered to be one of the handful of greatest defensive tackles ever to play in the NFL, Greene is also widely viewed as the most influential player in Pittsburgh Steelers history, with Andy Russell calling him "unquestionably, the NFL's best player in the seventies," and then adding, "No player had a greater impact or did more for his team."

Greene earned NFL Defensive Player of the Year honors twice. Courtesy of RMY Auctions

Hall of Fame defensive back Rod Woodson, who never had an opportunity to play with Greene in Pittsburgh, stated, "You start talking Pittsburgh Steelers and the first person that normally comes to mind for most people is Mean Joe Greene."

Former Denver Broncos head coach Dan Reeves commented, "It would be hard for me to come up with a Steelers player that you would put ahead of Mean Joe Greene. He was an unbelievable force to reckon with."

Mel Blount, who joined the Steelers one year after Greene arrived in Pittsburgh, had this to say:

> I had the honor of playing with Joe Greene and sharing those great Steeler Super Bowl victories with him. I am convinced that none of them would have happened without Joe and his leadership. He was a great leader on the field and in the locker room. His desire to win and positive attitude were contagious. Because of his physical play, he was known as "Mean" Joe Greene, but those of us who truly know Joe Greene know that he is a better person than he was a player, and that's saying a lot.

Franco Harris expressed similar sentiments when he said:

> By the time I was drafted by the Steelers, it was clear that Joe was the cornerstone of our team. With him in place, they drafted players to fit this new system and mentality. The results are now legendary, as we won four Super Bowls

and the Steelers became the new standard of professional football. Yes, Joe was the spark that ignited it all, and, as time passes, his role continues to shine brighter and brighter. There is no question in my mind that "Mean" Joe Greene is the greatest Steeler of all time!

As for how he would like to be remembered, Greene says, "I just want people to remember me as being a good player and not really mean. I want to be remembered for playing 13 years and contributing to four championship teams. I would like to be remembered for maybe setting a standard for others to achieve."

CAREER HIGHLIGHTS

Best Season

Although Greene performed brilliantly throughout his career, he made his greatest overall impact in Pittsburgh in 1972, when he led the Steelers to their first division title by making a career-high 11 sacks and registering 42 solo tackles, earning in the process NFL Defensive Player of the Year honors for the first of two times.

Memorable Moments/Greatest Performances

Greene turned in arguably the most memorable performance of his career during the latter stages of that 1972 campaign, when he led an injury-plagued Steelers squad to a 9–3 win over the Houston Oilers by recording five sacks, forcing a fumble, recovering another, and blocking an attempted field goal. The victory all but clinched the AFC Central Division title for Pittsburgh.

Greene once again starred against Houston on December 9, 1973, leading a Steeler defense that surrendered just 83 yards of total offense and created nine turnovers during a 33–7 win over the Oilers.

Greene recorded the only regular-season interception of his career during a 26–16 win over the Browns on November 17, 1974, subsequently returning the ball 26 yards into Cleveland territory.

After developing a new tactic of lining up at a sharp angle between the guard and center to disrupt the opposition's blocking assignments, Greene performed exceptionally well throughout the 1974 postseason, first helping to limit O. J. Simpson to only 48 yards rushing during Pittsburgh's 32–14 victory over Buffalo in the opening round of the playoffs, before recording a sack and contributing greatly to a superb defensive effort that held Oakland to just 29 yards rushing in the AFC championship game. Continuing his stellar play against Minnesota and perennial All-Pro center Mick Tingelhoff in Super Bowl IX, Greene recorded an interception, forced a fumble, and recovered another, in leading the Steelers to a convincing 16–6 victory over their NFC counterparts.

Greene also excelled against the Broncos in the 1978 playoffs, recording two sacks during the Steelers' 33–10 win over Denver in the divisional round of the postseason tournament.

Notable Achievements

- Ranks among Steelers career leaders with 78½ sacks (2nd) and 16 fumble recoveries (tied—7th).
- Played in 181 out of a possible 190 games, at one point appearing in 91 consecutive contests.
- Seven-time division champion (1972, 1974, 1975, 1976, 1977, 1978, and 1979).
- Four-time AFC champion (1974, 1975, 1978, and 1979).
- Four-time Super Bowl champion (IX, X, XIII, and XIV).
- 1969 NFL Defensive Rookie of the Year.
- 1970 Steelers MVP.
- Two-time NFL Defensive Player of the Year (1972 and 1974).
- 1979 NFL Man of the Year.
- 10-time Pro Bowl selection (1969, 1970, 1971, 1972, 1973, 1974, 1975, 1976, 1978, and 1979).
- Four-time First-Team All-Pro selection (1972, 1973, 1974, and 1977).
- Two-time Second-Team All-Pro selection (1975 and 1976).
- 10-time First-Team All-Conference selection (1970, 1971, 1972, 1973, 1974, 1975, 1976, 1977, 1978, and 1979).
- 1969 Second-Team All-Conference selection.
- Pro Football Hall of Fame All-1970s First Team.
- Pro Football Reference All-1970s First Team.
- Named to Super Bowl's Silver Anniversary Team in 1990.
- Named to NFL's 75th Anniversary Team in 1994.
- Named to Steelers' 75th Anniversary Team in 2007.
- #75 retired by Steelers.

- Named to *Sporting News* All-Century Team in 1999.
- Number 14 on the *Sporting News*' 1999 list of the 100 Greatest Players in NFL History.
- Number 13 on the NFL Network's 2010 list of the NFL's 100 Greatest Players.
- Elected to Pro Football Hall of Fame in 1987.

2

— JACK LAMBERT —

erhaps no other player has come to symbolize the "golden era" of Steelers football more than Jack Lambert, whose forceful personality drove the team to new heights. Intense, intimidating, highly motivated, and extremely talented, Lambert established himself as the Steelers' emotional leader shortly after he arrived in Pittsburgh, serving as a cornerstone of one of the greatest defenses in NFL history. A major contributor to all four Super Bowl championship teams of the 1970s, Lambert, who longtime teammate Jack Ham called "the most complete middle linebacker ever to play," earned nine straight trips to the Pro Bowl, seven All-Pro nominations, and nine All-AFC selections while wearing the Black and Gold, with his magnificent play also gaining him recognition in 1976 as the NFL's Defensive Player of the Year. And, after his playing career ended, Lambert received the additional honors of being named to the NFL's 75th Anniversary Team and the *Sporting News* All-Century Team, being ranked in the top 30 on both the *Sporting News*' and the NFL Network's lists of the 100 Greatest Players in NFL History, and being elected to the Pro Football Hall of Fame.

Born in Mantua, Ohio, on July 8, 1952, John Harold Lambert attended local Crestwood High School, where he acquired his signature gap-toothed look on the basketball court one day when a teammate's head collided with his mouth, knocking out his upper front four teeth. Starting for Crestwood High's football team at both quarterback and defensive back, Lambert left a lasting impression on head coach Gerry Myers, who recalled, "After a while, teams would stop running curl patterns in front of him. I can close my eyes now and see him hitting the split end from Streetsboro. Knocked his helmet and one shoe off."

Lambert continued to star on the gridiron after he enrolled at Kent State University, spending one season at defensive end, before earning All–Mid-American Conference honors twice as a middle linebacker. Yet, in spite of the success he experienced in college, most pro scouts considered the skinny 6'4" Lambert too small to play linebacker at the professional

Jack Lambert served as the centerpiece of Pittsburgh's famed "Steel Curtain" defense.
Courtesy of the Pittsburgh Steelers

level. Fortunately, Art Rooney Jr. and his cousin Tim felt differently, with the duo ultimately convincing the Steelers to select Lambert in the second round of the 1974 NFL Draft, with the 46th overall pick.

Despite spending his first year in the league playing at only 204 pounds, Lambert had an outstanding rookie season after supplanting Henry Davis as the starter at middle linebacker, recording two interceptions and leading the Super Bowl champion Steelers in tackles for the first of 10 straight times, with his exceptional play earning him NFL Defensive Rookie of the Year honors. He subsequently earned Pro Bowl and All-Pro honors for the first time by leading the Steelers to their second consecutive NFL title in 1975. However, Lambert may well have turned in his finest performance in 1976, when he led an injury-ravaged Steelers team that lost four of its first five games to nine straight wins and a playoff berth, earning in the process NFL Defensive Player of the Year honors.

Lambert truly established himself as Pittsburgh's emotional leader on defense during that 1976 campaign, with his intensity and aggressiveness giving the unit an edge it previously lacked. Priding himself on his ability to hit hard and intimidate the opposition, Lambert once stated, "Yes, I get satisfaction out of hitting a guy and seeing him lie there a while . . . I believe the game is designed to reward the ones who hit the hardest. If you can't take it, you shouldn't play."

Lambert's attitude made him one of the league's most intimidating players even though he barely weighed 220 pounds throughout most of his career. Bludgeoning opposing quarterbacks and running backs with vicious hits and frightening them with verbal taunts, Lambert struck fear into his opponents, with John Elway providing the following account of how he felt after Lambert and the rest of the Steelers knocked him out of his first game as a pro in 1983: "He had no teeth, and he was slobbering all over himself. I'm thinking, 'You can have your money back, just get me out of here. Let me go be an accountant.' I can't tell you how badly I wanted out of there."

As opposing quarterbacks crouched under center, Lambert typically pumped his legs up and down, thumping the turf like a war drum, while simultaneously mouthing threats to everyone in the offensive backfield. In explaining his behavior, Lambert said, "Because of my size, I have to be intense."

Praising his team's defensive leader for the level of intensity he displayed on the field, Steelers head coach Chuck Noll stated, "When you start talking about attitude and focus, Jack is the epitome. He was the most focused individual I've ever had."

Joe Greene added, "Jack didn't need to psyche himself to play. . . . He LIVED to play."

Meanwhile, in addressing the overall impact that Lambert made in Pittsburgh, Cleveland Browns head coach Sam Rutigliano stated emphatically, "Jack Lambert IS the Pittsburgh Steelers."

Lambert displayed a level of intensity few other players could match.
Courtesy of the Pittsburgh Steelers

Lambert's aggressive style of play eventually caused him to develop a reputation as something of a dirty player, which he strongly denied, saying, "It's beginning to get out of hand. All that stuff upsets me because I'm not a dirty football player. I don't sit in front of my locker thinking of fighting or hurting somebody. All I want to do is to be able to play football hard and aggressively, the way it's meant to be played."

Yet, despite the way others tended to view him, Lambert proved to be one of the league's most technically sound players, with teammate Andy Russell suggesting, "Lambert may have had the image of a wild man, but he killed you with his precision."

Blessed with a superb combination of speed, power, technique, and football intelligence, Lambert used his many attributes to ward off blockers, making him extremely effective in defending against the run. The franchise's all-time leader in tackles, Lambert, according to Steelers media guides, averaged 146 tackles per season his first 10 years in the league, finishing first on the team in that category in each of those campaigns.

In discussing Lambert's ability to play the run, former New York Jets linebacker Greg Buttle stated, "If that hole was there, he was in the hole. He made the tackle."

Former Denver Broncos coach Dan Reeves commented, "Jack was one of those guys that was in on a lot of tackles. He was the enforcer. He was a guy that was always trying to jaw with other people, but he backed it up."

Steelers radio announcer Bill Hillgrove noted, "There's a big difference between athletes and football players. Lambert had an instinct for the game that was unique."

As well as Lambert defended against the run, he proved to be equally effective in pass coverage, recording 28 interceptions over the course of his career, including six in both 1979 and 1981. Speaking of his former teammate's pass-coverage skills, Jack Ham said, "Of all the middle linebackers—Ray Nitschke, Willie Lanier, Dick Butkus—what set Jack apart was his ability to play the pass."

Expressing similar sentiments, Andy Russell told *Sports Illustrated* in 1983:

> Tough, raw-boned, intense—that's the way he'll be remembered, but I've seen a lot of guys like that come into the league. No, Jack's a whole lot more. The range he has—they put him in coverage 30 yards downfield. They gave him assignments the Bears or the Packers never would've dreamed of for Dick Butkus or Ray Nitschke. He brought a whole new concept to the position, and that's why, for me anyway, he's the greatest there has ever been. His first step is never wrong, his techniques have always been perfect. His greatness has nothing to do with his popular image.

Lambert continued to excel at middle linebacker for the Steelers until 1984, when he suffered a severe case of turf toe that limited him to only eight games and ultimately forced him to retire at season's end. In addition to intercepting 28 passes during his career, Lambert recorded "unofficial" totals of 1,479 tackles (1,045 solo) and 23½ sacks.

Following his playing days, Lambert, who remained a quiet and extremely private man off the field throughout his career, retreated to the hills of suburban Pennsylvania, where he continued to pursue his passions of bird-watching and fishing. After spending many years serving as a volunteer deputy wildlife officer in the tranquil woods near his home, Lambert now spends most of his time coaching youth baseball and basketball, tending to his land, and maintaining his town's ball fields.

Elected to the Pro Football Hall of Fame in 1990, Lambert expressed his love for football and the Steelers during his induction speech, proclaiming, "If I could start my life all over again, I would be a professional football player, and you damn well better believe I would be a Pittsburgh Steeler."

CAREER HIGHLIGHTS

Best Season

The 1976 campaign would have to be considered the finest of Lambert's career. After a rash of injuries caused the Steelers to begin the season with a record of just 1-4, the third-year linebacker assumed the mantle of leadership in Pittsburgh, telling his teammates at a "players only" meeting that "the only way we are going to the playoffs to defend our title is to win them all from here out." Not only did the Steelers win their final nine games, but they surrendered just two touchdowns and 28 total points the rest of the season, shutting out their opponents five times in the process. With the Steeler defense limiting the opposition to only 138 points the entire season—easily the franchise's lowest total since the NFL instituted a 14-game schedule in 1961—Lambert, who recorded two interceptions and a league-leading eight fumble recoveries over the course of the campaign, walked away with NFL Defensive Player of the Year honors.

Memorable Moments/Greatest Performances

Lambert recorded the first two interceptions of his career during a 34–24 win over the Kansas City Chiefs on October 13, 1974.

Displaying his penchant for always being around the football, Lambert recovered three fumbles during the Steelers' 16–10 victory over Oakland in the 1975 AFC championship game.

Lambert contributed greatly to a 13–3 win over the Oilers on December 3, 1978, by picking off Houston quarterback Dan Pastorini twice.

Lambert also proved to be a huge factor in Super Bowl XIV, recording a game-high eight tackles and making a key interception of a Vince Ferragamo pass that helped lead to a 31–19 victory over the Los Angeles Rams that gave the Steelers their fourth championship.

Lambert led a swarming Pittsburgh defense that sacked Steve Fuller eight times during a 35–14 win over the Chiefs on December 5, 1982, by getting to the Kansas City quarterback three times himself.

Lambert turned in another outstanding effort against Cincinnati on October 10, 1983, recording an interception and a sack during a 24–14 win.

Lambert played perhaps the greatest game of his career nearly two months later, when, during a 23–10 loss to the Bengals on December 4, 1983, he amazingly had a hand in 31 tackles. In discussing Lambert's performance, Mike Giddings, who operated a private scouting service that graded all NFL players, stated in a 1984 article that appeared in *Sports Illustrated*, "Last year, when the Bengals beat Pittsburgh, they ran off 75 plays. Lambert was in on 31 tackles. He had 22 at halftime. I don't see how his body could stand it."

Yet, Lambert will always be remembered most fondly by Pittsburgh fans for an incident that took place in Super Bowl X, when he delivered a clear message to the Dallas Cowboys. With the Steelers trailing the Cowboys by a score of 10–7 in the third quarter, Pittsburgh placekicker Roy Gerela missed a 33-yard field goal, after which Dallas defensive back Cliff Harris tapped him on the helmet and said, "Way to go." Observing Harris's act from a few feet away, Lambert grabbed the Dallas safety and threw him to the ground, providing an emotional lift to the Steelers that enabled them to ultimately come away with a 21–17 victory. When asked about the play after the game, Lambert said, "I felt we were intimidated a little. We weren't supposed to be intimidated. We're supposed to be the intimidators." Meanwhile, Chuck Noll told reporters, "Jack Lambert is a defender of what is right."

Notable Achievements

- Intercepted six passes in a season twice.
- Recorded more than 100 tackles nine times.
- Led NFL with eight fumble recoveries in 1976.
- Led Steelers in tackles 10 times and interceptions twice.

- Holds Steelers career record with 1,479 tackles (1,045 solo).
- Ranks among Steelers career leaders with 28 interceptions (10th) and 17 fumble recoveries (tied—5th).
- Eight-time division champion (1974, 1975, 1976, 1977, 1978, 1979, 1983, and 1984).
- Four-time AFC champion (1974, 1975, 1978, and 1979).
- Four-time Super Bowl champion (IX, X, XIII, and XIV).
- Steelers Defensive Captain for eight years.
- Two-time Steelers MVP (1976 and 1981).
- 1974 NFL Defensive Rookie of the Year.
- 1976 NFL Defensive Player of the Year.
- 1983 Newspaper Enterprise Association (NEA) NFL Defensive Player of the Year.
- Nine-time Pro Bowl selection (1975, 1976, 1977, 1978, 1979, 1980, 1981, 1982, and 1983).
- Six-time First-Team All-Pro selection (1976, 1979, 1980, 1981, 1982, and 1983).
- 1975 Second-Team All-Pro selection.
- Seven-time First-Team All-Conference selection (1975, 1976, 1978, 1979, 1980, 1982, and 1983).
- Two-time Second-Team All-Conference selection (1977 and 1981).
- Pro Football Hall of Fame All-1970s Second Team.
- Pro Football Hall of Fame All-1980s Second Team.
- Named to Super Bowl's Silver Anniversary Team in 1990.
- Named to NFL's 75th Anniversary Team in 1994.
- Named to Steelers' 75th Anniversary Team in 2007.
- #58 "unofficially" retired by Steelers.
- Named to *Sporting News* All-Century Team in 1999.
- Number 30 on the *Sporting News*' 1999 list of the 100 Greatest Players in NFL History.
- Number 29 on the NFL Network's 2010 list of the NFL's 100 Greatest Players.
- Elected to Pro Football Hall of Fame in 1990.

3

— JACK HAM —

Although Jack Ham's understated manner often caused him to be overshadowed by some of his more flamboyant Steeler teammates, he played his position as well as any other member of Pittsburgh's famed "Steel Curtain" defense. Perhaps the most complete outside linebacker in NFL history, Ham defended equally well against the run and the pass, using his quickness, intelligence, flawless technique, and superior football instincts to help shut down opposing offenses for 12 seasons. The league's all-time leader in takeaways by a non–defensive back, Ham helped lead the Steelers to seven division titles, four AFC championships, and four Super Bowl wins, earning in the process eight trips to the Pro Bowl, seven All-Pro selections, and nine All-AFC nominations. Ham's superb all-around play also earned him spots on the NFL's 75th Anniversary Team and the *Sporting News* All-Century Team, a number 47 ranking on that same publication's 1999 list of the 100 Greatest Players in NFL History, and a place in the Pro Football Hall of Fame.

Born in Johnstown, Pennsylvania, on December 23, 1948, Jack Raphael Ham Jr. attended local Bishop McCort High School, before continuing his education at Massanutten Military Academy in Woodstock, Virginia, for one post-graduate season. Offered an athletic scholarship by Penn State University, Ham spent three seasons starring at linebacker for the Nittany Lions, leading them to an overall record of 29-3 by recording a total of 251 tackles, with 143 of those being of the unassisted variety. Performing especially well while serving as team co-captain during his senior year of 1970, Ham earned All-America honors by making 91 tackles and intercepting four passes. In evaluating Ham's performance years later at his Pro Football Hall of Fame induction, legendary head coach Joe Paterno stated, "I've been asked 100 times in the last couple of weeks, 'Do you remember the greatest game Jack Ham ever played?' I can't. Jack never played a bad game for us. He had 10 or 11 tackles, he blocked a punt, he had an intercepted pass, he recovered a fumble because he was hustling. He was always consistent."

Many people consider Jack Ham to be the most complete outside linebacker in NFL history.
Courtesy of LegendaryAuctions.com

After being selected by the Steelers in the second round of the 1971 NFL Draft, with the 34th overall pick, the 6'1" Ham reported to his first pro training camp weighing only 210 pounds. However, he added 15 pounds onto his frame before long, thereby reaching the playing weight of 225 pounds at which he spent the remainder of his career. Ham then went on to have a solid rookie season for the team he followed as a youngster after laying claim to the starting left linebacker job with a three-interception performance against the New York Giants in the final preseason game. He followed that up with an outstanding sophomore campaign, earning Second-Team All-AFC honors in 1972 by recovering four fumbles and recording a team-leading seven interceptions, one of which he returned 32 yards for the first touchdown of his career. Ham then began an exceptional eight-year run during which he earned Pro Bowl and All-AFC honors each season, while also being named All-Pro seven times.

Blessed with tremendous quickness, Ham, according to Steelers head coach Chuck Noll and teammate Andy Russell, was "the fastest Steeler for the first 10 yards, including wide receivers and running backs." Ham's speed and mobility enabled him to excel in pass coverage, making him as effective in that role as most of the league's top safeties. Taking great pride in his ability to cover tight ends or running backs coming out of the backfield, Ham stated, "I loved playing pass coverage. Some people think of a linebacker only as a guy who can get to the right hole in a hurry and hit hard. To me, that's less than half of being a linebacker. You've got to do your job on pass coverage, or else you're a liability."

Ham then added, "I really loved the passing game. I loved man-to-man coverage, playing the tight end or a back out of the backfield. Trying to make plays downfield."

Proving to be equally effective against the run, Ham, who acquired the nickname "the Hammer" during his time in Pittsburgh, used his speed, intelligence, and ability to diagnose plays to always be around the football, with former NFL linebacker Maxie Baughan saying, "He was one of the more intelligent players to ever play that position. He was able to diagnose plays. You couldn't ever fool him."

Ham also drew praise from Andy Russell, who said of his former team-mate, "He was superb. I played the position for 14 years and watched film of every great linebacker you could mention. There was nobody better than Jack. People don't realize it, but, in a five-yard dash, Jack Ham was the fastest man in pro football. He had incredible acceleration that allowed him to come off a block, retain his balance, and explode. He'd make tackles look routine on plays where the rest of us would try to dive."

Rarely caught out of position, Ham invariably seemed to be at the right place at the right time, enabling him to make an inordinate number of big plays over the course of his career. In addition to ranking third all-time among NFL linebackers with 32 interceptions, Ham recovered 21 fumbles, with his 53 career takeaways representing the highest total ever amassed by a linebacker or defensive lineman. And, even though the NFL did not begin keeping an official record of quarterback sacks until Ham's final year in the league, the Steelers have credited him with an "unofficial" career total of 25 sacks. Ham even excelled on special teams, with his knack for blocking kicks making him a regular member of the Steelers' punt-return and field goal units.

Choosing to announce his retirement following the conclusion of the strike-shortened 1982 campaign, Ham ended his career having appeared in 162 out of a possible 169 contests, starting 160 of those at his familiar left-outside linebacker position. After retiring as an active player, Ham went into a career in broadcasting, first serving as a color commentator for national radio broadcasts of NFL games, before co-hosting a show in Pittsburgh with Mark Madden on ESPN Radio 1250 during the NFL season. Ham has since assumed the role of sports analyst for the Penn State Radio Network, and he also appears as an analyst on the Westwood One Radio Network.

Considered to be one of the NFL's most cerebral and consistent players during his playing days, Ham earned the undying respect of fellow Hall of Fame linebacker Jack Lambert, who said of his longtime Steelers teammate, "Jack Ham, in my opinion, is the greatest outside linebacker that ever played the game. Tremendous technique. He did everything right. He played the run the way you were supposed to play it. He played the pass the

Ham ranks third all-time among NFL linebackers with 32 career interceptions.
Courtesy of the Pittsburgh Steelers

way you were supposed to play it. Consummate. He was just the best that ever played the game. No question in my mind about it."

CAREER HIGHLIGHTS

Best Season

Ham performed magnificently for the Steelers in 1972, when he recorded a career-high seven interceptions, 83 interception-return yards, and four fumble recoveries. Nevertheless, he reached the apex of his career in 1975, when his brilliant all-around play prompted the Pro Football Writers of America to accord him NFL Defensive Player of the Year honors.

Memorable Moments/Greatest Performances

Ham recorded the first interception of his career during a 21–17 win over the San Diego Chargers on October 3, 1971.

Ham scored the first of his two career touchdowns during a lopsided 33–3 victory over the New England Patriots on October 22, 1972, when he picked off a Jim Plunkett pass, which he returned 32 yards for a TD.

Ham lit the scoreboard again on December 9, 1973, when he recovered a fumble in the end zone during a 33–7 win over the Houston Oilers.

Ham contributed to a 34–24 victory over the Kansas City Chiefs on October 13, 1974, by recording two of the seven interceptions the Steelers registered on the day.

Ham picked off another two passes in that year's AFC championship game, intercepting Oakland quarterback Ken Stabler twice during the Steelers' 24–13 victory over the Raiders, with his second interception, which he returned 19 yards to the Oakland 9-yard line, setting up Pittsburgh's go-ahead touchdown in the fourth quarter.

Ham displayed his all-around excellence during the Steelers' 28–10 win over the Baltimore Colts in their 1975 divisional round playoff game, recording an interception and two sacks.

Ham made a pair of interceptions during a 35–31 win over the Browns on November 13, 1977.

Ham helped lead the Steelers to a 24–7 victory over the San Francisco 49ers on November 27, 1978, by recording another two interceptions.

Ham turned in a tremendous all-around effort against Houston in the 1978 AFC championship game, leading the Steelers to a convincing 34–5 victory over their overmatched opponents by intercepting a pass, recording a sack, and recovering two fumbles.

Ham subsequently excelled against Dallas in Super Bowl XIII, making a team-high eight tackles during the Steelers' 35–31 win over the Cowboys.

Notable Achievements

- Scored two defensive touchdowns during career.
- Recorded at least five interceptions in a season twice.
- Finished third in NFL with seven interceptions in 1972.
- Led Steelers in interceptions twice.

- Ranks among Steelers career leaders with 32 interceptions (tied—7th) and 21 fumble recoveries (tied—2nd).
- Ranks third all-time among NFL linebackers with 32 career interceptions.
- Seven-time division champion (1972, 1974, 1975, 1976, 1977, 1978, and 1979).
- Four-time AFC champion (1974, 1975, 1978, and 1979).
- Four-time Super Bowl champion (IX, X, XIII, and XIV).
- 1975 Pro Football Writers of America NFL Defensive Player of the Year.
- Eight-time Pro Bowl selection (1973, 1974, 1975, 1976, 1977, 1978, 1979, and 1980).
- Six-time First-Team All-Pro selection (1974, 1975, 1976, 1977, 1978, and 1979).
- 1973 Second-Team All-Pro selection.
- Seven-time First-Team All-Conference selection (1973, 1974, 1975, 1976, 1977, 1978, and 1979).
- Two-time Second-Team All-Conference selection (1972 and 1980).
- Pro Football Hall of Fame All-1970s First Team.
- Pro Football Reference All-1970s First Team.
- Named to Super Bowl's Silver Anniversary Team in 1990.
- Named to NFL's 75th Anniversary Team in 1994.
- Named to Steelers' 75th Anniversary Team in 2007.
- #59 "unofficially" retired by Steelers.
- Named to *Sporting News* All-Century Team in 1999.
- Number 47 on the *Sporting News*' 1999 list of the 100 Greatest Players in NFL History.
- Number 60 on the NFL Network's 2010 list of the NFL's 100 Greatest Players.
- Elected to Pro Football Hall of Fame in 1988.

4

— MEL BLOUNT —

One of the greatest cornerbacks in NFL history, Mel Blount gained general recognition during his time in Pittsburgh as the prototype cornerback of his era, with longtime teammate Jack Ham stating emphatically, "When you create a cornerback, the mold is Mel Blount. I played in a lot of Pro Bowls. I never saw a cornerback like him. He was the most incredible athlete I have ever seen. With Mel, you could take one wide receiver and just write him off. He could handle anybody in the league."

A tremendous physical specimen with superior athletic skills and an extremely high football IQ, Blount excelled in all phases of the game, displaying an ability to blanket his man in any type of pass coverage, while also defending exceptionally well against the run. The Steelers' all-time leader in interceptions, Blount recorded a single-season franchise record 11 picks in 1975, when his superb play earned him NFL Defensive Player of the Year honors. One of the most important members of Pittsburgh's dominant teams of the 1970s, Blount helped the Steelers win seven division titles, four AFC championships, and four Super Bowls during the decade, earning in the process five trips to the Pro Bowl, four All-Pro selections, and six All-AFC nominations. And, following the conclusion of his playing career, Blount received the additional honors of being named to the NFL's 75th Anniversary Team and the *Sporting News* All-Century Team, being identified as one of the 100 greatest players in NFL history by both the *Sporting News* and the NFL Network, and being elected to the Pro Football Hall of Fame.

Born on his family's farm in Vidalia, Georgia, on April 10, 1948, Melvin Cornell Blount grew up in poverty, deriving most of his pleasure as a youth from playing sports. Establishing himself as an outstanding all-around athlete while attending Lyons Industrial High School, Blount excelled in baseball, basketball, football, and track, prompting Southern University in Baton Rouge, Louisiana, to offer him an athletic scholarship. Starring at safety and cornerback for the Jaguars the next few seasons, Blount earned All-America recognition at both positions from *Pro Scouts,* the *Sporting News,* and the *Pittsburgh Courier* during his time at Southern.

After being selected by the Steelers in the third round of the 1970 NFL Draft, with the 53rd overall pick, Blount struggled in a part-time role at cornerback his first two seasons in Pittsburgh, performing better on special teams, where he returned one punt for 52 yards and amassed 535 yards on 18 kickoff returns as a rookie. In fact, after being burned for several long touchdown receptions in 1971, Blount briefly considered leaving the game, later admitting, "Yeah, I thought about quitting. I thought a whole lot about it."

Returning to his home in Georgia during the subsequent offseason, Blount assessed his situation, recalling, "As I had time to sort things out, I realized that the football I had played at Southern hadn't given me the background I needed for pro football. In college, the game was so much less complex, but more physical. It was played on natural ability and very little else."

Blount continued, "I had to realize every mistake I made was a lesson. Instead of thinking about how many times I had been beaten, I decided to think of how many lessons I had learned."

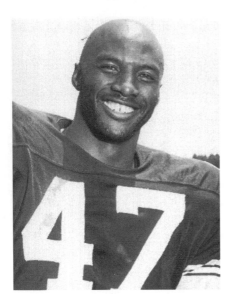

Arriving at training camp with a different attitude in 1972, Blount made a strong impression on Steelers defensive coordinator Bud Carson, who commented, "I know Mel is an outstanding prospect. He has great ability and speed. He shows all the physical requisites to be as good as anyone in the league."

After laying claim to the starting right cornerback job, Blount had an excellent season for the Steelers, recording three interceptions, recovering two fumbles, one of which he returned for a touchdown, and going the entire year without allowing an opposing receiver to score a single touchdown against him. Reflecting back on his

Mel Blount recorded more interceptions than anyone else in franchise history.
Courtesy of the Pittsburgh Steelers

remarkable turnaround, Blount says, "I owe it all to Bud Carson. He gave me something no one else on the staff ever did—he helped me believe in myself."

Blount continued his maturation over the course of the next two seasons, before emerging as the league's top corner in 1975, when he earned team MVP and Associated Press NFL Defensive Player of the Year honors by recording a league-leading 11 interceptions, which he returned for a total of 121 yards. Blount's superb play also earned him his first trip to the Pro Bowl and consensus First-Team All-Pro recognition. Upon learning that he had been named the league's most valuable defensive player, Blount stated, "I knew I was getting local publicity, but this is a national award and it makes you feel good about being recognized all over the country. I feel I played just as well the past two or three seasons as I did this year. But, to most people those years, I was just another ball player."

Blessed with tremendous natural ability, Blount stood 6'3" tall, weighed close to 220 pounds, and ran the 40-yard dash in 4.5 seconds. Equally effective in zone or man-to-man coverage, Blount employed an extremely physical style of play, with his combination of size and speed typically enabling him to overpower his opponent. Specializing in the then-popular "bump-and-run" type of pass defense, Blount took advantage of the rules of the day, which allowed a defensive back to maintain contact with a receiver until the quarterback released the ball.

In discussing the physicality of Blount's game, Steelers teammate Andy Russell said, "He would manhandle the wide receivers, take them and throw them out of bounds. Al Davis and Don Shula and people like that said it wasn't any fun to play the Steelers because you couldn't make a first down, so they changed the rules."

Pittsburgh offensive lineman Jon Kolb claimed that Blount's size and aggressiveness made him the league's most intimidating defensive back, stating, "A lot of cornerbacks want to be intimidators. They go through all kinds of things to be intimidating. Mel could just walk out there, look down on the guy, and then run side by side with him. That would be intimidating."

Revealing the attitude he took with him to the playing field, Blount said, "One of the things that I always wanted to do was let people know that this is my territory and, if you come in here, you're going to have to pay."

Backup quarterback Terry Hanratty suggested that Blount successfully conveyed his message to his opponent, stating, "Size, speed, quickness, toughness—that's what Mel had. If you gave Blount free reign to hit you, you were in trouble because, if he missed, he had the speed to catch up. A lot of receivers got short arms when they were in Mel's territory."

Meanwhile, in addressing the overall impact that Blount had on the outcome of games, Cincinnati Bengals tight end Bob Trumpy stated, "They had a receiver-stuffing cornerback who would also tackle. They could eliminate one half of the field basically . . . He was that strong, he was that good at what he did."

Blount's physical style of play prompted the NFL to institute what became known as the "Mel Blount Rule."
Courtesy of MEARSonlineauctions.com

Trumpy added:

> We'd go into the game thinking that we could get the ball
> to our wide receivers. And, after the game, we'd watch the
> tape and our wide receiver on Mel Blount's side would be
> in the concession stand. I mean, that's how far he shoved
> him. Everybody complained about what Pittsburgh was
> doing because Mel Blount was doing it so well. That's why
> the league had to come up with the Mel Blount Rule. You
> know, you get five yards and you get one chuck and then
> you gotta' let him alone because, seriously, it was like we
> were playing with 10 guys on offense.

When the NFL's competition committee instituted a new rule out-
lawing contact with receivers more than five yards beyond the line of
scrimmage, it insisted that it did so as a means of increasing overall scoring
throughout the league. However, Steelers coach Chuck Noll expressed the
belief that the committee had a different intent, suggesting, "They ganged
up on us and are trying to win the championship through legislation. But,
whatever the rules, you have to adjust to them and play with them."

Adapting extremely well to the new rules, Blount changed his coverage
tactics, playing behind the receiver, before closing in quickly to deflect or
intercept the pass intended for him. Proving to be equally effective over the
second half of his career, Blount earned Pro Bowl and All-Pro honors three
times between 1978 and 1981, with his outstanding play in the last of those
campaigns gaining him First-Team All-Pro recognition for the second time.

Blount spent two more years in Pittsburgh, announcing his retirement
following the conclusion of the 1983 campaign with career totals of 57
interceptions, 736 interception-return yards, 13 fumble recoveries, and four
defensive touchdowns. In addition to picking off more passes than anyone
else in franchise history, Blount ended his career having appeared in more
regular-season games (200) than any other Steelers player, missing just one
contest his 14 years in the league.

Upon learning of his election to the Pro Football Hall of Fame the first
time his name appeared on the ballot in 1989, Blount, who now serves
as director of player relations for the NFL, reflected on his playing career,
stating, "If the scales were balanced, there was nobody I couldn't cover.
That's what motivated me, drove me to be as good as I was. I was in front
of 50,000 people in the stands and millions on TV. I didn't want to be
embarrassed."

Blount then added, "I didn't want to be second to anyone. I wanted to set the standards for my position."

Many people feel that Blount achieved his goal.

CAREER HIGHLIGHTS

Best Season

Blount performed extremely well for the Steelers in 1981, recording six interceptions, one of which he returned for a touchdown, and amassing 106 interception-return yards. However, Blount had the greatest season of his career in 1975, when, en route to earning AP Defensive Player of the Year honors, he led the league with 11 interceptions, setting in the process a single-season franchise record that still stands.

Memorable Moments/Greatest Performances

Blount recorded the first interception of his career during a 23–10 win over the Buffalo Bills on October 11, 1970.

Although the Steelers suffered a 17–13 defeat at the hands of the Dallas Cowboys on October 8, 1972, Blount scored the first of his four career touchdowns when he returned a fumble 35 yards for a TD.

Blount crossed the opponent's goal line again on November 3, 1974, when he punctuated a 27–0 victory over the Eagles by returning an interception 52 yards for the game's final score.

Blount ended a Minnesota scoring threat in Super Bowl IX by picking off a Fran Tarkenton pass deep inside Pittsburgh territory late in the first half.

Blount recorded two interceptions for the first time in his career during a 42–6 manhandling of the Cleveland Browns on October 5, 1975.

Blount picked off two passes another two times that season, accomplishing the feat during a 28–3 victory over Kansas City on November 16, before intercepting Joe Namath twice during a 20–7 win over the Jets on November 30.

Blount contributed to a 31–17 victory over the Houston Oilers in the 1980 regular-season opener by picking off Ken Stabler twice.

Blount recorded another two interceptions during a 20–6 win over the New Orleans Saints on October 4, 1981, returning those picks a total of 58 yards.

Although the Steelers lost to the San Francisco 49ers by a score of 17–14 on November 1, 1981, Blount picked off a Joe Montana pass, which he returned 50 yards for a touchdown.

Blount scored the final touchdown of his career on November 6, 1983, when he returned a fumble three yards for a TD during a 26–3 win over the San Diego Chargers.

Notable Achievements

- Scored four defensive touchdowns during career.
- Recorded at least six interceptions four times.
- Surpassed 100 interception-return yards twice.
- Missed just one game in 14 seasons, at one point appearing in 132 consecutive contests.
- Led NFL with 11 interceptions in 1975.
- Led Steelers in interceptions four times.
- Holds Steelers single-season record for most interceptions (11 in 1975).
- Holds Steelers career record for most interceptions (57).
- Ranks among Steelers career leaders with: 736 interception-return yards (3rd); 14 seasons played (tied—3rd); and 200 games played (5th).
- Eight-time division champion (1972, 1974, 1975, 1976, 1977, 1978, 1979, and 1983).
- Four-time AFC champion (1974, 1975, 1978, and 1979).
- Four-time Super Bowl champion (IX, X, XIII, and XIV).
- 1975 Steelers MVP.
- 1975 Associated Press NFL Defensive Player of the Year.
- 1977 Pro Bowl MVP.
- Five-time Pro Bowl selection (1975, 1976, 1978, 1979, and 1981).
- Two-time First-Team All-Pro selection (1975 and 1981).
- Two-time Second-Team All-Pro selection (1978 and 1979).
- Four-time First-Team All-Conference selection (1975, 1976, 1977, and 1981).
- Two-time Second-Team All-Conference selection (1978 and 1979).
- Pro Football Reference All-1970s First Team.
- Pro Football Hall of Fame All-1980s First Team.
- Named to Super Bowl's Silver Anniversary Team in 1990.
- Named to NFL's 75th Anniversary Team in 1994.
- Named to Steelers' 75th Anniversary Team in 2007.

- #47 "unofficially" retired by Steelers.
- Named to *Sporting News* All-Century Team in 1999.
- Number 36 on the *Sporting News'* 1999 list of the 100 Greatest Players in NFL History.
- Number 44 on the NFL Network's 2010 list of the NFL's 100 Greatest Players.
- Elected to Pro Football Hall of Fame in 1989.

5

FRANCO HARRIS

The holder of virtually every Steelers career rushing record, Franco Harris established himself as the greatest running back in franchise history during his 12 seasons in Pittsburgh. Gaining more than 1,000 yards on the ground eight times, Harris set still-standing franchise marks for most yards rushing, yards from scrimmage, all-purpose yards, rushing touchdowns, and touchdowns scored, with his outstanding play helping the Steelers win eight division titles, four AFC championships, and four Super Bowls. An exceptional big-game performer who earned game MVP honors for his stellar play in Super Bowl IX, Harris also earned nine trips to the Pro Bowl, three All-Pro selections, and seven All-AFC nominations while wearing the Black and Gold. Yet, as much as Harris is remembered in Pittsburgh for the many contributions he made to the success of the Steelers through the years with his superb on-field play, he is equally beloved by Steeler fans for the tremendous impact that his larger than life persona had on the team and the city itself.

Born to an Italian mother and an African-American father in Fort Dix, New Jersey, on March 7, 1950, Franco Dok Harris starred on the gridiron while attending Rancocas Valley Regional High School in nearby Mount Holly Township. After enrolling at Penn State University, Harris spent most of his college career serving as a blocker for All-America running back Lydell Mitchell. Nevertheless, he still managed to rush for 2,002 yards and 24 touchdowns, catch 28 passes for 352 yards, and lead the Nittany Lions in scoring once, prompting the Steelers to select him in the first round of the 1972 NFL Draft, with the 13th overall pick.

Used somewhat sparingly by the Steelers during the early stages of the 1972 campaign, Harris became a starter in Week 5, after which he went on to earn NFL Offensive Rookie of the Year honors, Second-Team All-Pro recognition, and the first of his nine consecutive Pro Bowl selections by rushing for 1,055 yards and 10 touchdowns, amassing 1,413 all-purpose yards, scoring 11 touchdowns, and finishing second in the league with a

Franco Harris's Immaculate Reception helped change the fortunes of the Steelers forever.
Courtesy of the Pittsburgh Steelers

rushing average of 5.6 yards per carry. With Harris leading the way on offense, the Steelers advanced to the playoffs for the first time in franchise history. Although they ultimately suffered a 21–17 defeat at the hands of the Miami Dolphins in the AFC championship game, Harris gave them a dramatic 13–7 victory over the Oakland Raiders in the opening round of the postseason tournament when he scored a last-second touchdown on a play that later became known as "The Immaculate Reception."

Harris followed up his outstanding rookie season with a somewhat less productive sophomore campaign in which he rushed for only 698 yards and three touchdowns. However, he subsequently began an exceptional six-year run during which he posted the following numbers:

YEAR	RUSH YD	YD FROM SCRIMMAGE	RUSH TD	TD
1974	1,006	1,206	5	6
1975	1,246	1,460	10	11
1976	1,128	1,279	14*	14
1977	1,162	1,224	11	11
1978	1,082	1,226	8	8
1979	1,186	1,477	11	12

* Please note that any numbers printed in bold throughout this book indicate that the player led the NFL in that statistical category that year.

In addition to leading the NFL in rushing touchdowns and total touchdowns scored in 1976, Harris placed near the top of the league rankings in rushing yards all six seasons, finishing as high as second in 1975, with his excellent play earning him two All-Pro nominations and Pro Bowl and All-AFC honors each year. More importantly, the Steelers established themselves as the NFL's dominant team over the course of those six seasons, winning six consecutive division titles, four AFC championships, and four Super Bowls.

Although Pittsburgh's overwhelming defense received much of the credit for the tremendous success the Steelers experienced during that time, the offense more than held its own, with Harris serving as the catalyst on that side of the ball. After beginning the period as a run-first team that relied heavily on the 6'2", 230-pound Harris to wear down opposing defenses, the Steelers gradually transitioned into more of a passing offense that depended more on the powerful throwing arm of Terry Bradshaw and the brilliant pass-receiving skills of wide receivers Lynn Swann and John Stallworth. But, even as Pittsburgh began to place less emphasis on its running game, Harris remained a huge factor on offense, using his size and strength to bull his way past defenders and his speed to run away from them. Harris also proved to be a major contributor in the passing game, making at least 30 receptions five times and surpassing 200 receiving yards on six occasions, with the totality of his game prompting fellow Hall of Fame running back Jerome Bettis to say of his Steelers predecessor years later, "When you think about a running back, he was the cream of the crop."

Beyond his playing ability, though, Harris possessed a charismatic personality and a positive attitude that rubbed off on his teammates, giving the offense the same type of swagger that players such as Joe Greene and Jack Lambert provided to the defense. Meanwhile, Pittsburgh fans adopted Harris as one of their own, with the city's large Italian-American population dubbing themselves "Franco's Italian Army" and donning army helmets that featured his #32. In discussing the special bond that developed between himself, his teammates, and the city of Pittsburgh, Harris suggested, "A player should not be measured by statistics alone. He should be measured by something more special, such as the sharing of teammates and fans."

The lone criticism of Harris during his time in Pittsburgh came from outsiders such as Jim Brown, who found fault with the way he often tiptoed out of bounds instead of challenging oncoming tacklers. However, Harris responded by claiming that he avoided unnecessary contact so that he might extend his career and help his team win more championships.

Harris saw his string of six consecutive seasons with more than 1,000 yards rushing come to an end in 1980, when he gained 789 yards on the ground. He also failed to top the magical 1,000-yard mark in each of the next two campaigns, posting rushing totals of 987 and 604 yards in 1981 and 1982, respectively. However, he rushed for 1,007 yards in 1983, making him the first player in NFL history to surpass 1,000 yards rushing eight different times (he previously shared the record of seven with Jim Brown).

Unfortunately, the 1983 season ended up being Harris's last in Pittsburgh. With both him and Walter Payton closing in on Jim Brown's career rushing record, Harris asked the Rooney family for a pay raise during the subsequent offseason. Believing that the 34-year-old running back had very little left, the Rooney family refused, prompting Harris to threaten a hold-out. The Steelers then released him during training camp, after which he signed with the Seattle Seahawks. After gaining just 170 yards on the

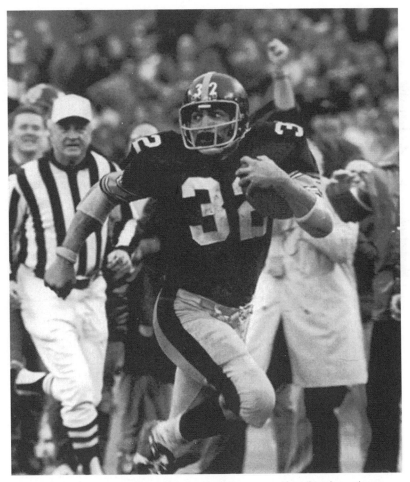

Harris gained more yards on the ground than any other Steelers player.
Courtesy of LegendaryAuctions.com

ground with Seattle in 1984, Harris retired at season's end, finishing his career with 12,120 rushing yards, 307 pass receptions, 2,287 receiving yards, 14,407 yards from scrimmage, 91 rushing touchdowns, 100 total touchdowns scored, and a rushing average of 4.1 yards per carry, compiling virtually all those numbers as a member of the Steelers. At the time of his retirement, Harris's 12,120 yards rushing represented the third-highest total in NFL history (he has since slipped to 15th on the all-time list). Always at his best when it mattered most, Harris held numerous Super Bowl and postseason records when he left the game, including most points scored (24) and most yards rushing (354) in Super Bowl competition, and most touchdowns scored (17) and most yards rushing (1,556) in postseason play. Commenting on his teammate's ability to perform well under pressure, Joe Greene proclaimed, "In a big game, there was no one better than Franco— no one." Meanwhile, Harris stated, "When someone tells me that a regular season game is the same as a championship game, not to me it isn't."

Following his playing days, Harris returned to Pittsburgh and became part-owner of Super Bakery, a company founded in 1990 to produce nutrition-oriented foods for schoolchildren. He also later became a co-owner of the Pittsburgh Passion and a paid representative for the Harrah's/ Forest City Enterprises casino plan for downtown Pittsburgh. After reconciling with the Rooneys, Harris received football's greatest honor in 1990, when he gained induction into the Pro Football Hall of Fame. Making an appearance during the pregame ceremonies for Super Bowl XL, at which the league honored the MVPs of the previous 39 contests, Harris delighted the pro-Steeler crowd by waving a "Terrible Towel" while being introduced. Although the Steelers have officially retired the uniform numbers of just two players (Ernie Stautner and Joe Greene), they have not reissued the numbers of several other exceptional players who have worn the Black and Gold. With Harris's #32 being among them, it is generally understood that no Steelers player will ever wear that number again.

STEELERS CAREER HIGHLIGHTS

Best Season

Harris played his best ball for the Steelers from 1975 to 1979, rushing for more than 1,000 yards and amassing more than 1,200 yards from scrimmage each year, while also scoring at least 10 touchdowns in four of those five seasons. Harris earned First-Team All-Pro honors for the only time in

1977, when he placed near the top of the league rankings with 1,162 yards rushing and 11 touchdowns. However, he averaged just 3.9 yards per carry. Harris rushed for 1,128 yards and a league-leading 14 touchdowns in 1976. But, once again, he averaged only 3.9 yards per carry. Harris, though, not only scored 11 touchdowns and finished second in the NFL with a career-high 1,246 yards rushing in 1975, but he also averaged 4.8 yards per carry, earning in the process one of his two Second-Team All-Pro nominations. Factoring everything into the equation, the 1975 campaign would have to be considered the finest of Harris's career.

Memorable Moments/Greatest Performances

Harris excelled in his first pro start, rushing for 115 yards and one touchdown during a 24–7 win over the Houston Oilers on October 15, 1972.

Harris topped that performance two weeks later, gaining 138 yards on 15 carries and scoring three touchdowns, in leading the Steelers to a 38–21 victory over Buffalo on October 29, 1972.

Harris continued his outstanding play against Kansas City on November 15 of that year, rushing for 134 yards and one touchdown during a 16–7 win.

Although the Steelers lost to Cleveland by a score of 26–24 just four days later, Harris gained 136 yards on the ground and scored one touchdown, which came on a career-long 75-yard run.

Harris had another big day against the Browns on November 17, 1974, rushing for a season-high 156 yards during a 26–16 Steelers win.

Harris helped propel the Steelers to a 32–14 victory over Buffalo in the divisional round of the 1974 playoffs by rushing for 74 yards and three touchdowns.

Harris followed that up with a strong performance against Oakland in the 1974 AFC championship game, leading the Steelers to a 24–13 win over the Raiders by gaining 111 yards on the ground and scoring a pair of touchdowns, which came on runs of eight and 21 yards.

Harris subsequently earned Super Bowl IX MVP honors by carrying the ball 34 times for 158 yards and one touchdown during Pittsburgh's 16–6 victory over Minnesota.

Harris had his two biggest games of the 1975 campaign in November, rushing for a season-high 157 yards during a 30–24 win over Cincinnati on the second of the month, before carrying the ball 21 times for 149 yards and two touchdowns during a 32–9 mauling of the Houston Oilers on November 24.

Harris turned in an outstanding effort against Baltimore in the divisional round of the 1975 playoffs, leading the Steelers to a 28–10 victory over the Colts by rushing for 153 yards and one touchdown, which came on an 8-yard run.

Harris helped the Steelers begin their nine-game winning streak in 1976 by rushing for 143 yards and two touchdowns during a 23–6 win over the Cincinnati Bengals on October 17.

Harris once again proved to be too much for Baltimore to handle in the 1976 playoffs, leading the Steelers to a lopsided 40–14 victory over the Colts in the divisional round of the postseason tournament by gaining 132 yards on 18 carries.

Harris starred during a 28–13 win over the Dallas Cowboys on November 20, 1977, rushing for a career-high 179 yards and two touchdowns, one of which came on a season-long 61-yard run.

Harris helped lead the Steelers to a 33–10 victory over the Denver Broncos in their 1978 divisional round playoff matchup by rushing for 105 yards and two touchdowns.

Harris performed exceptionally well throughout the month of October 1979, rushing for 153 yards and two touchdowns during a 51–35 win over the Browns, gaining 121 yards on 17 carries and scoring two touchdowns during a lopsided 42–7 victory over the Broncos, and leading the Steelers to a 14–3 win over the Cowboys by rushing for 102 yards and two touchdowns, one of which came on a 48-yard run.

Continuing his outstanding play in November, Harris proved to be the difference in a 33–30 overtime victory over Cleveland on November 25, 1979, rushing for 151 yards and two touchdowns, and scoring a third TD on a short pass from Terry Bradshaw.

Harris topped the 100-yard mark for the final time in his career on October 23, 1983, when he rushed for 132 yards and one touchdown during a 27–21 win over the Seattle Seahawks.

Still, there is little doubt that one moment stands out above all others as easily the most memorable of Harris's career. With the Steelers trailing the Oakland Raiders in the divisional round of the 1972 playoffs by a score of 7–6 with just 22 seconds left on the clock and in possession of the ball at their own 40-yard line, a scrambling Terry Bradshaw threw a desperation pass deep downfield for running back John "Frenchy" Fuqua. Just as the ball reached Fuqua, Oakland defensive back Jack Tatum delivered a jarring blow to him that separated him from the football, apparently resulting in an incomplete pass. However, Harris, who had been trailing the play, caught the ball just before it hit the ground and ran some 40 yards down the left sideline for a miraculous touchdown that gave the Steelers their first playoff victory ever. Looking back at the play, Harris said, "I was just doing my job going to the ball. I didn't see Tatum and Fuqua going up, but, all of a sudden, I saw the ball coming at me. I reached down and grabbed it around my knees and took off down the sideline. I didn't know if it was legal or not, but I wasn't going to stand around and ask." The play, which has become known as "The Immaculate Reception," remains one of the most famous in NFL history.

Notable Achievements

- Rushed for more than 1,000 yards eight times.
- Surpassed 1,000 yards from scrimmage nine times.
- Scored more than 10 touchdowns five times.
- Averaged more than 4.5 yards per carry three times, topping 5 yards per carry once (5.6 in 1972).
- Led NFL with 14 touchdowns in 1976.
- Finished second in NFL with rushing average of 5.6 yards per carry in 1972.
- Finished second in NFL with 1,246 yards rushing in 1975.
- Finished third in NFL in rushing touchdowns twice.
- Led Steelers in rushing 12 straight times.
- Holds Steelers single-season record for most rushing touchdowns (14 in 1976).
- Holds Steelers career records for most: rushing attempts (2,881); rushing yards (11,950); yards from scrimmage (14,234); all-purpose yards (14,449); rushing touchdowns (91); and touchdowns scored (100).
- Ranks fourth in Steelers history with 600 points scored.
- Retired as NFL's third-leading all-time rusher.
- Eight-time division champion (1972, 1974, 1975, 1976, 1977, 1978, 1979, and 1983).
- Four-time AFC champion (1974, 1975, 1978, and 1979).
- Four-time Super Bowl champion (IX, X, XIII, and XIV).
- 1972 NFL Offensive Rookie of the Year.
- 1972 Steelers MVP.
- Super Bowl IX MVP.
- 1976 NFL Man of the Year.
- Nine-time Pro Bowl selection (1972, 1973, 1974, 1975, 1976, 1977, 1978, 1979, and 1980).

- 1977 First-Team All-Pro selection.
- Two-time Second-Team All-Pro selection (1972 and 1975).
- Three-time First-Team All-Conference selection (1972, 1975, and 1977).
- Four-time Second-Team All-Conference selection (1974, 1976, 1978, and 1979).
- Pro Football Hall of Fame All-1970s Second Team.
- Pro Football Reference All-1970s Second Team.
- Named to Steelers' 75th Anniversary Team in 2007.
- #32 "unofficially" retired by Steelers.
- Number 83 on the *Sporting News'* 1999 list of the 100 Greatest Players in NFL History.
- Elected to Pro Football Hall of Fame in 1990.

6

— ROD WOODSON —

A tremendous all-around player who earned All-Pro honors as a cornerback, safety, and kick returner over the course of his career, Rod Woodson spent his first 10 NFL seasons in Pittsburgh, setting franchise records for most touchdown interceptions, punt-return yards, and kickoff-return yards. Excelling in all phases of the game, Woodson also ranks extremely high in team annals in interceptions, interception-return yards, tackles, forced fumbles, and fumble recoveries, leading the Steelers in picks four times and amassing more than 1,000 all-purpose yards on four separate occasions. Woodson, who starred at both cornerback positions during his time in Pittsburgh, earned seven trips to the Pro Bowl, five All-Pro selections, six All-AFC nominations, recognition as the 1993 NFL Defensive Player of the Year, and a spot on the NFL's 75th Anniversary Team while playing for the Steelers, helping them capture four division titles and one AFC championship in the process. And, after leaving Pittsburgh following the conclusion of the 1996 campaign, Woodson spent seven more years in the league starring for three other teams, with his exceptional play at each locale eventually landing him a top-50 spot on the NFL Network's 2010 list of the 100 Greatest Players in NFL History and a place in the Pro Football Hall of Fame.

Born to a Caucasian mother and an African-American father in Fort Wayne, Indiana, on March 10, 1965, Roderick Kevin Woodson grew up in that city's ghetto, where he often found himself being ridiculed by others for his mixed racial background. Establishing himself as an outstanding all-around athlete while attending local R. Nelson Snider High School, Woodson starred in basketball, track, and football, winning the high and low hurdles state championships in both his junior and senior years, while also gaining *Parade* magazine and *USA Today* All-America recognition for his stellar play at defensive back, wide receiver, and running back on the gridiron.

Continuing to excel in multiple sports after enrolling at Purdue University, Woodson earned All-America honors in both football and track, setting school records in both the 60- and 110-meter hurdles, and qualifying for the 1984 Olympic Trials in the latter event. Meanwhile, Woodson, who majored in criminal justice while at Purdue, starred for the Boilermakers on the gridiron as a cornerback and kick returner, earning All-America honors at both positions, while also seeing extensive action at running back and wide receiver. Displaying his extraordinary athletic ability in his final collegiate game, Woodson led Purdue to a victory over arch-rival Indiana by gaining over 150 combined rushing and receiving yards, recording 10 tackles, forcing a

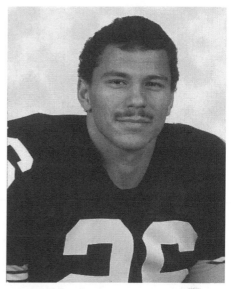

Rod Woodson starred at both cornerback positions during his time in Pittsburgh. Courtesy of the Pittsburgh Steelers

fumble, intercepting three passes, and returning two kickoffs for 46 yards and three punts for 30 yards.

Impressed with Woodson's brilliant all-around play, the Steelers made him the 10th overall pick of the 1987 NFL Draft, after which they used him primarily as a return man his first year in the league. Yet, even though Woodson made his greatest overall impact as a rookie returning punts and kickoffs, he also saw some action at cornerback, recording 20 tackles and one interception, which he returned 45 yards for the first touchdown of his career.

After laying claim to the starting right-cornerback job the following year, Woodson emerged as a force on the defensive side of the ball, recording four interceptions and finishing second on the club with 88 solo tackles, earning in the process team MVP honors for the first of three times. Also establishing himself as one of the NFL's most dangerous return men in 1988, Woodson ran back one kickoff 92 yards for a touchdown and placed near the top of the league rankings with a total of 1,131 return yards. Commenting on Woodson's outstanding play, then Steelers defensive coordinator Tony Dungy proclaimed, "Rod is a tremendous athlete. He is going to be a great player in this league if he keeps working."

Continuing to excel in his dual role of cornerback/return man from 1989 to 1991, Woodson earned Pro Bowl honors all three years and gained

First-Team All-Pro recognition in both 1989 and 1990. One of the NFL's most complete players throughout the period, Woodson finished second in the league in total return yards in each of those three seasons, while also compiling 11 interceptions, 217 solo tackles, and 10 fumble recoveries during that time.

Expressing his admiration for Woodson, Kansas City Chiefs head coach Marty Schottenheimer stated, "I can understand why he's been a successful performer in this league. He has tremendous personal pride in everything he does, including not only his play, but his preparation. He's got great ball skills . . . great hands."

The 6-foot, 200-pound Woodson also possessed intelligence, excellent instincts, good size, and tremendous speed, with Chuck Noll, who coached Woodson his first five years in the league, later saying of his star defensive back, "He was something special as an athlete. He had the great speed and the size."

Jerome Bettis, who spent one season in Pittsburgh playing with Woodson, also had high praise for his former teammate, stating, "He could run. He could jump. He was athletic. He could do it all."

Yet, as well as Woodson played at right corner under Noll from 1987 to 1991, he performed even better after he moved to the left side of the Steelers defense when Bill Cowher assumed head coaching duties in Pittsburgh in 1992. After earning Pro Bowl and First-Team All-Pro honors in Cowher's first year at the helm by recording four interceptions, four fumble recoveries, a career-high six sacks, and a team-leading 100 solo tackles, Woodson intercepted eight passes, amassed 138 interception-return yards, registered 95 solo tackles, and successfully defended 28 passes in 1993, earning in the process recognition as the NFL Defensive Player of the Year. He followed that up with another outstanding season, earning his sixth consecutive Pro Bowl selection and third straight All-Pro nomination in 1994, before tearing his ACL in the opening game of the ensuing campaign and subsequently undergoing reconstructive knee surgery that sidelined him for the rest of the regular season, although he returned to the Steelers in time to make a token appearance in Super Bowl XXX. Fully recovered by the start of the 1996 season, Woodson earned his seventh trip to the Pro Bowl by recording six interceptions, 121 interception-return yards, and 67 tackles, recovering three fumbles, and scoring a pair of touchdowns on defense.

Sadly, the 1996 campaign ended up being Woodson's last in Pittsburgh. With the Rooney family electing not to renew his contract at season's end, Woodson became a free agent, after which he signed with the San Francisco 49ers. Upon inking his deal with the 49ers, Woodson discussed the

Woodson holds franchise records for most TD interceptions, punt-return yards, and kickoff-return yards.
Courtesy of LegendaryAuctions.com

circumstances surrounding his departure from Pittsburgh and expressed his regrets over having to leave the city he had come to think of as home, saying:

> The new way of doing business in the NFL is not a pleasant business. Management thinks this is a young man's game. There is no consideration for what you have done,

only for what they think you can do. After the season last year, the Steelers wouldn't even talk to me. They never looked me in the face and said, "Rod, we don't think you can play anymore." They finally made me a low offer that they must have known I would refuse, to make me look like the guy that was running out of town. Well, I am leaving, and I have made this decision with my heart. Disappointed? Yes. But, more than that, I am hurt. And, if it hurts, then that says that this team and this city mean a lot to me.

Woodson then added, "I had great coaches in Pittsburgh—Chuck Noll, Tony Dungy, Rod Rust, John Fox, Dom Capers, and Dick LeBeau, just to name a few. I had great friends on the team and fans that even named their kids after me. For the next six months, I will eat, sleep, and live football. I will work toward the 49ers wanting me for years to come. . . . The 49ers expect a lot of me, but I expect even more. The Steelers don't think I can play anymore. Time will tell their story. And time will tell mine."

Steelers owner Dan Rooney also expressed a great deal of sadness over Woodson's impending departure, stating, "When Franco Harris went to Seattle, that was the most difficult. But this thing with Rod is right up there. Right up to now, I wanted Rod on our team. You can blame it on the salary cap. You can blame it on anything you want. I really wish he was finishing his career with us for a lot of reasons. It hurts."

Meanwhile, 49ers president Carmen Policy gleefully looked forward to Woodson's arrival, saying, "Woodson is the kind of player who can make other players better because he'll be able to show them how to position themselves, how to make plays."

Woodson ended up spending just one season in San Francisco, before moving on to Baltimore, where he recorded a total of 20 interceptions for the Ravens over the course of the next four years, earning in the process three more trips to the Pro Bowl. Adapting extremely well to his new position of free safety in 1999, Woodson led the NFL with seven interceptions and finished second in the league with 195 interception-return yards, before picking off four passes and recording 77 tackles for the Super Bowl champions the following year. Opting to sign with the Raiders following the conclusion of the 2001 campaign, Woodson spent his final two NFL seasons in Oakland, leading the league with eight interceptions in 2002, when he earned the last of his seven All-Pro nominations and 11 Pro Bowl selections, which represents a league record for defensive backs. Choosing to announce his retirement after the Raiders released him early in 2004, Woodson ended his career with 71 interceptions, 1,483 interception-return yards, 1,157 tackles, 20 forced fumbles, 32 fumble recoveries, and 12 touchdown interceptions, with his totals in each of the last two categories also representing NFL records. Woodson also scored four touchdowns on special teams, returned one fumble for a TD, and amassed 7,256 yards returning kickoffs and punts, giving him a total of 8,876 all-purpose yards. In his 10 years with the Steelers, Woodson intercepted 38 passes, amassed 779 interception-return yards, scored 10 of his 17 touchdowns, and recorded 671 tackles, 13½ sacks, 16 forced fumbles, 21 fumble recoveries, 7,256 punt and kickoff-return yards, and 8,104 all-purpose yards.

Woodson's brilliant all-around play prompted fellow Steelers Hall of Fame defensive back Mel Blount to say, "He, in my opinion, might be the greatest athlete that Chuck Noll ever drafted. And that's saying a lot when you think of all the Hall of Famers. This guy was special."

For his part, Woodson says, "I think that maybe when I played, in my timeframe, there may have been better cover corners, there might have been some better safeties, and I think there might have been some better kick returners. But, I think that, putting that all together in one package, I was proud of that."

After retiring as an active player, Woodson spent eight years working as an analyst for the NFL Network and the Big Ten Network, before briefly serving as cornerback coach for the Oakland Raiders. Returning to the broadcast booth in 2012, Woodson spent two years working for Westwood One radio, before resuming his coaching career as an assistant with the Raiders in 2014. He remained in Oakland until the end of 2017, when the Raiders dismissed him following the hiring of Jon Gruden as head coach. Woodson, who currently lives with his wife Nickie and their five children in Pleasanton, California, now coaches women's basketball at Valley Christian Senior High School in nearby Dublin, California.

Although Woodson left Pittsburgh feeling a certain amount of bitterness toward the team's front office, he still considers himself to be a Steeler at heart, telling Steelers.com:

> I spent 10 years there and people still see me as a player for the Steelers. I still see myself as a Steeler, wearing the black and gold. I wore black and gold when I was in high school. My college was black and gold, then I spent 10 years in black and gold with the Steelers. It is a part of who I am. It's the same colors I've been wearing since I was 14 years

old until I left Pittsburgh. . . . Normally, the people that do come up to me are Steelers fans. They are everywhere. No matter where you go, no matter what you do, you'll find a Steelers fan somewhere. When I moved out here to California, there was a Steelers flag flying right around the corner from my house. You realize that, if you wear black and gold, because I think that's the only city that their NFL, baseball, and hockey teams all have the same colors, you are part of the family. You are part of the community.

STEELERS CAREER HIGHLIGHTS

Best Season

Woodson played his best ball for the Steelers from 1992 to 1994, earning consensus First-Team All-Pro honors all three years by amassing a total of 16 interceptions and 337 interception-return yards during that time. Performing particularly well in 1993, Woodson gained recognition as the NFL Defensive Player of the Year by placing near the top of the league rankings with eight interceptions and 138 interception-return yards, while also recording 95 solo tackles, two sacks, two forced fumbles, one fumble recovery, one defensive touchdown, and 632 yards on special teams.

Memorable Moments/Greatest Performances

Woodson scored his first touchdown as a member of the Steelers during a 30–16 win over the Cincinnati Bengals on November 22, 1987, when he returned the first interception of his career 45 yards for a TD.

Woodson scored his first points on special teams during a 31–14 loss to the Phoenix Cardinals on October 9, 1988, when he returned a kickoff 92 yards for a touchdown.

Woodson lit the scoreboard again on November 19, 1989, returning a kickoff 84 yards for a touchdown during a 20–17 win over the San Diego Chargers.

In addition to earning AFC Defensive Player of the Week honors with his stellar play on that side of the ball, Woodson sealed a 20–9 victory over the Houston Oilers on September 16, 1990, by returning a punt 52 yards for a touchdown midway through the fourth quarter.

Woodson turned in another outstanding effort against Houston in the 1992 regular-season opener, leading the Steelers to a 29–24 win over the Oilers by recording a pair of interceptions, which he returned for a total of 73 yards.

Woodson starred during a 27–3 win over the Kansas City Chiefs on October 25, 1992, intercepting a pass and returning a punt 80 yards for a touchdown.

Woodson earned AFC Defensive Player of the Week honors for his performance during a 37–14 victory over the New Orleans Saints on October 17, 1993, when he picked off two passes, one of which he returned 63 yards for a touchdown.

Woodson helped lead the Steelers to a 23–10 win over the Buffalo Bills on November 14, 1994, by recording a sack and scoring a touchdown on a 37-yard interception return, earning in the process AFC Defensive Player of the Week honors once again.

Woodson crossed the opponent's goal line again during a 38–15 victory over the Cincinnati Bengals on December 4, 1994, when he returned an interception 27 yards for a touchdown.

Woodson scored the Steelers' first touchdown of the 1996 campaign in Week 2, when he returned an interception 43 yards for a TD during a 31–17 win over the Baltimore Ravens.

Woodson lit the scoreboard for the final time as a member of the Steelers during a 20–10 victory over Cincinnati on October 13, 1996, when he returned a fumble 42 yards for a touchdown.

Notable Achievements

- Scored six defensive touchdowns.
- Returned two punts and two kickoffs for touchdowns.
- Recorded at least five interceptions three times.
- Surpassed 100 interception-return yards three times.
- Recorded more than 100 tackles three times.
- Recorded six sacks in 1992.
- Amassed more than 1,000 all-purpose yards four times.
- Led NFL with average of 27.3 yards per kickoff return in 1989.
- Finished second in NFL in interception-return yards once and kickoff-return yards twice.
- Finished third in NFL in interceptions once and punt-return yards once.

- Led Steelers in interceptions four times.
- Holds Steelers career records for most: touchdown interceptions (5); punt-return yards (2,362); and kickoff-return yards (4,894).
- Ranks among Steelers career leaders with: 38 interceptions (4th); 779 interception-return yards (2nd); 671 tackles (9th); 16 forced fumbles (4th); and 21 fumble recoveries (tied—2nd).
- Holds NFL records for most interceptions returned for touchdowns (12) and most fumble recoveries by a defensive player (32).
- Ranks among NFL career leaders with: 17 non-offensive touchdowns (3rd); 71 interceptions (3rd); and 1,483 interception-return yards (2nd).
- Four-time division champion (1992, 1994, 1995, and 1996).
- 1995 AFC champion.
- Four-time AFC Defensive Player of the Week.
- 1993 Week 4 AFC Special Teams Player of the Week.
- 1993 NFL Defensive Player of the Year.
- Three-time Steelers MVP (1988, 1990, and 1993).
- Seven-time Pro Bowl selection (1989, 1990, 1991, 1992, 1993, 1994, and 1996).
- Five-time First-Team All-Pro selection (1989, 1990, 1992, 1993, and 1994).
- Five-time First-Team All-Conference selection (1989, 1990, 1992, 1993, and 1994).
- 1996 Second-Team All-Conference selection.
- Pro Football Hall of Fame All-1990s First Team.
- Pro Football Reference All-1990s First Team.
- Named to NFL's 75th Anniversary Team in 1994.
- Named to Steelers' 75th Anniversary Team in 2007.
- Number 87 on the *Sporting News'* 1999 list of the 100 Greatest Players in NFL History.
- Number 41 on the NFL Network's 2010 list of the NFL's 100 Greatest Players.
- Elected to Pro Football Hall of Fame in 2009.

7

TERRY BRADSHAW

A look at the career numbers of Terry Bradshaw might leave one wondering why he is often ranked as the finest quarterback of his time. Completing only 52 percent of his passes over the course of 14 NFL seasons, Bradshaw threw nearly as many interceptions (210) as he did touchdown passes (212). Furthermore, Bradshaw led NFL quarterbacks in a major statistical category just twice his entire career. But numbers tell only so much about Bradshaw, who, after struggling his first few years in Pittsburgh, gradually emerged as the offensive leader of Steeler teams that won eight division titles, four AFC championships, and four Super Bowls. A three-time Pro Bowl selection and three-time All-AFC nomination, Bradshaw also earned league MVP honors in 1978, when he led the Steelers to their third NFL title in five seasons. Yet, even though Bradshaw eventually established himself as an elite signal-caller in regular-season play, he built his reputation largely on his ability to perform well in the playoffs, with his four Super Bowl victories tying him with Joe Montana for the second-most by any quarterback in NFL history (Tom Brady has won six). A two-time Super Bowl MVP, Bradshaw earned a top-50 spot on both the *Sporting News'* and the NFL Network's lists of the 100 Greatest Players in NFL History with his outstanding postseason play, which ultimately gained him induction into the Pro Football Hall of Fame.

Born in Shreveport, Louisiana, on September 2, 1948, Terry Paxton Bradshaw spent his early childhood living in Camanche, Iowa, before moving back to Shreveport with his family as a teenager. Starring in multiple sports while attending Woodlawn High School, Bradshaw excelled as a quarterback on the gridiron and as a javelin thrower in track and field, once setting a national record by tossing the projectile 245 feet.

Choosing to accept a scholarship offer from Louisiana Tech University in nearby Ruston, Bradshaw spent three years calling the signals for the Bulldogs on offense and gained general recognition as the most outstanding quarterback in all of college football. After leading his team to a 9-2

Terry Bradshaw led the Steelers to eight division titles, four AFC championships, and four Super Bowl wins.
Courtesy of MEARSonlineauctions.com

record as a junior by amassing an NCAA-best 2,890 yards of total offense, Bradshaw passed for 2,314 yards in his senior year, making him the most sought-after player heading into the 1970 NFL Draft. With the 1-13

Steelers winning a tiebreaking coin flip with the equally inept Chicago Bears, they obtained the rights to the first overall pick, which they subsequently used to select Bradshaw.

Despite being heralded as "the NFL's next great quarterback," Bradshaw experienced a considerable amount of adversity his first few seasons in Pittsburgh. After winning just three of his eight starts while splitting time with second-year signal-caller Terry Hanratty as a rookie, Bradshaw went just 5-8 as a starter in his sophomore campaign of 1971. Although the Steelers compiled a record of 11-3 the following year, earning in the process their first playoff berth ever, they did so primarily on the strength of their running game and overpowering defense, with Bradshaw completing just 47.7 percent of his passes and throwing for only 1,887 yards and 12 touchdowns. The Steelers advanced to the playoffs once again in 1973, but Bradshaw started only nine games due to injury, finishing the year with 10 TD passes and 15 interceptions.

With Bradshaw continuing to perform erratically during the 1974 preseason, he lost his starting job to Joe Gilliam. But, after Gilliam failed to distinguish himself during the season's first half, Bradshaw assumed the mantle of leadership once again at midseason, posting a record of 5-2 as a starter the rest of the way. Nevertheless, Bradshaw remained mostly unimpressive, completing just 45.3 percent of his passes and throwing for only 785 yards and seven touchdowns.

Certainly, Bradshaw's inexperience contributed greatly to his early struggles. However, he also suffered from a lack of confidence and feelings of insecurity brought on by his frequent benchings and the manner with which the media often ridiculed him for his rural roots and perceived lack of intelligence. Eventually, though, Bradshaw learned to use the doubts that others had in him as motivational tools, stating years later, "The resentment, the anger I had for being called dumb and being put in and out of the lineup, you learn to use it as a tool."

Revealing the moment when he finally felt as if he belonged in the NFL, Bradshaw said, "When I got the confidence from that man (Coach Chuck Noll) was when I became a pro quarterback. Prior to that, I wasn't making any progress. I knew that when I made mistakes, I was going to be benched. But, when he said, 'Go make your mistakes, we're going to win with you,' that's when I became a quarterback."

Having received a vote of confidence from his head coach, Bradshaw displayed a new level of maturity during the 1974 postseason, leading the Steelers to their first NFL title by completing 58 percent of his passes, throwing for 394 yards, and tossing three TD passes and only one interception during victories over the Buffalo Bills, Oakland Raiders, and Minnesota Vikings. Bradshaw followed that up with a breakout 1975 campaign in which he earned Pro Bowl and Second-Team All-AFC honors by completing a career-high 57.7 percent of his passes, while also throwing for 2,055 yards and tossing 18 TD passes and just nine interceptions. He then guided the Steelers to their second consecutive NFL championship by leading them to playoff wins over the Baltimore Colts, Oakland Raiders, and Dallas Cowboys.

While the Steelers relied heavily on their potent running game and imposing "Steel Curtain" defense to capture their first two league championships, they also benefited greatly from having the strong-armed Bradshaw at quarterback. Able to loosen up opposing defenses with the threat of going deep with his powerful throwing arm, the 6'3", 215-pound Bradshaw provided the perfect complement to running backs Franco Harris and Rocky Bleier on offense. And, even though Bradshaw ran with the ball less as his career progressed, he also proved to be a capable runner, rushing for more than 200 yards in six different seasons, en route to amassing a total of 2,257 yards on the ground over the course of his career.

Limited to just eight starts by injuries to his neck and wrist in 1976, Bradshaw threw for only 1,177 yards and 10 touchdowns. However, a return to full health the following year enabled him to rank among the league leaders with 2,523 passing yards and 17 touchdown passes. No longer just a game-manager, Bradshaw subsequently reached the apex of his career, posting the following numbers over the course of the next four seasons:

YEAR	YD PASSING	TD PASSES	INT	COMP %	QBR
1978	2,915	**28**	20	56.3	84.7
1979	3,724	26	25	54.9	77.0
1980	3,339	24	22	51.4	75.0
1981	2,887	22	14	54.3	83.9

Bradshaw placed near the top of the league rankings in touchdown passes all four years, topping the circuit in that category in 1978, when he earned NFL MVP honors. He also ranked among the league leaders in passing yards and passer rating in three of those four seasons, with his strong play earning him two trips to the Pro Bowl and a pair of All-AFC nominations. More importantly, Bradshaw led the Steelers to the NFL championship in both 1978 and 1979, earning game MVP honors for his outstanding performances in Super Bowls XIII and XIV.

After failing to lead an aging Steelers team into the playoffs in either 1980 or 1981, Bradshaw played through pain throughout the strike-shortened 1982 campaign after injuring his elbow during training camp. Nevertheless, he still managed to tie for the league lead with 17 touchdown passes and complete 28-of-39 passes for 325 yards and two touchdowns during a 31–28 loss to San Diego in the opening round of the postseason tournament. Bradshaw subsequently appeared in just one game the following year after undergoing offseason elbow surgery, before announcing his retirement at season's end. In addition to his 212 touchdown passes, 210 interceptions, and 51.9 completion percentage, Bradshaw ended his career with 27,989 passing yards and a quarterback rating of 70.9. Although he passed for more than 300 yards in a game just seven times over the course of his career, he did so three times in the playoffs. Performing particularly well in his four Super Bowl appearances, Bradshaw threw for an impressive 932 yards and nine touchdowns, both of which represented Super Bowl records at the time of his retirement. Commenting on his ability to excel on football's grandest stage, Bradshaw stated, "In every fourth quarter of every Super Bowl, I came through with a big play. Go to Super Bowl XIV and take that touchdown pass at the end of the game to John Stallworth. That's who I am."

Following his retirement as an active player, Bradshaw spent six years serving as an NFL game analyst for CBS television, before joining that station's *NFL Today* pregame program in 1990. After co-hosting that show with Greg Gumbel for four years, Bradshaw joined the *Fox NFL Sunday* team of

Bradshaw's outstanding play earned him NFL MVP honors in 1978.
Courtesy of MEARSonlineauctions.com

analysts, where he has spent the last 25 years serving as a comic foil to his co-hosts.

Unfortunately, Bradshaw, who experienced frequent anxiety attacks during his playing days that ultimately led to him being diagnosed with clinical depression, found himself unable to return to Pittsburgh for many years once he left the game due to his fear of crowds, leading to an unintentional estrangement from the Steelers. Criticized for failing to attend Art Rooney's funeral in 1988, Bradshaw chose to pay homage to the Steelers' founder and longtime owner one year later during his Hall of Fame induction speech, when he pointed to the sky and said, "Art Rooney . . . boy, I tell you, I loved that man."

However, Bradshaw finally did return to the city of his greatest triumphs in September 2002, when he paid his respects to his longtime teammate and close friend Mike Webster following his passing. One month later, Bradshaw returned to the Steelers sideline for the first time in 20 years for a Monday night game between Pittsburgh and Indianapolis. He has since made a number of other appearances at Heinz Field, including taking his position on the Steelers All-Time Team during the franchise's 75th anniversary celebration in 2007.

CAREER HIGHLIGHTS

Best Season

Bradshaw had a big year for the Steelers in 1979, finishing third among NFL quarterbacks with a career-high 3,724 yards passing, while also ranking among the league leaders with 26 touchdown passes. However, he posted the best overall numbers of his career the previous season, earning 1978 NFL MVP honors and his lone First-Team All-Pro selection by throwing for 2,915 yards, leading the league with 28 TD passes, and finishing second in the circuit with a passer rating of 84.7.

Memorable Moments/Greatest Performances

Although the Steelers lost their November 14, 1971, meeting with the eventual AFC champion Miami Dolphins by a score of 24–21, Bradshaw threw three touchdown passes for the first time in his career, hitting Ron Shanklin with a 28-yard TD pass and collaborating with Dave Smith on scoring plays that covered 30 and 16 yards. Bradshaw finished the game with 25 completions in 36 attempts, for 253 yards.

Bradshaw gave the Steelers a dramatic 21–13 come-from-behind victory over Cincinnati on December 12, 1971, by coming off the bench to throw a pair of fourth-quarter touchdown passes.

Even though Bradshaw completed just eight of 19 passes for 80 yards and two TDs during a 28–7 win over the New Orleans Saints on November 25, 1974, he rushed for a career-high 99 yards and one touchdown, which came on an 18-yard scamper.

Bradshaw led the Steelers to a convincing 37–0 victory over San Diego in the 1975 regular-season opener by completing 21 of 28 pass attempts for 227 yards and two touchdowns, which came on a 40-yard connection with Frank Lewis and a 38-yard hookup with John Stallworth.

Bradshaw had another strong outing on November 9, 1975, passing for 219 yards and three touchdowns during a 24–17 win over the Houston Oilers.

Bradshaw led the Steelers to a 35–31 win over the Cleveland Browns on November 13, 1977, by passing for 283 yards and three touchdowns, the longest of which went 39 yards to Lynn Swann.

Bradshaw turned in a strong all-around effort against Seattle on December 4, 1977, leading the Steelers to a 30–20 victory over the Seahawks by passing for 158 yards and one touchdown, and scoring twice himself on a pair of short TD runs.

Just one week after passing for 242 yards and two touchdowns during a 28–3 win over Cincinnati, Bradshaw gave the Steelers a 15–9 overtime victory over Cleveland on September 24, 1978, by hitting Bennie Cunningham with a 37-yard TD pass during the overtime session.

Bradshaw continued to excel in his MVP season of 1978, throwing three touchdown passes during a 28–17 win over the Jets on October 1, before passing for 231 yards, completing one touchdown pass, and running for one score himself, in leading the Steelers to a lopsided 31–7 victory over the Atlanta Falcons one week later.

Bradshaw led the Steelers to a 42–7 rout of the Denver Broncos on October 22, 1979, by completing 18 of 24 pass attempts for 267 yards and two touchdowns, collaborating with Lynn Swann and Sidney Thornton on scoring plays that covered 11 and 17 yards, respectively.

Bradshaw had a huge day against Washington on November 4, 1979, passing for 311 yards and four touchdowns during a convincing 38–7 victory over the Redskins.

Bradshaw turned in another exceptional performance during a 33–30 overtime win over the Cleveland Browns on November 25, 1979, amassing more than 400 yards of total offense by throwing for a career-high 364 yards and gaining another 43 yards on the ground.

Bradshaw followed that up one week later by passing for 339 yards and two touchdowns during a 37–17 victory over Cincinnati, with his TD passes, both of which went to Lynn Swann, covering 58 and 42 yards.

Bradshaw led the Steelers to a 38–3 mauling of the Chicago Bears on September 28, 1980, by passing for 217 yards and four touchdowns, three of which went to Jim Smith.

Bradshaw passed for 253 yards and a career-high five touchdowns during a 34–20 win over the Atlanta Falcons on November 15, 1981, with two of his TD passes going to John Stallworth and the other three to Bennie Cunningham, Randy Grossman, and Lynn Swann.

Bradshaw had his last big game for the Steelers on September 19, 1982, when he led them to a 26–20 overtime victory over the Cincinnati Bengals by passing for 298 yards and three touchdowns, the last of which was a 2-yard toss to John Stallworth that won the game in OT.

Yet, Bradshaw is remembered more than anything for his exceptional postseason play, with his four Super Bowl victories making him one of just three quarterbacks in NFL history to hoist the Lombardi Trophy that many times. After being more of a game-manager in his first Super Bowl appearance, Bradshaw proved to be much more of a factor when the Steelers recorded a 21–17 victory over Dallas in Super Bowl X, passing for 209 yards and two touchdowns, with his 64-yard TD toss to Lynn Swann in the fourth quarter, which he released a split-second before being flattened by defensive tackle Larry Cole, being the game's most memorable play.

Bradshaw continued his postseason success the following year, completing 14 of 18 pass attempts for 264 yards and three touchdowns during Pittsburgh's lopsided 40–14 victory over Baltimore in the 1976 playoffs, with his longest completion of the day being a 76-yard TD connection with Frank Lewis on the Steelers' first possession of the game.

Bradshaw also performed extremely well during Pittsburgh's 33–10 win over Denver in the divisional round of the 1978 playoffs, throwing for 272 yards and two touchdowns, with his fourth-quarter TD passes of 45 yards to John Stallworth and 38 yards to Lynn Swann breaking the game wide open.

After being mocked before Super Bowl XIII by Dallas linebacker Thomas "Hollywood" Henderson, who questioned his intelligence by saying, "He couldn't spell 'Cat' if you spotted him the 'c' and the 'a'," Bradshaw gained a measure of revenge by passing for 318 yards and four touchdowns during the Steelers' 35–31 win over the Cowboys, earning in the process game MVP honors.

Bradshaw again performed brilliantly in Super Bowl XIV, earning game MVP honors for the second straight time by throwing for 309 yards and two touchdowns during the Steelers' 31–19 victory over the Los Angeles Rams. Bradshaw's touchdown passes came on a pair of spectacular second-half tosses to Lynn Swann and John Stallworth that covered 47 and 73 yards, respectively.

Notable Achievements

- Passed for more than 3,000 yards twice, topping 3,500 yards once (3,724 in 1979).
- Threw more than 20 touchdown passes four times.
- Posted touchdown-to-interception ratio of better than 2–1 once.
- Rushed for 346 yards and seven touchdowns in 1972.
- Averaged more than six yards per carry five times.
- Led NFL quarterbacks in: touchdown passes twice; game-winning drives twice; and fourth-quarter comebacks once.
- Finished second among NFL quarterbacks with passer rating of 84.7 in 1978.
- Finished third among NFL quarterbacks with 3,724 yards passing in 1979.
- Ranks second in Steelers history with: 3,901 pass attempts; 2,025 pass completions; 27,989 yards passing; and 212 touchdown passes.
- Ranks fifth in Steelers history with 32 rushing touchdowns.
- Eight-time division champion (1972, 1974, 1975, 1976, 1977, 1978, 1979, and 1983).
- Four-time AFC champion (1974, 1975, 1978, and 1979).
- Four-time Super Bowl champion (IX, X, XIII, and XIV).
- Two-time Steelers MVP (1977 and 1978).
- 1978 NFL MVP.
- 1978 Bert Bell Award winner as NFL Player of the Year.
- 1979 *Sports Illustrated* Sportsman of the Year.
- Two-time Super Bowl MVP (XIII and XIV).
- Three-time Pro Bowl selection (1975, 1978, and 1979).
- 1978 First-Team All-Pro selection.
- 1978 First-Team All-Conference selection.
- Two-time Second-Team All-Conference selection (1975 and 1979).

- Pro Football Hall of Fame All-1970s Second Team.
- Named to Steelers' 75th Anniversary Team in 2007.
- #12 "unofficially" retired by Steelers.
- Number 44 on the *Sporting News*' 1999 list of the 100 Greatest Players in NFL History.
- Number 50 on the NFL Network's 2010 list of the NFL's 100 Greatest Players.
- Elected to Pro Football Hall of Fame in 1989.

8

— MIKE WEBSTER —

Part of the extraordinary draft class of 1974 that also netted the Steelers Jack Lambert, Lynn Swann, and John Stallworth, Mike Webster went on to set franchise records for most seasons (15) and games (220) played, establishing himself during his time in Pittsburgh as arguably the greatest center in NFL history. A remarkably durable player, Webster began his career by appearing in 177 consecutive games, starting the final 150 of those at his familiar position of center. Along the way, Webster helped lead the Steelers to eight division titles, four AFC championships, and four Super Bowl wins, earning in the process nine trips to the Pro Bowl, six All-Pro selections, and nine All-AFC nominations. And, following the conclusion of his playing career, Webster received the additional honors of being included on both the *Sporting News'* and the NFL Network's lists of the 100 Greatest Players in NFL History, being named to the Steelers' 75th Anniversary Team, the NFL's 75th Anniversary Team, and the *Sporting News* All-Century Team, and being elected to the Pro Football Hall of Fame.

Born in Tomahawk, Wisconsin, on March 18, 1952, Michael Lewis Webster grew up on his family's farm, where his daily regimen as a teenager consisted of assisting his father with the early morning chores, before traveling 18 miles by bus to rural Rhinelander High School. After spending his final two years at Rhinelander High starring on the gridiron, Webster enrolled at the University of Wisconsin, where he earned All–Big Ten honors as a senior, prompting the Steelers to select him in the fifth round of the 1974 NFL Draft, with the 125th overall pick.

Entering the NFL at 6'2" tall and only 225 pounds, Webster found his ability to contend with the league's much larger defensive linemen being questioned by many when he first arrived in Pittsburgh. However, after adopting a year-round strength and weight program and developing a passion for health foods, Webster quickly bulked up to 250 pounds, enabling him to appear in every game his first two seasons with the Steelers. In addition to seeing a limited amount of duty as the backup to veteran

Mike Webster started 150 straight games at center for the Steelers.
Courtesy of the Pittsburgh Steelers

Ray Mansfield at the center position, Webster served as the long-snapper on all punts and kicks. Finally inserted into the starting lineup in the last game of the 1975 regular season, Webster subsequently began an amazing string of 150 consecutive starts that lasted until 1986, when he missed the first four games with a dislocated elbow.

Webster's toughness and durability left a lasting impression on Mansfield, who later said of his successor, "That's the toughness I like. Not a macho toughness, where you've got to strut it around, but an inner toughness, the John Wayne type who doesn't complain."

Webster also ingratiated himself to Pittsburgh's coaching staff with his versatility, which he displayed in 1976, when injuries to the Steelers' offensive line forced him to start six games at guard. Commenting on the flexibility that Webster offered the team, offensive line coach Dan Radakovich said prior to the start of the 1977 campaign, "He's got the quickness, strength, and intelligence to play center, guard, or tackle. Mike was the best center in the league last year. He's the best because he has great self-motivation."

Webster did indeed prove to be one of the league's most motivated players throughout his career, possessing a commitment to excellence second to none. The first Steelers player to arrive at training camp each year, Webster put in more practice hours than anyone else on the team, believing that the key to his success lay in his hard work and superior conditioning. In discussing the reasons that he pushed himself as hard as he did, Webster offered, "I'm not a very good athlete. I don't run very well, and I'm not very agile or nimble. The only chance I have to be successful is if I'm in better condition than the other guy."

Webster's dedication earned him the respect of every other member of the team, with Steelers guard Craig Wolfley saying of his teammate, "Every offensive lineman wants to grow up to be Mike Webster. But, when God made him, he used a different kind of material. There will never be another one like him."

Hall of Fame center Dermontti Dawson, who spent his first season in Pittsburgh being mentored by Webster, said of his former teammate, "Playing with Mike was the highlight of my career. I tried to emulate him by being No. 1 in the drills and making sure I was always first to the ball. Mike was such a hard worker and set such a high standard for us. Even in his 15th year, he was always hustling, always the first in line in the drills. It was an honor to play with him."

Revealing the thought process that he used to help motivate himself, Webster stated, "I always felt the best way to be able to do my best was to just get going and keep going for as long as I could. I had a coach tell me one time, 'You'll play much better if you just relax a little more between plays.' Well, he just doesn't understand. That guy over there on the other side of the line is trying to beat me up on every play. I'm not real calm about that. I do much better if I just keep a steady pace for as long as I can."

A strong, punishing blocker whose ability to pull and trap fit in perfectly with head coach Chuck Noll's running schemes, Webster also excelled in pass protection, with his superior strength and conditioning allowing him to ward off even the largest of defenders. In fact, after gradually increasing his playing weight to close to 260 pounds, Webster ended up winning the *NFL's Strongest Man* competition in 1980.

In addition to striking fear into his opponent with his bulging biceps, Webster often intimidated the opposition with the way he carried himself on the

Webster's superb blocking earned him spots on the NFL's 75th Anniversary Team and the *Sporting News* All-Century Team.
Courtesy of the Pittsburgh Steelers

playing field, with former Steelers assistant coach Bill Meyers once observing, "Watch any other lineman in the league; they all saunter up to the line. But Mike sprints to the line on every play. That's intimidating. He whipped your butt on the last play, and here he comes sprinting up to do it again."

Webster's many attributes made him the finest center of his time, enabling him to earn eight consecutive trips to the Pro Bowl from 1978 to 1985, a period during which Pittsburgh's coaching staff named him the team's offensive captain. Over the course of those eight seasons, Webster also made All-Pro six times, being accorded First-Team honors on five separate occasions. Continuing his string of 150 straight starts during that time, Webster drew praise from Chuck Noll, who said, "Mike has been the thing you work around. It's the one position we never had to concern ourselves with."

After missing the first four games of the 1986 campaign due to injury, Webster started the next 43 contests at center for the Steelers, before announcing his retirement when the team left him unprotected under the league's new Plan B free agency rules. However, Webster eventually chose to return to the field as a member of the Kansas City Chiefs, with whom he spent the 1989 and 1990 campaigns, before retiring from the game for good. Webster ended his career having played in a total of 245 games, 217 of which he started. Upon announcing his retirement, Webster stated, "It's been 17 wonderful years, but one thing you learn in this game is reality. It's time."

Unfortunately, Webster's life after football proved to be an unhappy one. After initially fielding several assistant coaching offers, Webster began to experience health and personal problems that remained with him for the rest of his life. Separated from his wife and children by the time the Pro Football Hall of Fame opened its doors to him in 1997, Webster lost all his money, briefly drifted into homelessness, began suffering from depression and memory loss, and became addicted to Ritalin, a drug commonly used to treat children with hyperactivity. Diagnosed in 1999 as having brain damage caused by repeated head injuries he suffered during his career, Webster often behaved erratically, with his son Garrett, with whom he spent his final days living in suburban Pittsburgh, telling the *Pittsburgh Post-Gazette*, "My dad has some health problems no one knows about and that I don't want to get into that much. But he has some brain injuries from football. I have to take care of my dad."

Webster's troubles ended on September 24, 2002, when he passed away at only 50 years of age. In paying homage to his former teammate, Franco

Harris said, "Mike was one of the main reasons we won four Super Bowls. Unfortunately, he had some turmoil and misfortune after his football career. He is now at peace. We do miss and love Mike."

Terry Bradshaw expressed his love and admiration for Webster some five years earlier, when, while presenting his longtime teammate at the latter's 1997 Hall of Fame induction, he stated, "There never has been and never will be another man as committed and totally dedicated to making himself the very best he could possibly be . . . Webby was the best ever."

STEELERS CAREER HIGHLIGHTS

Best Season

Webster earned consensus First-Team All-Pro honors four straight times between 1978 and 1981. Since the Steelers led the league in total offense and average yards per carry in 1979, we'll identify that as his finest season.

Memorable Moments/Greatest Performances

Webster dominated the middle of Kansas City's defensive line on November 7, 1976, enabling the Steelers to rush for a season-high total of 330 yards during a 45–0 blowout of the Chiefs.

Webster once again proved to be a force up front during Pittsburgh's lopsided 40–14 victory over the Baltimore Colts in the divisional round of the 1976 playoffs, helping the Steelers amass 526 yards of total offense, 225 of which came on the ground.

Webster dominated his opponent at the point of attack during a 51–35 win over the Browns on October 7, 1979, enabling the Steelers to gain a total of 522 yards, with 361 of those coming on the ground.

Webster and his line-mates manhandled New York's formidable defensive front otherwise known as "The Sack Exchange" on September 20, 1981, allowing the Steelers to amass 566 yards of total offense and 343 yards rushing during a 38–10 victory over the Jets.

Webster earned a game ball for his performance during a 20–0 win over the Houston Oilers on September 22, 1985, when, after sitting out the entire week of practice with an extremely painful back injury, he played every offensive down, helping the Steelers rush for a total of 233 yards.

Notable Achievements

- Holds share of Steelers record for most seasons played (15).
- Holds Steelers record for most games played (220).
- Missed just four games in 15 seasons, at one point appearing in 177 consecutive contests.
- Eight-time division champion (1974, 1975, 1976, 1977, 1978, 1979, 1983, and 1984).
- Four-time AFC champion (1974, 1975, 1978, and 1979).
- Four-time Super Bowl champion (IX, X, XIII, and XIV).
- Member of 1974 NFL All-Rookie Team.
- Nine-time Pro Bowl selection (1978, 1979, 1980, 1981, 1982, 1983, 1984, 1985, and 1987).
- Five-time First-Team All-Pro selection (1978, 1979, 1980, 1981, and 1983).
- 1984 Second-Team All-Pro selection.
- Five-time First-Team All-Conference selection (1978, 1979, 1980, 1981, and 1982).
- Four-time Second-Team All-Conference selection (1977, 1983, 1984, and 1985).
- Pro Football Hall of Fame All-1970s Second Team.
- Pro Football Hall of Fame All-1980s Second Team.
- Pro Football Reference All-1980s First Team.
- Named to NFL's 75th Anniversary Team in 1994.
- Named to Steelers' 75th Anniversary Team in 2007.
- #52 "unofficially" retired by Steelers.
- Named to *Sporting News* All-Century Team in 1999.
- Number 75 on the *Sporting News'* 1999 list of the 100 Greatest Players in NFL History.
- Number 68 on the NFL Network's 2010 list of the NFL's 100 Greatest Players.
- Elected to Pro Football Hall of Fame in 1997.

9
— TROY POLAMALU —

dentified by Bill Belichick as the player whom he considers to be the greatest Steeler of them all, Troy Polamalu helped revolutionize the position of strong safety during his time in the Steel City, with his tremendous versatility enabling him to assume many roles in the Pittsburgh defense. Equally effective against the run and the pass, Polamalu led the Steelers in interceptions five times and tackles once, ending his career as one of the franchise's all-time leaders in both categories. En route to helping the Steelers win five division titles, three AFC championships, and two Super Bowls, Polamalu earned eight Pro Bowl selections and six All-Pro nominations, also gaining recognition as the NFL Defensive Player of the Year in 2010. A member of the Steelers' 75th Anniversary Team, Polamalu will likely also be honored at some point in the next few seasons by being inducted into the Pro Football Hall of Fame.

Born in Santa Ana, California, on April 19, 1981, Troy Aumua Polamalu grew up with his four older siblings in a single-parent household after his Samoan mother and father divorced when he was just a toddler. Moving to the nearby suburb of Fountain Valley after his mother remarried, young Troy remained with his immediate family until the age of eight, when he went to live with his aunt and uncle in Oregon. Starring in baseball, basketball, and football while attending Douglas High School in Winston, Oregon, Polamalu earned All-State and All-League honors in all three sports, performing particularly well on the gridiron, where, after rushing for 1,040 yards, scoring 22 touchdowns, and recording eight interceptions as a junior, he rushed for 671 yards, scored nine touchdowns, and intercepted three passes in his senior year, even though an injury limited him to just four games.

Recruited by several major colleges while at Douglas, Polamalu ultimately chose to accept a scholarship from the University of Southern California, where he spent the next four years playing under head coaches Paul Hackett and Pete Carroll. Excelling at strong safety for the Trojans,

Troy Polamalu helped revolutionize the position of strong safety during his time in Pittsburgh.
Courtesy of the Pittsburgh Steelers

Polamalu recorded 278 tackles, six interceptions, four blocked punts, and three touchdowns during his college career, earning in the process First-Team All-America honors twice.

Subsequently selected by the Steelers with the 16th overall pick of the 2003 NFL Draft (after they traded away two later-round picks to move up 11 spots in the first round), Polamalu spent most of his rookie season playing on special teams and serving as a backup on defense, although he managed to make 38 tackles, record two sacks, and force one fumble. Inserted into the starting lineup the following year, Polamalu helped the Steelers compile a franchise-best regular-season record of 15-1 by recording 96 tackles, one sack, and one forced fumble, while also intercepting five passes, one of which he returned for a touchdown. With the Steelers finishing with the league's top-ranked defense, Polamalu earned Second-Team All-Pro honors and the first of his five straight trips to the Pro Bowl. Performing extremely well once again in 2005, Polamalu recorded 91 tackles, three sacks, two interceptions, and one touchdown for Pittsburgh's Super Bowl championship team, earning in the process First-Team All-Pro recognition for the first of four times.

As Polamalu rose to elite status among his NFL peers, he put on display for all to see his unique skill set that made him one of the league's most versatile defenders. Quick and strong, the 5'10", 213-pound Polamalu had the ability to either line up near the line of scrimmage when the Steelers expected the opposition to run the football or drop into coverage in passing situations. Extremely adept at blitzing the quarterback as well, Polamalu caused problems for opposing signal-callers, who never knew what to expect from him.

In discussing some of the issues he faced whenever he went up against Polamalu, veteran QB Charlie Frye said, "Troy Polamalu is a freak. They'll line him up at safety, at linebacker, or up on the line. You can't get a good read on where he's coming from."

Commenting on Polamalu's ability to impact a game in any number of ways, Steelers head coach Bill Cowher suggested, "He combines the athletic ability to cover, the explosion to be a great blitzer, he's an outstanding tackler and, on top of that, he's a very instinctive player."

Steelers teammate Brett Keisel stated, "He's one of those players that's special, that can make plays that no one else can make on the football field."

Bill Belichick added, "If you don't know where he is, he'll get you. . . . You make a mistake around him and he'll intercept it."

An extremely hard hitter who played the game with great passion, Polamalu inspired the following words from former USC teammate Carson Palmer, who later competed against him as a member of the Cincinnati Bengals: "Once he's on the football field and somebody is trying to take something away from him, his heart takes over. He's not going to let you complete a pass. He's going to smack you around, he's going to knock you out."

Yet, even though Polamalu's long hair and aggressive style of play caused others to sometimes view him as a wild man, he proved to be a true student of the game who excelled at breaking down opposing offenses, reading the quarterback, and making the suitable play. Furthermore, Polamalu always carried himself with grace, dignity, and humility off the playing field, explaining his somewhat contradictory behavior thusly: "I have developed

Polamalu earned NFL Defensive Player of the Year honors in 2010.
Courtesy of the Pittsburgh Steelers

the Samoan mentality—you have to be a gentleman everywhere but on the field. On the field, play like it is a game of life. Give everything you have. If you go out and play things safe, you can end up getting hurt. So, I always try to lay myself out on the line and sacrifice my body for the team."

Polamalu continued, "In football, you're taught to react by being aggressive, taught to react with violence. If you can't separate that on the field and off the field, you're going to be in a lot of trouble in your life . . . I take pride in my life—my wife, my family. I try my best not to have football define the person that I am."

Extremely spiritual, gentle, and soft-spoken off the playing field, Polamalu even surprised some of his own teammates with the paradoxical nature of his personality, with Jerome Bettis stating, "Troy Polamalu sat right next to me in the locker room. If you met Troy on the street you'd think, 'This dude is pretty quiet. Nice guy. Is he a priest?' But, sitting next to him every day, I got to see how intelligent and thoughtful Troy was about football. . . . On the field, I didn't recognize him. He was an animal. He was not the same guy. Literally, not the same person."

Despite being plagued by injuries in both 2006 and 2007, Polamalu earned Pro Bowl honors each year, before having one of his finest seasons in 2008, when he gained First-Team All-Pro recognition for the second time by recording 73 tackles and a team-leading seven interceptions for the eventual Super Bowl champions. After subsequently missing most of the 2009 campaign with a sprained MCL injury to his left knee, Polamalu returned with a vengeance the following year, earning team MVP, First-Team All-Pro, and NFL Defensive Player of the Year honors by picking off seven passes, recording 63 tackles, and scoring one touchdown. Praised for his exceptional play, Polamalu, said NFL veteran Trevor Pryce, "is the best I've ever seen."

Former Pro Bowl safety John Lynch suggested, "The guy is committed to the game of football and, obviously, is a tremendous talent. He makes their defense go."

Meanwhile, Carson Palmer said of his old college teammate, "In my eyes, he's the best defensive player in the league. He's a phenomenal player."

Performing well for the Steelers once again in 2011, Polamalu earned First-Team All-Pro honors for the final time by making 91 tackles, intercepting two passes, and recovering one fumble, which he returned for a touchdown. After appearing in only seven games the following season due to a severely strained calf, Polamalu spent two more years in Pittsburgh, making the last of his eight trips to the Pro Bowl in 2013, before announcing his retirement following the conclusion of the ensuing campaign after being told by the Steelers that they would release him if he decided to continue playing. Polamalu ended his career with 32 interceptions, 398 interception-return yards, 778 tackles (581 solo), 12 sacks, 14 forced fumbles, seven fumble recoveries, and five defensive touchdowns, which ties him with four other players for the second-most in franchise history.

Paying tribute to Polamalu after he made his announcement, Steelers head coach Mike Tomlin stated, "Troy is a shining example of a football man in the way he loved the game, the way he respected the game, and the way he played the game. It's a shining example of the window into who he is. He is a legendary Steeler and a legendary man. I congratulate him and wish him nothing but the best moving forward."

Steelers president Art Rooney II said, "On behalf of the entire Steelers organization and the Steelers Nation, I am happy to be able to publicly celebrate and thank Troy for his many contributions to the Steelers. His unique style of play will be remembered among the all-time Steelers. His passion for the game of football on the field and his willingness to be a contributor to the community make him a very special person."

Steelers chairman Dan Rooney added, "He's been a tremendous leader, really a leader by example, not only as a great football player but as a great person. He has influenced many people both on and off the field, which was really an important part. We've been fortunate to have great players throughout the years, but he, of course, would be one of the top players. He did everything with dignity and responsibility, and it was special to have Troy be a Steeler his entire career."

Some two years later, Bill Belichick expressed his admiration for Polamalu when he stated during an interview conducted prior to the October 23, 2016, meeting between the Steelers and his Patriots that, if he could choose just one player who ever donned a Pittsburgh uniform for his own team, he would pick Polamalu.

CAREER HIGHLIGHTS

Best Season

Polamalu performed extremely well for the Steelers in both 2004 and 2005, recording five interceptions, 96 tackles (67 solo), and one touchdown in the first of those campaigns, before picking off two passes, making 91 tackles (73 solo), recording three sacks, and recovering two fumbles, one of which he returned for a touchdown, in the second. However, he had his finest all-around season in 2010, earning AP Defensive Player of the Year honors by finishing second in the league with seven interceptions, amassing 101 interception-return yards, making 63 tackles, batting down 11 passes, forcing one fumble, recovering another, and scoring one touchdown on defense.

Memorable Moments/Greatest Performances

Polamalu turned in an outstanding all-around effort during a 13–3 win over the Miami Dolphins on September 26, 2004, making six tackles, deflecting a pass, and recording the first interception of his career during the contest.

Polamalu scored his first career touchdown during a 28–17 victory over the Cincinnati Bengals on October 3, 2004, when he returned an interception of a Carson Palmer pass 26 yards for a TD.

Polamalu earned AFC Defensive Player of the Week honors for the first of seven times by picking off two passes during a 24–10 win over the Cleveland Browns on November 14, 2004.

Polamalu helped lead the Steelers to a 20–17 victory over the New York Jets in their 2004 AFC divisional round matchup by making seven tackles and intercepting a Chad Pennington pass.

Polamalu had a big day against Houston on September 18, 2005, helping the Steelers record a 27–7 win over the Texans by making six solo tackles and setting an NFL record for the most sacks by a safety in a single game by getting to Houston quarterback David Carr three times.

Polamalu scored the second touchdown of his career when he returned a fumble 77 yards for a TD during a 20–10 win over the Green Bay Packers on November 6, 2005.

Polamalu starred during a 45–7 rout of the Kansas City Chiefs on October 15, 2006, earning AFC Defensive Player of the Week honors by recording 12 tackles (nine solo), deflecting three passes, and returning an interception 49 yards.

Polamalu sealed Pittsburgh's 23–14 victory over Baltimore in the 2008 AFC championship game by picking off a Joe Flacco pass and returning it 40 yards for a touchdown with just over four minutes remaining in regulation.

Polamalu earned AFC Defensive Player of the Week honors for the first of two straight times for his performance during a 13–10 win over the Ravens on December 5, 2010, when he recorded a sack, made five tackles, and forced a fumble.

Polamalu earned that distinction again the following week by recording a pair of interceptions, one of which he returned 45 yards for a touchdown, during a 23–7 win over the Bengals.

Polamalu contributed to a 23–20 victory over the Indianapolis Colts on September 25, 2011, by returning a fumble 16 yards for a touchdown.

Polamalu lit the scoreboard for the last time in his career when he picked off a Ryan Tannehill pass and returned it 19 yards for a TD during a 34–28 loss to Miami on December 8, 2013.

Notable Achievements

- Scored five defensive touchdowns.
- Recorded at least five interceptions three times.
- Surpassed 100 interception-return yards once (101 in 2010).
- Finished second in NFL in interceptions twice.
- Led Steelers in interceptions five times and tackles once.
- Ranks among Steelers career leaders with: 32 interceptions (tied—7th); 398 interception-return yards (9th); three touchdown interceptions (tied—5th); five defensive touchdowns (tied—2nd); 778 tackles (5th); and 14 forced fumbles (tied—7th).
- Five-time division champion (2004, 2007, 2008, 2010, and 2014).
- Three-time AFC champion (2005, 2008, and 2010).
- Two-time Super Bowl champion (XL and XLIII).
- Seven-time AFC Defensive Player of the Week.
- 2010 Steelers MVP.
- 2010 NFL Defensive Player of the Year.
- Eight-time Pro Bowl selection (2004, 2005, 2006, 2007, 2008, 2010, 2011, and 2013).

- Four-time First-Team All-Pro selection (2005, 2008, 2010, and 2011).
- Two-time Second-Team All-Pro selection (2004 and 2007).
- Two-time First-Team All-Conference selection (2004 and 2005).
- Pro Football Hall of Fame All-2000s Second Team.
- Named to Steelers' 75th Anniversary Team in 2007.

10

— BEN ROETHLISBERGER —

The holder of virtually every Steelers passing record, Ben Roethlisberger has established himself as one of the finest quarterbacks of his generation during his time in Pittsburgh. Ranking among the NFL's all-time leaders in several categories, "Big Ben," as he has come to be known, has passed for more than 3,000 yards 13 times, topping 4,000 yards six times and 5,000 yards once. Roethlisberger has also thrown more than 20 touchdown passes on 10 separate occasions, tossing at least 30 TD passes in three different seasons. A seven-time division champion, Roethlisberger has also led the Steelers to three AFC titles and two Super Bowl victories, with his exceptional play earning him six Pro Bowl selections and general recognition as the top signal-caller to come out of the outstanding draft class of 2004.

Born in Lima, Ohio, on March 2, 1982, Benjamin Todd Roethlisberger spent much of his youth away from his mother, living mostly with his father and stepmother after his parents divorced when he was 18 months old, before losing his mom to a car accident at the age of eight. Growing up dreaming of one day playing in the NBA, Roethlisberger set the Findlay High School career scoring record while playing point guard for the Trojans, earning in the process All-League and All-District honors. An outstanding all-around athlete, Roethlisberger also excelled in baseball and football, gaining All-League and All-District recognition for his play at shortstop, while serving as captain of his team in all three sports. Although Roethlisberger started at quarterback for the Trojans only as a senior, he made the most of his opportunity, being named Ohio's Division I Offensive Player of the Year after setting state records by throwing for 4,041 yards and 54 touchdowns.

After accepting a football scholarship from Miami University in Oxford, Ohio, the 6'5", 185-pound Roethlisberger spent his first season watching the action from the sidelines as a redshirt freshman while adding some much-needed bulk onto his frame. Laying claim to the starting quarterback job the following year, Roethlisberger earned Mid-American Conference Freshman of the Year honors by throwing for 3,105 yards and

Ben Roethlisberger holds virtually every Steelers passing record.
Courtesy of Keith Allison

25 touchdowns. Continuing to perform at an extremely high level in each of the next two seasons, Roethlisberger became just the third player in MAC history to throw for more than 3,000 yards in three seasons, with his extraordinary play in his junior year of 2003, which led the RedHawks to a 13-1 record and a number 10 ranking in the nation, gaining him Third-Team All-America and MAC Offensive Player of the Year recognition.

Feeling that he had nothing else to prove at the collegiate level, Roethlisberger decided to bypass his senior year at Miami and declare himself eligible for the 2004 NFL Draft, where the Steelers claimed him with the

11th overall pick, making him the third quarterback to be selected (Eli Manning went No. 1 and Philip Rivers went No. 4). After performing well at his first pro training camp, Roethlisberger replaced Tommy Maddox behind center in Week 2 of the regular season. He then went on to lead the Steelers to a perfect 13-0 record in his 13 starts, with his 2,621 yards passing, 17 TD passes, 66.4 completion percentage, and 98.1 passer rating earning him Associated Press NFL Offensive Rookie of the Year honors. Taking note of Roethlisberger's outstanding play his first year in the league, NFL veteran Mark Simoneau commented, "He's remarkable . . . he looks like a guy who's been around four or five years."

Despite missing four games due to a knee injury the following year, Roethlisberger had another solid season, throwing for 2,385 yards, tossing 17 TD passes and nine interceptions, completing 62.7 percent of his passes, and finishing third in the league with a passer rating of 98.6, before completing 62.4 percent of his passes and posting a passer rating of 101.7 during the Steelers' successful playoff run that earned them their fifth Super Bowl title. After being seriously injured in a motorcycle accident during the subsequent offseason, Roethlisberger experienced further adversity by undergoing an emergency appendectomy that sidelined him for the opening game of the 2006 campaign. He then suffered through the worst season of his career, completing just 59.7 percent of his passes, compiling a passer rating of only 75.4, and throwing a league-leading 23 interceptions. However, Roethlisberger rebounded nicely in 2007, earning his first trip to the Pro Bowl by throwing for 3,154 yards and ranking among the league leaders with 32 touchdown passes, a 65.3 completion percentage, and a 104.1 passer rating. Performing well once again in 2008, Roethlisberger led the Steelers to their second NFL championship in four years by passing for 3,301 yards and 17 touchdowns.

Successful during the early stages of his career despite his relative lack of experience, Roethlisberger relied heavily on his marvelous instincts, excellent vision, and outstanding composure to establish himself as one of the league's best young quarterbacks. Capable of delivering the ball accurately under extreme pressure, Roethlisberger moved well in the pocket, hung in until the last possible moment, and generally made excellent decisions, with Hall of Fame quarterback Dan Marino saying, "The thing that's impressive about Ben is his awareness in the pocket, his pocket presence, and his ability to move and still make throws downfield."

Also blessed with an extremely strong arm and great physical strength, the 6'5", 250-pound Roethlisberger drew praise from Patriots head coach Bill Belichick, who stated, "You can't knock him down, and he throws the ball as far as he wants to. There have been a lot of quarterbacks who have played 10 years and don't do as good a job."

Commenting on Roethlisberger's arm strength, former Steelers teammate Plaxico Burress claimed, "He can throw the ball 70 yards in the air. He can make all the throws."

Impressed with Roethlisberger's size, strength, and toughness, legendary Steelers linebacker Jack Ham said, "Roethlisberger, people just bounce off him. I had an opportunity to play some golf with him this summer. In my era, he might have played defensive tackle. He's 255, 260 pounds out there, and he absorbs a lot of punishment, and that's part of his DNA, I think. He's a guy who makes big plays right after someone bounces off him."

In discussing Roethlisberger's ability to create something out of nothing, NFL veteran Eric Smith stated, "When things break down and it becomes backyard football, that's when he's most dangerous."

Fellow quarterback Eli Manning also expressed his admiration for Roethlisberger when he said, "I have a lot of respect for him and how he plays the game and competes out there."

Continuing his success in 2009, Roethlisberger earned team MVP honors by throwing for 4,328 yards, tossing 26 touchdown passes, and completing 66.6 percent of his passes. After another solid year in 2010, Roethlisberger began a string of eight seasons that has represented the finest stretch of his career, compiling the following numbers during that time:

YEAR	YD PASSING	TD PASSES	INT	COMP %	QBR
2011	4,077	21	14	63.2	90.1
2012	3,265	26	8	63.3	97.0
2013	4,261	28	14	64.2	92.0
2014	**4,952**	32	9	67.1	103.3
2015	3,938	21	16	68.0	94.5
2016	3,819	29	13	64.4	95.4
2017	4,251	28	14	64.2	93.4
2018	**5,129**	34	**16**	67.0	96.5

Roethlisberger posted excellent figures in 2012 and 2015 even though he missed three contests in the first of those campaigns due to a shoulder injury and another four games in the second with an injured left knee. In addition to leading all NFL quarterbacks in yards passing in 2014 and 2018, Roethlisberger annually placed near the top of the league rankings in touchdown passes, with his outstanding play earning him Pro Bowl honors in five of those eight seasons. More importantly, the Steelers won three division titles and made five playoff appearances during that time, with Roethlisberger saying, "The biggest thing isn't necessarily how I play, but that we win. That's my number-one goal. I could be the worst quarterback out there, but, if we come out with a victory, that's all that matters to me."

Roethlisberger has led the Steelers to seven division titles, three AFC championships, and two Super Bowl wins.
Courtesy of Keith Allison

Remaining an admirer of Roethlisberger, Bill Belichick stated, "There's only one Ben Roethlisberger. . . . He can see over everything. He's got a tremendous arm. He can deliver with no wind-up or step into the throw. He can flat-footed fire it 50, 60 yards downfield. He's got great poise, great patience. He knows how long he can wait, and usually he waits until the bitter end and delivers the ball. . . . He's tough, really tough. I have a ton of respect for him."

Yet, even though Roethlisberger's playing ability, toughness, and leadership skills have earned him the respect of his teammates, opponents, and coaches throughout the league, he has been anything but a model citizen off the playing field, twice being accused of sexually assaulting women. The first such incident, which later caused him to be suspended for the first four games of the 2010 season for violating the NFL's personal conduct policy, allegedly took place in June 2008, with a woman claiming in a civil suit filed in Washoe County, Nevada, on July 17, 2009, that Roethlisberger assaulted her in the hotel room he occupied while competing in a celebrity golf tournament in Lake Tahoe. Roethlisberger found himself being accused of a similar act less than one year later, when police investigated a claim that he raped a 20-year-old college student inside the women's restroom of the Capital City nightclub located near the Georgia College & State University campus in Milledgeville, Georgia. Nevertheless, with criminal charges against Roethlisberger in both cases eventually being dropped due to a lack of evidence, it remains unclear as to what level of culpability he had in both incidents.

A fan favorite in Pittsburgh despite his somewhat sordid past, Roethlisberger can attribute much of his popularity to his franchise-record 4,616 pass completions, 56,194 passing yards, and 363 touchdown passes. He also ranks in the NFL's all-time top 10 in all three categories, with his many accomplishments virtually guaranteeing him a place in Canton once his playing career eventually comes to an end.

CAREER HIGHLIGHTS

Best Season

Roethlisberger posted impressive numbers for the Steelers in 2018, setting single-season franchise records for most pass attempts (675), pass completions (452), passing yards (5,129), and touchdown passes (34). He also performed extremely well in both 2007 and 2009, concluding the first of those campaigns with 3,154 yards passing, 32 TD passes, just 11 interceptions, and a career-best passer rating of 104.1, before throwing for 4,328 yards and 26 touchdowns, completing 66.6 percent of his passes, and compiling a passer rating of 100.5 two years later. However, Roethlisberger had his finest all-around season in 2014, when, in addition to leading all NFL quarterbacks with 4,952 yards passing, he ranked among the league leaders with 408 pass completions, 32 TD passes, a passer rating of 103.3, and a pass-completion percentage of 67.1, prompting *Pro Football Focus* to accord him All-Pro honors for the only time in his career.

Memorable Moments/Greatest Performances

Roethlisberger earned AFC Offensive Player of the Week honors for the first of 17 times by leading the Steelers on a pair of fourth-quarter touchdown drives that enabled them to overcome a 10-point deficit, giving them a 24–20 victory over the Dallas Cowboys on October 17, 2004. With the Steelers scoring the winning touchdown on a 2-yard run by Jerome Bettis with only 30 seconds remaining in regulation, Roethlisberger finished the contest with 21 completions in 25 attempts, for 193 yards and two TDs.

Roethlisberger led the Steelers to a 31–17 win over Cincinnati in the wild card round of the 2005 AFC playoffs by completing 14 of 19 pass attempts for 208 yards and three touchdowns, the longest of which went 43 yards to Cedric Wilson.

Roethlisberger made one of the more memorable plays of his career the following week, when he helped preserve the Steelers' 21–18 victory over the Colts in their divisional round playoff matchup by recording a game-saving tackle on Indianapolis defensive back Nick Harper, who headed toward the Pittsburgh end zone after recovering a Jerome Bettis fumble with less than two minutes remaining in regulation.

Roethlisberger gave the Steelers a 23–17 overtime win over the Cincinnati Bengals in the final game of the 2006 regular season when he collaborated with Santonio Holmes on a 67-yard scoring play just 1:33 into the overtime session.

Roethlisberger threw five touchdown passes in one game for the first time in his career during a 38–7 Monday night rout of the Baltimore Ravens on November 5, 2007, connecting with Heath Miller once and Santonio Holmes and Nate Washington twice each.

Roethlisberger passed for 309 yards and three touchdowns during a 26–21 victory over Jacksonville on October 5, 2008, hitting Hines Ward with a game-winning eight-yard TD pass with just 1:53 left in regulation.

Roethlisberger provided further heroics in Super Bowl XLIII, giving the Steelers a 27–23 win over Arizona by hitting Santonio Holmes with a 6-yard touchdown pass with only 35 seconds remaining in the fourth quarter. He finished the game 21-of-30, for 256 yards and that one TD.

Roethlisberger led the Steelers to a 27–14 win over Cleveland on October 18, 2009, by throwing for 417 yards and two touchdowns, the longest of which went to Hines Ward for 42 yards.

Roethlisberger outdueled Aaron Rodgers on December 20, 2009, passing for 503 yards and three touchdowns during a 37–36 win over the Packers, with his 19-yard TD toss to Mike Wallace on the game's final play giving the Steelers the victory.

Roethlisberger had a big game against Tennessee on October 9, 2011, pacing the Steelers to a 38–17 win over the Titans by passing for 228 yards and five touchdowns, the longest of which went 40 yards to Mike Wallace.

Roethlisberger again collaborated with Wallace on a long scoring play two weeks later, hitting the speedy receiver with a 95-yard TD pass during a 32–20 win over the Arizona Cardinals. He finished the game with 361 yards through the air and three touchdown passes.

Roethlisberger followed that up with another strong outing, throwing for 365 yards and two touchdowns during a 25–17 victory over the Patriots on October 30, 2011.

Roethlisberger turned in his finest performance of the 2013 campaign on November 17, passing for 367 yards and four touchdowns during a 37–27 win over the Lions.

Roethlisberger had a huge afternoon against Indianapolis on October 26, 2014, completing 40 of 49 passes for a career-high 522 yards and six touchdowns during a 51–34 victory over the Colts.

Roethlisberger retained his hot hand against Baltimore the following week, throwing for 340 yards and completing another six touchdown passes, in leading the Steelers to a convincing 43–23 win over the Ravens.

Roethlisberger turned in another strong effort against Cincinnati on December 7, 2014, passing for 350 yards and three touchdowns during a 42–21 victory over Cincinnati, with the longest of his TD tosses being a 94-yard connection with Martavis Bryant.

Almost exactly one year later, on December 6, 2015, Roethlisberger led the Steelers to a lopsided 45–10 victory over the Colts by throwing for 364 yards and four touchdowns, the longest of which went 68 yards to Bryant.

Roethlisberger paced the Steelers to a 43–14 win over the Chiefs on October 2, 2016, by completing 22 of 27 pass attempts for 300 yards and five touchdowns.

Roethlisberger followed that up with a similarly impressive performance against the Jets, passing for 380 yards and four touchdowns during a 31–13 Steelers win on October 9, 2016.

Although the Steelers lost to Dallas by a score of 35–30 on November 13, 2016, Roethlisberger starred in defeat, completing 37 of 46 pass attempts for 408 yards and three touchdowns.

Roethlisberger performed well during a 39–38 victory over the Baltimore Ravens on December 10, 2017, that marked the third consecutive game the Steelers won on a last-minute field goal by Chris Boswell, throwing for 506 yards and two touchdowns.

Although the Steelers suffered a 45–42 defeat at the hands of the Jacksonville Jaguars in the divisional round of the 2017 playoffs, Roethlisberger had another big game, passing for 469 yards and five touchdowns.

Roethlisberger torched the Kansas City secondary on September 16, 2018, throwing for 452 yards and three touchdowns during a 42–37 loss to the Chiefs.

Roethlisberger gave the Steelers a dramatic 28–21 win over Cincinnati on October 14, 2018, by hitting Antonio Brown with a 31-yard touchdown pass with only 10 seconds remaining in the contest.

Roethlisberger performed brilliantly during a 52–21 victory over Carolina on November 8, 2018, completing 22 of 25 pass attempts for 328 yards and five touchdowns.

Notable Achievements

- Has passed for more than 3,000 yards 13 times, topping 4,000 yards six times and 5,000 yards once.
- Has thrown more than 20 touchdown passes 10 times, topping 30 TD passes three times.
- Has posted touchdown-to-interception ratio of better than 2–1 nine times.
- Has completed more than 65 percent of passes six times.
- Has posted passer rating above 90.0 13 times, topping 100.0 on three occasions.
- Has averaged more than five yards per carry twice.
- Has led NFL quarterbacks in: pass completions once; passing yards twice; game-winning drives twice; and fourth-quarter comebacks three times.
- Finished second in NFL with passer rating of 104.1 in 2007.
- Has finished third in NFL in: pass completions once; touchdown passes once; pass completion percentage once; and passer rating twice.
- Holds NFL record for most touchdown passes thrown in consecutive games (12; Weeks 8 and 9 in 2014).
- Ranks among NFL career leaders with: 7,168 pass attempts (8th); 4,616 pass completions (7th); 56,194 passing yards (6th); and 363 touchdown passes (7th).
- Holds share of Steelers record for most seasons played (15).
- Holds Steelers single-game records for most: pass attempts (66); pass completions (44); passing yards (522); and touchdown passes (6).
- Holds Steelers single-season records for most: pass attempts (675 in 2018); pass completions (452 in 2018); passing yards (5,129 in 2018); and touchdown passes (34 in 2018).
- Holds Steelers career records for most: pass attempts (7,168); pass completions (4,616); passing yards (56,194); and touchdown passes (363).

- Seven-time division champion (2004, 2007, 2008, 2010, 2014, 2016, and 2017).
- Three-time AFC champion (2005, 2008, and 2010).
- Two-time Super Bowl champion (XL and XLIII).
- 17-time AFC Offensive Player of the Week.
- November 2013 AFC Offensive Player of the Month.
- 2004 AP NFL Offensive Rookie of the Year.
- 2009 Steelers MVP.
- Six-time Pro Bowl selection (2007, 2011, 2014, 2015, 2016, and 2017).
- 2014 *Pro Football Focus* Second-Team All-Pro selection.

11

— ERNIE STAUTNER —

One of the dominant defensive linemen of his era, Ernie Stautner spent his entire 14-year NFL career in Pittsburgh serving as an integral member of a punishing Steelers defense that typically ranked among the league's best. An extremely intense player with a burning desire to win, Stautner helped the Steelers forge a reputation of toughness that has been carried down through the years, influencing future generations of Pittsburgh players with his competitiveness and determination. The first player to have his number formally retired by the organization, Stautner earned nine trips to the Pro Bowl and nine All-Pro nominations during his career, which he ended with more fumble recoveries (23) than anyone else in franchise history. Stautner's spirited play also earned him spots on the NFL 1950s All-Decade Team and the Steelers' 75th Anniversary Team, as well as a place in the Pro Football Hall of Fame.

Born in Prienzing near Cham, Bavaria, in Germany on April 20, 1925, Ernest Alfred Stautner immigrated with his family to the United States at the age of three. Growing up in East Greenbush, New York, Stautner attended Columbia High School and Vincentian Institute, before serving in the US Marine Corps during World War II. After being discharged from the military following the war, Stautner enrolled at Boston College, where he spent the next four years starring at offensive and defensive tackle for the Eagles.

Selected by the Steelers in the second round of the 1950 NFL Draft, with the 22nd overall pick, Stautner earned a starting job immediately upon his arrival in Pittsburgh, laying claim to the left defensive tackle post as a rookie, before spending the next several seasons at right tackle. Though somewhat undersized at 6'1" and 235 pounds, Stautner quickly established himself as one of the league's elite defenders, earning All-Pro honors for the first of nine straight times in 1952. Serving as the cornerstone of Pittsburgh's defense, Stautner used his great strength and mobility to ward off blockers that typically outweighed him by 20 or 30 pounds. In discussing

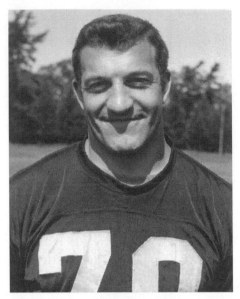

Ernie Stautner was the first Steelers player to have his number formally retired by the team.
Courtesy of the Pittsburgh Steelers

his longtime teammate, Steelers defensive back Jack Butler told the *Pittsburgh Post-Gazette*, "He was one of those Germans— know what I mean?—a tough dude. Quick off the ball, he'd explode off the ball, make great contact, and pound the hell out of offensive tackles. And he could chase."

Former Steelers chairman Dan Rooney, who saw quite a bit of Stautner in his youth, once noted, "Strength is what made Ernie Stautner special. He would be a little bit like Casey Hampton in that he was so strong. They didn't have strong guys in that era, the 1950s, because they didn't lift weights. They did running, mainly. He was quick, but strength was his biggest forte. And tough. He was a tough guy."

Rooney added, "He was a tremendous player. He was the first one who really made an impact from a defensive standpoint, almost in the whole league. I remember a game against the New York Giants at Forbes Field, and it was one of those games where it was close, and they were moving the ball, and he tackled the quarterback three straight times—first down, second down, third down—and then they had to punt. And we went on to win the game."

Stautner, who became known for his intensity, aggressiveness, and nastiness, defended his style of play by saying, "I gotta be mean. At my size, I can't afford to play any other way. Unless I'm meaner than these big guys, unless I can intimidate them, I'd have no chance in the world against them."

Although the Steelers, who posted a winning record just three times before Stautner joined them in 1950, finished above .500 in only four of the next 14 seasons, they developed a reputation for toughness during that time that he helped instill in them. Describing the overall impact that he made on the team, Stautner's Pro Football Hall of Fame biography reads:

> Blessed with excellent mobility and burning desire, the Boston College star went on to excel in the game of giants. For the next 14 years, Stautner was a fixture at defensive tackle, a veritable folk hero with long-suffering Steelers fans and a major factor in the Pittsburgh defense, one of the most punishing in the NFL at the time. . . . Yet Ernie's true worth on a football field could never be measured in lines in a record manual, for statistics can't measure such assets as competitive nature, team spirit, grim determination, and the will to win.

In addition to doing an outstanding job of controlling the opposing team's running game from the interior of Pittsburgh's defense, Stautner, who also spent a significant amount of time at right defensive end his last few years in the league, displayed a nose for the football throughout his career, intercepting two passes and retiring as the NFL's career leader in safeties, with three, while also ranking third in fumble recoveries, with 23. Stautner also proved to be one of the league's most durable players, exhibiting his toughness by missing only six games in 14 seasons despite suffering two broken shoulders, multiple cracked ribs, and having his nose broken several times.

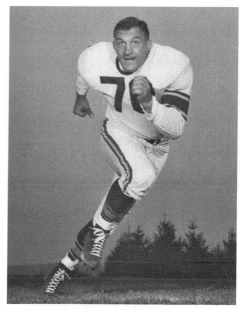

Choosing to announce his retirement following the conclusion of the 1963 campaign, Stautner became, on October 25, 1964, the first Steelers player to have his number (70) officially retired by the team. Five years later, he received the additional honor of being inducted into the Pro Football Hall of Fame the first time his name appeared on the ballot.

Remaining in the game long after he retired as an active player, Stautner joined the coaching staff of the Dallas

Stautner earned Pro Bowl and All-Pro honors nine times each as a member of the Steelers.
Courtesy of the Pittsburgh Steelers

Cowboys in 1966, serving as the team's defensive coordinator from 1973 to 1988. During that time, he helped develop the defensive skills of such standout performers as Randy White, Harvey Martin, and Ed "Too Tall" Jones, before spending his final two years in the organization scouting college players. From Dallas, Stautner moved on to Denver, where he spent four years coaching the Broncos defensive line. Returning to Germany in 1995, Stautner became head coach of the Frankfurt Galaxy of NFL Europe, whom he guided to consecutive World Bowls in 1995 and 1996, before retiring from football.

Unfortunately, Stautner began displaying symptoms of Alzheimer's shortly thereafter, eventually losing his battle with the dreaded disease some two months shy of his 81st birthday, on February 16, 2006. Upon learning of his passing, Steelers chairman Dan Rooney said, "The team in the 1950s was a lot better than anybody knew. They played well. They didn't win championships, but some of that was because of injuries. Our reputation for being a tough team started a little bit before Ernie, but not to the extent that he would take it to. . . . When people thought of the Steelers in the 1950s, they thought of Ernie Stautner."

CAREER HIGHLIGHTS

Best Season

Even though Stautner earned his lone First-Team All-Pro selection the following year, he had his finest all-around season in 1957, when he gained recognition as the NFL's Lineman of the Year by anchoring a Pittsburgh defense that led the league in fewest yards allowed and placed second in fewest points surrendered—a total of 178 that represented the lowest figure in team annals from 1947 to 1971.

Memorable Moments/Greatest Performances

Stautner recorded the first of his franchise-record three career safeties on October 1, 1950, when he put the finishing touches on a 26–7 victory over the Redskins by tackling Washington quarterback Harry Gilmer in the end zone.

Stautner starred during a 63–7 dismantling of the Giants on November 30, 1952, leading a Steelers defense that allowed New York just 15 yards rushing on 20 carries.

Stautner once again dominated his opponent at the line of scrimmage on October 24, 1953, contributing to a Pittsburgh defense that surrendered only 34 yards on the ground during a 31–14 win over the Packers.

Stautner and the rest of the Steeler defense turned in another superb effort against the Redskins in the 1956 regular-season finale, limiting the Washington offense to just 85 yards and five first downs during a convincing 23–0 Pittsburgh victory.

Stautner once again led the defensive charge on October 27, 1957, when the Steelers limited Philadelphia to 70 yards of total offense and zero yards passing during a 6–0 win.

Stautner contributed to a 27–24 victory over the Redskins in the final game of the 1962 regular season by recording the last of his two career interceptions.

Notable Achievements

- Recorded three safeties during career.
- Missed just six games in 14 seasons.
- Holds Steelers career record for most fumble recoveries (23).
- Tied for third in Steelers history in seasons played (14).
- 1957 NFL Best Lineman Award winner.
- Nine-time Pro Bowl selection (1952, 1953, 1955, 1956, 1957, 1958, 1959, 1960, and 1961).
- 1958 First-Team All-Pro selection.
- Eight-time Second-Team All-Pro selection (1952, 1953, 1954, 1955, 1956, 1957, 1959, and 1960).
- Two-time First-Team All-Conference selection (1957 and 1961).
- Pro Football Hall of Fame All-1950s First Team.
- Pro Football Reference All-1950s First Team.
- Member of Pittsburgh Steelers Legends Team.
- Named to Steelers' 75th Anniversary Team in 2007.
- #70 retired by Steelers.
- Elected to Pro Football Hall of Fame in 1969.

12

— HINES WARD —

Called "the most complete receiver in the NFL" by then–Steelers head coach Bill Cowher, Hines Ward proved to be both an excellent pass-catcher and a superb blocker over the course of his 14-year career, which he spent entirely in Pittsburgh. Arguably the greatest blocking wide receiver in league history, Ward, said longtime teammate Alan Faneca, changed the way the position was played with his physical style of play. An outstanding target in the passing game as well, Ward surpassed 90 receptions four times and 1,000 receiving yards on six occasions, ending his career as the Steelers' all-time leader in both categories. A three-time team MVP, Ward also earned four Pro Bowl selections and three All-Pro nominations during his time in the Steel City, with his exceptional all-around play helping the Steelers win six division titles, three AFC championships, and two Super Bowls.

Born in Seoul, South Korea, to a Korean mother and an African-American father on March 8, 1976, Hines Edward Ward Jr. lived a somewhat nomadic existence as a child. After moving with his parents to Forest Park, Georgia, at the age of one, young Hines went to live with his grandmother in Louisiana two years later, after his parents divorced. Ward remained with his grandmother until the age of seven, when he returned to his mom in Georgia. Having very little contact with his father as a teenager, Ward saw him only on the day he graduated from Forest Park High School. Unhappy throughout most of his childhood, Ward later said, "I was a lost child. I wasn't accepted in the black community because I was Korean, and I wasn't accepted in the Korean community because I was black."

Starring in football while at Forest Park High, Ward played quarterback in a high-powered shotgun offense for three seasons, amassing 3,581 passing yards and 2,500 rushing yards during that time, en route to earning Clayton County Offensive Player of the Year honors twice. Particularly effective in his senior year, Ward gained High School All-America

Hines Ward caught more passes for more yards than anyone else in franchise history.
Courtesy of the Pittsburgh Steelers

recognition from *Super Prep* and *USA Today* by throwing for more than 1,500 yards and running for more than 1,000 yards. Excelling in baseball as well, Ward performed well enough on the diamond to be selected by the Florida Marlins in the 73rd round of the 1994 MLB Draft.

Choosing to pursue a career in football instead, Ward enrolled at the University of Georgia, where, after transitioning from quarterback to wide receiver, he blossomed as a junior, making 52 receptions for 900 yards. Ward followed that up with an outstanding senior year, earning All-SEC honors by catching 55 passes for 715 yards and six touchdowns, thereby ending his college career with 149 receptions, 1,965 receiving yards, and 3,870 all-purpose yards.

Impressed with Ward's strong play his final two seasons at Georgia, the Steelers made him the 92nd overall pick of the 1998 NFL Draft when they selected him in the third round. Ward subsequently spent his first year in Pittsburgh playing mostly on special teams, making only 15 receptions for 246 yards as a backup wideout. Inserted into the starting lineup the following year, Ward had a solid sophomore season, catching 61 passes for 638 yards and seven touchdowns, before making 48 receptions for 672 yards and four touchdowns in 2000. With the Steelers having retooled their offense heading into the 2001 campaign, Ward began an exceptional six-year run during which he compiled the following numbers:

YEAR	REC	REC YD	TD
2001	94	1,003	4
2002	112	1,329	12
2003	95	1,163	10
2004	80	1,004	5
2005	69	975	11
2006	74	975	6

Ward's 94 catches in 2001 set a new single-season franchise record, which he broke the very next season, when he established career-high marks in receptions, receiving yards, and TD catches, placing near the top of the league rankings in all three categories. Developing into one of the NFL's best possession receivers during that time, Ward earned four Pro Bowl selections and three All-Pro nominations over the course of those six seasons, while also being named MVP of Super Bowl XL for his outstanding play during Pittsburgh's 21–10 victory over Seattle.

Although the 6-foot, 205-pound Ward possessed only average size and speed for a receiver, he made up for whatever he may have lacked in each of those areas with his intelligence, instincts, and ability to recognize coverages. Expressing his respect for Ward, perennial Pro Bowl cornerback Champ Bailey said, "One thing you know is, when you cover him, you're going to have to make a lot of tackles." Capable of making big plays downfield as well, Ward combined with Plaxico Burress, Antwaan Randle El, and Santonio Holmes at different times to give the Steelers one of the league's top wide receiver tandems.

Yet, as much of a factor as Ward proved to be in the passing game, he perhaps made an even bigger impact as a run-blocker, frequently delivering stunning blocks that helped spring teammates for long gains. Commenting on Ward's willingness to engage his opponent at the point of attack, veteran Kansas City Chiefs defensive end Eric Hicks suggested, "He probably loves hitting people more than catching passes."

In discussing Ward's blocking ability, Ben Roethlisberger stated, "He is an extra lineman out there in the run game."

Steelers assistant coach Bruce Arians noted, "For our running game to go, he has to block. He's that crucial. He's just like an offensive lineman."

Steelers head coach Mike Tomlin added, "He is just blessed with physical talent. He is probably more powerful than people think. Like a boxer, he delivers a great blow with a short punch. That is just who he is. It is part of what makes him unique."

However, Ward's ability to drive opposing defenders to the turf with jarring hits eventually caused him to develop something of a reputation as a dirty player, with his propensity for hitting defenders on their blindside drawing special criticism. The most notable instance of this occurred during a game against the Cincinnati Bengals on October 19, 2008, when he delivered a vicious blindside block to Keith Rivers that broke the rookie linebacker's jaw, causing him to miss the remainder of the season. It should be noted, though, that the NFL did not fine Ward for the hit, which it deemed legal, although it later passed a new rule banning such hits, with the so-called "Hines Ward Rule" making a blindside block illegal if it came from the blocker's helmet, forearm, or shoulder and landed to the head or neck area of a defender.

Suggesting that "all players should have their head on a swivel," Ward defended his actions by saying, "If you're going to talk stuff and try to take me out, I'm coming at you. Cleanly and fairly, but I'm coming. . . . Defensive backs are always trying to kill me, so I'm trying to get them first."

Ward earned team MVP honors three times.
Courtesy of the Pittsburgh Steelers

Looking back on the physical nature of his game after his playing career ended, Ward stated, "I didn't get incentives to block. I didn't get incentives to block the way I did. I didn't get paid extra money. I did it because I wanted to. I wanted to see what way I could impact the game when I didn't get the ball . . . I was an extra pulling guard for the Pittsburgh Steelers, and I took great pride in doing that."

Ward's exceptional blocking ability and superior pass-catching skills made him arguably the NFL's most complete wide receiver, with veteran cornerback Samari Rolle saying of his frequent foe, "I never look at him as a receiver. I look at him as a tough football player."

Expressing his appreciation for everything Ward contributed to the Steeler offense, Ben Roethlisberger said, "There are no words to describe how valuable Hines Ward has been to me."

Pittsburgh linebacker Joey Porter added, "We can't win without him."

Meanwhile, in assessing his value to the team, Ward stated, "I'm not the prototype wide receiver. But I like to think I'm one hell of a football player."

Ward's string of six straight seasons with at least 975 receiving yards ended in 2007, when he made 71 receptions for 732 yards and seven touchdowns. However, he topped 1,000 yards in each of the next two seasons, concluding the 2008 campaign with 81 catches for 1,043 yards and seven touchdowns, before making six TD grabs and ranking among the league leaders with 95 receptions and 1,167 receiving yards the following year. Ward spent two more seasons in Pittsburgh, making 105 receptions, amassing 1,136 receiving yards, and scoring seven touchdowns during that time, before being released by the Steelers in a salary cap move at the end of 2011. Choosing to retire rather than play for another team, Ward ended his career with 1,000 receptions, 12,083 receiving yards, 12,723 all-purpose yards, 85 TD catches, and 86 touchdowns, with each of those figures placing him among the franchise's all-time leaders. He also ranks extremely high in team annals in seasons played (14) and games played (217), missing a total of just seven contests his entire career.

Upon announcing his retirement, Ward told the assembled media, "I wanted to finish my career as a Steeler. I felt I just fit the mold as far as a blue-collar guy. I may not be the flashiest, most flamboyant wide receiver out there. But I get the job done for my team . . . I can say I'm a Steeler for life, and that's the bottom line. That's all I've really ever wanted."

Ward then added, "I want to go down as one of the greats to wear the black and gold, and that's how it should end . . . I want my legacy here to say, 'you know what, he was one hell of a football player who gave it his all.' I'm truly blessed. I played in three Super Bowls, won two Super Bowls, was Super Bowl MVP . . . what more could a player want out of his entire football career?"

Stepping away from the podium, Ward embraced Steelers owner Art Rooney II and said, "Thank you Mr. Rooney for giving a small-town boy from Forest Park, Georgia a chance."

Ward, who hosted the *Hines Ward Show* on Pittsburgh CBS O&O KDKA-TV from 2006 to 2012, signed with NBC Sports to be a football analyst shortly after he retired as an active player. He subsequently assumed a prominent role on that station's *Sunday Night Football* pregame show *Football Night in America* until 2016, when he became a studio analyst at CNN. Ward has also created the Hines Ward Helping Hands Foundation, which the Associated Press called "a foundation to help mixed-race children like himself in South Korea, where they have suffered discrimination."

CAREER HIGHLIGHTS

Best Season

While Ward had many outstanding seasons for the Steelers, the 2002 campaign stands out as the finest of his career. In addition to setting a then–single-season franchise record by making 112 receptions, Ward finished second in the league with 12 touchdown catches and amassed 1,329 receiving yards and 1,471 yards from scrimmage, earning in the process Second-Team All-Pro honors for the first of three straight times.

Memorable Moments/Greatest Performances

Ward scored his first career touchdown during a lopsided 43–0 victory over Cleveland in the 1999 regular-season opener when he caught a 1-yard TD pass from Mike Tomczak. He finished the game with three receptions for 51 yards.

Ward contributed to a 15–0 win over the Cincinnati Bengals on October 15, 2000, by making two catches for 91 yards and one touchdown, which came on a season-long 77-yard connection with Kent Graham on the Steelers' first possession of the game.

Ward went over 100 receiving yards for the first time in his career during a 20–7 win over the Jacksonville Jaguars on November 18, 2001, finishing the contest with nine receptions for 112 yards and one touchdown, which came on a 28-yard hookup with Kordell Stewart.

Ward turned in a similarly impressive performance against the Jets on December 9, 2001, catching 10 passes for 124 yards during an 18–7 win over New York.

Ward helped the Steelers forge a 34–34 tie with the Atlanta Falcons on November 10, 2002, by making 11 receptions for 139 yards and one touchdown.

Although the Steelers lost to the Tennessee Titans by a score of 31–23 the following week, Ward had a huge game, making 10 receptions for 168 yards and two touchdowns, one of which came on a 72-yard connection with Tommy Maddox on the first play from scrimmage.

Ward played a major role in the Steelers' 36–33 win over Cleveland in the 2002 AFC wild card game, making 11 catches for 104 yards and one touchdown, with his 5-yard TD grab with 3:06 left in regulation cutting Cleveland's lead to five points. The Steelers scored the game-winning TD a little over two minutes later on a 3-yard run by Chris Fuamatu-Ma'afala.

Ward starred during a 24–20 loss to Cincinnati on November 20, 2003, making a career-high 13 catches for 149 yards and one TD, which came on a 16-yard hookup with Tommy Maddox that gave the Steelers a three-point lead with only 1:05 left in regulation. Unfortunately, the Bengals won the game in the closing moments on an 18-yard TD pass from Jon Kitna to Matt Schobel.

Ward came up big for the Steelers in their 20–17 overtime win over the Jets in the divisional round of the 2004 AFC playoffs, making 10 catches for 105 yards and one touchdown, with his 4-yard TD grab tying the score at 17–17 with six minutes left in the final period of regulation.

Although the Steelers suffered a 23–20 defeat at the hands of the Patriots on September 25, 2005, Ward collaborated with Ben Roethlisberger on a career-long 85-yard scoring play during the contest, finishing the game with four receptions for 110 yards and two touchdowns.

Ward earned AFC Offensive Player of the Week honors for his performance during a 34–21 win over the Cleveland Browns on November 13, 2005, when he made eight catches for 124 yards and one touchdown, which came on a 51-yard pass from Antwaan Randle El.

Ward contributed to Pittsburgh's 21–10 victory over Seattle in Super Bowl XL by making five receptions for 123 yards and one touchdown, which came on a 43-yard hookup with Antwaan Randle El midway through the fourth quarter that gave the Steelers a commanding 11-point lead.

Ward starred in defeat on October 22, 2006, making eight receptions for 171 yards and three touchdowns during a 41–38 overtime loss to

Atlanta, with one of his TDs coming on a season-long 70-yard connection with Charlie Batch.

Ward helped lead the Steelers to a 27–14 win over Cleveland on October 18, 2009, by making eight catches for 159 yards and one TD, which came on a 52-yard pass from Ben Roethlisberger.

Ward topped 100 receiving yards for the final time in his career during a 23–22 win over Miami on October 24, 2010, finishing the game with seven receptions for 131 yards and one touchdown.

Notable Achievements

- Surpassed 90 receptions four times, topping 100 catches once (112 in 2002).
- Surpassed 1,000 receiving yards six times.
- Amassed more than 1,000 yards from scrimmage seven times.
- Scored at least 10 touchdowns three times.
- Missed just seven games in 14 seasons, at one point appearing in 88 consecutive contests.
- Finished second in NFL with 112 catches and 12 touchdown receptions in 2002.
- Led Steelers in receptions 11 times and receiving yards seven times.
- Holds Steelers career records for most: pass receptions (1,000); receiving yards (12,083); and touchdown receptions (85).
- Ranks among Steelers career leaders with: 14 seasons played (tied—3rd); 217 games played (2nd); 12,511 yards from scrimmage (2nd); 12,723 all-purpose yards (3rd); 86 touchdowns (2nd); and 526 points scored (6th).
- Six-time division champion (2001, 2002, 2004, 2007, 2008, and 2010).
- Three-time AFC champion (2005, 2008, and 2010).
- Two-time Super Bowl champion (XL and XLIII).
- 2005 Week 10 AFC Offensive Player of the Week.
- Three-time Steelers MVP (2002, 2003, and 2005).
- Super Bowl XL MVP.
- Four-time Pro Bowl selection (2001, 2002, 2003, and 2004).
- Three-time Second-Team All-Pro selection (2002, 2003, and 2004).
- 2002 First-Team All-Conference selection.
- Named to Steelers' 75th Anniversary Team in 2007.
- #86 "unofficially" retired by Steelers.

13

DERMONTTI DAWSON

I n speaking of Dermontti Dawson, former Pittsburgh Steelers head coach Bill Cowher stated, "To me, he was the best athlete to ever play that position (center). He was very powerful and explosive, just a rare combination of quickness, explosion, and he was a very dependable player. This guy hardly ever missed a game. He redefined the position."

Rivaling Mike Webster as the greatest offensive lineman in franchise history, Dermontti Dawson did indeed redefine the way the position of center is played in the National Football League. Using his great strength and tremendous athleticism to establish himself as the dominant center of his time, Dawson earned seven trips to the Pro Bowl, six First-Team All-Pro selections, and five First-Team All-AFC nominations during his 13 seasons in Pittsburgh, helping the Steelers win five division titles and one AFC championship in the process. An extremely durable player, Dawson started 170 consecutive games over parts of 12 seasons, starting every contest the Steelers played from 1989 to 1998, with his outstanding play and remarkable durability earning him a spot on the Steelers' 75th Anniversary Team and a place in the Pro Football Hall of Fame following the conclusion of his playing career.

Born in Lexington, Kentucky, on June 17, 1965, Dermontti Farra Dawson attended Bryan Station High School, where he spent his first two years starring in track and field in the discus throw and shotput. Choosing to apply his athletic skills to the football field as well after being recruited by the school's head football coach, Steve Parker, in his junior year, Dawson went on to earn All-State honors as an offensive tackle, with Parker later saying of his protégé, "He could make a bad step and still make a great block."

Subsequently offered a football scholarship by the University of Kentucky, Dawson spent three years splitting his time between the center and guard positions, gaining All–Southeastern Conference recognition as a senior in 1987. Impressed with Dawson's outstanding play at the collegiate level, the Steelers selected him in the second round of the 1988 NFL Draft, claiming him with the 44th overall pick.

Upon his arrival in Pittsburgh, Dawson spent his first year in the league being mentored by Mike Webster, starting five games at right guard, while also seeing some action at center. But, with Webster announcing his retirement at season's end, before ultimately returning to the league as a member of the Kansas City Chiefs, Dawson became the Steelers' starting center—a post he maintained for the rest of his career. Beginning a string of 10 straight seasons in which he started every game for Pittsburgh, Dawson quickly established himself as one of the league's elite players at his position, earning the nickname "Dirt" from his teammates for his ability to drive opposing defenders into the ground.

Dermontti Dawson used his strength and athleticism to establish himself as the dominant center of his time. Courtesy of the Pittsburgh Steelers

In discussing his former teammate, Tunch Ilkin, who played alongside Dawson on the Steelers' offensive line from 1988 to 1992, said, "Dermontti could just crank you. He had the ability, the explosive strength, and the athleticism to do it, to just knock guys out. He also had that stability to take on guys. He was strong enough to just absorb a 320-pound nose tackle and not give ground."

After failing to be accorded postseason honors in any of his first three years as a starter, Dawson earned the first of his seven consecutive trips to the Pro Bowl in 1992, before being named First-Team All-Pro for the first of six straight times the following year. And, as the individual accolades continued to mount for Dawson, the conversation eventually turned to whether he had surpassed the level of greatness Mike Webster had attained during his time in Pittsburgh. Tunch Ilkin, who played with both men, is one who believed that Dawson gave nothing away to his mentor, suggesting:

> In my day, the great debate was, who's better, Webster or Dwight Stephenson, the Dolphins' great center. Webbie's game was sheer toughness and strength; Dwight relied

more on his athletic ability. Put both those guys together, you've got Dermontti Dawson. He's scary strong, built like a Brahma bull. No neck, his trapezius muscles grow right into his ears. At the same time, he's so quick that he could bucket-step, cross-over step, do everything wrong from a technique standpoint, and still put a nose guard on his back. He's a genetic mutant. A freak of nature.

Weighing in on the debate, Chuck Noll, who coached Dawson his first four years in the league, said during a 1996 interview with CSNPhilly.com's Ray Didinger, "Dermontti is a much better athlete than Webster. Mike had great strength and power. Dermontti has it all: smarts, strength, quickness, and speed."

Revealing the amount of respect that Dawson garnered throughout the league, Didinger stated, "In 1996, the *Sporting News* polled pro personnel directors around the NFL and asked them to rank the players by position. Dawson received more first-place votes than any other player at any position, more than Jerry Rice at receiver, more than Emmitt Smith at running back."

Bill Cowher, who served as Dawson's head coach during the latter's final nine years in Pittsburgh, discussed some of the qualities that made his center so special, telling *Sports Illustrated* in 1998, "Other centers snap the ball, then move. Dermontti snaps *and* moves. It's all one motion. He is so much quicker than everyone else."

Years later, Cowher told the *Pittsburgh Courier-Journal* that Dawson redefined the center position, claiming, "As a player, I think he really took the position of center to another level. His athleticism—he would lead a basic run play we ran all the time. Dermontti allowed us to do blocking schemes that you never saw before in terms of a pulling center."

Former Steelers running back and current ESPN analyst Merril Hoge agreed with Cowher's assessment, stating, "What Dermontti did, which is what Mel Blount did, was change the game. You never had a center pull until Dermontti Dawson. He revolutionized and changed how teams ran the football in the NFL. I played with Mike Webster in my first year with the Steelers, and I never thought I would be able to say someone was better than Mike Webster at center. But Dermontti changed how we ran the ball."

Hall of Fame offensive tackle and CBS color analyst Dan Dierdorf also had high praise for Dawson, saying at the time of the latter's Hall of Fame induction, "He had all of the physical tools that were necessary—balance, strength, everything. The one thing that always impressed me was his ability to handle a nose tackle by himself. Most centers who play the game almost always need some sort of a double-team, or a rub from the guard next to them. The great centers, and there aren't many of them, block the nose tackle all by themselves, and Dermontti was one of those guys. That's what makes him so special."

Dawson's extraordinary quickness and tremendous strength enabled him to take on the nose tackle by himself even though, at 6'2" and 290 pounds, he often found himself giving away some 20 or 30 pounds to the man who lined up directly across from him at the line of scrimmage. In discussing Dawson's foot speed, Steel-

Dawson started every game the Steelers played for 10 straight seasons.
Courtesy of the Pittsburgh Steelers

ers running back Jerome Bettis said, "He's not the quickest center in the league, he's the quickest *lineman* in the league. He has the ability to snap the ball, pull, and lead a sweep."

Steelers offensive lineman Roger Duffy added, "He gets out in space, and he's as nimble as a defensive back. I've played center, but, when I watch Dermontti, it's like the tape is on a different speed."

Meanwhile, in addressing Dawson's great strength and aggressiveness at the point of attack, Jacksonville Jaguars defensive tackle John Jurkovic stated, "Dawson's initial punch is the best in the league. He does a little drop step and then launches a right, and it just rocks you. . . . Survive the initial onslaught and you may have a chance to make the play, because, after he blocks you, he's usually looking to go get someone else."

And, as for the size advantage that several of Dawson's opponents held over him, James Jones of the Baltimore Ravens noted, "It doesn't matter how big and strong you are. If a guy is on top of you before you're out of your stance, you're done."

Dawson's rare skill set prompted his high school coach, Steve Parker, to proclaim unabashedly, "Watching him develop in college and in the pros, I can say that he is the best center to ever play the game."

Dawson continued to dominate opposing defenders until 1998, when he earned the last of his six consecutive First-Team All-Pro selections. However, after being limited by severe hamstring injuries to a total of only 16 games the next two seasons, Dawson suffered the indignity of being released by the Steelers following the conclusion of the 2000 campaign. Choosing not to sign with another team, Dawson subsequently announced his retirement, ending his career having appeared in a total of 184 games as a member of the Steelers.

Returning to his hometown of Lexington, Kentucky, following his retirement, Dawson spent the next several years working as a real estate developer, before moving to San Diego, California, where he currently serves as a sales executive for a promotional products company.

Elected to the Pro Football Hall of Fame in 2012, Dawson expressed during his induction speech what his years in Pittsburgh meant to him, stating, "Being a Steeler meant being a blue-collar worker with an unwavering commitment to excellence. I hope I made Steeler nation proud." Dawson also revealed his basic philosophy toward life when he said, "Do everything with a purpose. Live, act, play, and work with a purpose, with a passion and, more importantly, with honor."

CAREER HIGHLIGHTS

Best Season

Dawson earned First-Team All-Pro honors six straight times from 1993 to 1998, with his outstanding play in the first of those campaigns, when the Steelers averaged 4.1 yards per carry en route to finishing sixth in the NFL in rushing, prompting the NFL Players Association to name him its co–Offensive Lineman of the Year. But Dawson and the rest of Pittsburgh's offensive line performed slightly better in 1996, when the Steelers placed second in the league in rushing, averaging 4.4 yards per carry, with Dawson being named NFL Alumni Offensive Lineman of the Year.

Memorable Moments/Greatest Performances

Dawson and his offensive line–mates dominated the opposition at the point of attack during a 31–21 win over the Indianapolis Colts on September 18, 1994, enabling the Steelers to amass 500 yards of total offense, with 261 of those coming on the ground.

Dawson helped lead the way for Steeler running backs to rush for 238 yards during a 29–9 victory over the Cleveland Browns in the divisional round of the 1994 playoffs.

Dawson anchored an offensive line that helped the Steelers amass a season-high total of 556 yards on offense during a 49–31 win over Cincinnati on November 19, 1995, with 191 of those yards coming on the ground.

Dawson and the rest of Pittsburgh's offensive line dominated their opponents once again at the line of scrimmage in the 1999 regular-season opener, enabling the Steelers to amass 464 yards of total offense and 217 yards rushing during a 43–0 blowout of the Cleveland Browns.

Notable Achievements

- Started 170 consecutive games at center over parts of 12 seasons.
- Five-time division champion (1992, 1994, 1995, 1996, and 1997).
- 1995 AFC champion.
- 1993 NFLPA co–AFC Offensive Lineman of the Year.
- 1996 NFL Alumni Offensive Lineman of the Year.
- Seven-time Pro Bowl selection (1992, 1993, 1994, 1995, 1996, 1997, and 1998).
- Six-time First-Team All-Pro selection (1993, 1994, 1995, 1996, 1997, and 1998).
- Five-time First-Team All-Conference selection (1994, 1995, 1996, 1997, and 1998).
- Pro Football Hall of Fame All-1990s First Team.
- Pro Football Reference All-1990s First Team.
- Named to Steelers' 75th Anniversary Team in 2007.
- #63 "unofficially" retired by Steelers.
- Elected to Pro Football Hall of Fame in 2012.

14

— ANTONIO BROWN —

One of the game's truly great receivers for much of the past decade, Antonio Brown has established himself as arguably the NFL's most potent offensive weapon since he joined the Steelers in 2010. After spending his first year in Pittsburgh functioning primarily as a punt and kickoff returner, Brown emerged as one of the league's top wideouts in his second season, since which time he has continued to perform at an elite level. In addition to catching more than 100 passes six times, Brown has gained more than 1,000 yards through the air on seven occasions, amassing in the process the second most receptions and receiving yards in franchise history. Brown has also accumulated more than 2,000 all-purpose yards three times and scored more than 10 touchdowns in four different seasons, with his extraordinary play, which helped lead the Steelers to four division titles and one AFC championship, earning him team MVP honors four times, seven trips to the Pro Bowl, and five All-Pro nominations.

Born in Miami, Florida, on July 10, 1988, Antonio Tavaris Brown attended Miami Norland High School, where he starred in football and track. The son of retired Arena Football League star Eddie Brown, Antonio excelled on the gridiron as a running back, quarterback, wide receiver, and punt returner, twice gaining Class 6A All-State recognition. Blessed with outstanding speed, Brown also competed in the 100-meter dash and ran the anchor leg on the Norland 4 × 100-meter relay team.

After being rejected by Florida State University for academic reasons following his graduation from Norland High, Brown enrolled at North Carolina Technical Academy, a prep school where he spent one season starting at quarterback, before being offered a scholarship by Florida International University. However, FIU rescinded its offer to him shortly thereafter when Brown became involved in an altercation with security before his freshman season began. Left with few other options, Brown subsequently enrolled at Central Michigan, where he started his college football career as a walk-on freshman, before eventually being granted a scholarship.

Transitioning from quarterback to wide receiver during his time at Central Michigan, Brown ended up setting the school record for most pass receptions (305), while also making 22 TD catches, scoring five touchdowns on special teams, and amassing 3,199 receiving yards, 2,612 kickoff-return yards, and 822 punt-return yards, with his exceptional play earning him All-MAC honors three straight times. Having also been named an All-American as a punt returner in both his sophomore and junior years, Brown decided

Antonio Brown has been arguably the NFL's most potent offensive weapon for most of the last decade.
Courtesy of the Pittsburgh Steelers

to forgo his senior season at Central Michigan and enter the 2010 NFL Draft, where the Steelers selected him in the sixth round, with the 195th overall pick.

Feeling that his small college background and relative lack of size caused pro scouts to overlook him, the 5'10", 181-pound Brown entered the league with a chip on his shoulder, later saying, "Being passed up by teams because of my size made me hungry. I've seen a lot of first-round guys who come in and never really do nothing because they may not appreciate the opportunity because everything has been given to them. I think guys who come from the bottom understand how hard it is, so they appreciate the opportunities more."

Spending his first year in Pittsburgh backing up starting wideouts Hines Ward and Mike Wallace, Brown made just 16 receptions for 167 yards and no touchdowns. However, he performed well on special teams, amassing a total of 674 all-purpose yards and scoring the first touchdown of his career on an 89-yard kickoff return. Given more playing time on offense his second year in the league, Brown earned his first Pro Bowl selection by becoming the first player in NFL history to record at least 1,000 receiving yards and 1,000 return yards in the same season. In addition to making 69 receptions for 1,108 yards and two touchdowns, Brown rushed for 41 yards and accumulated 1,062 yards on special teams, with his 2,211 all-purpose yards placing him second in the league rankings. Missing three games due to an injured ankle in 2012, Brown proved to be somewhat less productive, concluding the campaign with 66 catches, 787 receiving yards, 994 all-purpose yards, and five touchdowns. However, he subsequently began an extraordinary six-year run during which he posted the following numbers:

YEAR	REC	REC YD	ALL-PURPOSE YD	TD
2013	110	1,499	1,928	9
2014	**129**	**1,698**	2,030	14
2015	**136**	1,834	**2,074**	11
2016	106	1,284	1,456	12
2017	101	**1,533**	1,594	9
2018	104	1,297	1,297	15

Brown ranked in the league's top five in receptions and receiving yards in five of those six seasons, topping the circuit in each category twice. He also placed near the top of the league rankings in touchdown receptions four times, with his 15 TD grabs in 2018 leading the NFL. Putting up historic numbers during that time, Brown became the first player in NFL history to record at least 100 receptions in five straight seasons, accomplishing the feat six consecutive times. He also became the first player ever to lead his conference in receptions four straight times, with his 582 catches from 2013 to 2017 and 686 receptions over the course of those six seasons setting new NFL marks for most receptions over any five- or six-year span. In addition to earning Pro Bowl honors each year, Brown made All-Pro in five of those six seasons.

Although Brown lacks great size and has only slightly-above-average speed for an NFL wide receiver, his focus, exceptional work ethic, and tremendous feel for the game have enabled him to separate himself from other men who play his position, with fellow wideout Darrius Heyward-Bey suggesting, "That's what makes 84 so special. That's why he has a chance to be one of the greatest receivers to ever play the game. He is patient. He is poised. His concentration is better than anyone else in the league right now."

In discussing Brown, Baltimore Ravens cornerback Marlon Humphrey said, "Going up against 'A.B.', he's arguably the best in the game. A guy like that, he doesn't really get tired. If you watch him on film, he'll run his route, Big Ben starts scrambling, he just turns up field and is running around. It's a guy that you can tell is probably in the best shape of any of the receivers you play against. He doesn't really get tired. He does so much. He's a guy you've got to be aware of."

Meanwhile, Brown does not feel that his size has worked against him in any way, stating, "If you're not a first-round pick or you're not 6-2, they always say you can't be the best. But the only time there's a weight class is before the draft. This is the NFL. It's all about what you do. I can run past guys and get done what I need to. I can do everything the big guys can do."

Brown is the only player in NFL history to record at least 100 receptions in six straight seasons.
Courtesy of Keith Allison

Brown then added, "I don't think of myself as a small receiver, but you can't control what somebody says about you. It hasn't held me back—actually, I think I've changed the perception of smaller receivers."

However, while Brown proved to be a tremendous force for the Steelers between the white lines, he sometimes irritated his teammates and coaches with his selfish and unprofessional behavior, which head coach Mike Tomlin addressed on one occasion by stating, "AB is a competitor—we all know and understand that. But we've got to control it. He has to control it. If he does not, it can work against him, it can work against us. Those are the lessons you learn along the way. . . . Emotions can get away from you. It doesn't need to happen. It shouldn't happen. Hopefully, it won't moving forward . . . I'm not going to waste a lot of time talking to Antonio about not throwing water coolers and so forth. Be a professional."

Brown displayed his diva-like tendencies after the Steelers recorded an 18–16 victory over Kansas City in the divisional round of the 2016 playoffs. Although Ben Roethlisberger and Ramon Foster requested that their teammates "keep a low profile on social media" following the conclusion of the contest, Brown went against their wishes and violated NFL rules by broadcasting the team's locker room celebration on Facebook Live, thereby making public Coach Tomlin's vulgar rant on Pittsburgh's upcoming playoff opponent, the New England Patriots. Forced to apologize for his unsavory language, Tomlin expressed his dissatisfaction with Brown, whom he later disciplined.

Yet, those incidents paled in comparison to the events that transpired toward the end of the 2018 campaign, when Tomlin benched Brown for the regular-season finale after the star receiver failed to attend team meetings and practices in the week leading up to the contest. The *Pittsburgh Post-Gazette* later reported that Brown got into a confrontation with Ben Roethlisberger during a practice session, causing him to throw a football in the direction of his quarterback before leaving. Brown then failed to answer phone calls and text messages from his teammates, prompting Coach Tomlin to bench him for the final game of the regular season.

Expressing his displeasure with Brown's behavior a few days later, former Steelers teammate and current ESPN analyst Ryan Clark told ESPN Radio: "Antonio has done an extremely good job of tricking people. He's done a very good spin job of having us think, or making people think who don't know him, that it's all about the Pittsburgh Steelers, and that he is just a hard worker who's here to win football games. No, Antonio Brown loves Antonio Brown. If you listen to people talk about him, if you listen to the media, a lot of times the fans, they have an adoration for him that is not necessarily a depiction of who he is. He's like most receivers. He's selfish."

Meanwhile, Steelers president Art Rooney II stated that Brown's actions cast a dark shadow over his future in Pittsburgh, telling the *Pittsburgh Post-Gazette*, "There's not much we can do right now; we have time to make a decision. We'll look at all the options. We're not going to release him, that's not on the table."

Refusing to close the door on a possible return by Brown, Rooney added that the team's veteran leaders would have to agree to take him back, stating, "That's one of the questions we have to answer—whether we can get to a point where we all feel good about him being on the roster next year. We have a way to go before we feel good about that."

When asked about the likelihood of Brown participating in training camp in July, Rooney said, "As we sit here today, it's hard to envision that. But there's no sense in closing the door on anything today."

Finally deciding to part ways with Brown, the Steelers traded him to the Oakland Raiders for a pair of draft picks on March 11, 2019, ending the enigmatic wide receiver's nine-year stay in Pittsburgh. During his time in the Steel City, Brown made 837 receptions; amassed 11,207 receiving yards; caught 74 touchdown passes; accumulated 11,326 yards from scrimmage, 2,932 yards on special teams, and 14,258 all-purpose yards; and scored 79 touchdowns, placing him among the franchise's all-time leaders in each category.

STEELERS CAREER HIGHLIGHTS

Best Season

There are so many great seasons from which to choose, any of which could be classified as the finest of Brown's career. In addition to finishing second in the NFL with 110 receptions and 1,499 receiving yards in 2013, Brown rushed for four yards and amassed 425 yards on special teams, giving him a total of 1,928 all-purpose yards that placed him fifth in the league rankings. Brown followed that up with a brilliant 2014 campaign in which he led the NFL with 129 receptions and 1,698 receiving yards, while also placing near the top of the league rankings with 13 TD catches, 14 touchdowns, 319 punt-return yards, 1,711 yards from scrimmage, and 2,030 all-purpose yards. Brown once again posted exceptional numbers in 2017, making 101 receptions for a league-leading 1,533 yards, scoring nine touchdowns, and amassing 1,533 yards from scrimmage and 1,594 all-purpose yards. Nevertheless, Brown had his finest all-around season in 2015, when he established career-high marks in receptions (136), receiving yards (1,834), yards from scrimmage (1,862), and all-purpose yards (2,074), finishing either first or second in the league in each category. He also scored 11 touchdowns, with his fabulous performance gaining him First-Team All-Pro recognition for the second of four straight times.

Memorable Moments/Greatest Performances

Brown scored the first touchdown of his career the very first time he touched the ball as a pro, returning the opening kickoff 89 yards for a TD during a 19–11 win over the Tennessee Titans on September 19, 2010.

Brown registered his second touchdown on special teams on December 4, 2011, when he returned a punt 60 yards for a TD during a lopsided 35–7 win over Cincinnati, earning in the process AFC Special Teams Player of the Week honors for the first of three times.

Brown had his breakout game as a receiver on December 8, 2011, helping the Steelers record a 14–3 victory over Cleveland by making five receptions for 151 yards and one touchdown, which came on a career-long 79-yard connection with Ben Roethlisberger.

Although the Steelers lost to the Chicago Bears by a score of 40–23 on September 22, 2013, Brown had a huge game, making nine receptions for 196 yards and two touchdowns, which covered 33 and 21 yards.

Brown helped lead the Steelers to a 37–27 win over the Detroit Lions on November 17, 2013, by making seven receptions for 147 yards and two touchdowns, which came on hookups of 34 and 47 yards with Ben Roethlisberger.

Brown displayed his explosiveness during a 30–20 win over the Bengals on December 15, 2013, scoring twice in just a little over one minute in the first quarter, when, after catching a 12-yard TD pass, he returned a punt 67 yards for a touchdown 1:04 later.

Brown contributed to a 43–23 win over Baltimore on November 2, 2014, by catching 11 passes for 144 yards and one TD, which came on a 54-yard connection with Ben Roethlisberger.

Brown helped the Steelers clinch the division title with a 27–17 win over Cincinnati in the final game of the 2014 regular season by returning a punt 71 yards for a touchdown and making seven receptions for 128 yards and one TD, which covered 63 yards.

Brown torched the San Francisco defensive secondary for nine catches, 195 receiving yards, and one touchdown during a 43–18 rout of the 49ers on September 20, 2015.

Brown turned in a tremendous performance against Oakland on November 8, 2015, leading the Steelers to a 38–35 win over the Raiders by setting single-game franchise records for most receptions (17), receiving yards (284), and yards from scrimmage (306).

Brown starred during a 45–10 blowout of the Colts on December 6, 2015, catching eight passes for 118 yards and two touchdowns, while also scoring a third time on a 71-yard punt return.

Brown earned AFC Offensive Player of the Week honors for the first time by making 16 receptions for 189 yards and two touchdowns during a 34–27 victory over Denver on December 20, 2015, with his 23-yard TD grab with 3:24 left in regulation providing the winning margin.

Brown came up big for the Steelers in the 2015 regular-season finale, helping them clinch a playoff berth by catching 13 passes for 187 yards and one TD during a 28–12 win over Cleveland.

Although the Steelers suffered a 35–30 defeat at the hands of the Dallas Cowboys on November 13, 2016, Brown had another big game, making 14 receptions for 154 yards and one touchdown.

Brown proved to be the difference in a 28–7 win over the Colts on November 24, 2016, catching five passes for 91 yards and three TDs, which came on plays that covered 25, 33, and 22 yards.

Brown gave the Steelers a dramatic 31–27 victory over Baltimore on December 25, 2016, by catching a 4-yard TD pass from Ben Roethlisberger with only nine seconds remaining in regulation. He finished the contest with 10 receptions for 96 yards and that one touchdown.

Brown subsequently helped lead the Steelers to a 30–12 win over Miami in the 2016 AFC wild card game by catching five passes for 124 yards and two touchdowns, which came on plays that covered 50 and 62 yards.

Brown helped the Steelers begin the 2017 regular season on a positive note by making 11 receptions for 182 yards during a 21–18 win over Cleveland in Week 1.

Brown earned AFC Offensive Player of the Week honors for a second time by making 10 receptions for 144 yards and three touchdowns during a lopsided 40–17 victory over the Tennessee Titans on November 16, 2017.

On November 26, 2017, Brown contributed to a 31–28 victory over the Packers that the Steelers won on a last-second 53-yard field goal by Chris Boswell by making 10 receptions for 169 yards and two touchdowns, the longest of which covered 33 yards.

Although Boswell proved to be the hero once again two weeks later, giving the Steelers a 39–38 win over Baltimore by splitting the uprights from 46 yards out with just 42 seconds remaining in regulation, Brown contributed mightily to the victory by catching 11 passes for 213 yards.

Brown replaced Boswell as team hero on October 14, 2018, when he collaborated with Ben Roethlisberger on a 31-yard scoring play with just 10 seconds left in the fourth quarter to give the Steelers a dramatic 28–21 victory over the Cincinnati Bengals.

Although the Steelers suffered a heartbreaking 31–28 defeat at the hands of the New Orleans Saints on December 23, 2018, Brown turned in a tremendous effort, making 14 receptions for 185 yards and two touchdowns.

Notable Achievements

- Surpassed 100 receptions six times.
- Surpassed 1,000 receiving yards seven times, topping 1,500 yards three times.
- Amassed more than 2,000 all-purpose yards three times.
- Scored more than 10 touchdowns four times.
- Led NFL in: receptions twice; receiving yards twice; touchdown receptions once; and all-purpose yards once.
- Finished second in NFL in: receptions twice; receiving yards twice; touchdown receptions twice; yards from scrimmage once; and all-purpose yards once.
- Finished third in NFL in: touchdowns twice; all-purpose yards once; punt-return yards once; and punt-return average once.
- Led Steelers in receptions and receiving yards five times each.
- Holds Steelers single-game records for most: receptions (17); receiving yards (284); and yards from scrimmage (306), all vs. Oakland on November 8, 2015.
- Holds Steelers single-season records for most: pass receptions (136 in 2015); receiving yards (1,834 in 2015); and touchdown receptions (15 in 2018).
- Ranks among Steelers career leaders with: 837 receptions (2nd); 11,207 receiving yards (2nd); 11,326 yards from scrimmage (3rd); 14,258 all-purpose yards (2nd); 74 touchdown receptions (2nd); 79 touchdowns (4th); 482 points scored (tied—7th); and 1,759 punt-return yards (2nd).
- Four-time division champion (2010, 2014, 2016, and 2017).
- 2010 AFC champion.
- Three-time AFC Special Teams Player of the Week.

- Two-time AFC Offensive Player of the Week.
- Three-time AFC Offensive Player of the Month.
- 2017 *Sporting News* Offensive Player of the Year.
- Four-time Steelers MVP (2011, 2013, 2015, and 2017).
- Seven-time Pro Bowl selection (2011, 2013, 2014, 2015, 2016, 2017, and 2018).
- Four-time First-Team All-Pro selection (2014, 2015, 2016, and 2017).
- 2013 Second-Team All-Pro selection.

15

— JEROME BETTIS —

Nicknamed "The Bus" for his ability to carry multiple defenders on his back, Jerome Bettis arrived in Pittsburgh in 1996 after being acquired from the St. Louis Rams in arguably the greatest trade the Steelers ever made. Obtained for a pair of draft picks, Bettis went on to rush for the second-most yards in franchise history over the course of the next 10 seasons, gaining more than 1,000 yards on the ground six times. One of the NFL's all-time leading rushers, Bettis earned four trips to the Pro Bowl, two All-Pro selections, two All-AFC nominations, and NFL Comeback Player of the Year honors during his time in Pittsburgh, helping the Steelers win five division titles, one AFC championship, and one Super Bowl in the process. And, since retiring following the conclusion of the 2005 campaign, Bettis has been further honored by being named to the Steelers' 75th Anniversary Team and being inducted into the Pro Football Hall of Fame.

Born in Detroit, Michigan, on February 16, 1972, Jerome Abram Bettis grew up in poverty, spending his youth living with his parents and two older brothers in a tiny apartment in the city's ghetto. Looking back on his early years, Bettis recalls, "When I think about my childhood, one thing comes to mind: Love. We didn't have much money, but we had love in our house. The neighborhood where I grew up in Detroit was pretty rough. Our house was tiny. Man, everybody's house was tiny. In the kitchen, there was no space to move. I look back on it now and I realize how tight the conditions were. But, when you're a kid, you don't think anything of it. I'd say it was crude but effective."

Bettis continued, "If you met me when I was six, I was a chubby, mischievous kid. My saving grace was that my mom was a bowling teacher and she taught me and my two older brothers to play when we were real young. Bowling kept us busy, and, most importantly, inside. On the weekends, we traveled all over the state to bowling tournaments, and it kept us out of the streets. Our parents did a great job of shielding us from the reality of our neighborhood."

Despite being diagnosed with asthma at the age of 14, Bettis developed into an excellent athlete as a teenager, recalling, "As I got into my teens, I was big and fast, but I actually didn't play organized football until I got to high school. In middle school, we played football in the street right in front of the house. The streets weren't paved great, so you might be playing against 11 defenders—but they were like five guys and six potholes. The rule was, it was touch on the cement and tackle if you went into the grass. Well, sometimes it was tackle on the cement, too."

Jerome Bettis ranks second only to Franco Harris in franchise history in yardage gained on the ground.
Courtesy of the Pittsburgh Steelers

After enrolling at Mackenzie High School, Bettis established himself as a standout running back and linebacker, gaining recognition from the *Detroit Free Press* as the top player in the state as a senior, while also being named the Gatorade Circle of Champions Player of the Year. Offered numerous scholarship opportunities as he neared graduation, Bettis ultimately chose to attend the University of Notre Dame, where, as a sophomore in 1991, he rushed for 972 yards and set a school record by scoring 20 touchdowns in one season. Electing to forgo his final year of college and enter the 1993 NFL Draft after he gained 825 yards on the ground and scored 16 touchdowns as a junior, Bettis became the second running back taken in that year's draft (Garrison Hearst was first) when the Los Angeles Rams selected him with the 10th overall pick.

Performing brilliantly for the Rams his first year in the league, Bettis earned Pro Bowl, First-Team All-Pro, and NFL Offensive Rookie of the Year honors by rushing for 1,429 yards, amassing 1,673 yards from scrimmage, scoring seven touchdowns, and averaging a career-best 4.9 yards per carry. Although somewhat less productive in 1994, Bettis earned his second straight trip to the Pro Bowl by rushing for 1,025 yards and scoring four touchdowns. However, when the Rams changed head coaches after they relocated to St. Louis the following year, Bettis assumed a lesser role on offense, limiting him to just 637 yards rushing and three touchdowns.

With Bettis having fallen out of favor in St. Louis and the Steelers seeking to upgrade their running attack, the two teams worked out a trade on the day of the 1996 NFL Draft that sent Bettis and a third-round pick to the Rams for Pittsburgh's second- and fourth-round selections. Upon making the deal, St. Louis head coach Rich Brooks stated, "I wanted a little more speed at the position. Jerome is an outstanding player, and the Pittsburgh scheme will suit him more than my scheme will. It is a good move for Jerome."

The move ended up being an excellent one for both the Steelers and Bettis, who posted the following numbers over the course of the next six seasons:

YEAR	RUSH YD	YD FROM SCRIMMAGE	TD
1996	1,431	1,553	11
1997	1,665	1,775	9
1998	1,185	1,275	3
1999	1,091	1,201	7
2000	1,341	1,438	8
2001	1,072	1,120	4

Bettis finished third in the NFL in rushing in both 1996 and 1997, and he also ranked among the league leaders in yards from scrimmage twice and touchdowns scored once, with his 11 rushing TDs in 1996 placing him sixth in the league rankings. In addition to winning the NFL Comeback Player of the Year Award in the first of those campaigns, Bettis earned team MVP and Pro Bowl honors three times each during the period, while also gaining All-Pro recognition twice. More importantly, the Steelers captured the division title in three of those six seasons, although they failed to make it back to the Super Bowl, losing twice in the AFC championship game—once to the Denver Broncos, in 1997, and once to the New England Patriots, in 2001.

While the 5'11", 252-pound Bettis possessed tremendous straight-ahead power, he also had surprisingly quick feet for a man his size, making him even more difficult for opposing defenders to bring down. In discussing that aspect of Bettis's game, Steelers head coach Bill Cowher stated, "I have never seen a power back who was as light on his feet as Jerome was. He would make jump cuts in the hole and his shoulders were never anything but parallel to the line of scrimmage. He could see things and get there on his feet. He had the lightest feet for a big back I have ever seen playing the game."

Cowher continued, "The great thing about Jerome was you rarely saw him take a hit. He was always the one who initiated the hit. He had a great sense of balance, a great sense of forward lean. Most of the time, he was the one who was able to initiate hits. There were times in the fourth quarter when all he had to do was make a little snip-step and he could make people miss because they had to brace for him. I have never seen a guy who could make people miss in a hole better than him."

Longtime Steelers teammate Hines Ward added, "You look at his size and tenacity. To be that size and have quick feet was just amazing. Sometimes you found yourself as a teammate watching like a fan to see him get through a hole, side-step somebody, run over somebody, and then get up and do his patented 'The Bus' dance. That is what made him such a special running back. You don't see many guys be able to maneuver the holes and run somebody over."

Still, Bettis depended more than anything on his size and strength, which enabled him to wear down and intimidate his opponent as the game progresses. In describing his philosophy as a runner, Bettis explained, "I tried to inflict punishment on the defenders instead of just taking it. When I did that, I got defenders to turn away. After getting hit so many times, their mentality changed from being aggressive to just trying to get me on the ground. Then they had to play my game. I was able to make them miss me or bounce off them and keep going."

Bettis rushed for more than 1,000 yards six straight times as a member of the Steelers.
Courtesy of the Pittsburgh Steelers

Dermontti Dawson, who spent his final five seasons in Pittsburgh blocking for Bettis, expressed his appreciation for the many things the big running back brought to the Steeler offense, stating, "As an offensive line, you love to have a back like Jerome in the backfield. It doesn't take a very big hole for him to get through. People think you had to open big lanes for a back to run through, but Jerome somehow found a way. If you had a big crease or a small crease, he found his way through there. The advantage for us, Jerome was such a big back and was so powerful as a runner that he could give you those extra yards. As an offense, that is paramount in the success of the running game."

During his time in Pittsburgh, Bettis also emerged as a leader in the locker room, with Ben Roethlisberger relating in *The Bus: My Life in and out of a Helmet* the following story of how the veteran running back took him under his wing shortly after the Steelers selected him in the 2004 NFL Draft: "He opens up my notebook to the first page and writes down his phone numbers. He says, 'This is my home number; this is my cell number. If you ever need anything, give me a call.' When he walked away, I was like, 'Wow, I can't believe that just happened.' I was so in awe."

After suffering a serious hip and groin injury that sidelined him for the final five games of the 2001 campaign, Bettis missed another three contests in 2002, a season in which he rushed for only 666 yards, although he still managed to score nine touchdowns. Splitting time with Amos Zereoué and Duce Staley the next two seasons, Bettis amassed a total of 1,752 yards on the ground, with 941 of those coming in 2004, when his career-high 13 touchdowns helped him earn his sixth and final trip to the Pro Bowl. Bettis subsequently assumed the role of a short-yardage runner in 2005, rushing for 368 yards and nine touchdowns, before announcing his retirement immediately after the Steelers defeated the Seattle Seahawks in Super Bowl XL. Making his plans known to everyone while standing on the champions' podium following the conclusion of the contest, Bettis proclaimed, "I played this game for a championship. I'm a champion, and I think the Bus's last stop is here in Detroit." Bettis ended his career with 13,662 yards rushing, making him the NFL's fifth-leading all-time rusher at the time (he has since slipped to seventh). He also made 200 receptions for 1,449 yards, amassed 15,111 yards from scrimmage, and scored 94 touchdowns, with 91 of those coming on the ground. While playing for the Steelers, Bettis gained 10,571 yards on the ground and 806 yards on 125 pass receptions, accumulated 11,377 yards from scrimmage, scored 80 touchdowns, and threw three TD passes.

Bettis has remained in the public eye since retiring as an active player, spending three years serving as a studio commentator for NBC's *Football*

Night in America Sunday pregame show, before working for the NFL Network and, later, ESPN as an analyst. He also currently hosts *The Jerome Bettis Show*, which airs on WPXI-TV in Pittsburgh twice on Saturdays.

In analyzing Bettis's career and the contributions he made to the Steelers during his 10 years in Pittsburgh, Franco Harris said, "He was a bruiser. Wow, could he pound that football. He pounded and pounded. He was a great competitor, a great team player. He contributed greatly to those teams. He was one of the main reasons that those teams were successful and accomplished what they did. . . . We were completely different runners in our styles, but I loved to watch the way he ran. He was so effective."

Hines Ward stated, "To do the things he did at that size is amazing. I don't think there will ever be another big guy like Jerome who did it the way he did and for how long he did it."

Dermontti Dawson commented, "He was unusual because most backs weren't as big as Jerome. Usually a back of his size would come in on special situations, short-to-mid-range run plays. But he was a feature back for 13 years in the league. What made him unusual being a larger than normal back, he was so agile and strong that he could take the pounding and be the feature back all that time. He was a phenomenal runner."

Mel Blount perhaps summed up Bettis's time in Pittsburgh best when he said, "Jerome Bettis, to me, was a great player and a great ambassador for the Steelers. His play was reminiscent of the Steelers of the 1970s when we ran the ball, pounded it, and threw it when we had to. We lived and breathed and depended on the running game. That is championship football. You have to be able to run the football, and Jerome did it superbly."

STEELERS CAREER HIGHLIGHTS

Best Season

Bettis's first year in Pittsburgh proved to be a huge success, with the big running back earning 1996 NFL Comeback Player of the Year honors and his lone First-Team All-Pro selection as a member of the Steelers by ranking among the league leaders with 1,431 yards rushing, 1,553 yards from scrimmage, and 11 rushing touchdowns. Bettis also performed exceptionally well in 2000 and 2004, rushing for 1,341 yards and eight touchdowns in the first of those campaigns, before gaining 941 yards on the ground and finishing fourth in the league with 13 rushing touchdowns in the second. However, he had his finest all-around season in 1997, earning Second-Team

All-Pro honors by establishing career-high marks in rushing yards (1,665) and yards from scrimmage (1,775), while also scoring nine touchdowns.

Memorable Moments/Greatest Performances

Bettis went over 100 yards rushing for the first time as a member of the Steelers during a 31–17 win over the Baltimore Ravens on September 8, 1996, when he carried the ball 21 times for 116 yards and one touchdown.

Bettis followed that up with a strong performance against Buffalo, rushing for 133 yards and two touchdowns during a 24–6 win over the Bills, with one of his TD runs covering 43 yards.

Bettis starred against his former team on November 3, 1996, carrying the ball 19 times for 129 yards and two touchdowns during a 42–6 blowout of the St. Louis Rams, with one of his TDs coming on a season-long 50-yard run.

Bettis helped lead the Steelers to a 24–22 win over the Indianapolis Colts on October 12, 1997, by carrying the ball 30 times for 164 yards and one touchdown.

Bettis led the Steelers to a 23–17 overtime victory over Jacksonville on October 26, 1997, by rushing for 99 yards and scoring the game-winning TD on a 17-yard pass from Kordell Stewart.

Bettis earned AFC Offensive Player of the Week honors for his performance during a 26–20 overtime win over the Arizona Cardinals on November 30, 1997, when he carried the ball 36 times for 142 yards and three touchdowns, with his 10-yard TD run nearly five minutes into the overtime session giving the Steelers the victory.

Bettis provided much of the offensive punch during a 16–7 win over the Cincinnati Bengals on October 7, 2001, carrying the ball 21 times for 150 yards.

Bettis led the Steelers to a 15–12 overtime victory over the Cleveland Browns on November 11, 2001, by rushing for a season-high 163 yards.

Bettis earned AFC Offensive Player of the Week honors by gaining a season-high 149 yards on the ground during a 27–3 win over the Philadelphia Eagles on November 7, 2004.

Bettis earned that distinction again by carrying the ball 17 times for 101 yards and two touchdowns during a 21–9 win over the Chicago Bears on December 11, 2005.

Notable Achievements

- Rushed for more than 1,000 yards six straight times, topping 1,500 yards once (1,665 in 1997).
- Surpassed 1,500 yards from scrimmage twice.
- Rushed for more than 10 touchdowns twice.
- Averaged more than 4.5 yards per carry twice.
- Finished third in NFL in rushing twice.
- Finished fourth in NFL in rushing touchdowns once and yards from scrimmage twice.
- Led Steelers in rushing eight times.
- Ranks among NFL career leaders with: 3,479 rushing attempts (4th); 13,662 yards rushing (7th); and 91 rushing touchdowns (11th).
- Ranks second in Steelers history in: rushing attempts (2,683); rushing yards (10,571); and rushing touchdowns (78).
- Ranks among Steelers career leaders with: 11,377 yards from scrimmage (3rd); 11,377 all-purpose yards (4th); 80 touchdowns (3rd); and 482 points scored (tied—7th).
- Five-time division champion (1996, 1997, 2001, 2002, and 2004).
- 2005 AFC champion.
- Super Bowl XL champion.
- Three-time AFC Offensive Player of the Week.
- Three-time Steelers MVP (1996, 1997, and 2000).
- 1996 NFL Comeback Player of the Year.
- 1996 NFL Alumni Running Back of the Year.
- 2001 NFL Walter Payton Man of the Year.
- Four-time Pro Bowl selection (1996, 1997, 2001, and 2004).
- 1996 First-Team All-Pro selection.
- 1997 Second-Team All-Pro selection.
- Two-time First-Team All-Conference selection (1996 and 1997).
- Named to Steelers' 75th Anniversary Team in 2007.
- #36 "unofficially" retired by Steelers.
- Elected to Pro Football Hall of Fame in 2015.

16

JAMES HARRISON

Known for his angry demeanor and fierce competitive spirit, James Harrison carried on the Steeler tradition of intimidating right-outside linebackers, following in the footsteps of Greg Lloyd and Joey Porter. One of the NFL's toughest and meanest players throughout his career, Harrison spent parts of 14 seasons in Pittsburgh, displaying a relentlessness during that time that earned him the respect of his teammates and the scorn of the commissioner's office. The Steelers' all-time sacks leader, Harrison finished first on the club in that category six times, earning in the process team MVP honors twice and recognition as the NFL Defensive Player of the Year once. A five-time Pro Bowl selection and two-time First-Team All-Pro, Harrison helped the Steelers win seven division titles, three AFC championships, and two Super Bowls, with his 100-yard interception return in Super Bowl XLIII being one of the most electrifying plays in the history of the NFL's most celebrated event. Harrison accomplished all he did even though he spent his first few years in the league accomplishing very little after going undrafted by all 32 NFL teams.

Born in Akron, Ohio, on May 4, 1978, James Henry Harrison Jr. grew up rooting for the Cleveland Browns, who played their home games some 40 miles from where he lived. After briefly attending Archbishop Hoban High School as a freshman, Harrison transferred to Coventry High School, where, in addition to starring at linebacker and running back in football, he competed in several track and field events, including the shotput, high jump, and 4 × 100-meter relay.

Although Harrison developed a reputation as an outstanding all-around athlete while at Coventry, he also became known for his lack of maturity and combative disposition, failing to pay attention to his grades or college entrance exams, while also serving as a distraction to the football team. After being suspended for two games early in his senior year for challenging an assistant coach to a fight, Harrison later suffered a one-game suspension for making obscene gestures to the fans after he scored a

James Harrison recorded more sacks than anyone else in franchise history.
Courtesy of the Pittsburgh Steelers

touchdown. With the quality of Harrison's character coming into question, he failed to receive a scholarship offer from any major colleges, forcing him to enroll at Kent State University, whose football team he ended up making as a walk-on. Starring at linebacker/defensive end for the Golden Flashes his final two seasons, Harrison performed particularly well as a senior, earning First-Team Mid-American Conference honors by recording 15 sacks, 98 total tackles, and 20 tackles for loss.

Nevertheless, with pro scouts viewing the 6-foot, 242-pound Harrison as too short to play linebacker and too light to assume a position on the defensive line, all 32 teams bypassed him in the 2002 NFL Draft, prompting him to eventually sign with the Steelers as a free agent. Failing to make much of an impression upon his arrival in Pittsburgh, Harrison spent most of the next two seasons serving as a member of the practice squad, being released by the Steelers on three separate occasions. Commenting on the difficulties that Harrison encountered during the early stages of his career, veteran Steelers linebacker James Farrior later told the NFL Network, "He was a knucklehead that didn't know the plays. We'd be in practice, in training camp, and he might not know what he was doing, so he'd just stop and throw his hands up and tell the coaches to get him out of there. We thought the guy was crazy."

Re-signed by the Steelers during 2004 training camp after spending part of the previous season with the Rhein Fire of NFL Europe, Harrison earned a roster spot, after which he spent the next three years playing mostly on special teams, while also seeing some action at left-outside line-backer. Harrison, who recorded just four sacks and 110 tackles on defense between 2004 and 2006, later told the *Beaver County Times* that, had he not been successful in making the Pittsburgh roster in 2004, he planned to retire from football at age 26 and become a veterinarian.

Harrison finally broke into the starting lineup after the Steelers released Joey Porter following the conclusion of the 2006 campaign. Making the most of his opportunity after being shifted to the right side of the Pitts-burgh defense, Harrison earned Pro Bowl and All-Pro honors for the first of four straight times by forcing seven fumbles and recording a team-leading 8½ sacks and 98 tackles (76 solo). He followed that up with a dominating performance in 2008, gaining recognition as the NFL Defensive Player of the Year by making a career-high 101 tackles, forcing another seven fum-bles, and finishing fourth in the league with 16 sacks. Harrison continued to perform at an elite level the next two seasons, amassing 20½ sacks, 179 tackles, and 11 forced fumbles during that time, before missing five games in 2011 due to injury. Yet, even though he appeared in just 11 contests, Harrison still managed to tie for the team lead with nine sacks, earning in the process his fifth consecutive trip to the Pro Bowl.

One of the NFL's most intimidating players during that five-year period, Harrison played the game with a barely controlled rage that occa-sionally caused him to incur the wrath of the league office. Fined multiple times for delivering blows to his opponent's head, Harrison eventually came to feel that Roger Goodell sought to make an example of him, causing him to call the then-commissioner a "crook" and a "devil" during an interview with *Men's Journal* early in 2011. Although Harrison later apologized for his remarks and promised to exhibit more restraint on the playing field, he failed to do so, earning a one-game suspension in December 2011 for contacting Colt McCoy's facemask with his helmet a moment after the Cleveland quarterback released the football.

After missing all of training camp due to a knee injury and admitting that he had endured a dozen concussions over the course of his career, Harrison recorded just six sacks and 70 tackles (49 solo) in 2012, prompting the Steelers to insist that he take a pay cut at season's end. With Harrison refusing to do so,

Harrison earned NFL Defensive Player of the Year honors in 2008.
Courtesy of the Pittsburgh Steelers

Pittsburgh released him, after which the 34-year-old linebacker signed with the Cincinnati Bengals. Harrison ended up spending only one season in Cincinnati, recording just two sacks and 30 tackles for the Bengals in 2013, before being released by them on March 13, 2014. He subsequently announced his retirement on August 30 of that year, claiming that he based his decision primarily on his desire to spend more time with his family. Upon making his announcement, Harrison said, "My love for the game isn't strong enough to make up for missing one more birthday or first day of school. I am retiring as a man who is truly grateful for all of his blessings."

Choosing to end his retirement less than one month later, Harrison signed with the Steelers on September 23, 2014, after which he went on to spend three more productive seasons in Pittsburgh. Assuming a part-time role with the club from 2014 to 2016, Harrison amassed 15½ sacks and 140 tackles in helping the Steelers capture a pair of division titles. However, with the veteran linebacker seeing very little playing time in 2017, tensions mounted between himself, his teammates, and the organization, prompting the Steelers to release him during the latter stages of the campaign. Harrison left Pittsburgh having recorded 80½ sacks, 760 tackles (554 solo), seven interceptions, 33 forced fumbles, eight fumble recoveries, and one touchdown as a member of the team.

Just three days after being released by the Steelers, Harrison, who later found himself being accused of separating himself from the rest of the team, signed with the hated New England Patriots, causing him to draw a considerable amount of criticism from Pittsburgh fans, as well as many of his former teammates. Claiming that the blame for Harrison's departure lay squarely on his own shoulders, linebacker Bud Dupree stated, "Tweet this out to him. Deebo (Harrison's nickname) got released because he made himself get released. Deebo didn't get released because we just released him. Deebo did a lot of crap to get released."

Dupree continued, "Where has he been the whole season? How many times did he practice? I don't want to tarnish his character. He's a good dude at heart, but he let pride sort of get in his way."

Cornerback Artie Burns added, "Just the things that keep you on a team, on a great organization like this. You know, we're trying to win a Super Bowl over here, so we're not really trying to deal with all the small petty stuff. So, I guess they were aggravated with what he was doing, and they decided to release him."

Meanwhile, center Maurkice Pouncey went so far as to say that Harrison "erased his own legacy" with his selfish behavior and subsequent signing with the Patriots.

Responding to his critics with a lengthy message on Instagram, Harrison wrote:

> If anybody thought I signed a two-year deal with a team at age 39 to sit on the bench and collect a check and a participation trophy, they're mistaken. I didn't sign up to sit on the bench and be a cheerleader. I was clear about that when I signed, and I was told I would be on the field when I signed. When I was asking for reps in camp, I got none. I got lip service, though: "We know what you can do—you don't need the reps." But I know what my body needs to be in shape to compete, and I said so, but still zero reps.
>
> At the beginning of the season, when it was clear I didn't have a role anymore, I asked to be released. Throughout the season, I was told week in and week out that I'd be used. I wasn't. I started getting frustrated about the whole thing. I asked not to be dressed or take unnecessary practice reps if I wasn't going to play. That's what happened for a

couple of weeks, then we had a game week that I got solid reps in practice and everyone assumed I'd play. I got to the stadium four hours early as usual, and my locker was empty. Nobody said anything to me about being inactive, just an empty locker. I asked to be released, and again was told no.

A couple of weeks later, they dress me for the game, so I assume I'm going to play, and I get zero reps. Stood on the sideline the whole game. I asked to be released again, I was told no. Then, a few days later, they released me. I was never told I would be brought back, it was: "If I bring you back, be in shape." I cleared waivers, and they didn't call. New England called. Also, to be clear, ask Ryan (Shazier) if I came to see him in the hospital. I didn't help Bud (Dupree) or T.J. (Watt)? Ask T.J. if I helped him.

Maybe I didn't handle my frustration the best that I could have. If you haven't learned anything about me over the last 16 years, I'm a competitor to my core. I live and breathe competition. I do what it takes to keep my body and my mind ready to be on that field. I do it for me, I do it for my family, I do it for my team, and I do it for the fans. Nothing else to it. At the end of the day, they made a business decision and so did I.

Harrison appeared in four games with the Patriots, recording two sacks and five tackles in the final game of the regular season, before participating in all three of their postseason contests. He subsequently announced his retirement again on April 15, 2018, telling the *Pittsburgh Post-Gazette* at the time, "I have no problem with the Steelers family. I have no problem with the Rooneys. They made a business decision that was best for their organization. I made a business decision that was best for me and my family at the time. We went our separate ways. . . . Fans get mad because they're stuck with a team, one team, that's their team. At the end of the day, it's a business. Yes, you have loyalties to teams, but, when it comes down to it, it's a job, and when your job fires you, you need to find another job."

Harrison added, "There were a lot of things said. And I think a lot of guys said things because, hey, they were hurt, and when you're hurt, you say things you may not normally say."

Only time will tell if Harrison will eventually be welcomed back into the Steelers family.

STEELERS CAREER HIGHLIGHTS

Best Season

Harrison played his best ball for the Steelers from 2007 to 2011, having the greatest season of his career in 2008, when he earned NFL Defensive Player of the Year honors by recording 16 sacks, 101 tackles (67 solo), seven forced fumbles, one safety, and one interception.

Memorable Moments/Greatest Performances

Harrison recorded the first sack of his career during a 24–10 win over the Cleveland Browns on November 14, 2004.

Harrison scored his only regular-season touchdown in the final game of the 2004 campaign, when he returned a fumble 18 yards for a TD during a 29–24 win over the Buffalo Bills.

Harrison earned AFC Defensive Player of the Week honors for the first time for his performance during a 38–7 victory over Baltimore on November 5, 2007, when he intercepted a pass and recorded nine tackles, 3½ sacks, and three forced fumbles, one of which he recovered himself.

Harrison turned in another exceptional all-around effort in the 2008 regular-season opener, recording three sacks, eight tackles, and one forced fumble during a 38–17 win over Houston.

Harrison helped lead Pittsburgh to a 23–20 overtime win over Baltimore on September 29, 2008, by recording 10 tackles, 2½ sacks, and one forced fumble, which resulted in a Steelers TD.

Harrison performed magnificently during an 11–10 win over San Diego on November 16, 2008, earning AFC Defensive Player of the Week honors by forcing a fumble, recording a sack and a safety, and intercepting a pass, which he returned 33 yards.

Harrison starred during a 33–10 victory over the Patriots on November 30, 2008, recording two sacks, 10 tackles, and two forced fumbles on the day.

Harrison turned in another dominant performance against Detroit on October 11, 2009, earning AFC Defensive Player of the Week honors by recording three sacks, eight tackles, and one forced fumble during a 28–20 win over the Lions.

Harrison gained recognition as the AFC Defensive Player of the Week for the fourth and final time by recording two sacks, 11 tackles, two forced fumbles, and one fumble recovery during a 19–11 victory over the Tennessee Titans on September 19, 2010.

Harrison excelled during a lopsided 35–3 victory over the Oakland Raiders on November 21, 2010, intercepting a pass and recording two sacks and one forced fumble.

Harrison recorded three sacks and seven tackles during the Steelers' 31–24 win over Baltimore in the divisional round of the 2010 playoffs.

Harrison turned in a similarly dominant performance against Cincinnati on December 4, 2011, sacking Andy Dalton three times and making six tackles during a 35–7 Pittsburgh victory.

Harrison made the most memorable play of his career in Super Bowl XLIII, contributing to the Steelers' 27–23 win over the Arizona Cardinals by picking off a Kurt Warner pass at the goal line on the final play of the first half and returning the ball 100 yards for a touchdown that ended with him collapsing in the end zone from exhaustion, and remaining there several minutes as his teammates celebrated around him.

Notable Achievements

- Scored one regular-season defensive touchdown during career.
- Scored one defensive touchdown in playoffs during career.
- Finished in double digits in sacks three times.
- Recorded at least 100 tackles twice.
- Finished fourth in NFL with 16 sacks in 2008.
- Led Steelers in sacks six times and tackles once.
- Holds Steelers career record with 80½ sacks.
- Ranks among Steelers career leaders with: 33 forced fumbles (2nd); 760 tackles (6th); and 14 seasons played (tied—3rd).
- Seven-time division champion (2002, 2004, 2007, 2008, 2010, 2014, and 2016).
- Three-time AFC champion (2005, 2008, and 2010).
- Two-time Super Bowl champion (XL and XLIII).
- Four-time AFC Defensive Player of the Week.
- October 2009 AFC Defensive Player of the Month.
- Two-time Steelers MVP (2007 and 2008).
- 2008 NFL Defensive Player of the Year.
- Five-time Pro Bowl selection (2007, 2008, 2009, 2010, and 2011).
- Two-time First-Team All-Pro selection (2008 and 2010).
- Two-time Second-Team All-Pro selection (2007 and 2009).

17

— ALAN FANECA —

One of the NFL's premier offensive linemen for more than a decade, Alan Faneca spent 10 of his 12 years in the league with the Steelers, establishing himself during that time as the greatest guard in franchise history. A hard-working player who led by example, Faneca earned the respect of his teammates with his strong work ethic and exceptional on-field performance, which helped lead the Steelers to four division titles, one AFC championship, and one Super Bowl victory. Extremely durable, Faneca missed just two games his entire career, at one point starting 96 consecutive contests for the Steelers, with his many contributions to the team earning him seven trips to the Pro Bowl, seven All-Pro selections, five All-AFC nominations, and a spot on the franchise's 75th Anniversary Team.

Born in New Orleans, Louisiana, on December 7, 1976, Alan Joseph Faneca remained in his home state until the age of 14, when he traveled to Houston, Texas, where he spent the next four years attending Lamar Consolidated High School. Lettering in football and track and field while at Lamar Consolidated, Faneca earned All–Greater Houston, *Orlando Sentinel* All-South, and Touchdown Club of Houston Player of the Year honors as an offensive lineman, despite spending most of his high school years suffering from epileptic seizures.

After being placed on medication that enabled him to continue playing football, Faneca enrolled at Louisiana State University, where he went on to establish himself as one of the nation's top offensive linemen. Starring at right guard for the Tigers for three years, Faneca gained recognition from the *Knoxville News Sentinel* as the Southeastern Conference Freshman of the Year in 1995, before earning Second-Team All-America honors as a sophomore and consensus First-Team All-America honors as a junior in 1997.

Making an extremely favorable impression on everyone who saw him perform at LSU, Faneca drew praise from head football coach Gerry DiNardo, who said of his star guard, "He was one of the guys who was a great student of the game and his technique. He broke the game down more coach-like than player-like. It was really important to him. . . . He was a quiet guy, not a vocal leader. Everyone looked at him and really respected how hard he worked, how attentive to detail he was."

Meanwhile, LSU teammate Ben Bordelon stated, "You could tell from the first day of practice he was going to be something special. In walk-throughs, you could tell from his strength and footwork . . . he was athletic and a hard worker. He always led by example. He would teach the upperclassmen how to do it."

Having been named one of the three finalists for the 1997 Outland Trophy as the nation's best interior lineman in his junior year, Faneca chose to enter the 1998 NFL Draft, where the Steelers selected him in

Alan Faneca missed just two games his entire career.
Courtesy of Michael Rooney

the first round, with the 26th overall pick. Laying claim to the starting left guard job shortly after he arrived in Pittsburgh, Faneca performed well his first year in the league, being named the winner of the Joe Greene Award as the team's top rookie. After two more excellent seasons, Faneca earned the first of his nine consecutive trips to the Pro Bowl in 2001, while also earning All-Pro honors for the first of eight straight times.

Standing 6'5" and weighing close to 315 pounds, Faneca had good size and strength for an offensive lineman. But the things that really made him stand out were his superb technique, consistency, tremendous hustle, and dedication to his chosen profession. In discussing the last two qualities, longtime teammate Brett Keisel said, "I was immediately drawn to him because of how great a player he was. He was always working, even after consecutive Pro Bowls. Not only did he work hard in practice, but, in games, you always saw Alan hustling and making plays down the field, which is why we had such a great rushing attack when he was here."

Keisel continued, "The Steelers fans loved him. They were drawn by the way he plays the game, a no-nonsense player. When media or anyone would address him, he wouldn't sugarcoat anything. He would usually speak his mind on what he thought, which would sometimes cause controversy."

Fellow Steelers offensive lineman Trai Essex commented, "Watching film on Red was like watching art in motion. I never knew o-linemen could have moves until I saw him spin off a d-lineman en route to cutting a linebacker in order to open up a screen pass that went to the house. A great player and an even better leader. He absolutely changed and elevated the ceiling of the impact a guard can have on the game."

Former Steelers tight end Jerame Tuman added, "I think the main thing that Faneca had over other guards during his playing career was his athleticism and his versatility. Faneca was as good in space as he was at the line of scrimmage. He was arguably one of the top guys at his position for roughly a 10-year span."

After playing left guard almost exclusively his first five years in the league, Faneca moved to left tackle in 2003 to help compensate for the loss of Marvel Smith due to injury. Returning to his normal post the following year, Faneca helped the Steelers compile the second most rushing yards in the league, before serving as one of the key members of a Pittsburgh squad that won the NFL title in 2005.

Faneca remained with the Steelers for two more seasons, earning Pro Bowl and First-Team All-Pro honors in both 2006 and 2007, before

signing a lucrative five-year, $40-million free-agent deal with the New York Jets following the conclusion of the 2007 campaign. Inexplicably cut by the Jets in April 2010 after he made the Pro Bowl in each of his first two seasons in New York, Faneca subsequently signed with the Arizona Cardinals, with whom he spent one season, before announcing his retirement on May 10, 2011. Faneca ended his career with nine Pro Bowl appearances and eight All-Pro selections. Since retiring as an active player, Faneca has lost more than 100 pounds, enabling

Faneca earned Pro Bowl and All-Pro honors seven times each as a member of the Steelers.
Courtesy of Michael Rooney

him to successfully complete the New Orleans Rock 'n' Roll Marathon in 2014 with a finish time of 3:56:17.

Held in high esteem by the men he played with, Faneca inspired words of praise from former Steelers nose tackle Chris Hoke, who said, "Alan Faneca was an old school type guard who played hard-nosed and physical, the way that position was meant to be played. His ability to dominate the opponent at the point of attack and to also get out on the edge and blow open the hole to spring the running back to the next level is what makes him one of the best to ever do it."

Matt Cushing, who spent six seasons with Faneca in Pittsburgh, stated, "Alan was one of the most dominating linemen I had the opportunity to watch. Whether it was pulling, blocking one on one, coming off a double team to block a linebacker that should have had a speed advantage, or handling the stoutest of pass rushers, Alan got it done and got it done with an attitude befitting a Steelers lineman. Not only was he dominant, but he was consistently dominant, game in, game out, year in, year out. It was fun to be able to call him a teammate. And, on top of all that, he was a better person and friend."

STEELERS CAREER HIGHLIGHTS

Best Season

Faneca had arguably the finest season of his career in 2001, when he earned consensus First-Team All-Pro honors for the first of four times by helping the Steelers lead the league in total rushing yardage, with Pittsburgh running backs averaging 4.8 yards per carry.

Memorable Moments/Greatest Performances

Faneca served as the anchor of an offensive line that enabled Steeler running backs to rush for 211 yards during a 30–20 win over the Carolina Panthers on December 26, 1999.

Faneca's exceptional blocking at the line of scrimmage helped the Steelers rush for a season-high total of 275 yards during a 16–7 victory over the Cincinnati Bengals on October 7, 2001.

Faneca's outstanding lead blocking during a 27–3 win over the Philadelphia Eagles on November 7, 2004, helped the Steelers gain a season-high total of 252 yards on the ground, with Jerome Bettis earning AFC Offensive Player of the Week honors by rushing for 149 yards.

Faneca and his offensive line–mates turned in another dominant performance during a 27–7 win over the Cleveland Browns on December 7, 2006, enabling the Steelers to amass 528 yards of total offense, with 303 of those coming on the ground.

Yet, Faneca is perhaps remembered most in Pittsburgh for the pulling block he delivered during the Steelers' 21–10 victory over Seattle in Super Bowl XL that helped spring Willie Parker for a 75-yard touchdown run on the opening possession of the second half.

Notable Achievements

- Missed just two games in 10 seasons, at one point playing in 96 consecutive contests.
- Four-time division champion (2001, 2002, 2004, and 2007).
- 2005 AFC champion.
- Super Bowl XL champion.
- 2004 NFL Alumni Offensive Lineman of the Year.
- Seven-time Pro Bowl selection (2001, 2002, 2003, 2004, 2005, 2006, and 2007).
- Six-time First-Team All-Pro selection (2001, 2002, 2004, 2005, 2006, and 2007).
- 2003 Second-Team All-Pro selection.
- Five-time First-Team All-Conference selection (2001, 2002, 2003, 2004, and 2005).
- Pro Football Hall of Fame All-2000s First Team.
- Pro Football Reference All-2000s First Team.
- Named to Steelers' 75th Anniversary Team in 2007.

18

— LYNN SWANN —

S pending most of his time in Pittsburgh playing for Steeler teams that relied heavily on the run to wear down opposing defenses, Lynn Swann posted relatively modest numbers over the course of his career. Surpassing 50 receptions in just two of his nine NFL seasons, Swann never reached the magical 1,000-yard mark, amassing as many as 800 receiving yards just twice. Swann never finished any higher than seventh in the NFL in pass receptions, and he placed in the league's top five in receiving yards just once. Nevertheless, Swann always performed magnificently whenever the Steelers needed him to do so, contributing greatly to the success they experienced during the 1970s. A member of all four Chuck Noll Super Bowl winning teams, Swann established himself as one of the greatest big-game receivers in NFL history during his time in Pittsburgh, with his ability to perform well under pressure earning him spots on the NFL 1970s All-Decade Team and the Super Bowl's Silver Anniversary Team. A three-time Pro Bowler, three-time All-Pro, and three-time All-AFC selection, Swann also later received the additional honors of being named to the Steelers' 75th Anniversary Team and being elected to the Pro Football Hall of Fame.

Born in Alcoa, Tennessee, on March 7, 1952, Lynn Curtis Swann first demonstrated his amazing physical ability by walking at only seven months old. After moving with his family to San Mateo, California, at the age of two, Swann grew up in neighboring Foster City, where his mother, disappointed at not having a daughter, enrolled him in dance class. Developing much of the grace and dexterity that later became his trademarks on the football field, Swann told *Runner's World* years later, "People think football and dancing are so different. They think it's contradictory for a boy to dance, but dancing is a sport."

Excelling in multiple sports while attending Junipero Serra High School, Swann starred as a wide receiver in football and as both a pole vaulter and long jumper in track, once winning the California High School State Championship in the last event by leaping 25 feet, four inches.

Lynn Swann established himself as one of the greatest clutch receivers in NFL history during his time in Pittsburgh.
Courtesy of MEARSonlineauctions.com

Concentrating exclusively on football after enrolling at the University of Southern California in the fall of 1970, Swann spent three years playing under head coach John McKay, who said of his protégé, "He has speed, soft hands, and grace." After helping the Trojans compile a perfect record that earned them the National Championship in 1972, Swann received consensus All-America recognition as a senior the following year, prompting the

Steelers to select him in the first round of the 1974 NFL Draft, with the 21st overall pick.

Seeing very little action at wide receiver his first year in Pittsburgh, Swann made just 11 receptions for 208 yards and two touchdowns. However, he earned a spot on the NFL All-Rookie Team by leading the league with 577 punt-return yards, which represents a single-season franchise record. Swann also contributed to the Steelers' successful run to their first NFL championship by making five receptions for 77 yards and one touchdown during the playoffs, with his fourth-quarter TD grab against Oakland in the AFC championship game putting Pittsburgh ahead to stay.

Swann's role on offense increased dramatically in 1975, when, after becoming a starter, he ended up leading the Steelers with 49 receptions, 781 receiving yards, and 11 TD catches, with the last figure also placing him first in the league. Accorded Pro Bowl and All-Pro honors for the first time in his career, Swann capped off his outstanding season by making four receptions for 161 yards and one touchdown during Pittsburgh's 21–17 win over Dallas in Super Bowl X, earning in the process game MVP honors. Swann's brilliant performance came just two weeks after he suffered a severe concussion against Oakland in the AFC title game that forced him to spend two days in a hospital.

Swann proved to be somewhat less productive in 1976, making just 28 receptions for 516 yards and three touchdowns. But he earned Pro Bowl and All-Pro honors in each of the next two seasons by catching 50 passes for 789 yards and seven touchdowns in 1977, before establishing career-high marks with 61 receptions, 880 receiving yards, and 11 TD catches the following year.

Blessed with many natural gifts that helped make him one of football's consummate receivers, the 5'11", 185-pound Swann possessed outstanding speed, exceptional leaping ability, and tremendous agility and body control that often enabled him to make catches of a spectacular nature. Extremely graceful as well, Swann drew praise from Hall of Fame receiver Cris Carter, who said, "If there was one player after I became a wide receiver that I wanted to be like, it was Lynn Swann. The way he played with such grace— and I loved the way he played the game off the ground."

More than anything, though, Swann became known for his ability to perform well in big games, which he explained thusly: "People say I perform well in the 'big' games. Maybe that's because I have more fun in those games . . . when there is no next week, when six months of work is riding on every play and you come through, that's the ultimate. That's the rush we're all in this for."

Swann earned MVP honors for Super Bowl X.
Courtesy of MEARSonlineauctions.com

Swann had another excellent year for the Steelers in 1979, helping them capture their sixth consecutive division title by catching 41 passes, amassing 808 receiving yards, and scoring six touchdowns during the regular season, before making another 12 receptions for 180 yards and two touchdowns in the playoffs. He spent three more years in Pittsburgh, seeing his numbers gradually decline during that time, before announcing his retirement following the conclusion of the 1982 campaign. Ending his career with 336 receptions, 5,462 receiving yards, 6,284 all-purpose yards, 51 TD receptions, and 53 total touchdowns scored, Swann continues to rank among the franchise's all-time leaders in most receiving categories. At the time of his retirement, Swann also held Super Bowl records for most receiving yards (364) and most all-purpose yards (398).

Following his playing days, Swann, who began working as a commentator for ABC Sports while still active with the Steelers, moved seamlessly into a career in broadcasting. Spending the next two decades covering events such as weightlifting at the 1984 Summer Olympics in Los Angeles, bobsledding at the 1988 Winter Olympics in Calgary, Alberta, and ABC's *Wide World of Sports*, Swann remained with the station until 2006. After subsequently serving as part of the ownership team for Pittsburgh's AFL expansion franchise, the Pittsburgh Power, Swann accepted the position of athletic director at his alma mater, the University of Southern California, on July 1, 2016.

In addressing the roles that he and fellow wideout John Stallworth assumed during their time in Pittsburgh, Swann said, "We used to refer to ourselves as the 'Gamebreakers.' We weren't going to get a lot of opportunities, but, if they threw us the ball, we believed we could break the game wide open and make the big play."

Meanwhile, in discussing Swann's Steelers legacy, former teammate Joe Greene stated, "Lynn Swann didn't have the stats, but he sure as heck made an impact. No one made a bigger impact. It's like Gale Sayers. He didn't play a long time, but he made an impact. Lynn Swann had that impact. He played a lot of big games."

CAREER HIGHLIGHTS

Best Season

Although Swann had an extremely productive year for the Steelers in 1975, making 49 receptions for 781 yards and leading the NFL with 11 TD catches, he posted the best overall numbers of his career in 1978, earning his lone First-Team All-Pro selection by ranking among the league leaders with 61 receptions, 880 receiving yards, and 11 touchdowns.

Memorable Moments/Greatest Performances

Swann scored the first touchdown of his career in his first game as a pro, hauling in a 54-yard TD pass from Joe Gilliam during a 30–0 win over the Baltimore Colts in the 1974 regular-season opener.

Swann lit the scoreboard for the second time in his career when he returned a punt 64 yards for a touchdown during a 28–7 victory over the New Orleans Saints on November 25, 1974.

Swann went over 100 receiving yards for the first time during a 42–6 blowout of the Cleveland Browns on October 5, 1975, making five receptions for 126 yards and one TD, which came on a 43-yard pass from Joe Gilliam.

Swann contributed to a 30–24 victory over the Cincinnati Bengals on November 2, 1975, by making six receptions for 116 yards and two touchdowns, collaborating with Terry Bradshaw on scoring plays that covered 37 and 25 yards.

Swann helped lead the Steelers to a 35–31 win over Cleveland on November 13, 1977, by making five catches for 129 yards and one touchdown, which came on a 39-yard hookup with Bradshaw.

Swann proved to be the difference in a 28–17 victory over the Jets on October 1, 1978, making seven receptions for 100 yards and two touchdowns, the longest of which covered 26 yards.

Swann torched the San Francisco defensive secondary for eight catches, 134 receiving yards, and two touchdowns during a 24–7 win over the 49ers on November 27, 1978.

Swann made five catches for a career-high 192 yards and two touchdowns during a 37–17 victory over Cincinnati on December 2, 1979, hooking up with Terry Bradshaw on scoring plays that covered 58 and 42 yards.

Swann had another huge game on November 16, 1980, making nine receptions for 138 yards and one touchdown during a 16–13 win over the Browns, with his 3-yard TD reception in the fourth quarter providing the margin of victory.

Swann gave the Steelers a 27–21 overtime victory over the New England Patriots on September 27, 1981, when he hauled in a 24-yard touchdown pass from Terry Bradshaw during the overtime session. He finished the game with three catches for 68 yards and that one TD.

Swann began to establish himself as a tremendous big-game receiver in Super Bowl X, when he earned game MVP honors by making four receptions for 161 yards and one touchdown during the Steelers' 21–17 victory over Dallas. In addition to scoring the game-winning touchdown on a 64-yard fourth-quarter connection with Terry Bradshaw, Swann made a spectacular leaping sideline grab in which he seemingly defied the laws of nature by keeping both feet in bounds while pulling the ball back onto the playing field. In discussing the play, teammate Mike Wagner recalled, "That sideline catch, I was actually looking down, and I'm going, 'How did he do that?'" Swann made another remarkable reception during the contest, exhibiting his amazing body control by out-leaping Dallas cornerback Mark Washington for a Bradshaw aerial thrown deep down the middle, tipping the ball into the air, and gaining possession of it as he fell to the ground.

Swann continued his postseason success during Pittsburgh's 40–14 victory over Baltimore in the divisional round of the 1976 playoffs, making five catches for 77 yards and two touchdowns, which came on Bradshaw passes that covered 29 and 11 yards.

Swann again performed extremely well in the 1978 AFC championship game, contributing to the Steelers' lopsided 34–5 win over the Houston Oilers by making four receptions for 98 yards and one touchdown, which came on a 29-yard second-quarter connection with Bradshaw.

Swann subsequently dominated the Dallas defensive secondary for a second time in Super Bowl XIII, making seven receptions for 124 yards and one touchdown during the Steelers' 35–31 victory over the Cowboys, with his TD coming on a superb 18-yard grab in the back of the Dallas end zone.

Swann also contributed significantly to the Steelers' 31–19 win over the Los Angeles Rams in Super Bowl XIV, making five catches for 79 yards and one touchdown, which came on a 47-yard hookup with Terry Bradshaw.

Notable Achievements

- Surpassed 50 receptions twice.
- Topped 800 receiving yards twice.
- Made 11 touchdown receptions twice.
- Returned one punt for a touchdown.
- Led NFL in touchdown receptions once and punt-return yards once.
- Finished second in NFL in touchdown receptions once.
- Led Steelers in receptions five times and receiving yards four times.
- Ranks among Steelers career leaders with: 336 receptions (6th); 5,462 receiving yards (6th); 51 touchdown receptions (4th); and 53 touchdowns (6th).
- Six-time division champion (1974, 1975, 1976, 1977, 1978, and 1979).
- Four-time AFC champion (1974, 1975, 1978, and 1979).
- Four-time Super Bowl champion (IX, X, XIII, and XIV).
- Member of 1974 NFL All-Rookie Team.
- Super Bowl X MVP.
- 1981 NFL Man of the Year.
- Three-time Pro Bowl selection (1975, 1977, and 1978).
- 1978 First-Team All-Pro selection.
- Two-time Second-Team All-Pro selection (1975 and 1977).
- Three-time First-Team All-Conference selection (1975, 1977, and 1978).
- Pro Football Hall of Fame All-1970s First Team.
- Named to Super Bowl's Silver Anniversary Team in 1990.
- Named to Steelers' 75th Anniversary Team in 2007.
- #88 "unofficially" retired by Steelers.
- Elected to Pro Football Hall of Fame in 2001.

19

─ JOHN STALLWORTH ─

Immediately preceded on this list by the man with whom he combined to form one of the greatest wide receiver tandems in NFL history, John Stallworth teamed up with Lynn Swann to give the Steelers the league's most dynamic pass-receiving duo for much of the 1970s. Posting more impressive career numbers than his sidekick, Stallworth retired at the end of 1987 with more pass receptions, receiving yards, and touchdown catches than anyone else in franchise history. En route to earning three trips to the Pro Bowl, one All-Pro selection, and two All-AFC nominations, Stallworth surpassed 70 receptions and 1,000 receiving yards three times each, with his outstanding play helping the Steelers win eight division titles, four AFC championships, and four Super Bowls. And, despite being overshadowed by Swann much of the time, Stallworth eventually landed a spot on the Steelers' 75th Anniversary Team and a place in the Pro Football Hall of Fame.

Born in Tuscaloosa, Alabama, on July 15, 1952, Johnny Lee Stallworth experienced a considerable amount of adversity as a child, finding himself temporarily paralyzed on one side after he suffered a viral infection at the age of eight. Told by doctors that he likely would never walk again, Stallworth remained steadfast in his commitment to regaining full mobility, stating years later that his terrifying experience with paralysis "brought out a motivation in me to really extend myself." Yet, even after recovering from his malady, Stallworth hardly resembled a future NFL star, with his clumsiness often causing him to trip over his own two feet.

Developing into an excellent athlete by the time he reached his teens, Stallworth received his introduction to organized football while attending Tuscaloosa High School, where he spent three years playing running back. After subsequently failing to make much of an impression on legendary Alabama head coach Paul "Bear" Bryant, who chose not to offer him a scholarship, Stallworth ended up enrolling at Division II Alabama A&M, with whom he earned All–Southern Intercollegiate Athletic Conference honors as a wide receiver in 1972 and 1973. Later noting that Bryant's rejection of him turned out to be a blessing in disguise, Stallworth stated, "Looking back, I wouldn't change a thing. Hindsight is always 20-20, but I could have been lost in the shuffle at Alabama. They weren't throwing the ball a whole lot in those days."

Having set Alabama A&M school records for most career and single-game receptions, Stallworth entered the 1974 NFL Draft, where the Steelers selected him in the fourth round, with the 82nd overall pick. With Pittsburgh having selected the more highly touted Lynn Swann three rounds earlier in that year's draft, Franco Harris later claimed that Stallworth arrived at his first pro training camp taking nothing for granted, saying, "He was a very unassuming guy who didn't come in with much fanfare. But you noticed that he steadily kept working hard, pounding away. He just grew into greatness."

Stallworth ended up accomplishing very little his first three years in Pittsburgh, catching only 16 passes for 269 yards and one touchdown in a backup role as a rookie, before totaling just 29 receptions, 534 receiving yards, and seven touchdowns while battling through injuries the next two seasons. However, Stallworth emerged as an offensive weapon after he became a full-time starter in 1977, finishing second on the team with 44 receptions, 784 receiving yards, and seven touchdowns. He followed that up with a similarly productive 1978 campaign, making 41 receptions for 798 yards and nine touchdowns, before earning Pro Bowl, First-Team All-Pro, and team MVP honors in 1979 by catching 70 passes, scoring eight touchdowns, and finishing second in the league with 1,183 receiving yards. At his very best in that year's playoffs, Stallworth helped the Steelers capture their fourth NFL title in six seasons by making 12 receptions for 259 yards and three touchdowns during the postseason, with his sensational

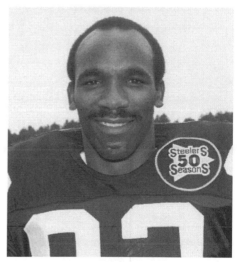

John Stallworth combined with Lynn Swann to give the Steelers one of the most dynamic pass-receiving duos in NFL history.
Courtesy of the Pittsburgh Steelers

73-yard TD grab against Los Angeles in Super Bowl XIV providing much of the impetus for the Steelers to defeat the Rams by a score of 31–19.

Although Stallworth perhaps lacked some of Swann's suppleness, he possessed more size, speed, and broken-field running ability, making him

Stallworth retired with more pass receptions, receiving yards, and TD catches than anyone else in franchise history.
Courtesy of the Pittsburgh Steelers

more dangerous after he caught the football. Standing 6'2" and weighing 195 pounds, Stallworth ran the 40-yard dash in 4.5 seconds when he first entered the league, with his ability to accelerate and separate himself from his defender making him one of the NFL's top deep threats. Stallworth also had exceptional hands, outstanding leaping ability, and incredible concentration in tight coverage, with his extraordinary skill set eventually making him Terry Bradshaw's most trusted receiver. In discussing the chemistry that developed over time between himself and Bradshaw, Stallworth said, "I know that I'm the primary receiver on every route. Even if the quarterback looks elsewhere first, I know I'll be open and he'll come back to me."

Meanwhile, former Bengals wide receiver and current NFL analyst Cris Collinsworth noted, "You could just see that Terry Bradshaw believed that John Stallworth, when he needed it the most, was going to make a play."

After establishing himself as one of the NFL's elite wideouts in 1979, Stallworth missed virtually the entire 1980 season with a broken leg. Returning to action the following year, Stallworth had one of his most productive seasons, catching 63 passes for 1,098 yards and five touchdowns, before earning his second trip to the Pro Bowl by making 27 receptions for 441 yards, and finishing third in the league with seven TD catches during the strike-shortened 1982 campaign.

Unfortunately, the injury bug bit Stallworth once again in 1983, limiting him to only four games and eight receptions. However, he remained healthy the next two seasons, totaling 155 receptions, 2,332 receiving yards, and 16 touchdowns during that time, with his outstanding play in 1984 earning him Pro Bowl, team MVP, and NFL Comeback Player of the Year honors. Playing perhaps the best ball of his career that season, Stallworth placed second in the league with 1,395 receiving yards, and he also finished fourth in the circuit with 80 receptions and 11 TD catches.

Stallworth spent two more years in Pittsburgh, but he found himself being plagued by various leg and ankle injuries. Choosing to announce his retirement following the conclusion of the 1987 campaign, Stallworth ended his career with 537 receptions, 8,723 receiving yards, and 63 touchdown receptions, all of which represented Steelers team records at the time. He also rushed for 111 yards and one touchdown during his career. A tremendous big-game performer, Stallworth had 12 touchdown receptions and a string of 17 straight games with at least one reception in postseason play, with his career (24.4 yards) and single-game (40.33 yards) per-catch averages in Super Bowl play both representing all-time records.

Embarking on an extremely successful business career following his playing days, Stallworth, in 1986, founded Madison Research Corporation

(MRC), which specializes in providing engineering and information technology services to government and commercial clients. After seeing MRC grow to more than 650 employees and $69.5 million in revenues by 2006, Stallworth sold his business to Wireless Facilities, Inc., enabling him to subsequently pursue other interests, which included becoming part-owner of the Pittsburgh Steelers on March 23, 2009.

Stallworth, who received induction into the Pro Football Hall of Fame in 2002, had the honor of presenting his longtime teammate Lynn Swann at the latter's induction ceremony one year earlier. In explaining his decision to have Stallworth present him, Swann stated, "John had had such a quietly successful life after football that maybe they (the Hall of Fame voters) needed to see John and hear from John and understand how great John Stallworth really was."

Speaking on behalf of his former teammate during his acceptance speech, Swann said, "I don't think I could be in the Hall of Fame unless there was a John Stallworth. The competition between John and me, the things that we made each other do in terms of working and getting ready, I knew I always had to be ready."

In discussing the extraordinary pass-catching duo, fellow Steelers Hall of Famer Mel Blount opined, "When you look at what they accomplished, I don't think there was a better one-two combination in the game. If you had either one of them, you had a big-time receiver. We had both of them."

CAREER HIGHLIGHTS

Best Season

Stallworth earned his lone First-Team All-Pro nomination in 1979, when he ranked among the league leaders with 70 receptions, 1,183 receiving yards, and eight touchdown catches. However, he had his finest all-around season in 1984, when he established career-high marks in receptions (80), receiving yards (1,395), and touchdown receptions (11), earning in the process First-Team All-Conference and NFL Comeback Player of the Year honors.

Memorable Moments/Greatest Performances

Stallworth had his breakout game in the 1974 regular-season finale, helping the Steelers record a 27–3 victory over the Cincinnati Bengals by making six receptions for 105 yards and scoring the first touchdown of his career on a 5-yard pass from Terry Bradshaw.

Although the Steelers lost the opening game of the 1976 regular season to the Oakland Raiders by a score of 31–28, Stallworth made six catches for 94 yards and scored the only rushing touchdown of his career on a 47-yard run in the third quarter.

Stallworth starred during a 35–31 win over the Cleveland Browns on November 13, 1977, making six receptions for 126 yards and two touchdowns, which came on Terry Bradshaw passes that covered 38 and nine yards.

Stallworth turned in another outstanding performance on October 8, 1978, when he helped lead the Steelers to a 31–7 victory over the Atlanta Falcons by making six catches for 114 yards and one touchdown, with one of his receptions going for a season-long 70-yard catch-and-run.

Stallworth proved to be a huge factor in the Steelers' 33–10 win over Denver in the divisional round of the 1978 playoffs, making 10 receptions for 156 yards and one touchdown, which came on a 45-yard fourth-quarter connection with Terry Bradshaw.

Stallworth subsequently made two touchdown catches during Pittsburgh's 35–31 win over Dallas in Super Bowl XIII, displaying his explosiveness by taking a short seam pass 75 yards for one of his scores.

Stallworth excelled once again in Super Bowl XIV, leading the Steelers to a 31–19 victory over the Los Angeles Rams by making three receptions for 121 yards and one touchdown, which came on a brilliant over the shoulder 73-yard catch-and-run that put Pittsburgh ahead to stay in the fourth quarter. In describing his TD catch to *Sports Illustrated*, Stallworth said, "My 73-yard catch-and-run put us up 24–19 and triggered a sigh of relief on our sideline. Not only had the play worked, but it broke the Rams' backs too. We knew we were ahead to stay."

Stallworth had a big day against New Orleans on October 4, 1981, making seven receptions for 158 yards and one touchdown during a 20–6 win over the Saints, with his 47-yard TD grab in the fourth quarter sealing the victory for the Steelers.

Although the Steelers lost the 1982 AFC wild card game to the San Diego Chargers by a score of 31–28, Stallworth again exhibited his ability to perform well in big games, making eight catches for 116 yards and one touchdown.

Stallworth starred in defeat once again in the 1984 regular-season opener, making eight receptions for 167 yards and one touchdown during a 37–27 loss to the Kansas City Chiefs.

Stallworth scored three touchdowns in one game for the first time in his career during a 35–7 victory over the Houston Oilers on November 4, 1984, hooking up with Mark Malone on scoring plays that covered 43, 17, and 39 yards. He finished the contest with four catches for 109 yards.

Stallworth duplicated that feat three weeks later, making seven receptions for 116 yards and three touchdowns during a 52–24 win over the San Diego Chargers on November 25.

Stallworth turned in his last great performance for the Steelers on September 30, 1985, making a career-high 11 receptions for 151 yards and one touchdown during a 37–24 loss to the Cincinnati Bengals, with his TD coming on a 17-yard pass from Mark Malone.

Notable Achievements

- Surpassed 60 receptions four times, topping 70 catches three times and 80 catches once.
- Surpassed 1,000 receiving yards three times.
- Made 11 touchdown receptions in 1984.
- Finished second in NFL in receiving yards twice.
- Finished third in NFL with seven touchdown receptions in 1982.
- Finished fourth in NFL in receptions once and touchdown receptions twice.
- Led Steelers in receptions five times and receiving yards five times.
- Ranks among Steelers career leaders with: 537 receptions (fourth); 8,723 receiving yards (3rd); 8,834 yards from scrimmage (5th); 63 touchdown receptions (3rd); 64 touchdowns (5th); 384 points scored (11th); and 14 seasons played (tied—3rd).
- Eight-time division champion (1974, 1975, 1976, 1977, 1978, 1979, 1983, and 1984).
- Four-time AFC champion (1974, 1975, 1978, and 1979).
- Four-time Super Bowl champion (IX, X, XIII, and XIV).
- Two-time Steelers MVP (1979 and 1984).
- 1984 NFL Comeback Player of the Year.
- Three-time Pro Bowl selection (1979, 1982, and 1984).
- 1979 First-Team All-Pro selection.
- Two-time First-Team All-Conference selection (1979 and 1984).
- Named to Steelers' 75th Anniversary Team in 2007.
- #82 "unofficially" retired by Steelers.
- Elected to Pro Football Hall of Fame in 2002.

20

— JACK BUTLER —

A hard-hitting, ball-hawking defensive back who excelled at both corner-back and safety for the Steelers, Jack Butler spent his entire nine-year NFL career in Pittsburgh, amassing the second most interceptions in franchise history. The Steelers' all-time leader in interception-return yards, Butler returned four picks for touchdowns during his career and tied an NFL record that still stands by intercepting four passes in one game in 1953. The versatile Butler also made four touchdown receptions for the Steelers, with his exceptional all-around play earning him four trips to the Pro Bowl, four All-Pro nominations, spots on the NFL's 50th Anniversary Team and the Steelers' 75th Anniversary Team, and a place in the Pro Football Hall of Fame. Butler accomplished all he did even though he entered the NFL as an undrafted free agent after never having played football prior to college.

Born in Oakland, Pennsylvania, on November 12, 1927, John Bradshaw Butler grew up some 50 miles southeast, in the city of Pittsburgh, where he spent his youth rooting for the hometown Pirates and Steelers. After attending Mount Carmel High School in Canada, Butler enrolled at St. Bonaventure University, where he played football for the first time at the suggestion of the school's athletic director, Father Silas Rooney, who also happened to be the brother of Steelers founder Art Rooney. Although Butler ended up having an extremely successful collegiate career as a wide receiver for the Bonnies, he never seriously considered turning pro, especially when he went undrafted by all 12 teams in the 1951 NFL Draft. But, while attending graduate school at St. Bonaventure in the hope of eventually becoming either a Catholic priest or an electrician, Butler received a telephone call from Pittsburgh Steelers scout Fran Fogarty, who contacted him on the recommendation of Father Silas.

Looking back at the events that transpired at the time, Butler told the *Buffalo News*, "I fully intended to go back to school. Fran Fogarty called from the Steelers and asked me if I wanted to try out for the team. I

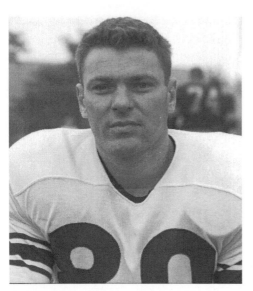

Jack Butler ranks second in franchise
history in career interceptions.
Courtesy of the Pittsburgh Steelers

thought, 'Hey, this is a terrific way to spend my summer. I won't make the team, but it will be a great way to pass the time.' I never went back to school."

Butler continued, "Job-wise, I didn't know what I wanted to do, but I knew what I didn't want to do. I guess what I didn't want to do was go to work. . . . If Father Silas had never called Mr. Rooney and said, 'Take a look at this guy,' that would have been the end of it."

Butler ended up surprising himself by making the Steelers roster after being moved from wide receiver to defensive back by Pittsburgh's coaching staff, who he impressed with his aggressiveness and outstanding athleticism. A starter by Week 3, Butler later recalled, "I didn't play defensive back until someone got hurt in about the third game or so. I'll tell you one thing: No one got behind me that game. I was so far back no one could. That was the best thing that ever happened to me."

Performing well as a rookie, Butler concluded the 1951 campaign with five interceptions, 142 interception-return yards, and one defensive touchdown, which came on a 52-yard pick-six. Establishing himself as one of the NFL's top cornerbacks over the course of the next two seasons, Butler ranked among the league leaders with seven interceptions and 168 interception-return yards in 1952, before once again placing near the top of the league rankings with nine picks and 147 interception-return yards in 1953. After another solid season in 1954, Butler earned Pro Bowl honors for the first of four straight times the following year, even though he failed to record a single interception during the campaign.

Proving to be a huge asset to the Steelers with his aggressiveness, versatility, and athleticism, the 6'1", 200-pound Butler fit in perfectly with Pittsburgh's bruising defense, with current Steelers owner Art Rooney Jr. once commenting, "He hit so hard he would hurt himself." A superb tackler who did an exceptional job of wrapping up, Butler also knew how to use the rules of the day to his advantage, noting years later, "You could bump 'em and push 'em and do things. You could grab onto the receiver's jersey so he didn't get far from you. You could hold on a little bit."

A fierce competitor, Butler added, "I just loved the game and loved to play. Everything was a challenge. I mean, I loved it. Playing the Browns was great—Mac Speedie or Dante Lavelli, playing whomever, covering so and so. He wasn't going to beat me; I was going to beat him. I thought that way anyway."

Butler's quickness, sure hands, and intelligence also allowed him to double as a wide receiver from time to time, with the former college wide-out making seven receptions for 102 yards and four touchdowns over the course of his career.

In addressing Butler's unique skill set, Joe Gordon, the club's director of communications and marketing from 1968 to 1998, stated, "The first thing I can recall as a young fan of the Steelers in the 1950s is that he was such an outstanding player on mediocre and poor teams. Probably the things that stood out the most were his toughness and versatility."

Art Rooney Jr. also had high praise for Butler, revealing, "Jim Finks once told me that Jack Butler was one of the greatest athletes he had ever seen. As you might know, Jim was a pretty good talent evaluator."

Butler continued to perform at an extremely high level after the Steelers moved him to safety in 1956, amassing a total of 25 interceptions over the course of the next three seasons (including a league-leading 10 in 1957), en route to earning Pro Bowl and All-Pro honors all three years. However, he suffered a crippling knee injury during the 1959 campaign that brought his career to a premature end, later recalling, "It was a freaky thing. It happened on a play away from me. It was a little slot pass. (Eagles receiver) Pete Retzlaff stumbled and fell and hit me on the knee on his way down. He hit me right below the knee. That was it. I'd been hit a lot harder many times."

Forced to retire with 52 interceptions, 827 interception-return yards, 10 fumble recoveries, and five defensive touchdowns, Butler ended his career with the second-most picks in NFL history at the time. Subsequently named to the NFL 1950s All-Decade Team, Butler later received the additional honors of being named one of the 300 greatest players in the history of professional football and being elected to the Pro Football Hall of Fame by the members of the Senior Committee in 2012.

After retiring as an active player, Butler briefly worked as an assistant on the coaching staff of the Buffalo Bills of the newly formed American Football League, before spending the next 50 years in scouting, with 44 of those coming as director of the scouting combine known as BLESTO, which

Butler starred at both cornerback and
safety for the Steelers.
Courtesy of the Pittsburgh Steelers

helped revolutionize how the league evaluated talent.

Unfortunately, Butler spent most of his post-playing career suffering from the after-effects of his knee injury, requiring a knee replacement and battling repeated staph infections, one of which took his life at the age of 85, on May 11, 2013, three years after he retired from scouting. Upon learning of his passing, Art Rooney Jr. said, "Jack Butler was one of the all-time great Steelers. He devoted his entire life to the NFL and made contributions to many teams and many players through his work with BLESTO and player personnel matters."

Steve Perry, president and executive director of the Pro Football Hall of Fame, described Butler as "one of the finest cornerbacks ever to step on an NFL field."

And former Steelers linebacker Bill Priatko payed homage to his one-time teammate by stating, "Jack was most certainly a great football player and a truly humble man. He would always say that he loved the game of football. He never looked at what he accomplished as being so great. . . . He had such a presence about him. He was so genuine. I call him a pure definition of a man's man."

CAREER HIGHLIGHTS

Best Season

It could be argued that Butler played his best ball for the Steelers in 1952 and 1953, amassing a total of 16 interceptions and 315 interception-return yards over the course of those two seasons. Nevertheless, he failed to earn Pro Bowl or All-Pro honors in either of those campaigns. On the other hand, after Butler led the NFL with a career-high 10 interceptions in 1957, he appeared in the Pro Bowl and made First-Team All-Pro for the first of three straight times, prompting me to identify that as his finest season.

Memorable Moments/Greatest Performances

Butler crossed the opponent's goal line for the first time in his career on October 28, 1951, when he sealed a 28–14 victory over the Chicago Cardinals by returning an interception 52 yards for a TD during the latter stages of the fourth quarter.

Butler recorded the first of his four career touchdown receptions during a 29–28 loss to the Cleveland Browns on November 16, 1952, when he hauled in a 7-yard pass from quarterback Jim Finks.

Butler contributed to a 63–7 mauling of the Giants on November 30, 1952, by collaborating with Pittsburgh quarterback Gary Kerkorian on a 20-yard scoring play.

Butler again proved to be a thorn in the side of the Giants on November 15, 1953, when he hooked up with Jim Finks on a 33-yard TD pass in the fourth quarter that provided the margin of victory in a 14–10 win over New York.

Although the Steelers lost to the Philadelphia Eagles by a score of 24–22 on October 9, 1954, Butler recorded the second pick-six of his career when he returned an interception 23 yards for a touchdown.

Butler once again displayed his playmaking ability the following week, returning an interception 41 yards for a touchdown during a 55–27 victory over the Cleveland Browns.

Butler made the last touchdown reception of his career during a 23–0 win over the Washington Redskins in the 1956 regular-season finale, when he collaborated with Ted Marchibroda on a 10-yard scoring play.

Butler scored his last defensive touchdown on November 18, 1956, when he recovered a fumble, which he returned six yards for a TD during a 14–7 win over the Chicago Cardinals.

Butler turned in the finest performance of his career in the final game of the 1953 regular season, when he led the Steelers to a 14–13 victory over the Washington Redskins by picking off four passes, one of which he returned five yards for the game-winning touchdown in the fourth quarter. Describing the last of his four picks, Butler recalled, "Bill Dudley was with the 'Skins then, and he ran a down-and-out. He was at the end of his career; I was on the right corner. But it was a down-and-out and (Washington quarterback Eddie) LeBaron threw it to him and I came up and it was an easy pick and I went straight down the field. I just don't remember much more about it. I remember that play, but I just never thought four interceptions was that great of a thing."

Notable Achievements

- Scored five defensive touchdowns during career.
- Recorded at least seven interceptions four times.
- Surpassed 100 interception-return yards four times.
- Led NFL with 10 interceptions in 1957.
- Finished second in NFL with nine interceptions in 1958.
- Finished third in NFL with 142 interception-return yards in 1951.
- Finished fourth in NFL in interception-return yards twice.
- Led Steelers in interceptions five times.
- Holds Steelers career record for most interception-return yards (827).
- Ranks among Steelers career leaders with: 52 interceptions (2nd); four touchdown interceptions (tied—3rd); and five defensive touchdowns (tied—2nd).
- Tied NFL record by intercepting four passes vs. Washington Redskins on December 13, 1953.
- Four-time Pro Bowl selection (1955, 1956, 1957, and 1958).
- Three-time First-Team All-Pro selection (1957, 1958, and 1959).
- 1956 Second-Team All-Pro selection.
- Four-time First-Team All-Conference selection (1956, 1957, 1958, and 1959).
- Pro Football Hall of Fame All-1950s Team.
- Pro Football Reference All-1950s First Team.
- Named to NFL's 50th Anniversary Team in 1969.
- Member of Pittsburgh Steelers Legends Team.
- Named to Steelers' 75th Anniversary Team in 2007.
- Elected to Pro Football Hall of Fame in 2012.

21

─ ANDY RUSSELL ─

T he first in a long line of exceptional Steeler linebackers, Andy Russell set a standard for future generations of players who manned that position in Pittsburgh. Persevering through the dark days of the 1960s, Russell proved to be a key figure in the Steelers' rise to prominence during the 1970s, using his intelligence, toughness, and leadership ability to help establish a winning culture in Pittsburgh. Spending his entire 12-year NFL career in the Steel City, Russell served as team captain his final 10 seasons, helping to lead the Steelers to four division titles, two AFC championships, and two Super Bowl victories. A two-time MVP of the Pittsburgh defense, Russell also earned seven Pro Bowl selections, two All-Pro nominations, and six All-Conference selections while wearing the Black and Gold, prompting Steelers fans to later elect him to the franchise's 75th Anniversary Team.

Born in Detroit, Michigan, on October 29, 1941, Charles Andrew Russell grew up in the New York area, before moving with his family to St. Louis while still just a freshman in high school. Starring at fullback, defensive end, and linebacker while attending Ladue Horton Watkins High School, Russell earned All-State honors as a senior, prompting several out-of-state universities to offer him an athletic scholarship. However, Russell ultimately chose to remain close to home, accepting a scholarship from the University of Missouri, where he spent three seasons playing under head coach Dan Devine. Continuing to play on both sides of the ball while at Mizzou, Russell excelled as a fullback on offense and a linebacker on defense, helping to lead the Tigers to an overall record of 25-3-3 in his three years as a starter.

After being selected by the Steelers in the 16th round of the 1963 NFL Draft, with the 220th overall pick, Russell ignored his father's wishes and elected to pursue a career in pro ball, stating years later, "My father did not want me to play professional football because he felt it would 'embarrass' the family to play a game for a living. You have to be a worker."

Andy Russell started the legacy of outstanding linebacker play in Pittsburgh.
Courtesy of the Pittsburgh Steelers

Laying claim to the starting right-outside linebacker job immediately upon his arrival in Pittsburgh, Russell performed well his first year in the league, earning a spot on the NFL All-Rookie Team by intercepting three passes and recovering one fumble. But he ended up spending the next two years in the military after he joined the Army to fulfill his ROTC commitment, recalling, "In 1964 and 1965, I was in Germany as an Army Lieutenant. I got back in 1966." Russell, though, continued to play football while in the service, gaining recognition as the Most Outstanding Player of the USAREUR (US Army Europe) Football League in 1964.

Returning to the NFL following his discharge in 1966, Russell reclaimed his starting right-outside linebacker job, which he maintained for the next 11 seasons. Unfortunately, the Steelers experienced very little success from 1966 to 1971, compiling an overall record of just 23-58-3 during that time. Nevertheless, Russell remained one of the team's few bright spots, earning two First-Team All-Conference selections and three Pro Bowl nominations over the course of those six seasons, while also being named the Steelers MVP on defense in both 1968 and 1970, and the team's Most Valuable Player in 1971.

A smart and instinctive player, the 6'2", 225-pound Russell defended well against both the run and the pass, even though he lacked foot speed. Rarely caught out of position, Russell did an excellent job of filling holes, turning plays inside, and applying pressure to opposing quarterbacks via the blitz. Although the NFL did not begin keeping an official record of sacks until well after Russell's playing days ended, the Steelers have credited him with an "unofficial" career total of 30½, many of which came before Chuck Noll insisted that he adopt a more disciplined positional style of defense when he assumed control of the team in 1969.

Russell served as team captain his last 10 years in Pittsburgh.
Courtesy of the Pittsburgh Steelers

An exceptional leader as well, Russell served as team captain from 1967 to 1976, a period during which many outstanding young players joined him on the Pittsburgh defense, including Jack Ham and Jack Lambert, who combined with him to form arguably the greatest linebacking trio in NFL history. Continuing to excel during the 1970s, Russell earned four more trips to the Pro Bowl and four more First-Team All-Conference selections. Meanwhile, the Steelers emerged as the NFL's dominant team during the latter stages of Russell's career, winning the Super Bowl in two of his last three years in the league.

Choosing to announce his retirement following the conclusion of the 1976 campaign, Russell ended his career having never missed a game over the course of his 12 NFL seasons, appearing in 168 consecutive regular-season contests during that time. In addition to his 30½ sacks, Russell recorded 18 interceptions, which he returned for a total of 238 yards, recovered 10 fumbles, and scored two defensive touchdowns.

After he retired from professional football, Russell devoted his undivided attention to the business ventures he began during his playing days, stating:

> Back when I played, you knew you were not going to make any money playing football, so I had to get a real job. When I got back from the military, I went and got my MBA. I convinced my father that I needed to play a couple more years of professional football to pay for my MBA. Then I started my own business in 1969 selling limited partner investments for Wall Street. In the first year, I was making dramatically more money than the Steelers were paying me. I didn't retire until after the 1976 season. I would go to meetings before practice, after practice. I would go to work on Monday. It was 24/7. I loved every minute. I am not complaining. I started an investment bank called Russell, Rea and Zappala. We ultimately sold that to J.P. Morgan.

Russell also later created the Andy Russell Charitable Foundation, which contributes funds to children's charities, and he is currently involved with the Ray Mansfield Steelers Smoker to raise money for the Boys and Girls Clubs of western Pennsylvania, of which he says, "I am the chairman of that. Ray Mansfield was my best Steeler buddy and he passed away hiking the Grand Canyon. I replaced him as the chairman of that."

When asked about his chances of eventually gaining induction into the Pro Football Hall of Fame, Russell, who currently lives in western Pennsylvania, says:

> That is something I leave to others to think about. There have been some things that I have done in my career that would not impress the Hall of Fame voters. For example, I

was the Steeler captain for 10 years. I think that is a Steeler record. That was not selected by the players. It was not a popularity contest. It was selected by the coaches. I never missed a game my entire football career; high school, college, Army or pro. It is obviously a lot of luck to avoid all those injuries. I played hurt a lot with broken fingers and thumbs, and things like that. But, you played. In those days, the biggest badge of honor was to play hurt. That is not so anymore.

CAREER HIGHLIGHTS

Best Season

Russell had several outstanding seasons, with his strong play prompting his teammates to name him the Steelers Most Valuable Player in 1971 and earning him Second-Team All-Pro honors in both 1968 and 1972. However, he perhaps played his best ball for the Steelers in 1970, when his career-high three interceptions and 64 interception-return yards earned him consensus First-Team All-AFC honors.

Memorable Moments/Greatest Performances

Russell recorded the first of his 18 career interceptions during a 23–10 win over the St. Louis Cardinals on September 29, 1963.

Russell also victimized the Cardinals for the first touchdown of his career on November 13, 1966, when he returned a blocked punt 14 yards for a TD during a 30–9 Steelers win.

Russell crossed the opponent's goal line again on September 30, 1973, when he returned an interception 45 yards for a touchdown during a 36–7 victory over the Houston Oilers.

Russell contributed to a 40–14 win over the Colts in the divisional round of the 1976 playoffs by sacking Baltimore quarterback Bert Jones twice.

Yet, Russell made the most memorable play of his career against the Colts one year earlier, when, during Pittsburgh's 28–10 home win over Baltimore in the 1975 playoffs, he recovered a fumble and returned the ball 93 yards for the game's final score. Reminiscing about the play at the Steelers' 75th Anniversary celebration, Russell recalled, "It was the most elapsed time on a single play in NFL history. Ray Mansfield said that the network cut to a commercial and was still able to show the touchdown."

Notable Achievements

- Scored two regular-season touchdowns during career.
- Scored one touchdown in playoffs.
- Ranks third all-time among Steeler linebackers with 18 career interceptions.
- Never missed a game entire career, appearing in 168 consecutive contests.
- Four-time division champion (1972, 1974, 1975, and 1976).
- Two-time AFC champion (1974 and 1975).
- Two-time Super Bowl champion (IX and X).
- Member of 1963 NFL All-Rookie Team.
- Steelers Team Captain for 10 years.
- Two-time Steelers Defensive MVP (1968 and 1970).
- 1971 Steelers MVP.
- 1972 Byron "Whizzer" White NFL Man of the Year.
- Seven-time Pro Bowl selection (1968, 1970, 1971, 1972, 1973, 1974, and 1975).
- Two-time Second-Team All-Pro selection (1968 and 1972).
- Six-time First-Team All-Conference selection (1967, 1970, 1972, 1973, 1974, and 1975).
- NFL 1970s All-Decade Team.
- Named to Steelers' 75th Anniversary Team in 2007.
- #34 "unofficially" retired by Steelers.

22

─── DONNIE SHELL ───

A hard-hitting safety who spent his entire 14-year NFL career in Pittsburgh, Donnie Shell helped the Steelers win eight division titles, four AFC championships, and four Super Bowls, initially contributing to their success with his stellar play on special teams, before establishing himself as one of the NFL's premier strong safeties. An extremely opportunistic player, Shell scored four defensive touchdowns during his career and led the Steelers in interceptions five times, recording a total of 51 picks as a member of the team that places him third in franchise history. A member of the NFL's Silver Anniversary Super Bowl Team, Shell also earned five trips to the Pro Bowl, four All-Pro selections, four All-Conference nominations, and spots on the Pro Football Reference All-1980s Second Team and the Steelers' 75th Anniversary Team.

Born in Whitmire, South Carolina, on August 26, 1952, Donnie Shell attended local Whitmire High School, where he played on state championship teams in baseball (as a left-handed pitcher) and basketball, ran track, and excelled in football at linebacker. Proving to be particularly proficient on the gridiron, Shell led a defense that limited its opponents to no touchdowns his entire senior year, with his 13-tackle, one-interception performance in one contest prompting South Carolina State head coach Oree Banks to offer him a full athletic scholarship.

After spending his first few seasons at S.C. State playing linebacker, Shell switched positions at the suggestion of new head coach Willie Jeffries prior to the start of his senior year, with Jeffries recalling, "When we got there, he was wearing No. 90 and playing linebacker. I said, 'Donnie, we got those young defensive backs; we need you leading them. Besides, linebacker is nothing but a glorified strong safety.'"

Moving to strong safety, Shell emerged as the dominant player at his position in the Mid-Eastern Athletic Conference, earning All-MEAC honors, while also being named to the Associated Press and *Pittsburgh Courier* All-America teams.

Yet, in spite of the success Shell achieved at the collegiate level, no team selected him in the 1974 NFL Draft, leaving him to subsequently ponder free-agent offers made by the Denver Broncos and Pittsburgh Steelers. Shell ultimately chose to sign with the Steelers, on the recommendation of Jeffries, who told him that "they were a blue-collar team that would give him a chance." Jeffries, who briefly coached under Chuck Noll in Pittsburgh, later said, "That's one thing I liked about Coach Noll. He didn't care what round you were taken in, he didn't care if you were first round, last round, or free agent. Are you self-motivated, can you help the team win, and are you a good team member? That is what he cared about."

Shell ended up spending his first three seasons in Pittsburgh serving as a backup to Mike Wagner at the strong safety position and starring on special teams, where he earned the nickname "Torpedo" for the jarring hits he delivered with his 5'11", 190-pound frame. Shell finally received his big break in 1977, when he became the starting strong safety after Wagner suffered an injury that sidelined him for most of the year. Taking full advantage of the opportunity afforded him, Shell recorded three interceptions and defended so well against the run that the Steelers traded away two-time Pro Bowl safety Glen Edwards at season's end to make room for him in the starting defensive backfield the following year.

With Wagner shifted to free safety upon his return to the team in 1978, Shell became the full-time starter at strong safety, a role that he maintained for the next 10 seasons. Making significant contributions to the Super Bowl champion Steelers in both 1978 and 1979, Shell picked off eight passes and recovered seven fumbles over the course of those two seasons, earning in the process one All-Pro selection, two All-AFC nominations, and two trips to the Pro Bowl.

Donnie Shell ranks third in franchise history with 51 career interceptions.
Courtesy of the Pittsburgh Steelers

Although the retirements of several key players caused

the Pittsburgh dynasty to come to an end during the early 1980s, Shell continued to perform at an elite level, earning All-Pro honors three straight times from 1980 to 1982 and continuing his string of five straight Pro Bowl selections, with his seven interceptions and 135 interception-return yards in 1980 gaining him recognition as the Steelers Most Valuable Player. Commenting on his former teammate's play, NFL Hall of Famer Tony Dungy, who spent his first two years in the league in Pittsburgh, later told Rick Gosselin of the Talk of Fame Network, "Donnie played in the box and was like

Shell led the Steelers in picks five times.
Courtesy of MEARSonlineauctions.com

another linebacker as a run defender. He was probably the most physical player on a physical defense, and he also had 51 interceptions. He covered Hall-of-Fame tight ends like Ozzie Newsome man-to-man and covered wide receivers in the nickel package. He patrolled the deep zones. He could do it all."

Displaying a willingness throughout his career to launch himself into running backs much larger than himself, Shell became known for his head-on-collisions with Houston Oilers fullback Earl Campbell, with Steelers tight end Bennie Cunningham recalling one particular on-field meeting between the two men: "Earl hit the line and went into a spin, and Donnie put his helmet in his rib cage. A form tackle; nothing illegal about it. But I'd never seen Earl have to leave the field until that time."

Although Shell posted a less-than overwhelming time of 4.6 seconds in the 40-yard dash, he possessed superior closing speed, stating, "Some guys were faster but played slower in a game. I might not have had blazing speed, but I was faster on the field.

Shell remained the Steelers' starting strong safety for five more years, having one of his finest seasons in 1984, when he matched his career high by recording seven interceptions. Gradually assuming a leadership role on the club, Shell helped mentor several young defensive backs during his time in Pittsburgh, including Tony Dungy and Rod Woodson, who played alongside Shell in the latter's final season. In discussing the sense of responsibility he felt toward the team's younger players, Shell said, "When I got here, we didn't have player development, so the veterans took you under their wing and taught you the nuances of the National Football League." After identifying Mel Blount, Joe Greene, and Jon Kolb as Pittsburgh players who helped him adjust to life in the pros, Shell recalled that he tried to return the favor to one young player years later, saying, "It was Tony Dungy. He was my roommate my third year. I got to know him in a great way. He was an All-American quarterback and switched to defensive back. The things that Mel Blount, Joe Greene, and Jon Kolb sewed into me, I tried to sew those things into him being his mentor and helping him to establish himself."

Choosing to announce his retirement following the conclusion of the 1987 campaign, Shell ended his career with 51 interceptions, 490 interception-return yards, and 19 fumble recoveries, with his totals in all three categories placing him among the franchise's all-time leaders. He also ranks extremely high in team annals in seasons (14) and games (201) played. Meanwhile, Shell's 51 picks represented the highest total ever amassed by an NFL strong safety at the time of his retirement.

Following his playing days, Shell served as director of player development for the Carolina Panthers from 1994 to 2009, before taking on the position of director of spiritual life at Johnson C. Smith University in Charlotte, North Carolina, where he currently serves.

CAREER HIGHLIGHTS

Best Season

Shell had his finest season for the Steelers in 1980, when his career-high seven interceptions and 135 interception-return yards earned him team MVP honors and one of his three First-Team All-Pro selections.

Memorable Moments/Greatest Performances

Shell recorded the first interception of his career during the Steelers' 27–3 win over Cincinnati in the 1974 regular-season finale.

Shell scored the first of his four career touchdowns during a 27–24 win over the Kansas City Chiefs on October 29, 1978, when he recovered a fumble, which he returned 17 yards for a TD.

Shell helped lead the Steelers to a 31–17 victory over the Houston Oilers in the opening game of the 1980 regular season by picking off two passes, which he returned for a total of 76 yards.

Shell intercepted another two passes during Pittsburgh's 23–17 win over Minnesota on October 5, 1980, recording two of the five picks the Steelers registered against Tommy Kramer.

Shell had a huge game against Cleveland on November 22, 1981, recording a career-high three interceptions during the Steelers' 32–10 victory over the Browns.

Shell earned AFC Defensive Player of the Week honors for his performance during a 38–17 win over the Cincinnati Bengals on October 1, 1984, when he picked off two passes, one of which he returned 52 yards for a touchdown.

Shell recorded another two interceptions during Pittsburgh's 13–7 victory over the Los Angeles Raiders in the 1984 regular-season finale, earning in the process AFC Defensive Player of the Week honors for the second and final time.

Although the Steelers lost to the Browns by a score of 34–10 on September 20, 1987, Shell scored the third touchdown of his career when he returned a fumble 19 yards for a TD.

Shell crossed the opponent's goal line for the final time during a 35–24 loss to the Miami Dolphins on November 1, 1987, racing 50 yards for a TD after he intercepted a Dan Marino pass.

Notable Achievements

- Scored four defensive touchdowns during career.
- Recorded at least five interceptions six straight times.
- Surpassed 100 interception-return yards once (135 in 1980).
- Led NFL with two non-offensive touchdowns in 1987.
- Finished second in NFL with five interceptions in 1982.
- Led Steelers in interceptions five times.
- Ranks among Steelers career leaders with: 51 interceptions (3rd); 490 interception-return yards (8th); 19 fumble recoveries (4th); 14 seasons played (tied—3rd); and 201 games played (4th).
- Eight-time division champion (1974, 1975, 1976, 1977, 1978, 1979, 1983, and 1984).

- Four-time AFC champion (1974, 1975, 1978, and 1979).
- Four-time Super Bowl champion (IX, X, XIII, and XIV).
- 1980 Steelers MVP.
- Two-time AFC Defensive Player of the Week.
- Five-time Pro Bowl selection (1978, 1979, 1980, 1981, and 1982).
- Three-time First-Team All-Pro selection (1979, 1980, and 1982).
- 1981 Second-Team All-Pro selection.
- Two-time First-Team All-Conference selection (1979 and 1980).
- Two-time Second-Team All-Conference selection (1978 and 1981).
- Pro Football Reference All-1980s Second Team.
- Named to NFL Silver Anniversary Super Bowl Team in 1991.
- Named to Steelers' 75th Anniversary Team in 2007.
- #31 "unofficially" retired by Steelers.

23

— GREG LLOYD —

Bridging the gap between two distinct eras of Steelers football, Greg Lloyd spent 10 seasons in Pittsburgh, establishing himself as the NFL's most intimidating linebacker and most feared defensive player. Possessing tremendous determination and a burning desire to win, Lloyd brought violence and nastiness back to the Steeler defense, serving as the cornerstone of a unit that earned the nickname "Blitzburgh" during the 1990s. Whether running down an opposing ball-carrier or applying pressure to an opposing quarterback, Lloyd inspired his teammates with his aggressive style of play, helping to lead the Steelers to five division titles and one AFC championship. A two-time team MVP, five-time Pro Bowler, and three-time All-Pro, Lloyd led the Steelers in sacks twice and tackles three times, while also forcing more fumbles than anyone else in franchise history. Named to the Steelers' 75th Anniversary Team following the conclusion of his playing career, Lloyd accomplished all he did even though he spent his entire time in Pittsburgh playing with an ACL missing in one knee, and another ACL basically stapled together in his other knee.

Born in Miami, Florida, on May 26, 1965, Gregory Lenard Lloyd grew up in Georgia, where he attended Peach County High School. After enrolling at tiny Fort Valley State University, a historically black college located in Fort Valley, Georgia, Lloyd went on to earn All–Southern Intercollegiate Athletic Conference (SIAC) and team Defensive MVP honors three straight times, with his outstanding play also gaining him recognition as the SIAC Player of the Year as a senior. Displaying during his time at Fort Valley the intensity and volatile temperament for which he later became so well known, Lloyd occasionally had to be held out of practice so that he didn't hurt his teammates, with head coach Doug Porter recalling, "We'd say, 'Hold off on the quarterbacks.' And Greg would say, 'You better keep him out of here, then.'" In fact, Lloyd thrived on playing at an extremely high emotional level to such an extent that he often purposely picked a fight with his girlfriend on game day so that he could take his anger with him to the stadium.

Greg Lloyd served as the cornerstone of a Pittsburgh defensive unit that acquired the nickname "Blitzburgh."
Courtesy of George Kitrinos

Due to his small college background, Lloyd ended up lasting until the sixth round of the 1987 NFL Draft, where the Steelers selected him with the 150th overall pick. He subsequently missed most of his first two seasons after suffering two separate knee injuries that forced him to sit out the entire 1987 campaign and much of the following season as well.

Nevertheless, even though Lloyd started just four contests in 1988, he managed to make his presence felt, earning an ejection from his first pro game after he punched Denver Broncos quarterback Gary Kubiak.

Laying claim to the starting right-outside linebacker job in 1989, Lloyd helped the Steelers improve their record from 5-11 to 9-7 by recording three interceptions and a team-leading seven sacks and 92 tackles. After performing well once again in 1990, Lloyd earned Pro Bowl honors for the first of five straight times the following season by forcing six fumbles and recording eight sacks and 76 tackles. Lloyd then helped the Steelers capture their first division title in nearly a decade in 1992 by registering 96 tackles and a team-high 6½ sacks, before beginning a string of three straight seasons in which he gained First-Team All-Pro recognition. Playing the best ball of his career from 1993 to 1995, Lloyd forced 16 fumbles and recorded 314 tackles and 22½ sacks during that time, in leading the Steelers to two more division titles and one AFC championship.

Establishing himself as the emotional leader of the Steelers defense shortly after he joined the starting unit, Lloyd brought to the team a level of intensity it had not seen since the days of Jack Lambert and "Mean" Joe Greene during the championship years of the 1970s. Absolutely relentless, the 6'2", 230-pound Lloyd set the tone for the Pittsburgh defense with his aggressive style of play and pursuit of opposing ball-carriers. Able to alter the outcome of games with the sheer force of his will, Lloyd instilled fear into his opponents, and even his own teammates, whom he held to the same high standard as himself. Demanding nothing less than a 100 percent effort from every member of the team, Lloyd often admonished those he believed failed to play as hard as he did, with his teammates accepting his criticism because they knew how much he wanted to win.

Revealing the attitude with which he approached the game, Lloyd once said, "This isn't one of those games—unlike the commissioner and all those SOBs want it to be—to put on PBS so all the little kids can watch it, and they can show in the classroom. It's not a game like that. It's a violent damn game. It's a game that players play with anger, frustration, and emotion. And that's how I play the game. If people don't like it, so be it."

On another occasion, Lloyd stated, "If you want to be the best, don't let there be any discrepancy about being the best. If we have to bite, we'll bite. If we have to spit, we'll spit. If we have to scratch, we'll do that."

Often criticized for his attitude, curt responses to questions, and questionable on-field behavior, Lloyd responded to his detractors by stating, "When you play football for 60 minutes the way I do, you don't have to answer to anybody."

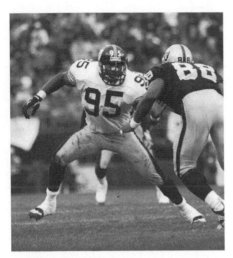

Lloyd forced more fumbles than anyone else in franchise history.
Courtesy of George Kitrinos

Lloyd's combative disposition, total disdain for his opponent, and outstanding talent made him the most feared player in the league. One of the first linebackers that had the brute force of a pass-rusher, as well as the athleticism to cover tight ends and chase down opposing running backs, Lloyd treated opposing quarterbacks so roughly that the league eventually had to create new rules to protect them.

Called a "monster that can move" by 49ers running back Ricky Watters and "nasty, basically" by teammate Levon Kirkland, Lloyd made an extremely strong impression on Steelers running back Erric Pegram, who said, "I watch the guy play, and one of the main reasons I love him to death is because of the way he gets on the field. He has a way of hitting you."

Unfortunately, Lloyd's days as a dominant player came to an end in 1996, when he suffered a season-ending knee injury in Week 1. Although Lloyd returned to the Steelers the following year, he failed to regain his earlier form, recording just 3½ sacks and 52 tackles, before seriously injuring his ankle during a 23–20 loss to the Philadelphia Eagles in Week 13. Subsequently plagued by a staph infection, Lloyd lost more than 20 pounds, forcing him to sit out the remainder of the year. With Lloyd still hobbled by the injury in 1998, the Steelers cut him just before training camp, after which he signed with the Carolina Panthers. Lloyd spent one year in Carolina, recording 64 tackles, one interception, and one sack, before announcing his retirement at season's end with career totals of 54½ sacks, 791 tackles (707 solo), 11 interceptions, 35 forced fumbles, and 16 fumble recoveries. In addition to holding the Steelers' career record for most forced fumbles (34), Lloyd ranks among the franchise's all-time leaders in sacks (53½), tackles (727), and fumble recoveries (15).

Continuing to display his volatile temperament after retiring as an active player, Lloyd ran afoul of the law in 2001, when he was accused of sticking a gun in his 12-year-old son's mouth due to the youngster's bad grades in school. Although a pair of subsequent trials ended in hung juries,

Lloyd's aggressive behavior toward his son resulted in the two becoming estranged from one another. The elder Lloyd also pleaded no contest to simple battery charges made against him for pointing a gun at his ex-wife Rhonda Lloyd's head in 2002.

While Lloyd's inappropriate actions cannot be justified in any way, it is his fiery disposition that helped him reach the level of excellence he attained during his playing career. Trying to explain the anger he carried with him to the playing field, Lloyd once said, "You've got to have attitude, gentlemen, to play this ballgame. You've got to go out and play like somebody robbed your house and is running down the street with your television on their back. That's the way you've got to play this game."

STEELERS CAREER HIGHLIGHTS

Best Season

Lloyd performed exceptionally well for the Steelers in both 1993 and 1994, recording six sacks and a career-best 111 solo tackles in the first of those campaigns, before earning UPI AFC Defensive Player of the Year honors the following season by registering 87 tackles (69 solo) and a career-high 10 sacks. However, Lloyd made his greatest overall impact in 1995, when, after Rod Woodson suffered a season-ending injury in Week 1, he helped compensate for the loss of his Hall of Fame teammate by making 6½ sacks, intercepting three passes, forcing six fumbles, and recording 116 tackles (88 solo), earning in the process First-Team All-Pro honors for the third straight time.

Memorable Moments/Greatest Performances

Lloyd helped lead the Steelers to a 13–0 shutout of the New York Jets on December 10, 1989, by recording an interception and a sack.

Lloyd got to Kansas City quarterback Dave Krieg twice during a 27–3 victory over the Chiefs on October 25, 1992.

Lloyd earned AFC Defensive Player of the Week honors for the first of four times for his performance during a 16–3 win over the Chargers on October 10, 1993, when he recorded a sack and applied constant pressure to San Diego quarterbacks John Friesz and Stan Humphries.

Lloyd repeated as AFC Defensive Player of the Week after he sacked Steve DeBerg twice during a 21–20 victory over the Miami Dolphins on December 13, 1993.

Lloyd turned in an outstanding all-around performance against Cincinnati on December 4, 1994, recording an interception and a sack during a 38–15 win over the Bengals.

Lloyd contributed to a 37–34 overtime victory over the Chicago Bears on November 5, 1995, by setting up a Steelers touchdown when he intercepted a pass, which he returned 52 yards to the Chicago 4-yard line.

Lloyd recorded two sacks and an interception during a 20–3 win over Cleveland on November 13, 1995, earning in the process AFC Defensive Player of the Week honors for the third time.

Lloyd earned that distinction for the final time by making a game-high 12 tackles during a 41–27 win over the New England Patriots on December 16, 1995.

Notable Achievements

- Recorded 10 sacks in 1994.
- Surpassed 100 tackles four times.
- Led Steelers in sacks twice and tackles three times.
- Holds Steelers career record for most forced fumbles (34).
- Ranks among Steelers career leaders with: 53½ sacks (8th); 727 tackles (8th); and 15 fumble recoveries (9th).
- Five-time division champion (1992, 1994, 1995, 1996, and 1997).
- 1995 AFC champion.
- Four-time AFC Defensive Player of the Week.
- Two-time Steelers MVP (1991 and 1994).
- 1994 UPI AFC Defensive Player of the Year.
- Five-time Pro Bowl selection (1991, 1992, 1993, 1994, and 1995).
- Three-time First-Team All-Pro selection (1993, 1994, and 1995).
- Three-time First-Team All-Conference selection (1993, 1994, and 1995).
- Pro Football Reference All-1990s Second Team.
- Named to Steelers' 75th Anniversary Team in 2007.

24

— L. C. GREENWOOD —

Spending his entire 13-year NFL career in Pittsburgh, L. C. Greenwood combined with "Mean" Joe Greene to give the Steelers a dominant tandem on the left side of their defensive line. An excellent pass-rusher, Greenwood led the Steelers in quarterback sacks six times, amassing an unofficial total of 73½ sacks over the course of his career that continues to place him among the franchise's all-time leaders. Outstanding against the run as well, Greenwood displayed a nose for the football during his time in Pittsburgh, recovering a total of 14 fumbles that also ranks him extremely high in team annals. Greenwood's stellar all-around play, which helped the Steelers win seven division titles, four AFC championships, and four Super Bowls, earned him six trips to the Pro Bowl, six All-AFC nominations, two All-Pro selections, and spots on the NFL 1970s All-Decade Team and the Steelers' 75th Anniversary Team.

Born in Canton, Mississippi, on September 8, 1946, L. C. Henderson Greenwood attended local Rogers High School, where he began playing football mostly as a means of escaping the constant chores that awaited him at home. Looking back at that period of his life, Greenwood recalled, "My dad wasn't satisfied unless I was working all the time. My dad left home at six o'clock in the morning, and he didn't get back until six in the evening. And then, after dinner, he'd leave the house and go to work somewhere else from eight to midnight. Plus, he kept a farm for us, and he was a lay preacher on weekends. Football wasn't important. Keeping the family fed was."

After graduating from high school in 1966, Greenwood fielded multiple scholarship offers, ultimately turning down an offer to study pharmacy at Clarke College in Atlanta, Georgia, for the opportunity to play football in Pine Bluff (Jefferson County) at Agricultural, Mechanical, and Normal College (AM&N), now known as the University of Arkansas at Pine Bluff. A four-year starter at AM&N, Greenwood excelled at both defensive end and defensive tackle, although a knee injury caused him to slide to

L. C. Greenwood combined with Joe
Greene to give the Steelers a dominant left
side of the defensive line.
Courtesy of the Pittsburgh Steelers

the 10th round of the 1969 NFL Draft, where the Steelers finally selected him with the 238th overall pick.

Greenwood subsequently spent his first two seasons in Pittsburgh playing mostly on special teams, while also serving as a backup to starting defensive ends Ben McGee and Lloyd Voss. However, after gradually bulking up to his pro playing weight of 245 pounds, the 6'6" Greenwood became the Steelers' starting left end in 1971, continuing to function in that capacity for the remainder of his career.

Rapidly developing into an elite pass-rusher, Greenwood recorded a team-high 8½ sacks and recovered five fumbles in his first year as a full-time starter, helping the Steelers improve their record to 6-8 in the process. He followed that up with two more solid seasons, before earning First-Team All-Pro honors for the first of two straight times in 1974 by recording a career-high 11 sacks for the Super Bowl champion Steelers.

Combining tremendous strength with superior speed, Greenwood used his great quickness to outmaneuver offensive tackles and bring down quarterbacks and running backs in the opposing backfield. Greenwood also proved to be very much a showman, displaying a considerable amount of style over the course of his playing career. While recovering from an ankle injury in 1973, Greenwood donned a pair of high-top cleats that a friend painted gold. Although Greenwood went back to his regular footwear after the ankle healed, he eventually decided to wear the gold cleats as a way of distinguishing himself from his more highly publicized teammate, Joe Greene, who he lined up next to on Pittsburgh's defensive line.

Greenwood often found himself being overshadowed by Greene, whom the Steelers selected nine rounds earlier in the 1969 NFL Draft. But Greene later credited his longtime teammate with much of the success he experienced at left tackle, stating, "I leaned on L. C. a lot. Some of the things I was able to do on the field were definitely because of his presence. We helped each other out. He was one of those special guys—special as a player, special as a person."

Greenwood continued to excel for the Steelers at left defensive end for several more years, earning First-Team All-Pro honors again in 1975, Pro Bowl honors six times between 1973 and 1979, and six All-Conference nominations over that same period. Meanwhile, the Steelers won six consecutive division titles and four Super Bowls between 1974 and 1979, with Greenwood's contributions to their

Greenwood led the Steelers in sacks six times.
Courtesy of the Pittsburgh Steelers

"Steel Curtain" defense proving to be a huge factor in the success they experienced during that time.

Nevertheless, with Greenwood limited by knee problems to just five starts in 1981, the Steelers chose to release him prior to the start of the ensuing campaign, after which the 36-year-old veteran announced his retirement. Greenwood, who appeared in 170 out of a possible 190 games during his 13 seasons in Pittsburgh, ended his playing career with an unofficial total of 73½ sacks that currently places him fourth in team annals, behind only James Harrison, Joe Greene, and Jason Gildon.

After retiring as an active player, Greenwood remained in Pittsburgh, where he became a successful businessman, heading Greenwood Enterprises, which owned six companies, including Monaloh Basin Engineers, a construction and engineering firm for which he served as executive vice president. Greenwood also later established Greenwood Manufacturing, which distributed packing materials.

Greenwood, who, according to the *Pittsburgh Tribune-Review*, had 21 operations on his back, experienced numerous health problems later in life, spending his final days using a walker to go from one place to another. After undergoing one of his many surgeries in September of 2013, Greenwood remained in the hospital for another two weeks, before dying of kidney failure at the age of 67, on September 29, 2013.

Following his passing, Steelers chairman Dan Rooney said in a prepared statement, "L.C. was one of the most beloved Steelers during the most successful period in team history, and he will be missed by the entire organization."

Meanwhile, former teammates Joe Greene and Jack Ham railed against the Pro Football Hall of Fame's exclusion of Greenwood, with Greene telling the *Pittsburgh Tribune-Review*, "I don't know what my career would have been without him. He should absolutely be in the Hall of Fame. Bottom line, he's being cheated."

Ham took things one step further, suggesting that there is a bias against the Steelers among the Hall of Fame voters, claiming, "I've heard people say, 'What are we gonna do, build a wing out here for all the Steelers from back then?' I wouldn't be in the Hall of Fame without L.C. and the work he did on the field. The fact that he isn't in there too has everything to do with politics."

Art Rooney Jr. agreed, stating upon learning of Greenwood's passing, "The saddest thing is, he never got into the Hall of Fame. To me, it's terribly sad. He deserves to be there."

CAREER HIGHLIGHTS

Best Season

Greenwood earned First-Team All-Pro and consensus First-Team All-AFC honors in both 1974 and 1975, with his "unofficial" and career-high total of 11 sacks in the first of those campaigns prompting me to identify that as his finest season.

Memorable Moments/Greatest Performances

Greenwood scored the only points of his career during a 21–17 victory over the Patriots on December 8, 1974, when he tackled Jim Plunkett in the end zone for a safety.

Greenwood proved to be a huge factor in Super Bowl IX, applying constant pressure to Minnesota quarterback Fran Tarkenton and knocking down three of his passes, in helping the Steelers limit the Vikings to just 119 yards of total offense.

Greenwood turned in another dominant performance in Super Bowl X, sacking Dallas quarterback Roger Staubach four times during the Steelers' 21–17 win over the Cowboys.

Greenwood helped lead the Steelers to a 33–30 overtime victory over the Browns on November 25, 1979, by recording a career-high 4½ sacks against Cleveland quarterback Brian Sipe.

Notable Achievements

- Recorded 11 sacks in 1974.
- Finished second in NFL with five fumble recoveries in 1971.
- Led Steelers in sacks six times.
- Recorded four sacks in Super Bowl X.
- Ranks among Steelers career leaders with 73½ sacks (4th) and 14 fumble recoveries (tied—10th).
- Seven-time division champion (1972, 1974, 1975, 1976, 1977, 1978, and 1979).
- Four-time AFC champion (1974, 1975, 1978, and 1979).
- Four-time Super Bowl champion (IX, X, XIII, and XIV).
- Six-time Pro Bowl selection (1973, 1974, 1975, 1976, 1978, and 1979).
- Two-time First-Team All-Pro selection (1974 and 1975).
- Five-time First-Team All-Conference selection (1973, 1974, 1975, 1978, and 1979).
- 1976 Second-Team All-Conference selection.
- Pro Football Hall of Fame All-1970s Second Team.
- Pro Football Reference All-1970s Second Team.
- Named to Super Bowl's Silver Anniversary Team in 1990.
- Named to Steelers' 75th Anniversary Team in 2007.
- #68 "unofficially" retired by Steelers.

25

— CARNELL LAKE —

An extremely athletic, intelligent, and versatile defensive back who starred at both safety and cornerback during his time in Pittsburgh, Carnell Lake helped lead the Steelers to five division titles and one AFC championship during the 1990s. Earning postseason honors at both positions, Lake appeared in four Pro Bowls, gained All-Pro recognition three times, and received five All-AFC nominations while wearing the Black and Gold, before being further honored following the conclusion of his playing career by being named to the NFL 1990s All-Decade Team and the Steelers' 75th Anniversary Team. And, after spending his final two years in the league playing for other teams, Lake eventually returned to Pittsburgh, where he continued to contribute to the success of the Steelers by serving as their defensive backs coach for seven seasons.

Born in Salt Lake City, Utah, on July 15, 1967, Carnell Augustino Lake grew up primarily in Southern California, although he also lived in the San Francisco Bay area from 1979 to 1981, a period during which he attended Bowditch Middle School in Foster City. After excelling as a tailback and cornerback in Pop Warner Football while living by the Bay, Lake made a name for himself as a standout running back and linebacker at Culver City High School, gaining more than 1,000 yards as a junior, and rushing for 956 yards and 12 touchdowns as a senior, before dislocating his elbow at midseason. Subsequently offered a scholarship by UCLA, Lake spent the next four years starring at outside linebacker for the Bruins, recording career totals of 25½ sacks and 45½ tackles for loss, with both figures placing him among the school's all-time leaders.

In discussing the qualities that made Lake so successful at the collegiate level, UCLA head coach Terry Donahue stated, "Carnell Lake is one of the top athletes on our football team. He has tremendous speed, good instincts, and competitiveness."

Donahue then added, "I thought he could be a fine offensive running back. And I still do. We talked to him about it in the spring and let him know the option was available."

Impressed with Lake's superb play at UCLA and his 4.37 speed in the 40-yard dash, the Steelers selected him in the second round of the 1989 NFL Draft, with the 34th overall pick. After moving to strong safety upon his arrival in Pittsburgh, Lake spent his first pro training camp studying the team's defensive backs, paying particularly close attention to Rod Woodson. Recalling his earliest days as a pro, Lake said, "I watched Rod Woodson like a hawk. I just sat there and watched everything I could and picked it up like a sponge. And it was good enough to earn me a starting spot my first year."

Carnell Lake starred in the Steelers' defensive secondary during the 1990s. Courtesy of the Pittsburgh Steelers

After laying claim to the starting strong safety job, Lake went on to have a solid rookie season, recording 70 tackles, one interception, one sack, and two forced fumbles, and finishing third in the league with six fumble recoveries. Commenting on Lake's strong play during the latter stages of the campaign, Kansas City Chiefs defensive coordinator Tony Dungy noted, "I really liked Carnell coming out of college. I saw a lot of Lester Hayes in him. Lester was the same type of guy in college—an outside, walkaway linebacker at Texas A&M. Both Lester and Carnell had great athletic ability and toughness. I thought Carnell would end up at corner, but he's playing really well for them at strong safety."

Although Lake eventually proved Dungy prophetic by moving to cornerback, he remained at strong safety for five more years, establishing himself as one of the league's best players at that position. After earning Second-Team All-AFC honors in 1990 by recording 67 tackles, one sack, and one interception, Lake began a string of four straight seasons in which he made at least 80 stops, performing particularly well in 1993, when, in addition to bringing down opposing ball-carriers 91 times, he picked off four passes and recorded five sacks.

Even though Lake recorded just 16 interceptions during his time in Pittsburgh, his speed and quickness made him an excellent pass defender. Meanwhile, his college experience at linebacker made him a terror against the run. A notoriously hard hitter, Lake often launched his 6'1", 210-pound frame into opposing running backs, making him one of the league's most feared tacklers among defensive backs. Lake's aggressiveness and superior athletic ability also enabled him to apply pressure to opposing quarterbacks in blitz situations, with his 21½ career sacks as a member of the Steelers placing him among the franchise's all-time leaders among players who roamed the secondary.

After earning Pro Bowl, First-Team All-AFC, and Second-Team All-Pro honors for his outstanding play at strong safety in 1994, Lake moved to right cornerback the following year when Rod Woodson sustained a season-ending injury in Week 1. Excelling at his new post, Lake helped the Steelers advance to the Super Bowl, while simultaneously continuing his string of four straight seasons in which he gained Pro Bowl and First-Team All-Conference recognition. Lake subsequently returned to his more familiar position of strong safety in 1996, before spending his final two seasons in Pittsburgh at cornerback. Playing on an injured left foot in 1998, Lake later recalled:

> I thought my play was better than it had ever been. The only problem was I got injured in '98, and that was the year I really felt my cornerback skills were at the top of my game. We didn't have anybody else, and I just wanted to see if I could play through it. I should've stopped to take one or two weeks off, recovered, and come back. Playing injured, you have to do that, but playing hurt is not recommended, and that's the only regret I have because it lingered on even when I went to Jacksonville.

Signing with the Jacksonville Jaguars as a free agent following the conclusion of the 1998 campaign, Lake left Pittsburgh with career totals of 734 tackles (677 solo), 21½ sacks, 16 interceptions, 15 forced fumbles, and 16 fumble recoveries. He also scored five defensive touchdowns as a member of the Steelers, which represents one of the highest totals in team annals.

Lake played for five division championship teams during his time in Pittsburgh.
Courtesy of the Pittsburgh Steelers

Lake ended up spending just one season in Jacksonville, before sitting out the entire 2000 campaign due to recurring problems with his left foot. He then joined the Baltimore Ravens, assuming a backup role with them in 2001, before announcing his retirement at season's end with career totals of 822 tackles (756 solo), 25 sacks, 16 interceptions, 15 forced fumbles, and 17 fumble recoveries.

Although Lake spent his last two years in the league with other teams, his heart remained in Pittsburgh, later saying, "I played with some of the best players that have ever played the game. I played in a city that has a history of winning. A fan base that is probably the best in the NFL by far, around the world. I couldn't have asked for a better experience."

More than a decade after he played his last game for the Steelers, Lake returned to Pittsburgh in 2011 as the team's defensive backs coach. He remained in that position until February 7, 2018, when he made the following announcement:

> I have decided to return to California to be able to be a part of my youngest son's last year of high school football. I want to thank Mr. Art Rooney II and the Rooney family, Coach Mike Tomlin, Kevin Colbert, the coaching staffs I have worked with throughout my time in Pittsburgh, and the entire Steelers organization. It has been a privilege and honor to play and coach for the Pittsburgh Steelers. I also want to thank all the players I have coached during my seven years with the team—it truly was an honor to work with them.

STEELERS CAREER HIGHLIGHTS

Best Season

Lake had an excellent year for the Steelers in 1993, recording four interceptions, five sacks, and a career-high 91 solo tackles. He also performed extremely well in 1996, earning Pro Bowl and First-Team All-AFC honors by scoring a pair of defensive touchdowns and leading the NFL with 85 fumble-return yards. However, Lake had his finest all-around season in 1997, when he earned his lone First-Team All-Pro nomination and AFC Defensive Player of the Year honors as voted on by a 101-member panel of NFL sportswriters known as the Kansas City Committee of 101 by intercepting three passes, forcing two fumbles, scoring one touchdown on defense, and recording 60 tackles and a career-high six sacks.

Memorable Moments/Greatest Performances

Lake recovered a fumble, made five tackles, and recorded the first interception of his career during a 17–7 win over the Cleveland Browns on October 15, 1989, earning in the process AFC Defensive Player of the Week honors.

Lake played a key role in the Steelers' 21–20 win over Miami on December 13, 1993, recording a sack and an interception, which he returned 26 yards.

Lake put the finishing touches on Pittsburgh's 29–9 victory over Cleveland in the divisional round of the 1994 playoffs by sacking Vinny Testaverde in the end zone for a fourth-quarter safety.

Lake made a pair of big plays in the divisional round of the 1995 playoffs as well, intercepting a pass and recovering a fumble during the Steelers' 40–21 win over Buffalo.

Lake contributed to a 26–20 overtime victory over the Arizona Cardinals on November 30, 1997, by recording a career-high three sacks.

Lake sealed a 17–12 win over the Chicago Bears in Week 2 of the 1998 campaign by intercepting quarterback Erik Kramer's third-down pass at the Pittsburgh 16-yard line with just 44 seconds remaining in regulation. Commenting on Lake's game-saving pick, Steelers defensive coordinator Jim Haslett said, "Big-time players make big-time plays. He made it in the right situation, too."

Lake scored the first of his five career touchdowns during a 34–17 win over the Houston Oilers on September 10, 1995, when he returned an interception 32 yards for a TD.

Lake lit the scoreboard again on September 16, 1996, when he returned an interception 47 yards for a touchdown during a 24–6 victory over the Buffalo Bills.

Lake crossed the opponent's goal line again on November 17, 1996, when he returned a fumble 85 yards for a touchdown during a 28–3 win over Jacksonville.

Lake proved to be a major factor in the Steelers' 24–22 win over Indianapolis on October 12, 1997, recording a sack and returning a fumble 38 yards for a touchdown.

Although the Steelers lost to the Cincinnati Bengals by a score of 25–24 on December 20, 1998, Lake scored the final points of his career when he returned an interception 15 yards for a touchdown.

Notable Achievements

- Scored five defensive touchdowns during career.
- Surpassed 100 tackles once.
- Recorded at least five sacks in a season twice.
- Missed just six games in 10 seasons.
- Led NFL with 85 fumble-return yards in 1996.

- Finished second in NFL with two non-offensive touchdowns in 1996.
- Finished third in NFL with six fumble recoveries in 1989.
- Led Steelers with six sacks in 1997.
- Ranks among Steelers career leaders with: 734 tackles (7th); 15 forced fumbles (tied—5th); 16 fumble recoveries (tied—7th); three touchdown interceptions (tied—5th); and five defensive touchdowns.
- Five-time division champion (1992, 1994, 1995, 1996, and 1997).
- 1995 AFC champion.
- 1989 Week 6 AFC Defensive Player of the Week.
- 1997 Kansas City Committee of 101 AFC Defensive Player of the Year.
- Four-time Pro Bowl selection (1994, 1995, 1996, and 1997).
- 1997 First-Team All-Pro selection.
- Two-time Second-Team All-Pro selection (1994 and 1995).
- Four-time First-Team All-Conference selection (1994, 1995, 1996, and 1997).
- 1990 Second-Team All-Conference selection.
- Pro Football Hall of Fame All-1990s Second Team.
- Pro Football Reference All-1990s First Team.
- Named to Steelers' 75th Anniversary Team in 2007.

26

— LE'VEON BELL —

The NFL's finest all-purpose back for much of his career, Le'Veon Bell spent five seasons in Pittsburgh, amassing the second most yards from scrimmage of any player in the league during that time. An exceptional runner and outstanding receiver coming out of the backfield, Bell gained more than 1,000 yards on the ground and 600 yards through the air three times each, with his dynamic playmaking ability helping the Steelers win three division titles. A two-time team MVP, Bell led the Steelers in rushing four times and caught more passes than any other running back in franchise history, earning in the process three Pro Bowl selections and three All-Pro nominations. Yet, even though Bell arguably performed as well as any other back in the league during his time in Pittsburgh, the Steelers refused to meet his salary demands in 2018, prompting the two sides to sever their relationship following the conclusion of the campaign.

Born in Reynoldsburg, Ohio, on February 18, 1992, Le'Veon Andrew Bell grew up with his four siblings in a single-parent household, being raised by his mother, Lisa A. Bell, who often struggled to make ends meet. Starring in multiple sports while attending Madison High School in nearby Groveport, Bell excelled in football, basketball, and track, gaining Second-Team All-OCC Ohio Division recognition on the hardwood as a junior, while also competing in the 100- and 200-meter dashes and the high jump, where he recorded a personal-best jump of six feet, eight inches. Even more proficient on the gridiron, Bell concluded his high school career with 3,222 yards rushing and 43 rushing touchdowns, performing particularly well as a senior, when he earned First-Team All-OCC honors by amassing 1,750 all-purpose yards and scoring 25 touchdowns.

Choosing to accept a scholarship offer from Michigan State University, Bell spent three seasons starring in the Spartan backfield, rushing for 3,346 yards, making 78 receptions for another 531 yards, scoring 34 touchdowns, and accumulating a total of 4,114 all-purpose yards during that time. A consensus All–Big Ten Conference First-Team choice after

Le'Veon Bell caught more passes than any other running back in franchise history.
Courtesy of the Pittsburgh Steelers

gaining 1,793 yards on the ground as a junior in 2012, Bell also received All-America honorable mention recognition from *Sports Illustrated*, prompting him to forgo his senior year at MSU and declare himself eligible for the 2013 NFL Draft.

Lauded by pro scouts for his quick feet, powerful 6'1", 225-pound frame, exceptional lower body strength, and outstanding cutback ability, Bell lasted until just the second round of the draft, when the Steelers claimed him with the 48th overall pick. Expressing his satisfaction with his former team's selection after training camp opened, Jack Ham stated, "Doing Penn State games, I watched this kid play at Michigan State, and the thing people don't realize is he's a good route runner out of the backfield, and they get mismatches and line him up in the slot, and, when you catch 80-some balls like he did last year, that's a great outlet for Roethlisberger to get him the football in space. I don't think they realized how complete a running back Bell is until they got him here. I think that was a great draft to bring him in."

After missing the first three games of his rookie campaign due to a right foot injury he suffered during the preseason, Bell made Ham look like a genius, rushing for 860 yards and eight touchdowns, while also making 45 receptions for 399 yards, with his 1,259 yards from scrimmage establishing a new single-season franchise record for a rookie. Improving upon those numbers the following year, Bell earned Pro Bowl and First-Team All-Pro honors by making 83 receptions for 854 yards, scoring 11 touchdowns, and finishing second in the league with 1,361 yards rushing, 2,215 yards from scrimmage, and 2,215 all-purpose yards. In addition to becoming just the second Pittsburgh player ever to surpass 2,000 yards from scrimmage in a single season, Bell joined Marshall Faulk on an extremely exclusive list of NFL players who have rushed for 1,350 yards and recorded 850 receiving yards in the same season.

Subsequently suspended by the NFL for the first two games of the 2015 regular season after being arrested with then-teammate LeGarrette Blount on DUI and marijuana possession charges in August 2014, Bell nevertheless performed well after he returned to action in Week 3, rushing for 556 yards and amassing 692 yards from scrimmage over his first six games. However, his season ended abruptly in early November when he tore the MCL in his right knee during a 16–10 loss to the Cincinnati Bengals, prompting the Steelers to put him on injured-reserve for the rest of the year.

Suspended by the NFL once again at the start of the ensuing campaign for violating the league's substance abuse policy, Bell missed the first three games of the 2016 regular season. Yet, he still managed to make 75 receptions for 616 yards, score nine touchdowns, and place near the top of the league rankings with 1,268 yards rushing, 1,884 yards from scrimmage, 1,888 all-purpose yards, and a rushing average of 4.9 yards per carry, with his fabulous performance gaining him Pro Bowl and Second-Team All-Pro recognition. Continuing to perform at an elite level after being given the franchise tag prior to the start of the 2017 season, Bell once again earned Pro Bowl and All-Pro honors by catching 85 passes for 655 yards, scoring 11 touchdowns, and finishing in the league's top three with 1,291 yards rushing, nine rushing TDs, 1,946 yards from scrimmage, and 1,946 all-purpose yards.

However, even though Bell remained focused on the playing field throughout the 2017 campaign, he grew increasingly disenchanted with the Steelers as the season wore on for placing the franchise tag on him, prompting him to announce at season's end that he would seriously consider sitting out the 2018 campaign or retiring from the NFL if the team chose to pursue the same course of action once again. Bell, who reportedly turned down a two-year deal worth $30 million in 2016, added that he wanted to be paid in relation with his value to the team, saying, "I just want to be valued where I'm at . . . I'm not going to settle for anything. I know what I do and what I bring to the table. I'm not going out here getting the ball 400 times if I'm not getting what I feel I'm worth."

Amending his comments somewhat after news of his earlier statements broke across the Internet, Bell later tweeted: "I'm trying to win a Super Bowl . . . I can care less about what happens after this season . . . my biggest thing I'm focused on is this team I'm on right now, playing for/with my brothers, and bringing back a seventh ring! What happens next year is irrelevant to my goals."

Bell holds single-season franchise records for most yards from scrimmage and most all-purpose yards.
Courtesy of Scot Tumlin

Refusing to cater to Bell's wishes, the Steelers subsequently placed the franchise tag on him, forcing him to accept a salary of $14.5 million if he wished to continue playing with them in 2018. Although Bell elected not to sign the franchise tag, he participated in team activities until contract negotiations stalled on July 16. Remaining away from the team from that point on, Bell missed the first nine games of the regular season and then failed to report to the Steelers prior to the league's November 13 deadline, thereby making him ineligible to play at all in 2018. With Bell's behavior making him appear selfish to many, he became persona non grata to his teammates, some of whom expressed their displeasure with him to the local media. Offensive lineman Ramon Foster proved to be Bell's harshest critic, stating, "He's making seven times what I make, twice as much as Al (Villanueva) is making, and we're the guys who do it for him."

Center Maurkice Pouncey added, "Obviously, it's Le'Veon over the Steelers, and we are the Steelers."

With Bell having reached a point of no return with the Steelers, he signed as a free agent with the New York Jets on March 13, 2019, leaving Pittsburgh with career totals of 5,336 rushing yards, 35 rushing touchdowns, 312 receptions, 2,660 receiving yards, seven TD catches, and 7,996 yards from scrimmage. In addition to making more receptions than any other running back in team annals, Bell holds several other franchise records, including single-game and single-season marks for most yards from scrimmage. Still only 27 years old as of this writing, Bell figures to add significantly to his career totals over the course of the next several seasons.

STEELERS CAREER HIGHLIGHTS

Best Season

Bell had an outstanding year for the Steelers in 2017, rushing for 1,291 yards and nine touchdowns, while also making 85 receptions for 655 yards and two TDs, with his exceptional play earning him Pro Bowl and First-Team All-Pro honors. However, he posted slightly better overall numbers in 2014, when, in addition to finishing second in the NFL with 1,361 yards rushing, he caught 83 passes for 854 yards, scored 11 touchdowns, averaged nearly one more yard per carry than he did three years later (4.7 to 4.0), and established single-season franchise records for most yards from scrimmage and most all-purpose yards (2,215).

Memorable Moments/Greatest Performances

Bell scored the first two touchdowns of his career on a pair of short runs during a 34–27 loss to the Minnesota Vikings on September 29, 2013, finishing the game with 57 yards rushing and four receptions for 27 yards.

Bell went over 100 yards rushing for the first time as a pro on December 22, 2013, when he helped lead the Steelers to a 38–31 win over Green

Bay by carrying the ball 26 times for 124 yards, with his 1-yard TD run with just 1:25 left in regulation providing the margin of victory.

Bell averaged a robust seven yards per carry during a 37–19 win over Carolina on September 21, 2014, concluding the contest with 147 yards on 21 carries, including a career-long 81-yard run.

Bell proved to be the difference in a 27–24 victory over the Tennessee Titans on November 17, 2014, carrying the ball 33 times for 204 yards and one touchdown.

Although the Steelers lost to New Orleans by a score of 35–32 on November 30, 2014, Bell performed brilliantly, amassing 254 yards of total offense, with 95 of those coming on the ground and the other 159 on eight pass receptions.

Bell earned AFC Offensive Player of the Week honors for the first time the following week by accumulating 235 yards of total offense and scoring two touchdowns during a 42–21 win over Cincinnati, with 185 of those yards coming on the ground.

Bell gave the Steelers a dramatic 24–20 victory over the San Diego Chargers on October 12, 2015, by scoring the game-winning touchdown from one yard out on the game's final play. He finished the contest with 111 yards rushing and that one TD.

Bell carried the ball 18 times for 144 yards and made five receptions for another 34 yards during a convincing 43–14 victory over the Kansas City Chiefs on October 2, 2016.

Bell proved to be a one-man wrecking crew on November 20, 2016, accounting for 201 of the 313 yards of total offense the Steelers accumulated during a 24–9 win over the Browns, with 146 of those yards coming on the ground and the other 55 on eight pass receptions.

Bell had a career-day on December 11, 2016, leading the Steelers to a 27–20 win over Buffalo by rushing for a franchise-record 236 yards and three touchdowns, while also making four receptions for 62 yards, with his 298 yards of total offense earning him AFC Offensive Player of the Week honors.

Bell played a key role in Pittsburgh's 30–12 victory over Miami in their 2016 AFC wild card game matchup, rushing for 167 yards and two touchdowns.

Bell followed that up by carrying the ball 30 times for 170 yards, in leading the Steelers to an 18–16 victory over Kansas City in the divisional round of the postseason tournament, with his 170 yards on the ground setting a new franchise record for most yards rushing in a playoff game.

Starring once again against Kansas City on October 15, 2017, Bell earned AFC Offensive Player of the Week honors by carrying the ball 32 times for 179 yards and one touchdown during a 19–13 win over the Chiefs.

Notable Achievements

- Rushed for more than 1,000 yards three times.
- Surpassed 75 receptions three times.
- Surpassed 600 receiving yards three times, topping 800 yards once (854 in 2014).
- Amassed more than 1,000 yards from scrimmage four times, topping 2,000 yards once (2,215 in 2014).
- Scored more than 10 touchdowns twice.
- Averaged more than 4.5 yards per carry three times.
- Finished second in NFL in: rushing once; yards from scrimmage twice; and all-purpose yards twice.
- Finished third in NFL in: rushing once; rushing touchdowns once; yards from scrimmage once; and all-purpose yards once.
- Led Steelers in rushing four times.
- Holds Steelers single-game records for most yards rushing (236) and most yards from scrimmage (298), both vs. Buffalo on December 11, 2016.
- Holds Steelers single-season records for most yards from scrimmage (2,215) and most all-purpose yards (2,215), both in 2014.
- Holds Steelers record for most yards rushing in a single postseason (357 in 2016).
- Holds Steelers career record for most receptions by a running back (312).
- Ranks among Steelers career leaders with: 5,336 yards rushing (4th); 7,996 yards from scrimmage (6th); 7,996 all-purpose yards (6th); 312 receptions (8th); 35 rushing touchdowns (tied—3rd); and 42 touchdowns (tied—10th).
- Three-time division champion (2014, 2016, and 2017).
- Three-time AFC Offensive Player of the Week.
- Two-time AFC Offensive Player of the Month.
- Two-time Steelers MVP (2014 and 2016).
- Three-time Pro Bowl selection (2014, 2016, and 2017).
- Two-time First-Team All-Pro selection (2014 and 2017).
- 2016 Second-Team All-Pro selection.

27

— MAURKICE POUNCEY —

One of the NFL's premier players at his position for most of the last decade, Maurkice Pouncey has excelled at center for the Steelers ever since he arrived in Pittsburgh in 2010. Accorded Pro Bowl honors in seven of his first nine years in the league, Pouncey has failed to earn that distinction only in those seasons when injuries forced him to miss most of his team's games. A five-time All-Pro selection, Pouncey has served as the anchor of Pittsburgh's offensive line throughout his career, with his stellar play helping the Steelers win four division titles and one AFC championship.

Born in Bartow, Florida, on July 24, 1989, LeShawn Maurkice Pouncey attended Lakeland High School, where he starred as a two-way lineman for the school's football team. A two-time All-State selection, Pouncey joined his twin brother, Mike, in leading Lakeland to 45 straight victories, three consecutive Florida Class 5A State Championships, and two straight *USA Today* National Championships. Considered a four-star recruit by Rivals .com, Pouncey fielded offers from Florida State, Clemson, Miami, and Michigan, before accepting an athletic scholarship to attend the University of Florida, where he spent the next three seasons playing under head coach Urban Meyer.

Continuing to dominate the opposition at the collegiate level, Pouncey spent his first year at Florida playing right guard, gaining Freshman First-Team All-America recognition from both Rivals.com and the *College Football News*, while also being named to the Freshman All–Southeastern Conference team by the league's coaches and the *Sporting News*. Moved to center prior to the start of his sophomore season, Pouncey helped the Gators win the BCS National Championship, earning in the process First-Team All-SEC honors. Performing even better as a junior, Pouncey became the first player in school history to win the prestigious Rimington Award, presented annually to the nation's best center. After also being accorded First-Team All-SEC and First-Team All-America honors, Pouncey chose to skip his senior year at Florida and declare himself eligible for the 2010 NFL Draft, where the Steelers selected him in the first round, with the 18th overall pick.

In discussing the selection of Pouncey, Steelers director of football operations Kevin Colbert stated, "Pouncey is just that good. It was evident early in the evaluation process that this was someone who was going to be interesting to us where we were going to be picking."

Elated with the selection of Pouncey, head coach Mike Tomlin said, "Pouncey is a young guy with a great deal of experience at playing high quality football in the SEC. He has the type of playing demeanor that we covet. He's a finisher. He's a physical foot-

Maurkice Pouncey has continued the tradition of outstanding play at center in Pittsburgh.
Courtesy of the Pittsburgh Steelers

ball player. He likes to play the game, but not only as he's playing the game. When you do your research on this young man, he likes the things that come with being a professional football player and being a football player period. He likes to work out, he likes to compete in the weight room, he likes to work on his craft, and those are things, of course, that we're looking for."

Giving Pouncey his full endorsement, Urban Meyer said of his former protégé, "I'm proud for Maurkice and his family. He has worked so hard to put himself in this position. He loves the game of football, and he loves to compete. His passion for the game shows on and off the field, and I know a number of NFL teams told us they loved his attitude and his skill set."

Meanwhile, Pouncey expressed his joy over being drafted by the Steelers by stating, "I wanted this from day one. I'm so happy to be a Pittsburgh Steeler. I'm so happy they picked me. I just like the Steelers so much. All the fans and the city; that's the team I met with at the combine and I fell in love with. They weren't my favorite team growing up, but now, since I've been to the combine and I've watched all the great years they've had, I about fell in love with the Pittsburgh Steelers. I can't wait to get there. It's unexplainable."

Laying claim to the starting job immediately upon his arrival in Pittsburgh, Pouncey started every game at center for the Steelers his first year in the league, helping to pave the way for running back Rashard Mendenhall to rush for a career-high 1,273 yards. Called for only one penalty all year long, Pouncey earned a spot on the NFL All-Rookie Team, a trip to the Pro Bowl, and Second-Team All-Pro honors, with his Pro Bowl selection making him the first Pittsburgh offensive lineman to be so honored as a rookie since 1956.

Continuing his superb play in 2011 and 2012, Pouncey gained Pro Bowl and All-Pro recognition both years, establishing himself over the course of those two seasons as arguably the league's finest center. Doing an excellent job of using his size and strength to drive defenders off the line of scrimmage, the 6'4", 304-pound Pouncey excelled as a run-blocker from the time he first entered the league. Before long, he also developed into an outstanding pass-protector, making good use of his quick feet, superior agility, and mean streak to build a reputation as one of the NFL's most complete interior offensive linemen.

Unfortunately, Pouncey missed a significant amount of playing time in two of the next three seasons, appearing in only one game in 2013 after tearing his right ACL and MCL in Week 1 against the Tennessee Titans, and sitting out all of 2015 after breaking his fibula when Green Bay Packers safety Ha Ha Clinton-Dix rolled onto the back of his right ankle during a preseason contest. In between, though, Pouncey helped the Steelers capture the division title in

Pouncey earned Pro Bowl honors in seven of his first nine years in the league.
Courtesy of the Pittsburgh Steelers

2014, earning in the process his fourth trip to the Pro Bowl and fourth All-Pro selection.

Remaining relatively healthy since 2016, Pouncey has missed just two games over the course of the past three seasons, earning during that time three more Pro Bowl selections and his fifth All-Pro nomination. And, with Pouncey attaining veteran status the past few years, he has emerged as one of Pittsburgh's team leaders, as Steelers All-Pro right guard David DeCastro acknowledged when he said, "Pounce, he raises my game. He's a natural leader, a natural kind of alpha male type guy. He's a rises-tide-lifts-all-ships kind of player. . . . A guy I love being in there with."

One of the most prominent figures in Pittsburgh's locker room, Pouncey often expresses the feelings of many of his teammates, as he did when James Harrison signed with the New England Patriots after being released by the Steelers in 2017 and Le'Veon Bell chose to sit out the entire 2018 campaign after failing to come to terms with the team on a new contract. Criticizing both men for their actions, Pouncey subsequently drew support from virtually all his teammates, who admire and respect him for his leadership skills and team-first mentality, which will likely continue to put him in high standing his remaining time in Pittsburgh.

CAREER HIGHLIGHTS

Best Season

Pouncey had perhaps his two finest seasons for the Steelers in 2011 and 2014, earning First-Team All-Pro honors in each of those campaigns. However, while Pouncey missed two games in 2011, he started all 16 contests three years later, with his exceptional play at center helping the Steelers set numerous single-season franchise records, including most points scored (436), total yards gained on offense (6,577), and total first downs made (379). All things considered, Pouncey turned in his most dominant performance for the Steelers in 2014.

Memorable Moments/Greatest Performances

Pouncey anchored an offensive line that enabled the Steelers to rush for a season-high 264 yards during a 37–19 win over the Carolina Panthers on September 21, 2014.

Pouncey's exceptional blocking helped the Steelers rush for 240 yards and amass 460 yards of total offense during a 27–20 victory over the Buffalo Bills on December 11, 2016, with Le'Veon Bell setting a single-game team record by gaining 236 of those yards on the ground.

Pouncey helped pave the way for Bell to rush for 170 yards during a hard-fought 18–16 victory over Kansas City in the divisional round of the 2016 AFC playoffs.

Notable Achievements

- Four-time division champion (2010, 2014, 2016, and 2017).
- 2010 AFC champion.
- Member of 2010 NFL All-Rookie Team.
- Seven-time Pro Bowl selection (2010, 2011, 2012, 2014, 2016, 2017, and 2018).
- Two-time First-Team All-Pro selection (2011 and 2014).
- Three-time Second-Team All-Pro selection (2010, 2012, and 2018).

28

— HEATH MILLER —

The greatest tight end in franchise history, Heath Miller spent his entire 11-year NFL career in Pittsburgh serving as a key contributor to Steeler teams that won four division titles, three AFC championships, and two Super Bowls. An outstanding blocker and dependable receiver, Miller surpassed 50 receptions six times and 750 receiving yards on three occasions, retiring with the second most catches and third most receiving yards in team annals. Extremely durable, Miller missed just eight games his entire career, with his consistently excellent play earning him team MVP honors once and two trips to the Pro Bowl. Meanwhile, Miller's humility and sense of selflessness made him tremendously popular with his teammates and the fans of Pittsburgh, who honored him after every catch he made with chants of "HEEEEATH!"

Born in Richlands, Virginia, on October 22, 1982, Earl Heath Miller grew up in nearby Swords Creek, where he attended tiny Honaker High School. Starring at quarterback and defensive back for the Honaker Tigers football team, Miller earned AP All-State honors twice and gained recognition as the AP Player of the Year as a senior, when he led the school to its first state championship. Displaying his willingness to share the spotlight with his teammates while calling the signals for Honaker, Miller later drew praise from his high school coach, Doug Hubbard, who told *Pittsburgh Magazine*, "That was the kind of leader he was. There would be times when we ran the option and Heath could have just strolled right into the end zone. But, instead, he tossed the ball back to a teammate and blocked for him so that he could score." An outstanding all-around athlete, Miller also excelled in baseball and basketball at Honaker, earning All-Region honors as a first baseman on the diamond and a forward on the hardwood.

After accepting an athletic scholarship from the University of Virginia, Miller spent his college career playing for head coach Al Groh, making the transition from quarterback to tight end as a freshman in 2001. Performing exceptionally well at his new post, Miller ended up setting ACC records for most career receptions (144), yards (1,703), and touchdowns (20) by a tight end, earning along the way unanimous All-America honors as a junior, when he also won the Mackey Award as the nation's best player at that position. Commenting on his teammate's superb play, Anthony Poindexter stated, "He isn't a rah-rah guy. You spend 24 hours around him and you might not hear him say three sentences. . . . He's the same on the field. His game speaks for him. They call him 'Big Money' because he comes through with so many big plays. But he doesn't brag; he doesn't show off. He scores a touchdown and he doesn't spike the ball, he just flips it to the ref."

Choosing to leave college after his junior year, Miller entered the 2005 NFL Draft, where the Steelers selected him in the first round, with the 30th overall pick. Laying claim to the starting tight end job immediately upon his arrival in Pittsburgh, Miller earned a spot on the NFL All-Rookie Team by making 39 receptions for 459 yards and six touchdowns, helping the Steelers capture their first NFL title in 26 years in the process. He followed that up with three more solid seasons, totaling 129 receptions, 1,473 receiving yards, and 15 touchdowns from 2006 to 2008, a period during which he gradually established himself as Ben Roethlisberger's security blanket.

Although wide receivers Hines Ward and Santonio Holmes typically

amassed more yards through the air, Miller developed a chemistry with Roethlisberger that frequently prompted the big quarterback to turn to him when he needed a key reception to be made. Sure-handed and extremely reliable, Miller proved to be particularly effective on routes of the short-to-intermediate variety, providing an outstanding target over the middle for Roethlisberger. Meanwhile, even though the Steelers drafted the 6'5", 256-pound Miller primarily for his pass-catching skills, he eventually became known as one of the best blocking tight ends in the league. Crediting his improvement in that area to time he put in on the practice field,

Heath Miller established himself as one of the most popular players in franchise history during his 11 years in Pittsburgh. Courtesy of the Pittsburgh Steelers

Miller told *Pittsburgh Magazine*, "The longer I've been in this league, the more I've realized that hard work is the way you stick around. Every year, you see so many talented guys come and go. I take pride in doing whatever I'm asked to help the team win."

Miller's dedication to his profession, selfless attitude, and humility prompted Roethlisberger to call him his "greatest teammate," with Big Ben telling the *Pittsburgh Tribune-Review*, "I'll come off to the sideline and ask him if he was open on a play, and he will tell me 'No.' I'll go look at it on film, and he was wide open."

Miller ranks among the Steelers' all-time leaders in every major pass-receiving category.
Courtesy of the Pittsburgh Steelers

Miller's modesty and understated manner often caused him to be overlooked in favor of more spectacular pass-receiving tight ends such as Antonio Gates and Tony Gonzalez when it came time for postseason honors to be handed out. However, Miller earned his first trip to the Pro Bowl in 2009, when he made 76 receptions for 789 yards and six touchdowns. After totaling 93 receptions, 1,143 receiving yards, and four touchdowns the next two years, Miller earned team MVP honors and his second trip to the Pro Bowl in 2012 by making 71 receptions for 816 yards and eight touchdowns.

Miller subsequently suffered a torn MCL and ACL early in 2013 that required him to undergo reconstructive surgery to repair three torn ligaments. Nevertheless, he ended up missing just two games, finishing the season with 58 catches, 593 receiving yards, and one touchdown. Miller remained with the Steelers for two more years, making 66 receptions for 761 yards and three touchdowns in 2014, before catching 60 passes, accumulating 535 receiving yards, and scoring two touchdowns the following season. Yet, even though Miller performed well for the Steelers both years, he elected to announce his retirement following the conclusion of the 2015 campaign, ending his career with 592 receptions, 6,569 receiving yards, and 45 TD catches—all of which place him among the franchise's all-time leaders. In making his decision known to the public, Miller said:

> Today, I informed the Steelers of my plans to retire. I realize how extremely fortunate and grateful I am to have spent my entire career as a Pittsburgh Steeler. I would like to thank the Rooney Family, Kevin Colbert, Bill Cowher, Mike Tomlin, James Daniel and the rest of the Steelers organization for giving me the opportunity to live out my childhood dream. I will always cherish and value the special bonds that I formed with my teammates. It was truly an honor for me to take the field with them. I am also appreciative of my entire family and all the coaches who helped me along the way. Additionally, I want to thank Steelers Nation, the best fans in the NFL!

In explaining his decision to retire when he did, Miller stated:

> For me, it was a number of reasons. Obviously, I played in the league a long time, 11 years. And I always wanted to be able to walk away from the game with my health, for the most part, and I feel like I'm doing that. I didn't want to stick around too long and continue to play when I felt like I wasn't able to play to the level that I'm accustomed to playing. I also have a growing family, and, once you have kids, it gets harder and harder to be away from them. A lot of signs told me the time is right, so I made the decision.

Upon learning of Miller's decision, Steelers president Art Rooney II said, "On behalf of the entire Steelers organization and Steelers Nation around the world, I would like to congratulate and thank Heath for his many contributions to the Steelers. The chants of 'HEEEEATH' will be missed at Heinz Field and around the entire NFL. Heath is the most accomplished tight end in team history and his efforts will not soon be forgotten."

Steelers GM Kevin Colbert added, "Heath Miller was as great a combination of character and football player as I have ever been around. Heath helped us win many games, including two Super Bowl Championships, while also being an important part of our community."

When asked how he would like to be remembered by his teammates, Miller responded, "Most important to me, I always wanted to have the respect of the guys in the locker room. And I think you earn that respect by coming to work every day, being prepared, being ready to sacrifice whatever it is for the betterment of the team. I hope that's the way the guys I played with have felt about me. I know that every day I came to work, and did the best that I could, and put it all on the line, and there's a certain level of comfort in that."

CAREER HIGHLIGHTS

Best Season

Miller earned his first trip to the Pro Bowl in 2009, when he recorded a career-high 76 receptions, amassed 789 receiving yards, and scored six touchdowns. However, he proved to be slightly more productive in 2012, catching 71 passes and establishing career-high marks with 816 receiving yards and eight touchdowns.

Memorable Moments/Greatest Performances

Miller topped 100 receiving yards for the first time in his career during a 28–17 victory over the Miami Dolphins in the 2006 regular-season opener, making three receptions for 101 yards and one touchdown, which came on a career-long 87-yard reception of a pass thrown by Charlie Batch.

Miller made five receptions for 71 yards and one touchdown during a 31–28 win over the Cleveland Browns on November 11, 2007, with his 2-yard TD grab late in the fourth quarter providing the margin of victory.

Miller contributed to a 38–28 win over the San Diego Chargers on October 4, 2009, by catching eight passes for 70 yards and two touchdowns.

Miller helped the Steelers record a 37–36 victory over the Green Bay Packers on December 20, 2009, by making seven receptions for a career-high 118 yards.

Miller made five receptions for 97 yards and one touchdown during a 23–20 win over the Baltimore Ravens on December 2, 2012, with his 7-yard TD grab midway through the final period tying the score at 20–20. The Steelers won the game some seven minutes later when Shaun Suisham kicked a 42-yard field goal as time expired.

Although the Steelers lost to the Tampa Bay Buccaneers by a score of 27–24 on September 28, 2014, Miller made a career-high 10 catches for 85 yards and one touchdown during the contest.

Miller hauled in seven passes for 112 yards and one touchdown during a 51–34 win over the Indianapolis Colts on October 26, 2014, with his 11-yard fourth-quarter connection with Ben Roethlisberger giving the Pittsburgh quarterback his sixth TD pass of the game.

Miller equaled his single-game career-high in receptions when he made 10 catches for 105 yards during a 16–10 loss to the Cincinnati Bengals on November 1, 2015.

Notable Achievements

- Surpassed 50 receptions six times, topping 60 catches four times and 70 catches twice.
- Surpassed 800 receiving yards once (816 in 2012).
- Made eight touchdown receptions in 2012.
- Missed just eight games in 11 seasons.
- Led Steelers with 71 receptions in 2012.
- Ranks among Steelers career leaders with: 592 receptions (3rd); 6,569 receiving yards (4th); 6,577 yards from scrimmage (7th); 45 touchdown receptions (5th); and 45 touchdowns (8th).
- Four-time division champion (2007, 2008, 2010, and 2014).
- Three-time AFC champion (2005, 2008, and 2010).
- Two-time Super Bowl champion (XL and XLIII).
- Member of 2005 NFL All-Rookie Team.
- 2012 Steelers MVP.
- Two-time Pro Bowl selection (2009 and 2012)

29

— LEVON KIRKLAND —

ombining great size and strength with extraordinary quickness for a man of his proportions, Levon Kirkland established himself as one of the NFL's finest all-around linebackers during his nine seasons in Pittsburgh. Excelling against both the run and the pass, Kirkland used his powerful frame and keen instincts to record more than 100 tackles six times, leading the Steelers in that category on three separate occasions. Meanwhile, Kirkland's speed and agility enabled him to also excel in pass coverage, with his unique skill set making him a key contributor to Steeler teams that won five division titles and one AFC championship during the 1990s. A two-time team MVP, Kirkland earned two trips to the Pro Bowl and two All-Pro selections during his time in Pittsburgh, before being named to the NFL 1990s All-Decade Team following the conclusion of his playing career.

Born in Lamar, South Carolina, on February 17, 1969, Lorenzo Levon Kirkland attended Lamar High School, where he starred in multiple sports, playing basketball in the winter, competing in track and the high-jump in the spring, and excelling on the gridiron as a wide receiver, tight end, linebacker, and kickoff returner. Choosing to remain close to home, Kirkland accepted a scholarship offer from Clemson University, which he helped lead to 39 victories over the course of the next four years as he gradually increased his weight from 205 to 240 pounds. Developing into an exceptional pass-rushing outside linebacker while at Clemson, Kirkland emerged as a finalist for the Butkus Award as the nation's top linebacker as a junior in 1990.

Subsequently selected by the Steelers in the second round of the 1992 NFL Draft, with the 38th overall pick, Kirkland spent his first season in Pittsburgh playing exclusively on special teams as he learned the nuances of playing linebacker in the NFL. Commenting on the adjustments Kirkland had to make after he entered the league, former Steelers director of football operations Tom Donahue said, "He played pretty much like a

Levon Kirkland recorded more than 100 tackles for the Steelers six times.
Courtesy of the Pittsburgh Steelers

defensive end in college. So, he had a lot to learn when he came here, and we moved him inside. He had to switch from a down position to standing up, from the outside to the inside. That took his entire first season. The only times he played were on special teams, but he was learning during all that time."

Replacing Hardy Nickerson as the starter at left-inside linebacker his second year in the league, Kirkland had an outstanding season, finishing second on the team with 103 solo tackles, while also forcing four fumbles and recovering two others, one of which he returned for a touchdown. Performing well once again in 1994, Kirkland recorded 100 tackles (70 solo), three sacks, and two interceptions for a Steelers team that won the division title for the first of four straight times.

With the strong play of Kirkland and Chad Brown on the inside enabling outside linebackers Greg Lloyd and Kevin Greene to rush the quarterback with abandon, the quartet emerged as the league's most terrifying linebacker unit during their time together, which, unfortunately, lasted just three seasons. But, regardless of whom Kirkland played alongside, he remained a tremendous force on defense, annually ranking among the team leaders in tackles, while also proving to be surprisingly effective in pass coverage considering his unusually large frame for a linebacker. Although listed at 6'1" and 275 pounds, Kirkland played much closer to 300 pounds, with his speed and nimbleness belying his size.

In discussing his teammate's exceptional all-around play and freakish athletic ability, Earl Holmes stated, "The guy, he knows the game. That guy has unbelievable instincts. Incredible. He's just there. To me, he's the best inside linebacker in the NFL. . . . He's just a big-boned guy. He does everything that a receiver or a running back can do. People think because he's big like that, he can't run. But we see it. He can run."

Steelers head coach Bill Cowher added, "We bring our inside linebackers a lot as blitzers, and we also have them drop back—so he has to do a lot. It's something special for a guy who has that kind of size to be able to do that."

After starting every game for the Steelers for the first of six straight times in 1995, Kirkland earned Pro Bowl and Second-Team All-Pro honors the following year by recording four sacks, a career-high four interceptions, and a team-leading 113 tackles (75 solo). With Greg Lloyd missing virtually the entire season with a knee injury, Kirkland also assumed the mantle of leadership on defense, which he maintained his remaining years in Pittsburgh.

Kirkland continued to perform at an elite level the next four seasons, recording more than 100 tackles on three occasions, en route to leading the team in that category two more times. Particularly effective in 1997, Kirkland earned his second consecutive trip to the Pro Bowl and his lone First-Team All-Pro nomination by picking off two passes and recording a career-high five sacks and 126 tackles. Yet, surprisingly, the Steelers elected to release him prior to the start of the 2001 campaign due to salary cap reasons. Kirkland left Pittsburgh having recorded 11 interceptions, 14

Kirkland contributed to five division championship teams during his time in Pittsburgh.
Courtesy of the Pittsburgh Steelers

forced fumbles, eight fumble recoveries, 18½ sacks, and 849 tackles (639 solo), with the last figure representing the fourth-highest total in franchise history.

After being waived by the Steelers, Kirkland signed with the Seattle Seahawks, with whom he spent one season, before ending his career in 2002 as a member of the Philadelphia Eagles, whom he helped lead to a berth in the NFC championship game. Kirkland recorded another 174 tackles after he left Pittsburgh, giving him a career total of 1,023 stops (771 solo).

Following his playing days, Kirkland returned to his alma mater of Clemson University, where he worked as the recruitment coordinator for the admissions department until 2009. Since leaving that post, Kirkland has spent the last several years coaching at the high school and collegiate levels, serving at different times as linebacker coach for Wade Hampton High School in Greenville, South Carolina, assistant head coach at Woodmont High School in South Carolina, and head coach for Shannon Forest Christian School in Greenville, South Carolina, before accepting the position of linebacker coach at Florida A&M University in 2013. But, wherever he has gone, Kirkland has continued to hold the Steelers close to his heart, stating on one occasion, "They say once you are a Steeler you are always a Steeler. I really do believe that. It's a team I will always cheer for. I enjoyed being a Steeler, the tradition, the black and gold everywhere. The Rooney family is outstanding."

Kirkland then added, "There was a certain pride there. The organization was more like a family than a business. I have been to other teams, and it wasn't the same feel. I was so blessed and fortunate to play here, where you had such a tradition of great linebackers."

STEELERS CAREER HIGHLIGHTS

Best Season

Kirkland played his best ball for the Steelers in 1997, when he earned his lone First-Team All-Pro selection and NFL Alumni Linebacker of the Year honors by intercepting two passes, forcing one fumble, recovering another, and recording a career-high five sacks and 126 tackles (95 solo).

Memorable Moments/Greatest Performances

Kirkland scored the only points of his career during a 16–3 win over the San Diego Chargers on October 10, 1993, when he returned a fumble 16 yards for the game's only touchdown.

Kirkland recorded his first career sack during a 37–14 victory over the New Orleans Saints on October 17, 1993.

Kirkland contributed to a 14–10 win over the Cincinnati Bengals on October 16, 1994, by recording eight tackles and the first interception of his career.

Although the Steelers lost Super Bowl XXX to the Dallas Cowboys by a score of 27–17 due largely to a pair of key interceptions thrown by quarterback Neil O'Donnell, Kirkland performed extremely well, making 10 tackles, recording a sack of Troy Aikman, and leading a Pittsburgh defense that limited Dallas to just 15 first downs and 56 yards rushing.

Kirkland helped lead the Steelers to a 24–6 win over the Buffalo Bills on September 16, 1996, by intercepting two passes for the only time in his career.

Kirkland led the defensive charge during a 20–10 victory over Cincinnati on October 13, 1996, recording two of the 10 sacks the Steelers registered against Bengals quarterback Jeff Blake.

Kirkland recorded a sack, forced a fumble, and made five tackles during a 13–10 win over Seattle on September 27, 1998, earning in the process AFC Defensive Player of the Week honors.

Kirkland again earned that distinction for his performance during a 30–20 victory over the Carolina Panthers on December 26, 1999, when he recorded a sack and a team-high nine tackles.

Notable Achievements

- Scored one defensive touchdown during career.
- Intercepted four passes in 1996.
- Surpassed 100 tackles six times.
- Led Steelers in tackles three times.
- Ranks among Steelers career leaders with 849 tackles (4th) and 14 forced fumbles (tied—7th).
- Five-time division champion (1992, 1994, 1995, 1996, and 1997).
- 1995 AFC champion.
- Two-time AFC Defensive Player of the Week.
- 1997 NFL Alumni Linebacker of the Year.
- Two-time Steelers MVP (1998 and 1999).
- Two-time Pro Bowl selection (1996 and 1997).
- 1997 First-Team All-Pro selection.
- 1996 Second-Team All-Pro selection.
- Two-time First-Team All-Conference selection (1996 and 1997).
- Pro Football Hall of Fame All-1990s Second Team.

30

— JAMES FARRIOR —

Arguably the best free-agent acquisition in franchise history, James Farrior joined the Steelers in 2002 after spending his first five years in the NFL with the New York Jets. Over the course of the next 10 seasons, Farrior served as the defensive captain of Steeler teams that won five division titles, three AFC championships, and two Super Bowls, establishing himself during that time as one of the best inside linebackers ever to play for the Black and Gold. A smart and instinctive player who helped stabilize Pittsburgh's defense from his left-inside linebacker position, Farrior led the Steelers in tackles five times, ending his career as the second-leading tackler in team annals. The Steelers' 2004 team MVP, Farrior also earned two trips to the Pro Bowl, two All-Pro selections, and one All-AFC nomination during his time in the Steel City.

Born in Ettrick, Virginia, on January 6, 1975, James Alfred Farrior attended Matoaca High School, where he starred in multiple sports, lettering three times in football, track, and wrestling. Proving to be particularly proficient on the gridiron, Farrior excelled at both fullback and linebacker, earning *Parade* magazine High School All-America, All-State, and *Richmond Times-Dispatch* Co-Player of the Year honors as a senior by posting 78 tackles, 11 sacks, four forced fumbles, and two interceptions, while also carrying the ball 105 times for 1,006 yards and 22 touchdowns.

Choosing to remain close to home following his graduation from Matoaca High, Farrior accepted a scholarship from the University of Virginia, where he spent the next four years starring at linebacker for the Cavaliers. Amassing a total of 381 tackles during his time at Virginia, Farrior earned All–Atlantic Coast Conference Second-Team honors as a junior, before being named to the First Team as a senior in 1996.

Subsequently selected by the Jets with the eighth overall pick of the 1997 NFL Draft, Farrior struggled his first few years in the league while assuming a part-time role as an outside linebacker in New York's 3-4 defense. However, he improved his performance dramatically after New

York switched to a 4-3 alignment in 2001, recording two interceptions, three forced fumbles, and a team-leading 142 tackles (106 solo). Yet, despite his outstanding play, the Jets elected not to re-sign him when he became a free agent at season's end, with Farrior later stating, "It was more of a business decision than anything else. They wanted to go in another direction. I wasn't mad about it. I just had to accept it and move on."

Looking back at the five years he spent in New York, Farrior said, "It was definitely a great learning experience for me. It just really taught me what it takes to be a professional football player in the league. Being in New York, it definitely taught me how to deal with the media. It can be pretty brutal up there in New York. So, I had to learn fast that when things are going good it's fine and okay. But, when it's going bad, you've got to be prepared for the worst."

After signing with the Steelers, Farrior returned to his more familiar college position of inside linebacker in Pittsburgh's 3-4 defensive scheme, where, playing alongside Kendrell Bell, Joey Porter, and Jason Gildon, he thrived as never before. After bringing down opposing ball-carriers 82 times his first year in Pittsburgh, Farrior recorded a team-leading 141 tackles (96 solo) in 2003. He followed that up with another outstanding season, earning Pro Bowl and First-Team All-Pro honors in 2004 by making 94 tackles, picking off four passes, which he returned for a total of 113 yards, forcing three fumbles, recovering three others, and scoring one touchdown, with his fabulous performance also earning him a runner-up finish to Baltimore's Ed Reed in the NFL Defensive Player of the Year voting.

James Farrior served as defensive captain of the Steelers for 10 seasons.
Courtesy of Douglas A. Smith

Commenting on his exceptional play his first few years with the Steelers, Farrior said, "I feel like coming to Pittsburgh was a rebirth for me. It's allowed me to do a lot of things that I knew I could always do; be a playmaker and make plays in the NFL. I never doubted my ability, but it was just me getting the opportunity and getting a chance. I love it here, and I think it's a perfect fit for me."

Although the 6'2", 235-pound Farrior appeared somewhat smallish for an inside linebacker, his speed, intelligence, and superior instincts allowed him to do an excellent job of getting to the football, making him an outstanding defender against the run. Meanwhile, his quickness and athleticism also enabled him to excel in pass coverage and as an occasional blitzer.

As Farrior established himself as arguably the Steelers' best defender, he also gradually emerged as their leader on the defensive side of the ball, using his intelligence and relatively calm demeanor to provide guidance to his teammates. In discussing the prominent role that Farrior assumed on the team, Steelers head coach Mike Tomlin stated, "Our unquestioned leader is James Farrior. I think, if you polled anybody, player or coach, equipment man or receptionist, they realize he sets the tone for this outfit."

Tomlin added, "He's the kind of leader I embrace, very flat-lined emotionally. He doesn't ride the emotional roller coaster. He is very consistent on a day-to-day basis on how he approaches his business, and really kind of a blueprint for doing it at a high level for a long time in this league."

Embracing his new role, Farrior said, "It's a good feeling to know that you run the ship out there. I take a lot of pride in that. I know that I have a lot of responsibility. At the end of the day, I have to get those guys lined up and get them to do what they do best."

Continuing his outstanding play in 2005, Farrior began an exceptional six-year run during which he compiled more than 100 tackles all but once. Performing especially well from 2006 to 2008, Farrior recorded 126 tackles and four sacks in the first of those campaigns, before making 94 tackles and a career-high 6½ sacks the following year. He then earned Pro Bowl and Second-Team All-Pro honors in 2008 by registering 133 tackles and 3½ sacks for the Super Bowl champion Steelers.

In addition to performing at an elite level throughout the period, Farrior served as a mentor to the other members of Pittsburgh's young linebacking corps, assisting in the development of LaMarr Woodley, Lawrence Timmons, and James Harrison, who earned NFL Defensive Player of the Year honors in 2008. Commenting on the impact that Farrior made on the team's younger players, Mike Tomlin stated, "I think a lot of our young players look up to him. A lot of guys gravitate to him. A lot of guys not only look to him in terms of how they prepare to play football games, but how they prepare over a 12-month calendar. . . . This is a guy who is in great physical condition 12 months a year, takes a couple of weeks off, and then gets back about the business of preparing himself for the next one."

Backup linebacker Stevenson Sylvester added, "I don't know how to explain it. He's just a guy that you want to be around. James, he gets you

Farrior ranks second in franchise history with 1,078 career tackles.
Courtesy of Scot Tumlin

going, the kind of leader you can really bond with, your friend and your coach at the same time. When you need influence, you go to him; he's a guy you just want on your side in a fight."

James Harrison also had high praise for Farrior, saying, "He is the nuts and bolts of our defense. He makes the calls on our defense and how we are going to run them. We need him out there."

After recording more than 100 tackles in each of the three previous seasons, Farrior brought down opposing ball-carriers just 78 times in 2011, prompting the Steelers to release him at season's end. Rather than signing with another team, the 37-year-old veteran elected to announce his retirement, ending his career with 1,412 tackles (983 solo), 35½ sacks, 11 interceptions, 225 interception-return yards, 18 forced fumbles, 12 fumble recoveries, and one touchdown. In his 10 years with the Steelers, Farrior recorded 1,078 tackles (731 solo), 30 sacks, eight interceptions, 141 interception-return yards, 12 forced fumbles, 10 fumble recoveries, and his only touchdown.

After retiring as an active player, Farrior teamed up with his brother, Matt, to create The James Farrior Foundation, which runs a variety of programs that assist those in need through all stages of life. In addition to providing guidance and mentoring for students, the foundation offers college financial assistance to eligible students and aids families in need. The Farrior brothers also work with the National Bone Marrow Registry.

Looking back fondly at his 10 seasons with the Steelers, Farrior says, "I felt like Pittsburgh was my home. I felt like this was the place where I was born to play."

STEELERS CAREER HIGHLIGHTS

Best Season

Farrior performed exceptionally well for the Steelers through the years, making a career-high 141 tackles (96 solo) in 2003, recording 94 tackles (64 solo) and a career-best 6½ sacks in 2007, and earning Second-Team All-Pro honors in 2008 by recording 3½ sacks and 133 tackles (87 solo). However, he had his finest all-around season in 2004, earning team MVP honors and his lone First-Team All-Pro nomination by recording three sacks, 94 tackles (65 solo), three forced fumbles, three fumble recoveries, and four interceptions, one of which he returned 14 yards for the only touchdown of his career.

Memorable Moments/Greatest Performances

Farrior contributed to a 34–15 win over the Baltimore Ravens in the 2003 regular-season opener by making a team-leading 13 tackles.

Farrior earned AFC Defensive Player of the Week honors for his performance during a 24–20 victory over the Cowboys on October 17, 2004, when he recorded two sacks in one game for the first time in his career.

Farrior helped lead the Steelers to a convincing 27–3 win over the Philadelphia Eagles on November 7, 2004, by recording a sack of Donovan McNabb and intercepting one of his passes, which he subsequently returned 41 yards.

Farrior recorded another interception during a 19–14 victory over the Cincinnati Bengals two weeks later, picking off a Carson Palmer pass and returning the ball 14 yards for his only career touchdown.

Farrior played a key role in Pittsburgh's 21–18 win over Indianapolis in the 2005 playoffs, recording 2½ sacks and a team-leading 10 tackles, with one of his sacks setting up the touchdown that put the Steelers ahead by a score of 21–3.

Farrior turned in an outstanding all-around effort against Cincinnati on October 19, 2008, recording a sack and a game-high 11 tackles (six solo) during a 38–10 win over the Bengals.

Farrior had another strong game two weeks later, recording ½ sack and a season-high 12 solo tackles during a 23–6 victory over the Washington Redskins on November 3.

Farrior turned in his finest performance of the 2009 campaign on October 25, when he recorded a sack and 15 tackles (nine solo) during a 27–17 win over the Minnesota Vikings.

Notable Achievements

- Scored one defensive touchdown during career.
- Intercepted four passes in 2004.
- Amassed 113 interception-return yards in 2004.
- Recorded at least six sacks in a season twice.
- Surpassed 100 tackles six times.
- Led Steelers in tackles five times.
- Ranks second in Steelers history with 1,078 tackles (731 solo).
- Five-time division champion (2002, 2004, 2007, 2008, and 2010).
- Three-time AFC champion (2005, 2008, and 2010).
- Two-time Super Bowl champion (XL and XLIII).
- 2004 Week 6 AFC Defensive Player of the Week.
- 2004 Steelers MVP.
- Finished second in 2004 NFL Defensive Player of the Year voting.
- Two-time Pro Bowl selection (2004 and 2008).
- 2004 First-Team All-Pro selection.
- 2008 Second-Team All-Pro selection.
- 2004 First-Team All-Conference selection.
- Pro Football Reference All-2000s Second Team.

31

— DWIGHT WHITE —

Nicknamed "Mad Dog" for the level of intensity he exhibited on the playing field, Dwight White spent all 10 of his NFL seasons in Pittsburgh, establishing himself during that time as one of the key members of the Steelers' famed "Steel Curtain" defense. A "high-motor" player who gave 100 percent effort on every play, White did an excellent job of defending against both the run and the pass, recording 46 sacks, four interceptions, seven fumble recoveries, and two safeties over the course of his career. An outstanding big-game player, White registered nine sacks in 18 postseason contests and scored the first points the Steelers tallied in any Super Bowl when he sacked quarterback Fran Tarkenton in the end zone for a safety during Pittsburgh's 16–6 victory over Minnesota in Super Bowl IX. In all, White helped lead the Steelers to seven division titles, four AFC championships, and four Super Bowl wins, earning in the process two Pro Bowl selections, four All-AFC nominations, and a spot on the franchise's 75th Anniversary Team.

Born in Hampton, Virginia, on July 30, 1949, Dwight Lynn White moved with his parents and two younger siblings to Dallas, Texas, at the age of 10. Developing a love for people and an appreciation for the importance of church and the community as a teenager, White attended James Madison High School, before enrolling at East Texas State University (since renamed Texas A&M University–Commerce), where he earned First-Team All–Lone Star Conference honors as a senior in 1971.

Subsequently selected by the Steelers in the fourth round of the 1971 NFL Draft, with the 104th overall pick, White became an immediate starter at right end upon his arrival in Pittsburgh, joining L. C. Greenwood (left end), Joe Greene (left tackle), and Lloyd Voss (right tackle) on the defensive line. After acquiring his "Mad Dog" moniker shortly after he joined the Steelers, White went on to have a solid rookie season, before earning a trip to the Pro Bowl and First-Team All-AFC honors for the first of three times in his sophomore campaign of 1972. He followed that up

Dwight White acquired the nickname "Mad Dog" for the level of intensity he displayed on the playing field.
Courtesy of the Pittsburgh Steelers

with another strong performance in 1973, helping the Steelers advance to the playoffs for the second straight time by recording two interceptions, registering one safety, and applying constant pressure to opposing quarterbacks, with his solid all-around play once again earning him Pro Bowl and All-Conference honors.

With the Steelers subsequently establishing themselves as the NFL's dominant team by winning four of the next six Super Bowls, White proved to be a huge factor in their rise to the top of the football world, earning two more All-AFC nominations, while annually ranking among the team leaders in sacks. White, who often said that playing on the defensive line was like having a "dog's life," served as the perfect complement to Joe Greene and L. C. Greenwood on the right side of Pittsburgh's defensive front. Although the 6'4", 255-pound White lacked Greene's overwhelming strength and Greenwood's tremendous quickness, he proved to be the equal of both men in terms of intensity and willingness to help the team in any way possible, exhibiting both qualities in Super Bowl IX, when he played virtually the entire game after spending most of the previous week in a hospital bed suffering from pneumonia.

White remained one of the key members of Pittsburgh's defense until 1979, when injuries forced him to relinquish his starting job to John Banaszak. He spent one more year with the Steelers, appearing in only seven games in 1980, before announcing his retirement at season's end. White's unofficial career total of 46 sacks places him ninth in team annals.

Following his playing days, White became a prominent stockbroker in Pittsburgh and one of the most successful former Steelers in the business world, at one point serving as a company board member of W.R. Lazard & Co, before becoming senior managing director of public finance for Mesirow Financial in Pittsburgh. Unfortunately, White lived only until the age of 58, passing away on June 6, 2008, when he suffered a blood clot in his lung after undergoing back surgery.

Upon learning of his passing, Steelers chairman Dan Rooney said, "Dwight White was one of the greatest players to ever wear a Steelers uniform. He was a member of the greatest defensive line in NFL history."

Rooney added, "He played with a relentlessness that led us to four Super Bowl titles in the 1970s. Dwight refused to be denied, as was evidenced when he walked out of the hospital with pneumonia to play in Super Bowl IX and had an outstanding game. Dwight will be remembered by those who knew him even more for being a wonderful and caring person."

White recorded the first points the Steelers scored in any Super Bowl. Courtesy of the Pittsburgh Steelers

CAREER HIGHLIGHTS

Best Season

White played his best ball for the Steelers from 1972 to 1975, posting 33½ of his 46 career sacks over the course of those four seasons. Since he earned consensus First-Team All-AFC honors for the only time in 1973, we'll identify that as his finest season.

Memorable Moments/Greatest Performances

White performed extremely well in his first playoff appearance, recording two sacks during the Steelers' 13–7 victory over Oakland in the 1972 divisional round postseason contest that is remembered primarily for Franco Harris's "Immaculate Reception."

White continued to be a thorn in the side of the Raiders on November 11, 1973, picking off a pair of Daryle Lamonica passes, recording three sacks, and making nine solo tackles, in leading the Steelers to a 17–9 win.

White recorded the second of his two career safeties during a 32–9 victory over the Oilers on November 24, 1975, when he sacked Houston quarterback Dan Pastorini in the end zone for the game's first points.

White had a big game against Dallas in Super Bowl X, recording two of the seven sacks the Steelers registered against Roger Staubach during their 21–17 win.

White picked off two passes for the second time in his career on October 23, 1977, when he intercepted Dan Pastorini twice during a 27–10 victory over the Houston Oilers.

Yet, White is remembered most for his heroic performance in Super Bowl IX, when he climbed out of a hospital bed to help lead the Steelers to a 16–6 win over Minnesota. White, who entered the contest having lost 18 pounds after being diagnosed with pneumonia and a lung infection, played nearly the entire game, making three key tackles early on, before scoring the game's first points when he pounced on Fran Tarkenton in the end zone for a safety following a fumbled snap from center. Recalling his effort years later, White said, "I was so sick . . . I don't think guys play in that condition anymore. I don't know how much I was getting paid, but it wasn't enough."

Notable Achievements

- Recorded safety in Super Bowl IX.
- Ranks ninth in Steelers history with 46 sacks.
- Seven-time division champion (1972, 1974, 1975, 1976, 1977, 1978, and 1979).
- Four-time AFC champion (1974, 1975, 1978, and 1979).
- Four-time Super Bowl champion (IX, X, XIII, and XIV).
- Two-time Pro Bowl selection (1972 and 1973).
- Three-time First-Team All-Conference selection (1972, 1973, and 1975).
- 1974 Second-Team All-Conference selection.
- Named to Steelers' 75th Anniversary Team in 2007.

32

— JOEY PORTER —

A fierce competitor whose style of play very much resembled that of Greg Lloyd, Joey Porter served as the emotional leader of Steeler teams that won three division titles, one AFC championship, and one Super Bowl. An extremely intense player who intimidated the opposition with his verbal taunts and terrorized opposing quarterbacks with his pass-rushing ability, Porter established himself as one of the NFL's most feared players during his eight seasons in Pittsburgh. Before moving on to Miami and, later, Arizona, Porter recorded more than 10 sacks twice as a member of the Steelers, earning in the process Pro Bowl, All-Pro, and All-AFC honors three times each. And, after leaving Pittsburgh, Porter received the additional distinctions of being named to the NFL 2000s All-Decade Team and the Steelers' 75th Anniversary Team.

Born in Bakersfield, California, on March 22, 1977, Joey Eugene Porter attended local Foothill High School, where he lettered in football and basketball, starring on the gridiron as a lineman on defense and as both a wide receiver and running back on offense. After earning All-Conference honors as a senior by carrying the ball 86 times for 1,086 yards, Porter found himself being courted by several colleges for his offensive prowess. Choosing to accept a scholarship offer from Colorado State University, Porter began his college career as an H-back, before finally being moved to the defensive side of the ball in his junior year. Excelling at defensive end his final two seasons at CSU, Porter registered a total of 22 sacks, with his 53 tackles, 15 sacks, eight quarterback pressures, and 12 tackles-for-loss as a senior earning him Third-Team All-America and First-Team All–Western Athletic Conference honors.

Selected by the Steelers in the third round of the 1999 NFL Draft, with the 73rd overall pick, Porter played mostly on special teams as a rookie, although he also managed to record two sacks, 10 tackles, and one forced fumble, which he recovered himself and returned for his first career touchdown. Replacing Carlos Emmons at starting right-outside linebacker

Joey Porter served as the emotional leader of the Steelers during his time in Pittsburgh.
Courtesy of the Pittsburgh Steelers

the following year, Porter finished second on the team with 10½ sacks, while also making 60 tackles (43 solo), forcing two fumbles, recovering another, picking off one pass, registering a safety, and scoring another touchdown. Performing especially well during the month of October, Porter helped lead the Steelers to a perfect 5-0 record, earning in the process recognition as the AFC Defensive Player of the Month.

Continuing his outstanding play in 2001, Porter recorded nine sacks, 59 tackles (45 solo), and four forced fumbles, before earning Pro Bowl and First-Team All-Pro honors the following year by leading the Steelers with nine sacks, 88 tackles, and four interceptions. Even though Porter missed the first two games of the 2003 regular season after he suffered a gunshot wound to his backside during an incident outside a Denver bar on August 31, he put together another solid season, before gaining Pro Bowl and Second-Team All-Pro recognition in each of the next two seasons, recording a total of 17½ sacks and 109 tackles during that time.

One of the most physically gifted linebackers in the NFL, the 6'2", 250-pound Porter possessed outstanding size and speed, with former Steelers running back Chris Fuamatu-Ma'afala stating, "Porter was so fast and could run you over. He was so athletic."

Meanwhile, as Porter established himself as one of the league's top outside linebackers, he also emerged as the vocal leader of the Steelers, both on and off the field, with former teammate Mike Logan saying, "Joey Porter had to be the biggest character that I played with. He always had something to say. But his desire to be the best and play the game at 150 percent made you love him."

Noting that Porter demanded as much from his teammates as he did from himself, Steelers linebacker Andre Frazier stated, "If you didn't run to the ball, Porter gave you that look."

Porter ranks fifth in franchise history with 60 career sacks.
Courtesy of Keith Allison

In discussing the factors that motivated him to play at the highest level possible, Porter said, "That position (linebacker) has to be good. The people that play for us are always going to be measured to some great ones. It doesn't matter how far you go back. From the beginning, with Lambert and Ham, and everybody who started it, it's a long list after those guys who came to Pittsburgh and played linebacker."

An extremely emotional player who enjoyed exchanging barbs with the opposition, Porter followed in the footsteps of Greg Lloyd in that regard, displaying a similar level of intensity on the playing field. However, Porter occasionally took things a bit too far, as he did on November 14, 2004, when he found himself being ejected from a game against the Browns before the contest even began when he and Cleveland running back William Green exchanged blows on the field during pregame practice.

Porter remained in Pittsburgh through the end of the 2006 season, when the Steelers chose to release him rather than pay him $1 million in signing bonuses. Upon announcing the move, Steelers spokesman Dave Lockett said, "It's a business decision that was made." Porter ended his time in Pittsburgh with career totals of 60 sacks, 446 tackles (323 solo), 10 interceptions, 214 interception-return yards, 17 forced fumbles, eight fumble recoveries, and three touchdowns.

After being released by the Steelers, Porter signed a five-year, $32 million deal with the Miami Dolphins, with whom he ended up spending the next three seasons. Having arguably the finest season of his career for the Dolphins in 2008, Porter earned Second-Team All-Pro honors and the last of his four Pro Bowl selections by finishing second in the league with 17½ sacks. That same year, Porter became the first player in NFL history to record at least 10 career interceptions and 70 career sacks. Released by the Dolphins following the conclusion of the 2009 campaign, Porter signed a three-year deal with the Arizona Cardinals on March 19, 2010, just one week before police arrested him on the suspicion of drunken driving and assault on a California Highway Patrol officer. Porter remained in Arizona for two seasons, before being released by the Cardinals early in 2012. He subsequently announced his retirement, but only after he signed a one-day contract with the Steelers that enabled him to officially retire as a member of the team. Upon inking his deal with the Steelers, Porter, who ended his career with 98 sacks, 665 tackles (498 solo), 12 interceptions, 233 interception-return yards, 25 forced fumbles, 10 fumble recoveries, and three touchdowns, said, "This is home. Even when I left—it was okay to go and play for Miami and Arizona—but there's nothing like home. Pittsburgh, once you come through here, it's a special place in your heart here, in Pittsburgh. That void wouldn't have been filled if I didn't come back and retire as a Steeler."

Unfortunately, Porter has continued to run afoul of the law since retiring as an active player, being arrested in Las Vegas in 2012 for passing a bad check at a casino, being accused of punching former Cincinnati Bengals offensive tackle Levi Jones outside a casino that same year, and being arrested at a Pittsburgh bar known as The Flats on Southside early in 2017. Initially charged with aggravated assault, simple assault, resisting arrest, public drunkenness, and disorderly conduct, Porter later had four of the five charges dropped. Yet, despite his numerous run-ins with the law, Porter remains a prominent figure in Pittsburgh, where he currently serves as the Steelers' outside linebacker coach.

STEELERS CAREER HIGHLIGHTS

Best Season

Although Porter recorded 10½ sacks for the Steelers in both 2000 and 2005, he had his finest all-around season for them in 2002, when he earned his lone First-Team All-Pro nomination by registering nine sacks, two forced fumbles, two fumble recoveries, and a career-high four interceptions, 153 interception-return yards, and 88 tackles (60 solo).

Memorable Moments/Greatest Performances

Porter recorded the first sack of his career during a 43–0 manhandling of the Cleveland Browns in the 1999 regular-season opener.

Porter scored his first career touchdown during a 47–36 loss to the Tennessee Titans in the final game of the 1999 regular season, when he forced and recovered a Neil O'Donnell fumble, which he returned 46 yards for a TD.

Porter turned in a tremendous all-around effort against Cincinnati on October 15, 2000, leading the Steelers to a 15–0 win over the Bengals by recording seven solo tackles, three sacks, four quarterback hurries, a safety, and a forced fumble.

Although the Steelers lost to the Philadelphia Eagles in overtime by a score of 26–23 on November 12, 2000, Porter returned a fumble 32 yards for his second career touchdown.

Porter earned AFC Defensive Player of the Week honors for the first time for his performance during a 17–10 win over the Tampa Bay Buccaneers on October 21, 2001, when he recorded four sacks and six tackles.

Although the Steelers suffered a 30–17 defeat at the hands of the Oakland Raiders on September 15, 2002, Porter once again earned AFC

Defensive Player of the Week honors by recording three sacks, seven tackles, and two interceptions, which he returned for a total of 114 yards.

Porter earned that distinction again by recording three sacks, four tackles, and two forced fumbles during a 34–20 victory over the New England Patriots on October 31, 2004.

Porter helped lead the Steelers to a 41–0 rout of the Cleveland Browns on December 24, 2005, by recording three sacks and forcing a fumble, earning in the process AFC Defensive Player of the Week honors for the fourth and final time.

Porter sealed a 28–17 victory over the Miami Dolphins in the 2006 regular-season opener by returning an interception 42 yards for a touchdown with just under three minutes remaining in the fourth quarter.

Notable Achievements

- Scored three defensive touchdowns during career.
- Intercepted four passes in 2002.
- Amassed 153 interception-return yards in 2002.
- Surpassed 10 sacks in a season twice.
- Led Steelers in sacks twice and tackles once.
- Ranks among Steelers career leaders with 60 sacks (5th) and 17 forced fumbles (3rd).
- Three-time division champion (2001, 2002, and 2004).
- 2005 AFC champion.
- Super Bowl XL champion.
- Four-time AFC Defensive Player of the Week.
- October 2000 AFC Defensive Player of the Month.
- 2002 Steelers Co-MVP.
- Three-time Pro Bowl selection (2002, 2004, and 2005).
- 2002 First-Team All-Pro selection.
- Two-time Second-Team All-Pro selection (2004 and 2005).
- Three-time First-Team All-Conference selection (2002, 2004, and 2005).
- Pro Football Hall of Fame All-2000s Second Team.
- Pro Football Reference All-2000s Second Team.
- Named to Steelers' 75th Anniversary Team in 2007.

33

— CASEY HAMPTON —

The greatest nose tackle in Steelers history, Casey Hampton spent 12 seasons in Pittsburgh serving as the anchor of a defense that annually ranked among the league's best. Proving to be a force on that side of the ball, "Big Snack," as he came to be known, used his considerable girth and tremendous strength to help control the running games of opposing offenses, earning in the process five trips to the Pro Bowl and a place on the franchise's 75th Anniversary Team. Meanwhile, Hampton's stellar play on the interior of Pittsburgh's defense helped the Steelers win six division titles, three AFC championships, and two Super Bowls.

Born in Galveston, Texas, on September 3, 1977, Casey Hampton Jr. attended Ball High School, where he lettered in football and track. Starring on the gridiron at linebacker, Hampton twice earned District Defensive Player of the Year honors, gaining recognition as a Texas Class 5A All-State First-Team selection in his senior year. Also excelling as a shotputter and discus-thrower in track and field, Hampton registered top throws of 16.13 meters in the shotput and 48.08 meters in the discus throw.

After enrolling at the University of Texas, Hampton established himself as one of the nation's premier defensive linemen, recording 329 tackles (177 solo), 56 quarterback pressures, and nine forced fumbles while starting 37 consecutive games for the Longhorns between 1997 and 2000. Accorded consensus First-Team All-America honors in both his junior and senior years, Hampton drew praise from teammate Greg Brown, who said, "I have never seen him take a down off, he's just so intent on destroying people that he never takes time to rest. It's gotta be a gift."

In discussing his relentless style of play, Hampton told the *Daily Texan*, the university's student paper, "The way I see it, you never know when your last play is going to be. So, you should go hard all the time. There's no reason to take a play off."

Meanwhile, in addressing the level of dominance he achieved at the collegiate level, Hampton stated, "No one guy can block me. Two guys can probably get it done, but never one guy. I can always overpower one."

Hampton's exceptional play at Texas prompted the New York Jets to select him in the first round of the 2001 NFL Draft, with the 19th overall pick. However, New York ended up trading him and two later-round picks to the Steelers for wide receiver Santana Moss, who Pittsburgh tabbed with the 16th overall pick of that year's draft.

Laying claim to the starting nose tackle job shortly after he arrived in Pittsburgh, Hampton put together a solid rookie season, helping the Steelers finish first in the NFL in total yards allowed on defense with his outstanding play at the point of attack. Although Hampton recorded just one sack and 22 tackles his first year in the league, he occupied multiple blockers on virtually every play, thereby allowing the other members of Pittsburgh's front seven to frequently bring down opposing ball-carriers near the line of scrimmage.

Yet, Hampton, who played alongside fellow defensive tackle and future NFL star Shaun Rogers in a 4-3 scheme at Texas, later admitted that it took

him some time to adjust to the role he assumed in Pittsburgh's 3-4 defense, saying, "It took a while. Probably took into my second year to realize every play isn't for me to make and I'm not supposed to be out there making plays; just playing within the defense. . . . It's tough, man, when you're used to making plays and getting up the field, and you're pretty good at it, and they ask you to do something entirely different. But you've just got to be unselfish and see the bigger picture."

After recording two sacks, 40 tackles, two forced fumbles, and one fumble recovery in his sophomore campaign of 2002, Hampton earned Pro Bowl honors for the first of five times the following year by registering one sack and 39 tackles.

Casey Hampton anchored the Steelers defense from his nose tackle position for 12 seasons.
Courtesy of the Pittsburgh Steelers

A torn ACL in his right knee subsequently limited Hampton to just six games in 2004. But he returned the following year to help lead the Steelers to their first NFL championship in 26 seasons, earning in the process the first of his three consecutive Pro Bowl selections.

Over the course of his first few seasons in Pittsburgh, Hampton came to very much enjoy performing for the fans at Heinz Field, stating during a 2002 interview with texas sports.com, "This is a football town. When we win, everyone is happy, but when we lose, everyone is mad. It's the type of town you want to be in. Every game is sold out, and they are

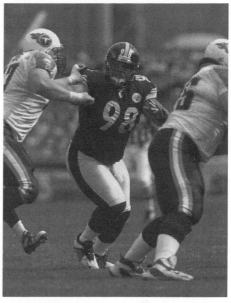

Hampton played for two Super Bowl championship teams during his time in Pittsburgh.
Courtesy of the Pittsburgh Steelers

die-hard up here. It's a very fun place to play."

Hampton also established himself as one of the league's best run-stuffers during his early years with the Steelers. Extremely difficult to move out of the middle, Hampton played low to the ground and typically occupied the center and either guard, thereby allowing the inside linebackers to make an inordinate number of tackles. A three-down lineman in his prime, Hampton also did a good job of applying pressure up the middle to opposing quarterbacks, making him arguably the NFL's finest all-around nose tackle.

Although listed at 6'1" and 325 pounds, Hampton weighed much closer to 350 pounds throughout most of his career. Admitting that he paid little attention to his weight, Hampton said, "I don't talk about weight. It doesn't do any good. If I say I weigh something, then somebody says I don't weigh that. It becomes a back-and-forth thing . . . I come into camp at a certain weight, and I lose what I need to lose. I don't weigh in. I never have. I've never been fined for my weight."

Hampton then added, "I've never been ashamed of my size. I'm a big dude. But I'm a smooth big guy. I'm not like a big fat guy. I got some swag to myself. You've got to have a little swag, and you've got to know how to carry it. I know how to do that."

Continuing to serve as the anchor of Pittsburgh's defense for seven more seasons, Hampton missed just nine games between 2006 and 2012, earning three trips to the Pro Bowl during that time, while helping the Steelers win two more AFC championships and one more Super Bowl. But, after Hampton became a free agent following the conclusion of the 2012 campaign, the Steelers chose not to re-sign him. Failing to receive a contract offer from any other team, Hampton elected to announce his retirement, ending his career with nine sacks, 373 tackles (205 solo), four forced fumbles, and two fumble recoveries, which he returned for a total of 36 yards. During his 12 seasons in Pittsburgh, the Steelers finished with the NFL's number one ranked defense in terms of points allowed four times and yards allowed six times, placing first in both categories on three separate occasions.

In discussing the role he assumed in Pittsburgh's defense and the legacy he left behind during a 2018 interview with the Talk of Fame Network, Hampton said, "Nobody plays the true nose-tackle position like I played it because the game has changed so much. I mean, I was like a two-gapper all the time. That's what I did. And I don't think guys really do that anymore . . . I think it's more up-the-field and get-to-the quarterback because it's such a passing league now. So, I think what I did is almost entirely extinct now. It's still the nose-tackle position, but it's entirely different the way they play it now."

Hampton then added that he derived a great deal of pleasure from disrupting opposing offenses, stating, "It was something I ended up taking a lot of pride in. I had a lot of great linebackers that played behind me, and it was just fun to see those guys go out there and make plays. That's pretty much what I got my joy out of—watching those guys do their thing and watching our defense be successful."

CAREER HIGHLIGHTS

Best Season

Hampton had his finest overall season for the Steelers in 2009, earning one of his five trips to the Pro Bowl by recording a career-high 2½ sacks and 43 tackles (23 solo), while clogging up the middle for a Pittsburgh defense that allowed the third fewest rushing yards in the league.

Memorable Moments/Greatest Performances

Hampton turned in an outstanding all-around effort during a 30–14 win over Carolina on December 15, 2002, recording a sack and anchoring a defense that surrendered just 50 yards on the ground and 131 yards of total offense to the Panthers.

Hampton and the rest of Pittsburgh's defensive front dominated New England at the point of attack on October 31, 2002, holding the Patriots to just five yards rushing during a 34–20 win.

Hampton and his line-mates once again dominated the opposition on November 7, 2004, limiting Philadelphia to only 23 yards rushing and 113 yards of total offense during a 27–3 victory.

Hampton made a key play during the Steelers' 21–10 win over Seattle in Super Bowl XL, helping them protect their slim 14–10 fourth-quarter lead by sacking Matt Hasselbeck for a 5-yard loss at the Pittsburgh 34-yard line, leading to an Ike Taylor interception two plays later.

Notable Achievements

- Six-time division champion (2001, 2002, 2004, 2007, 2008, and 2010).
- Three-time AFC champion (2005, 2008, and 2010).
- Two-time Super Bowl champion (XL and XLIII).
- 2005 Steelers Co-MVP.
- Five-time Pro Bowl selection (2003, 2005, 2006, 2007, and 2009).
- Named to Steelers' 75th Anniversary Team in 2007.

34

— JON KOLB —

emembered primarily for his tremendous physical strength, Jon Kolb spent most of his career protecting Terry Bradshaw's blind side from his left tackle position, which he manned for the Steelers for the better part of 11 seasons. Serving as the starter at that post from 1971 to 1981, Kolb contributed significantly to Pittsburgh teams that won seven division titles, four AFC championships, and four Super Bowls, with his consistently excellent play earning him one All-Pro selection, five All-AFC nominations, and a spot on the Steelers' 75th Anniversary Team.

Born in Ponca City, Oklahoma, on August 30, 1947, Jon Paul Kolb grew up on his family's farm milking cows and doing field work. After attending Owasso High School, where he earned All-State honors as a senior for his performance on the gridiron, Kolb enrolled at Oklahoma State University. Starting at center for the Cowboys for three seasons, Kolb earned two All–Big Eight selections and All-America recognition in his senior year of 1968.

Subsequently selected by the Steelers in the third round of the 1969 NFL Draft, with the 56th overall pick, Kolb spent his first two seasons in Pittsburgh playing almost exclusively on special teams, before finally breaking into the starting lineup in 1971. Laying claim to the starting left tackle job that year, Kolb remained at that post for the next 11 seasons, starting 125 out of a possible 130 contests between 1971 and 1979.

Stationed immediately next to left guard Sam Davis throughout that nine-year period, Kolb combined with Davis to provide solid pass protection and excellent lead-blocking on the left side of the line for a dominant Steelers team that gradually transitioned from a run-first offense to a more balanced attack. Making good use of his great physical strength, tremendous balance, and outstanding technique, Kolb allowed quarterback Terry Bradshaw to survey the field for open receivers, while also opening holes in the running game for backs Franco Harris, Rocky Bleier, and John Fuqua. Playing his best ball for Pittsburgh from 1974 to 1979, Kolb earned one

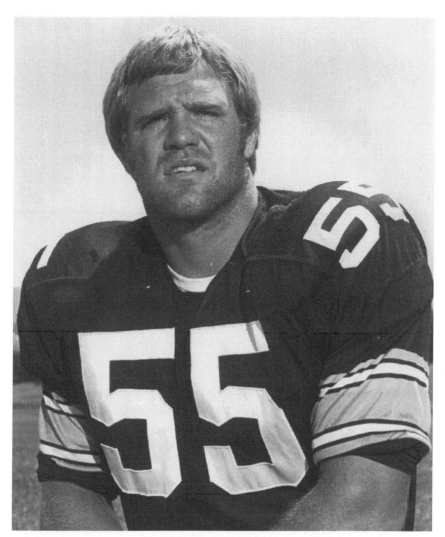

Jon Kolb started at left tackle for the Steelers from 1971 to 1981.
Courtesy of the Pittsburgh Steelers

All-Pro nomination and five All-Conference selections over the course of those six seasons, in helping the Steelers win four NFL championships.

Yet, as much as Kolb contributed to the success of the Steelers with his exceptional blocking, he became equally well known for his appearances in the *World's Strongest Man* competition, placing in the top three in both 1978 and 1979. Kolb also won the *NFL's Strongest Man Contest* in 1978, before finishing second to teammate Mike Webster two years later.

Kolb earned five All-AFC nominations while playing for the Steelers.
Courtesy of the Pittsburgh Steelers

Kolb, who stood 6'2" tall and weighed 262 pounds, would certainly be considered small for an offensive lineman by today's standards. Nevertheless, he rivaled anyone in the league in terms of sheer physical strength during his playing days, combining with teammates Steve Furness, Mike Webster, and Steve Courson to form the "500 Club," which typically gathered in the Red Bull Inn to conduct bench press routines of 500 pounds or more. Unfortunately, both Webster and Courson ended up passing away at relatively young ages, with Courson admitting to using steroids before he died, and Webster being suspected of doing the same. Whether or not Kolb artificially enhanced his performance in any way remains very much an open question.

After Kolb missed just three games the previous 11 seasons, injuries to his neck, shoulder, and ankles limited him to only seven contests in 1980. Having lost his starting job to Ray Pinney, Kolb started just six games in 1981, before announcing his retirement at season's end. Upon announcing his decision, Kolb stated, "Every time I scratch my head and my shoulder hurts, I know I've made the right decision. I enjoyed my 13 years as a Steeler player, and they'll always be a part of me. The hardest part about retirement is leaving the people I had as teammates. There's just an intangible closeness that you cannot explain. . . . In thinking about this, the things I'm going to miss are the Joe Greenes, the Sam Davises, the Dwight Whites, and the Mike Wagners. Those are the guys who I think of as the Steelers."

Following his playing days, Kolb spent several seasons serving on Chuck Noll's coaching staff, working at different times with the offensive line, tight ends, and defensive line, while also serving as the team's strength and conditioning coach. After leaving the game, Kolb, who currently resides with his wife in Hermitage, Pennsylvania, became a physical therapist and sports performance coach. He also teaches part-time in the Human Performance and Exercise Science department at Youngstown State University.

CAREER HIGHLIGHTS

Best Season

Kolb had his finest all-around season in 1979, when the Newspaper Enterprise Association accorded him First-Team All-Pro honors after he helped the Steelers finish first in the NFL in total offense. In addition to leading the way for Steeler running backs to amass the second-most rushing yards in the league (2,603), Kolb did an exceptional job of protecting Terry Bradshaw's blind side, enabling him to throw for a career-high 3,724 yards.

Memorable Moments/Greatest Performances

Kolb helped Steeler running backs rush for a season-high 230 yards during a 26–9 win over the Cleveland Browns on November 7, 1971.

Kolb and his offensive line–mates did a superb job of blocking up front during a 24–7 victory over the Houston Oilers on October 15, 1972, enabling the Steelers to gain a season-high 249 yards on the ground.

Kolb excelled once again during a 28–7 win over the New Orleans Saints on November 25, 1974, helping the Steelers amass a total of 272 yards on the ground.

Kolb and the rest of Pittsburgh's offensive line turned in another dominant performance during a 33–30 overtime victory over the Browns on November 25, 1979, enabling the Steelers to amass 606 yards of total offense, with 255 of those coming on the ground.

Notable Achievements

- Missed just three games in first 11 seasons, appearing in every contest in each of first eight seasons.
- Seven-time division champion (1972, 1974, 1975, 1976, 1977, 1978, and 1979).
- Four-time AFC champion (1974, 1975, 1978, and 1979).

- Four-time Super Bowl champion (IX, X, XIII, and XIV).
- 1979 NEA First-Team All-Pro selection.
- Two-time First-Team All-Conference selection (1975 and 1978).
- Three-time Second-Team All-Conference selection (1974, 1976, and 1979).
- Named to Steelers' 75th Anniversary Team in 2007.

35

— MIKE WAGNER —

Perhaps the most overlooked and underappreciated member of Pittsburgh's dominant defense of the 1970s, Mike Wagner spent the entire decade serving as the cerebral quarterback of the Steelers' defensive backfield. Despite being overshadowed much of the time by the other members of Pittsburgh's "Steel Curtain" defense, Wagner did an outstanding job of patrolling the secondary from his safety position, helping to lead the Steelers to four AFC championships and four Super Bowl wins. Wagner's consistently strong play ended up earning him two trips to the Pro Bowl, one All-Pro selection, four All-AFC nominations, and a spot on the Steelers' 50th Anniversary Team.

Born in Waukegan, Illinois, on June 22, 1949, Michael Robert Wagner attended Carmel High School, a Catholic school in the suburban Chicago area, where he starred on the gridiron as a wide receiver and defensive lineman. Looking back at his days at Carmel High, Wagner says, "It was very comparable to Western Pennsylvania high school football. I was a skinny kid and didn't get any scholarship offers, so I went to Western Illinois and just tried out for the team."

After earning a spot on the Western Illinois University football team as a walk-on, Wagner had to wait until his junior year to be awarded a scholarship, recalling, "Until the beginning of my junior year, WIU did not have athletic scholarships to offer its student athletes. I had to convince Coach (Darrell) Mudra to give me a scholarship in 1969 when WIU began funding athletic scholarships."

Wagner continued, "He did not want to give me one, saying that I was already there, and he could use it to bring another player to the school. I told him my dad was a factory worker raising two more boys behind me, that my mom went to work to help pay for my schooling, and that I deserved one. I had to threaten him that I would not play or transfer unless he gave me one."

Mike Wagner spent 10 seasons quarterbacking the Steelers' defensive
secondary from his safety position.
Courtesy of the Pittsburgh Steelers

Finally granted a scholarship by Mudra, Wagner went on to earn NAIA
All-America honors as a junior, with former WIU assistant coach Pete
Rodriguez later saying of his protégé, "Mike Wagner was the All-American
boy. He had all the attributes to be a fine player. You don't find someone
like him at Western Illinois usually. He got overlooked by a lot of people
and bigger schools. He really blossomed at Western."

Wagner, who began his college career as a 6'1", 185-pound defensive end, revealed that he first began thinking about playing football professionally during his junior year, stating, "I felt I had a shot at the pros. I felt I was fast enough, tough enough, and big enough. I wasn't sure what they (the Steelers) were thinking, but they drafted me at the right time when they were rebuilding."

Selected by the Steelers in the 11th round of the 1971 NFL Draft, with the 268th overall pick, Wagner got an early look at wide receiver, before Pittsburgh's coaching staff moved him to the defensive side of the ball. Establishing himself as the team's starting strong safety by the start of the regular season, Wagner performed well as a rookie, making two interceptions, which he returned for a total of 53 yards, before missing the final two games of the campaign with an injury. Looking back at his first NFL season, Wagner recalls, "I learned under fire." Wagner followed that up by intercepting six passes in 1972, before earning First-Team All-AFC honors for the first of three times the next season by leading the NFL with eight interceptions.

Considered the leader of Pittsburgh's young defensive secondary by 1974, Wagner became known for his intelligence and football acumen, with longtime teammate Andy Russell later saying, "I think Mike was the best safety the Steelers ever had. He was intelligent."

In addressing the manner with which he came to be viewed, Wagner suggests, "People hang tags on you. There is a certain amount of thinking on the football field. Coaches love talent, and I don't think I was the most talented, but I tried not to make mental mistakes. I didn't have the quickest step, but I put myself in the correct position, then I would be able to make plays, and I accepted that challenge."

Wagner added, "My theory on being a defensive back is that there might be a breakdown in coverage. I would play soft, where most coaches would say take care of your business and do what you're supposed to do."

In addition to doing an excellent job in pass coverage, the 6'1", 200-pound Wagner proved to be a sure tackler who opposing wide receivers feared coming over the middle.

Wagner continued to perform well for the Steelers at strong safety until 1977, when he fractured three vertebrae in his neck while making a tackle in Week 3, bringing his season to a premature end. Moved to free safety upon his return to the team in 1978, Wagner helped the Steelers win their third Super Bowl in five years, later saying of that championship campaign, "It was the season when most of the media and the fans were saying that we were too old and not hungry enough. There were a lot of challenges to

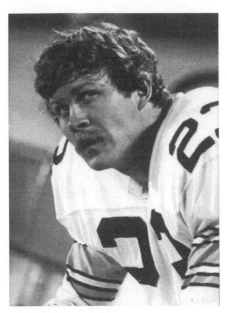

Wagner led the NFL with eight interceptions in 1973.
Courtesy of the Pittsburgh Steelers

win that game at the time. I just thought it was the best thing all the way around."

Wagner remained in Pittsburgh two more years, before announcing his retirement after finishing second on the team with six interceptions in 1980. He ended his career with 36 interceptions, 491 interception-return yards, and 12 fumble recoveries, ranking among the franchise's all-time leaders in each of the first two categories.

Following his playing days, Wagner spent many years working in the financial industry, serving as vice president of the Private Banking Group for First National Bank in Pittsburgh, where he provided personalized services for affluent households. Now retired, Wagner looks back fondly on his playing career, taking special pride in the contributions he made to the success of the Steelers. In discussing the legacy that the Steeler teams of the 1970s left behind, Wagner says, "From our perspective, we are the standard that others use to determine their position behind us. No other team has yet to win four Super Bowl championships in six years, and we won under the 'old rules' and the 'new' rules."

Wagner continued, "What set us apart was that we didn't do a lot of different things offensively or defensively, we just did them better than other teams. A lot of that had to do with Chuck Noll and his staff's stubbornness to stick to fundamentals, to take care of your own responsibility, and to make as few mental mistakes as possible. Of course, it did help that we had nine NFL Hall of Famers, and a couple more yet to be honored, on those '70s teams."

Wagner then added, "One of the really great things about being a Pittsburgh Steeler from those championship teams is the gleam that people get in their eyes when they recognize us. There's a great sense of pride in how the fans bonded with the team and vice-versa."

CAREER HIGHLIGHTS

Best Season

Although Wagner earned All-Pro honors for the only time in his career in 1976, he made his greatest overall impact in 1973, when he led the NFL with eight interceptions and placed near the top of the league rankings with 134 interception-return yards and five fumble recoveries.

Memorable Moments/Greatest Performances

Wagner recorded the first interception of his career during a 27–17 loss to the Cleveland Browns on October 10, 1971.

Wagner contributed to a 38–21 win over the San Diego Chargers on October 7, 1973, by intercepting a pass and scoring the only touchdown of his career when he recovered a fumble in the end zone on special teams.

Wagner recorded three interceptions in one game twice, accomplishing the feat for the first time during a 20–13 win over the Cincinnati Bengals on October 28, 1973.

Wagner had another big day against Cincinnati on November 2, 1975, picking off two passes and amassing 83 interception-return yards during a 30–24 victory.

Wagner picked off three passes in one game for the second time in his career on September 28, 1980, doing so during a 38–3 rout of the Chicago Bears.

Wagner played a key role in Pittsburgh's 16–10 victory over Oakland in the 1975 AFC championship game, intercepting Raiders quarterback Ken Stabler twice.

Wagner also recorded an interception in each of Pittsburgh's first two Super Bowl appearances, with his pick and subsequent 19-yard return in the fourth quarter of Super Bowl X, which helped set up a field goal that increased the Steeler lead to five points, being perhaps the most memorable play of his career.

Notable Achievements

- Scored one touchdown during career.
- Recorded at least six interceptions three times.
- Surpassed 100 interception-return yards twice.
- Led NFL with eight interceptions in 1973.

- Finished third in NFL with 84 fumble-return yards in 1974.
- Finished fourth in NFL with five fumble recoveries in 1973.
- Led Steelers in interceptions once.
- Ranks among Steelers career leaders with 36 interceptions (6th) and 491 interception-return yards (7th).
- Seven-time division champion (1972, 1974, 1975, 1976, 1977, 1978, and 1979).
- Four-time AFC champion (1974, 1975, 1978, and 1979).
- Four-time Super Bowl champion (IX, X, XIII, and XIV).
- Two-time Pro Bowl selection (1975 and 1976).
- 1976 Second-Team All-Pro selection.
- Three-time First-Team All-Conference selection (1973, 1975, and 1976).
- 1978 Second-Team All-Conference selection.
- Named to Steelers' 50th Anniversary Team in 1982.

36

— BUDDY DIAL —

The first Steelers player to surpass 1,000 receiving yards in a season, Buddy Dial spent five of his eight NFL seasons in Pittsburgh, establishing himself during that time as one of the league's most dynamic offensive players. A threat to score from anywhere on the field, Dial averaged 21.6 yards per reception as a member of the Steelers, leading the league in that category twice. The sure-handed Dial also annually placed near the top of the league rankings in receptions, receiving yards, and touchdown receptions, earning in the process two trips to the Pro Bowl and one All-Pro nomination. And, more than 50 years after he appeared in his last NFL game, Dial's career average of 20.8 yards per catch remains the second-best in league history.

Born in Ponca City, Oklahoma, on January 17, 1937, Gilbert Leroy Dial grew up in Magnolia, Texas, where he attended Magnolia High School. Excelling as an end/linebacker in six-man football while in high school, Dial earned All-District honors three times, helping to lead his team to bi-district victories his junior and senior years. Continuing to star on the gridiron after enrolling at Rice University, Dial made 21 receptions for 357 yards and five touchdowns in 1956, while also performing so well on defense that he gained recognition as the sophomore lineman of the year in the Southwest Conference. Dial followed that up with two more outstanding seasons for the Owls, earning All–Southwest Conference honors as a junior, before receiving consensus All-America and Columbus Touchdown Club Lineman of the Year honors as a senior in 1958.

Subsequently selected by the New York Giants in the second round of the 1959 NFL Draft, with the 22nd overall pick, Dial failed to appear in a single game with the Giants, who waived him prior to the start of the regular season. Immediately picked up by the Steelers, Dial soon showed that the New York coaching staff made an error in judgment, making 16 receptions for 428 yards and six touchdowns in somewhat limited duty as a rookie in 1959. Emerging as one of the NFL's top deep threats the following season, Dial began an outstanding four-year run during which he posted the following numbers:

YEAR	REC	REC YD	TD REC	YDS/REC
1960	40	972	9	**24.3**
1961	53	1,047	12	19.8
1962	50	981	6	19.6
1963	60	1,295	9	**21.6**

In addition to leading the NFL in average yards per reception in two of those four seasons, Dial finished second in the league in receiving yards twice and TD catches once, earning in the process two trips to the Pro Bowl, one First-Team All-Conference nomination, and one Second-Team All-Pro selection. Teaming up with quarterback Bobby Layne, Dial formed one-half of one of the NFL's deadliest passing combinations, collaborating with Layne on four scoring plays that covered at least 70 yards, two of which went for more than 80 yards.

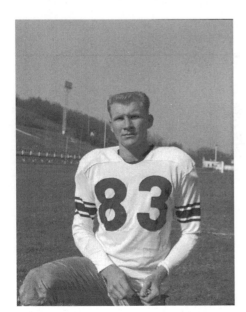

Buddy Dial's 1,047 receiving yards in 1961 made him the first player in Steelers history to top the magical 1,000-yard mark.
Courtesy of the Pittsburgh Steelers

Developing a reputation as one of the league's most difficult men to cover, Dial drew praise from opposing defensive back Jimmy Hill, who said, "He catches every damn thing that comes to him."

In discussing the attributes that made the 6'1", 194-pound Dial one of the league's most successful wideouts, former Steelers halfback Dick Hoak raved, "Buddy Dial was a heck of a receiver. He was the real deal. He had some speed, the moves, had great hands and no fear—he could catch the ball over the middle. He had all the things you want in a receiver. He had pretty good size too for the position. He was very good."

Nevertheless, the Steelers decided to part ways with Dial following the conclusion of the 1963 campaign, trading him to the Dallas Cowboys for the rights to Dallas's first-round draft pick, Scott Appleton, the All-America defensive tackle from the University of Texas whom the Cowboys had selected with the fourth overall pick of the 1964 NFL Draft. But, with the Houston Oilers also using their first-round pick in that year's AFL Draft to claim Appleton, the Texas native chose to remain

Dial averaged a franchise-best 21.6 yards per reception during his time in Pittsburgh. Courtesy of the Pittsburgh Steelers

close to home and joined the Oilers. With Appleton never appearing in a single game with the Steelers, the Pittsburgh-Dallas deal subsequently became known as the "Buddy Dial for nothing" trade.

Dial, who left the Steelers with career totals of 219 receptions, 4,723 receiving yards, and 42 TD catches, ended up accomplishing very little as a member of the Cowboys over the course of the next three seasons, making just 42 receptions for 713 yards and two touchdowns, before announcing his retirement at the end of 1966 after suffering a serious back injury. Yet, Dial, who started Christian devotional services during his time in Pittsburgh, contributed significantly to the moral fiber of the Dallas community, greatly increasing the number of individuals in the area who joined the Fellowship of Christian Athletes.

Following his playing career, Dial settled in the Houston suburb of Tomball, where he continued his work for the Lord, becoming a prominent speaker for many local civic, church, and charity groups. Unfortunately, Dial's addiction to pain pills that he developed during his time in Dallas eventually caused him to suffer from kidney failure, which, combined with prostate cancer, ended up taking his life. Dial died at the age of 71, on February 29, 2008. Upon learning of his passing, Steelers chairman Dan Rooney said, "He came at a time when you were really switching over to the modern-day game. He was a great receiver for us, and he played extremely well and gave us an opportunity to play in that transition."

STEELERS CAREER HIGHLIGHTS

Best Season

Dial earned his first trip to the Pro Bowl in 1961 by making 53 receptions for 1,047 yards and finishing second in the NFL with 12 touchdown receptions. However, he posted the best overall numbers of his career in 1963, earning his lone All-Pro selection by placing near the top of the league rankings with 60 receptions, 1,295 receiving yards, nine TD catches, and 1,300 all-purpose yards, while also topping the circuit with an average of 21.6 yards per catch.

Memorable Moments/Greatest Performances

Dial scored the first touchdown of his career during a 21–16 loss to the Giants on October 25, 1959, when he collaborated with quarterback Bobby Layne on a 35-yard TD pass late in the fourth quarter. He finished the game with four receptions for 146 yards and that one touchdown.

Dial contributed to a 35–28 win over the expansion Dallas Cowboys in the 1960 regular-season opener by making two catches for 84 yards and one touchdown, which came on a season-long 70-yard connection with quarterback Tom Tracy.

Dial helped the Steelers forge a 27–27 tie with the Washington Redskins on October 23, 1960, by making seven receptions for 187 yards and one touchdown, which came on a 27-yard hookup with Rudy Bukich in the fourth quarter.

Although the Steelers lost their October 22, 1961 meeting with the Cleveland Browns by a score of 30–28, Dial had a huge afternoon, making nine receptions for a career-high 235 yards and two TDs, one of which went for 88 yards.

Dial helped lead the Steelers to a convincing 37–7 win over the Cowboys on November 12, 1961, by making six receptions for 148 yards and two touchdowns, which covered 15 and 73 yards.

Dial torched the St. Louis secondary for seven catches and a season-high 186 receiving yards during a 19–7 victory over the Cardinals on December 2, 1962.

Dial served as a key figure in Pittsburgh's 38–27 win over Washington on October 20, 1963, making six catches for 155 yards and one touchdown, with his 4-yard hookup with Ed Brown late in the fourth quarter sealing the victory for the Steelers.

Dial turned in another outstanding effort the following week, leading the Steelers to a 27–21 win over the Dallas Cowboys by making seven receptions for 162 yards, and scoring all three Pittsburgh touchdowns on pass plays that covered 83, 25, and 14 yards.

Yet, even though the Steelers suffered a 42–27 home loss to the Cowboys on October 21, 1962, Dial experienced the most famous (or infamous) moment of his career during the contest. After Dial, who finished the game with nine catches for 157 yards and two touchdowns, gathered in one of his TD passes, he entered the Dallas end zone, only to be startled by the explosion of a large cannon Pittsburgh's cheerleading squad set off right in front of him (a Steelers tradition). Captured on film, the incident has appeared on the "NFL's Greatest Follies" countless times through the years.

Notable Achievements

- Surpassed 50 receptions three times.
- Surpassed 1,000 receiving yards twice, topping 900 yards two other times.
- Made 12 touchdown receptions in 1961.
- Averaged more than 20 yards per reception three times.
- Never missed a game in five seasons with Steelers.
- Led NFL in average yards per reception twice.
- Finished second in NFL in receiving yards twice and touchdown receptions once.
- Led Steelers in receptions four times and receiving yards four times.
- Holds Steelers career record for most yards per reception (21.6).
- Ranks among Steelers career leaders with 4,723 receiving yards (8th) and 42 touchdown receptions (6th).
- Two-time Pro Bowl selection (1961 and 1963).
- 1963 Second-Team All-Pro selection.
- 1961 First-Team All-Conference selection.

37

— RAY MANSFIELD —

Perhaps remembered most as the man who immediately preceded Mike Webster as the starting center in Pittsburgh, Ray Mansfield spent 13 of his 14 NFL seasons with the Steelers, establishing a legacy of durability during that time that he passed on to other players who have since manned that post for the Black and Gold. Appearing in a franchise-record 182 consecutive contests, Mansfield never missed a game his entire career, helping the Steelers win four division titles, two AFC championships, and their first two Super Bowls. And, although Mansfield, who began his professional career as a defensive lineman, never appeared in the Pro Bowl or gained All-Pro recognition, he earned All-AFC honors twice, with his veteran leadership making him one of the most valued members of the Steelers for much of the 1970s.

Born in Bakersfield, California, on January 21, 1941, Bert James Ray Mansfield grew up in Kennewick, Washington, where he attended Kennewick High School. After starring on the gridiron in high school, Mansfield accepted an athletic scholarship from the University of Washington, where he spent his final two seasons starting at center for head coach Jim Owens, who later called him "one of the top linemen ever at Washington."

Making an extremely favorable impression on his Husky teammates as well, Mansfield drew praise from quarterback Bob Schloredt, who described him as "a very intense player and a very smart player. He had good size and quickness. He was a big center who could snap the ball and move. He had great instincts."

Mansfield's strong play in college earned him First-Team All-Coast and Third-Team All-America honors as a senior in 1962, prompting the Philadelphia Eagles to select him in the second round of the 1963 NFL Draft, with the 18th overall pick. Also selected by the Denver Broncos in the fifth round of that year's AFL Draft, with the 37th overall pick, Mansfield ultimately chose to sign with the Eagles, who used him at defensive tackle his first year in the league.

Acquired by the Steelers during the subsequent offseason, Mansfield spent his first two seasons in Pittsburgh at left defensive tackle, before being shifted to the offensive side of the ball in 1966. Returning to his more natural position of center, Mansfield remained the starter at that post for the next 10 seasons, serving as the anchor of Pittsburgh's offensive line. Despite being surrounded by very little talent from 1966 to 1971, the 6'3", 250-pound Mansfield developed a reputation as one of the NFL's better offensive linemen, with his solid play earning him respect throughout the league. Mansfield, who acquired the nick-

Ray Mansfield immediately preceded Mike Webster as Pittsburgh's starting center. Courtesy of the Pittsburgh Steelers

name "Ranger" due to his love of the outdoors, also gradually emerged as one of the leaders in the Pittsburgh locker room, with his fun-loving, cigar-smoking, comedic ways making him arguably the team's most popular player.

More than anything, though, Mansfield became known for his strong work ethic and extraordinary durability, never missing a game in a 25-year amateur and pro playing career. Displaying his toughness on one occasion in 1974, Mansfield played an entire game with an ankle sprained so badly that it puffed up to twice its normal size, hiding the injury from his teammates and coaches.

Remaining a fixture at center after the Steelers emerged as an NFL powerhouse during the early 1970s, Mansfield made huge contributions to the success they experienced from 1972 to 1976, earning Second-Team All-Conference honors in two of those five seasons. Mansfield also spent his final three seasons in Pittsburgh mentoring young offensive lineman Mike Webster, who ended up replacing him as the team's starting center in 1976. Choosing to announce his retirement in July 1977, Mansfield ended his career having played in 196 consecutive games as a pro, with 182 of those coming as a member of the Steelers.

Mansfield appeared in a franchise-record 182 straight games.
Courtesy of the Pittsburgh Steelers

After retiring as an active player, Mansfield became a successful insurance broker in the Pittsburgh area, devoting much more of his time to the job he previously held during the offseason. Unfortunately, Mansfield's life ended abruptly on November 3, 1996, when he died while hiking in the Grand Canyon with his son and another companion. The 55-year-old Mansfield, who began experiencing problems with one of his ankles, told the others to go on without him, stating that he would catch up with them later that evening at the campsite. However, he never showed up, with his body subsequently being found the following morning sitting with his back against a big rock, cigar in hand, facing a magnificent vista where the sun would have set the previous evening. With Mansfield's family history of cardiac illness, the Coconino County Park Service declared that he likely died of natural causes, apparently of a heart attack.

Upon learning of his onetime teammate's passing, former Steelers defensive lineman John Banaszak said, "He was an adventurer. That was his element. That was his form of competition . . . recreation and relaxation."

Banaszak then called Mansfield a role model on and off the field who frequently told tales of their days together on the Steelers, stating, "I can see him with a big cigar telling those stories, and it brings a smile to my face right now."

Meanwhile, former Steelers head coach Chuck Noll remembered Mansfield as "a special person," saying, "He was one of the guys who was a Steeler when I arrived in 1969, and he was great in the locker room. He was a guy that everybody rallied around. He always had a certain amount of levity, but he was a tremendous football player."

STEELERS CAREER HIGHLIGHTS

Best Season

Mansfield did his best job of blocking at the point of attack in 1972, when, en route to earning All-Conference honors for one of two times, he helped the Steelers compile the second-most rushing yards in the NFL (2,520) and post the highest rushing average in the league (5.1 yards per carry).

Memorable Moments/Greatest Performances

Mansfield and the rest of Pittsburgh's offensive line turned in a dominant performance against Chicago in the 1967 regular-season opener, enabling Steeler running backs to rush for a season-high 195 yards and three touchdowns during a lopsided 41–13 victory.

Mansfield and his line-mates once again dominated the opposition on October 22, 1972, helping Steeler running backs gain 243 yards on the ground during a convincing 33–3 win over the New England Patriots.

In perhaps his greatest performance, Mansfield anchored a Pittsburgh offensive line that led the way for Steeler backs to rush for 249 yards during the team's 16–6 victory over the Minnesota Vikings in Super Bowl IX.

Mansfield is also remembered for kicking the extra point on the Steelers' final touchdown of their 40–14 win over the Baltimore Colts in the divisional round of the 1976 postseason tournament. Mansfield, who doubled as a placekicker in college, found himself pressed into duty after Roy Gerela pulled a groin muscle earlier in the contest.

Notable Achievements

- Never missed a game in 13 seasons with Steelers, appearing in franchise-record 182 consecutive contests during that time.
- Four-time division champion (1972, 1974, 1975, and 1976).
- Two-time AFC champion (1974 and 1975).
- Two-time Super Bowl champion (IX and X).
- Two-time Second-Team All-Conference selection (1972 and 1975).

38

— JOHN HENRY JOHNSON —

While the Steeler defenses of the 1950s and early 1960s became known for their bruising style of play, John Henry Johnson used his punishing running style and devastating blocking to bring the same type of physicality to the Pittsburgh offense. Blessed with a rare combination of speed, power, and superior blocking ability, Johnson drew praise from none other than the great Jim Brown, who once called him the greatest running back he had ever seen. Often described as the perfect NFL fullback, Johnson became, in 1962, the first Steelers running back to rush for more than 1,000 yards in a season, a feat he duplicated two years later at the age of 35. In all, Johnson led the Steelers in rushing in four of his five full seasons in Pittsburgh, earning in the process three trips to the Pro Bowl and one All-Pro nomination. And, even though Johnson did not truly emerge as one of the NFL's elite running backs until after he joined the Steelers at the rather advanced age of 30, he ended up earning a place in the Pro Football Hall of Fame with his exceptional all-around play as a member of the team.

Born in the tiny Mississippi River delta cotton-farming community of Waterproof, Louisiana, on November 24, 1929, John Henry Johnson grew up during a time of segregation, in a town that did not make high school available to black students. Leaving Waterproof at 16 years of age to live with an older brother stationed at Camp Stoneman in Pittsburg, California, Johnson told the *Pittsburgh Post-Dispatch* in 1986, "My parents wanted to give me a chance for an education, so they sent me to live with my brother. Anything was better than Waterproof."

After enrolling in Pittsburg Junior High School as a ninth-grader in the spring of 1946, Johnson began competing in organized sports for the first time, eventually establishing himself as the area's finest all-around athlete. In addition to earning All–Contra Costa County Athletic League honors three straight times for his outstanding play on the gridiron, Johnson excelled in basketball, track and field, and baseball, twice leading the league in scoring on the hardwood, winning the state discus championship in 1949 and establishing new meet records in the shotput and 180-yard low hurdles at the North Coast champion- ships, and batting over .500 in the one season he played baseball.

Following his graduation from Pittsburg Junior High, Johnson enrolled at nearby St. Mary's College, where he spent the next two years, earning during that time the praise of local sportswriters, who called him "one of the fleetest and finest players on the Pacific Coast." Choosing to transfer to Arizona State University when St. Mary's dropped its football program prior to the start of the 1951 campaign, Johnson sat out his

John Henry Johnson led the Steelers in rushing in four of his five full seasons in Pittsburgh.
Courtesy of the Pittsburgh Steelers

junior year due to restrictions placed on transfer students, before earning All–Border Conference honors as a senior in 1952 by excelling as a halfback on offense, a safety on defense, and a punt-returner on special teams.

Subsequently selected by the Steelers in the second round of the 1953 NFL Draft, with the 18th overall pick, Johnson instead elected to join the Calgary Stampeders of the Canadian Football League, with whom he captured league MVP honors in 1953, before returning to the United States the following year after the Steelers traded his NFL rights to the San Francisco 49ers. Johnson had an outstanding rookie season for the 49ers, earning a trip to the Pro Bowl by finishing second in the league with 681 yards rushing and nine rushing touchdowns. Yet, even though Johnson did an excellent job of running with the football his first year in the league, the 49ers chose to employ him primarily as a blocker for fellow "Million Dollar Backfield" runners Joe Perry and Hugh McElhenny in each of the next two seasons, limiting him to a total of only 370 yards rushing during that time.

Dealt to the Detroit Lions early in 1957, Johnson ended up spending three years in the Motor City, helping the Lions capture the NFL title his first year there by ranking among the league leaders with 621 yards rushing and five rushing touchdowns. After assuming more of a supporting role in each of the next two seasons, Johnson found himself headed for Pittsburgh when the Lions traded him to the Steelers following the conclusion of the 1959 campaign.

Serving as his new team's featured runner, Johnson posted the best numbers of his career over the course of the next five seasons, annually finishing among the league's leading rushers. After gaining 621 yards on the ground, scoring three touchdowns, and averaging a career-best 5.3 yards per carry in 1960, Johnson rushed for 787 yards and six touchdowns the following year. He then earned Pro Bowl honors for the first of three straight times in 1962 by finishing second in the NFL with 1,141 yards rushing, becoming in the process the first player in Steelers history to surpass the magical 1,000-yard mark. Johnson also ranked among the league leaders with 1,367 yards from scrimmage (5th), seven rushing touchdowns (4th), and nine touchdowns (10th). After another solid season in which he gained 773 yards on the ground, the 35-year-old Johnson became the oldest man ever to rush for more than 1,000 yards in a season to that point by finishing third in the league with 1,048 yards rushing in 1964.

Possessing good size, tremendous power, and outstanding speed, the 6'2", 210-pound Johnson ran equally well inside and outside the tackles, using his great strength to bowl over opposing defenders and his quickness to out-run them. Often preferring to run to contact, Johnson proved to be one of the league's most aggressive running backs, describing his mindset thusly: "Football is like a combat zone. I was always told that you carry the impact to the opponent. If you wait for it, the impact will be on you. . . . You've got to scare your opponent. It sort of upsets their concentration. I find I can run away from a lot of guys after I get them afraid of a collision with me."

In discussing his running style years later, Johnson stated, "If you were a good running back and you were a threat to them, they'd do everything to try to punish you, try to scare you, try to intimidate you—they'd twist your arm, twist your leg, they'd bite you, they'd rub their hands in your eyes—they'd do everything to try to intimidate you. So, you have to counter-attack them. So, I'd hit them with my elbow."

Noting that Johnson succeeded in doling out his fair share of punishment over the course of his career, Detroit Lions linebacker Wayne Walker commented, "All the defensive guys said, 'Watch him.' Because, if you didn't keep your eye on him, next thing you know, you'd have your jaw wired."

In addition to his exceptional running, Johnson proved to be the NFL's finest blocking fullback.
Courtesy of the Pittsburgh Steelers

Also known for his bone-crunching blocks, Johnson developed a repu-tation throughout the league as the finest blocking back in the game, with quarterback Bobby Layne, who played with him in Detroit and Pittsburgh, once saying, "John Henry is my bodyguard. Half the good runners will get a passer killed if you keep them around long enough. But a quarterback hits the jackpot when he gets a combination runner-blocker like Johnson."

Revealing the pride he took in his blocking, Johnson suggested, "There's far more to playing fullback than just running with the football. Everybody wants to run with the ball, that's the quickest way to get the headlines and lots of newspaper space. But how many times does a back peel off a long run by himself? I'll tell you—absolutely none."

Serving as a testament to Johnson's toughness, Bobby Layne included him on his list of "Pro Football's 11 Meanest Men" in an article he wrote for *SPORT* magazine in 1964. Yet, Layne tempered his remarks by stating, "By 'mean,' I mean vicious, unmanageable, consistently tough. I don't mean dirty." And, years later, Layne told the *Beaver County* (Pa.) *Times*, "John Henry was maybe the meanest player around on the football field, but he is one of the best friends a guy could have. We were, and still are, real close. Friends in real life, not just on the football field. He's the greatest."

Author Dave Newhouse echoed Layne's sentiments in his book entitled *The Million Dollar Backfield*, writing, "Away from football, he was as nice and cozy as a warm soft bed. But, dress him in football gear, and he was a bed of nails."

In addressing the image that others had of him, Johnson told Newhouse, "I know I wasn't dirty. I just enjoyed hitting."

After Johnson missed virtually the entire 1965 campaign due to injury, he spent the following year with the American Football League's Houston Oilers, before announcing his retirement at season's end. Johnson ended his career with 6,803 yards rushing, 8,281 yards from scrimmage, 48 rushing touchdowns, 186 receptions, 1,478 receiving yards, seven TD catches, and a rushing average of 4.3 yards per carry. During his time in Pittsburgh, he rushed for 4,381 yards and 26 touchdowns, made 106 receptions for 814 yards and six touchdowns, and averaged 4.4 yards per carry.

Following his retirement, Johnson settled in the Pittsburgh area, where he took a job as coordinator of urban affairs for the Columbia Gas Company. He also later worked in collections for Time-Warner Cable and in the community relations department of Allegheny County, before retiring to private life in 1989 and moving with his second wife to her hometown of Cleveland. Unfortunately, Johnson had already begun to exhibit the symptoms of severe head trauma by that time, with his wife, Leona, telling Dave Newhouse, "By then, he was seriously ill. He couldn't remember where his offices were. He'd get lost on the freeway. He couldn't find the grocery store. He got so he was afraid to leave the house."

After Leona died in 2002, Johnson returned to California to live with his oldest daughter, Kathy, with whom he spent the rest of his life. Confined to a wheelchair by dementia his last few years, Johnson passed away at

81 years of age, on June 3, 2011. His daughter subsequently authorized that his brain be donated to a study being conducted at Boston University for the effects of head trauma, including the neurodegenerative disease chronic traumatic encephalopathy, or CTE, which may be related to blows suffered to the head while playing football.

STEELERS CAREER HIGHLIGHTS

Best Season

Johnson performed exceptionally well for the Steelers in 1964, finishing third in the NFL with 1,048 yards rushing and seven rushing touchdowns, while also ranking among the league leaders with 1,117 yards from scrimmage. However, he posted slightly better overall numbers in 1962, earning All-Pro honors for the only time in his career by placing near the top of the league rankings with 1,141 yards rushing, seven rushing TDs, nine touchdowns, and 1,367 yards from scrimmage.

Memorable Moments/Greatest Performances

Johnson went over 100 yards rushing for the first time as a member of the Steelers on November 27, 1960, when he carried the ball 18 times for 109 yards during a 22–10 victory over the Washington Redskins.

Johnson turned in a tremendous all-around effort against the Philadelphia Eagles two weeks later, leading the Steelers to a 27–21 win over the eventual NFL champions by throwing a 15-yard TD pass to Buddy Dial, making a seven-yard TD reception, and recording a career-long 87-yard touchdown run. In addition to having a hand in all three Steeler touchdowns, Johnson finished the game with 182 yards on 19 carries.

Johnson had another big game against the Eagles on October 6, 1962, leading the Steelers to a 13–7 victory over their Eastern Division rivals by carrying the ball 22 times for 128 yards and gaining another 32 yards on five pass receptions.

Johnson starred during a 26–17 win over the St. Louis Cardinals on November 11, 1962, carrying the ball 25 times for 138 yards and one touchdown.

Johnson contributed to a lopsided 31–0 victory over the New York Giants on September 22, 1963, by rushing for 123 yards and one touchdown.

Johnson keyed a 9–7 win over the Cleveland Browns on November 10, 1963, by carrying the ball 27 times for a season-high 131 yards.

Johnson saved the finest performance of his career for an October 10, 1964, head-to-head matchup with the great Jim Brown, leading the Steelers to a 23–7 victory over the Cleveland Browns by gaining 200 yards on 30 carries and scoring three touchdowns, which came on runs that covered 33, 45, and five yards.

Notable Achievements

- Rushed for more than 1,000 yards twice.
- Surpassed 1,000 yards from scrimmage three times.
- Averaged more than 4.5 yards per carry three times, topping 5 yards per carry once (5.3 in 1960).
- Finished second in NFL with 1,141 yards rushing in 1962.
- Finished third in NFL in rushing yards once and rushing touchdowns once.
- Led Steelers in rushing four times.
- Ranks among Steelers career leaders with 4,381 yards rushing (5th) and 26 rushing touchdowns (tied—7th).
- Retired as NFL's fourth-leading all-time rusher.
- Three-time Pro Bowl selection (1962, 1963, and 1964).
- 1962 Second-Team All-Pro selection.
- Member of Pittsburgh Steelers Legends Team.
- #35 "unofficially" retired by Steelers.
- Elected to Pro Football Hall of Fame in 1987.

39

LAWRENCE TIMMONS

The backbone of the Steelers defense for nearly a decade, Lawrence Timmons spent 10 seasons in Pittsburgh, during which time he established himself as one of the best inside linebackers in franchise history. Starting at right-inside linebacker for the Steelers for eight seasons, Timmons amassed more than 100 tackles six times, ending his career as the third-leading tackler in team annals. One of Pittsburgh's emotional leaders throughout his tenure in the Steel City, Timmons anchored a defense that annually ranked among the NFL's best, earning in the process one trip to the Pro Bowl and one All-Pro nomination. Along the way, Timmons helped lead the Steelers to five division titles, two AFC championships, and one Super Bowl win.

Born in Florence, South Carolina, on May 14, 1986, Lawrence Olajuwon Timmons attended local Wilson High School, where he played football and ran track. Excelling on the gridiron at both linebacker and tight end, Timmons earned All-State First-Team and Defensive Player of the Year honors as a senior by recording more than 150 tackles, while also catching 47 passes for over 800 yards and five touchdowns. Starring in track as well, Timmons competed in the long jump and served as a member of his school's 4 × 100-meter and 4 × 200-meter relay squads. Ranked as the fifth best outside linebacker prospect in the nation, Timmons received scholarship offers from several major colleges, including North Carolina, Florida, and Tennessee, before ultimately committing to Florida State University. Timmons spent the next three seasons performing well for the Seminoles at linebacker and on special teams, proving to be particularly effective as a junior, when he earned Third-Team All-America and First-Team All–Atlantic Coast Conference honors by recording 79 tackles and five sacks.

Choosing to forgo his final year of college eligibility, Timmons entered the 2007 NFL Draft, where the Steelers selected him in the first round, with the 15th overall pick, Timmons spent his first season in Pittsburgh playing mostly on special teams, before assuming a more prominent role the following year, when he joined veterans James Harrison, Larry Foote,

James Farrior, and LaMarr Woodley in giving the Steelers the league's deepest and most talented linebacking corps. Serving as a rotational player in 2008, Timmons recorded five sacks, 65 tackles (43 solo), and one interception, with his strong play prompting the Steelers to release Foote at season's end and turn over the starting right-inside linebacker job to Timmons.

Performing well in his first year as a full-time starter, Timmons registered seven sacks, 78 tackles (56 solo), and four forced fumbles in 2009, before helping to lead the Steelers to the AFC title the following year by recording three sacks, two interceptions, two forced fumbles, and a team-leading 135 tackles (96 solo). After bringing down opposing ball carriers 93 times in 2011, Timmons began a string of five straight seasons in which he recorded more than 100 tackles, leading the team in that category on four separate occasions. Particularly effective in 2012 and 2014, Timmons concluded the first of those campaigns with 106 tackles, six sacks, and three interceptions, before earning Pro Bowl and Second-Team All-Pro honors two years later by making a career-high 139 tackles.

Although the 6'1", 234-pound Timmons lacked the size of a prototypical inside linebacker, he possessed excellent speed and quickness, outstanding instincts, and a nose for the football, making him a veritable tackling machine. Blessed with strong leadership skills as well, Timmons gradually emerged as the leader of the Pittsburgh defense, although he preferred to lead by example, stating on one occasion, "I like to let my work ethic speak for itself, just things of that nature, like the way I go about practice and show these guys how to do it."

Lawrence Timmons ranks as the third-leading tackler in franchise history.
Courtesy of the Pittsburgh Steelers

Establishing himself before long as a mentor to the team's younger players, Timmons said, "A lot of guys, especially the young guys, I try to do anything I can for them—on the field, off the field, anything."

Meanwhile, in describing how he viewed himself and his

Timmons helped lead the Steelers to five division titles, two AFC championships, and one Super Bowl win.
Courtesy of the Pittsburgh Steelers

role on the team, Timmons stated, "I look at myself as a game-changer, and I try to make that a facet of my game . . . I just want to be great. I want to stand out, be a great leader for this defense, and I'm just trying to leave it all out on the field."

Making a strong impression on several of his younger teammates, Timmons drew praise from Le'Veon Bell, who stated, "He's a great cover linebacker—one of the best in the business. Timmons is a Pro Bowler. He's a great player, and he's been around for a long time. We both make each other better."

Extremely durable as well, Timmons missed just two games in his 10 seasons with the Steelers, starting every game for them from 2010 to 2016.

Unfortunately, the 2016 campaign ended up being Timmons's last in Pittsburgh. Allowed to depart via free agency at season's end, Timmons signed a two-year, $12 million contract with the Miami Dolphins, leaving the Steelers with career totals of 988 tackles (680 solo), 35½ sacks, 12 interceptions, 274 interception-return yards, 13 forced fumbles, seven fumble recoveries, and one touchdown. Timmons subsequently spent one turbulent season in Miami, being suspended for one week during the early stages of the 2017 campaign after leaving the team without notifying anyone, before being released by the Dolphins on March 13, 2018. Since that time, Timmons has failed to catch on with any other NFL team.

STEELERS CAREER HIGHLIGHTS

Best Season

Timmons had a big year for the Steelers in 2014, earning Pro Bowl and Second-Team All-Pro honors by recording two sacks and a team-leading 139 tackles (90 solo). He also performed extremely well in each of the previous two seasons, recording three interceptions, six sacks, 106 tackles (75 solo), and one touchdown in 2012, before picking off two passes, registering three sacks, and making 126 tackles (86 solo) in 2013. However, Timmons had his finest all-around season in 2010, when, in addition to making two interceptions, recording three sacks, and amassing a team-high 135 tackles (96 solo), he deflected 10 passes, forced two fumbles, and recovered two others, prompting *Pro Football Focus* to rate him higher than any other inside linebacker in the game and accord him First-Team All-Pro honors.

Memorable Moments/Greatest Performances

Timmons contributed to a 23–20 overtime win over Baltimore on September 29, 2008, by recording four tackles and the first sack of his career.

Timmons helped lead the Steelers to a 38–10 victory over the Cincinnati Bengals on October 19, 2008, by recording two sacks and nine tackles (six solo).

During a 33–10 win over the Patriots on November 30, 2008, Timmons recorded his first career interception, which he subsequently returned 89 yards to the New England 1-yard line.

Timmons starred during a 19–11 victory over the Tennessee Titans on September 19, 2010, recording a season-high 15 tackles (12 solo) and forcing a fumble.

Timmons earned AFC Defensive Player of the Week honors by recording an interception, two sacks, and 11 tackles (nine solo) during a 28–10 win over Cleveland on October 17, 2010.

Although the Steelers lost to the Browns by a score of 20–14 on November 25, 2012, Timmons scored the only touchdown of his career on a 53-yard interception return of a Brandon Weeden pass.

Timmons excelled during a 19–16 win over the Baltimore Ravens on October 20, 2013, making a career-high 17 tackles (12 solo).

Timmons had another big game exactly one year later, recording a sack and a game-high 12 tackles during a 30–23 win over the Houston Texans on October 20, 2014.

Timmons made a key play during the Steelers' 24–14 win over the Giants on December 4, 2016, intercepting an Eli Manning pass at the Pittsburgh 2-yard line and returning the ball 58 yards to the New York 40.

Timmons proved to be a huge factor in Pittsburgh's 30–12 victory over Miami in the 2016 AFC wild card game, recording two sacks and a team-leading 14 tackles (eight solo).

Notable Achievements

- Scored one defensive touchdown during career.
- Surpassed 100 tackles six times.
- Recorded seven sacks in 2009.
- Led Steelers in tackles five times and sacks once.
- Ranks third in Steelers history with 988 tackles (680 solo).
- Five-time division champion (2007, 2008, 2010, 2014, and 2016).
- Two-time AFC champion (2008 and 2010).
- Super Bowl XLIII champion.
- 2010 Week 6 AFC Defensive Player of the Week.
- 2014 Pro Bowl selection.
- 2014 Second-Team All-Pro selection.

40

BILL DUDLEY

Although Bill Dudley spent parts of only three seasons in Pittsburgh, he earned a place on this list with the tremendous versatility he displayed during his relatively brief stay in the Steel City. The only player ever to throw a TD pass and score a touchdown on a run, a pass reception, a punt return, a kickoff return, an interception return, and a fumble return, Dudley did a little bit of everything for the Steelers, earning NFL MVP honors in 1946, when he became the only player to lead the league in rushing and interceptions in the same season. Easily the most impactful player to don a Steelers uniform during the first two decades of their existence, Dudley led the NFL in rushing in each of his two full seasons in Pittsburgh, while also topping the circuit in all-purpose yards twice and punt-return average, interceptions, interception-return yards, and fumble recoveries once each, with his unmatched ability to perform well in all phases of the game prompting Steelers founder Art Rooney to call him, "the best all-around football player I've ever seen."

Born in Bluefield, Virginia, on December 24, 1921, William McGarvey Dudley attended Graham High School, where he starred on the gridiron, earning him an athletic scholarship from the University of Virginia, which he entered in the fall of 1938. After beginning his college career as a punter and placekicker, Dudley eventually moved to halfback, where he made a name for himself his final two seasons, leading the Southern Conference in total offensive yards as a junior, before becoming the first Virginia player to earn All-America honors the following year. Named winner of the prestigious Maxwell Award as College Football Player of the Year following the conclusion of his senior year, Dudley drew praise from University of Pittsburgh coach Wes Fesler, who stated, "I've never seen him caught from behind. He's a great defensive man and one of the deadliest tacklers I've ever watched."

Subsequently selected by the Steelers with the first overall pick of the 1942 NFL Draft, Dudley elected to turn pro after his parents refused to sign the consent form that would have allowed him to fulfill his desire of

becoming a navy pilot. Looking back at his decision to sign
with the Steelers for $5,000,
Dudley recalled, "There was a
war coming on, and I wanted
to get a little bit of money
until I went into the service."

Performing exception-
ally well as a rookie, Dudley
earned a runner-up finish to
Green Bay's Don Hutson in
the NFL MVP voting by leading the league with 696 yards
rushing, 271 punt-return
yards, and 1,349 all-purpose
yards, while also throwing two
TD passes, recording three
interceptions on defense, and
ranking among the league
leaders with six touchdowns,
298 kickoff-return yards, and averages of 4.3 yards per carry and 13.6 yards
per punt return.

Bill Dudley earned NFL MVP honors in 1946.
Courtesy of the Pittsburgh Steelers

With the nation's involvement in World War II intensifying, Dudley
chose to enlist in the Army Air Corps toward the tail end of 1942, temporarily putting his football career on hold. He then spent virtually all of the
next three years contributing to the war effort as a fighter pilot instructor
in the Pacific and as a member of the US Armed Forces All-Star Team.
Discharged from the military in November 1945, Dudley returned to the
Steelers for the final month of the season, during which time he amassed
204 yards rushing, scored three touchdowns, and intercepted two passes.

Fully dedicated to his chosen profession by the start of the 1946 campaign, Dudley performed brilliantly for the Steelers, earning First-Team
All-Pro and NFL MVP honors by passing for 452 yards, scoring five
touchdowns, throwing two TD passes, averaging 40.2 yards per punt, and
leading the league with 604 yards rushing, 385 punt-return yards, 1,650
all-purpose yards, an average of 14.3 yards per punt return, 10 interceptions, 242 interception-return yards, and seven fumble recoveries. Dudley's
outstanding play enabled the Steelers to improve their record from 2-8 to
5-5-1, with Art Rooney later noting, "He instantly made our team better
with his versatility and all-around football skills."

Dudley managed to do an excellent job on both sides of the ball even though he stood just 5'10" tall, weighed only 182 pounds, and lacked superior running speed. Commenting on his frequent adversary's skill set, Washington Redskins Hall of Famer Sammy Baugh suggested, "He doesn't seem to be able to do anything real well, but he's a helluva football player. I'd say Bill is a real specialist—specializing in everything."

Dudley, himself, stated long after his playing career ended, "I never considered myself a great football player. I considered myself a good one. I wasn't fast, and I wasn't big. Every time I walked onto the field, I felt I had something to prove."

Typically lining up as a tailback in Pittsburgh's single-wing offense, Dudley usually took the snap directly from center, before either running with the ball himself or handing it off to one of his teammates. Extremely intelligent, Dudley relied heavily on his ability to read blocks, change speeds, and cut quickly to avoid opposing defenders. He also possessed a winning attitude and provided leadership to his teammates, who he chastised if they failed to give less than a 100 percent effort.

Dudley's many intangible qualities and all-around ability earned him the undying respect of team owner Art Rooney, who called him "a Jimmy Brown on offense and a 'Night Train' Lane on defense." Rooney added, "Steve Owens of the Giants and Greasy Neale of the Eagles imposed an automatic fine on their quarterbacks if they called a pass play into Dudley's territory."

Yet, at the very height of his career, Dudley chose to announce his retirement at only 25 years of age due, at least in part, to the physical abuse he endured over the course of that 1946 campaign. Reflecting back on his decision years later, Dudley revealed, "I was playing 50 minutes a game, had hurt my knee in the last game of the season, and I was definitely going to retire. I don't think anyone could take that beating. I had written a letter to Mr. Rooney and told him I'm not asking to be traded, but I don't feel I can come back and take the physical beating I had taken."

However, newspaper accounts suggested that Dudley based most of his decision on the stormy relationship he shared with new Steelers head coach Jock Sutherland, with whom he spent the entire year feuding. The veracity of those stories came to light when Dudley elected to return to the game months later after Rooney traded him to the Detroit Lions for wingback Paul White and quarterback Bob Cifers.

Dudley ended up spending three years in Detroit and another three in Washington, never again reaching the heights he attained while wearing the Black and Gold, although he did manage to earn two trips to the Pro Bowl as a member of the Redskins. Retiring for good following the conclusion of the 1953 campaign, Dudley ended his career with 3,057 yards rushing, 123 receptions, 1,383 receiving yards, 8,217 all-purpose yards, 18 rushing touchdowns, 18 TD catches, five special team touchdowns, six touchdown passes, 23 interceptions, 459 interception-return yards, 17 fumble recoveries, three defensive touchdowns, 33 field goals in 66 attempts, and an average of 37.8 yards per punt. His numbers as a member of the Steelers include 1,504 rushing yards, 133 receiving yards, 3,335 all-purpose yards, 14 total touchdowns scored, 15 interceptions, 349 interception-return yards, and seven fumble recoveries.

Dudley is the only player ever to lead the league in rushing and interceptions in the same season.
Courtesy of RMYAuctions.com

Looking back at his years with the Steelers, Dudley said, "I thoroughly enjoyed my time in Pittsburgh. I'm sorry I couldn't have continued my whole career there. We played a good football game, got some good crowds in Pittsburgh, and I think the football we played kept the fans happy, both in '42 and '46."

Dudley added, "I'm very, very fond of Pittsburgh. It's where I like to be remembered as playing ball. Nothing against Washington or Detroit, it was just my first stop, and I became friends with Mr. Rooney. He was an employer who later turned into a very good friend."

Following his retirement, Dudley briefly coached at the University of Virginia, before returning to Pittsburgh for one year, where he served as an assistant under head coach Walt Kiesling. He also did some scouting for the Steelers and Lions, before going into the insurance business with his brother in Virginia, where he later spent four terms serving in the Virginia House of Delegates.

Inducted into the Pro Football Hall of Fame in 1966, Dudley lived a long and fulfilling life, which sadly came to an end on February 4, 2010, five days after he suffered a massive stroke at 88 years of age. Upon learning of his passing, Steelers president Art Rooney II said, "Bill was truly an NFL and Steelers legend as one of the great players to wear a Steelers uniform. Bill's dedication to the game of football and to the game he loved will never be forgotten."

Dan Rooney added, "We lost one of the all-time great Steelers. My father knew Bill very well and admired him as both a player and as a member of society. I became very close to Bill through the years. He was a dear friend who will be missed by anyone who knew him."

STEELERS CAREER HIGHLIGHTS

Best Season

Dudley made a huge impact in Pittsburgh as a rookie in 1942, helping the Steelers compile the first winning record in franchise history by leading the NFL with 696 yards rushing, 271 punt-return yards, and 1,349 all-purpose yards. However, he performed even better in 1946, when he led the NFL in eight different categories, including yards rushing (604), all-purpose yards (1,650), interceptions (10), interception-return yards (242), and fumble recoveries (7), with his superb all-around play earning him recognition as the league's Most Valuable Player.

Memorable Moments/Greatest Performances

Although the Steelers suffered a 24–14 defeat at the hands of the Philadelphia Eagles in the 1942 regular-season opener, Dudley excelled in his first game as a pro, accounting for all of Pittsburgh's points with a 44-yard touchdown run the second time he touched the ball and a 24-yard TD pass.

Dudley performed heroically during a 28–14 loss to the Washington Redskins the following week, when, after injuring his ankle so badly in the first half that he had to be carried off the field, he later returned to run back the second-half kickoff 84 yards for a touchdown that momentarily knotted the score at 7–7.

Dudley sealed a 17–9 win over the New York Giants on November 1, 1942, with a touchdown run of 66 yards in the fourth quarter. He finished the contest with 135 yards on 24 carries.

Dudley led the Steelers to a lopsided 35–7 victory over the Detroit Lions one week later by throwing a 9-yard touchdown pass to Tom Brown and scoring himself on a 37-yard run.

Although the Steelers lost to the Packers by a score of 17–7 on October 20, 1946, Dudley gained a season-high 133 yards on the ground, scoring Pittsburgh's only points of the game on a 31-yard touchdown run in the second quarter.

Dudley turned in an exceptional all-around effort one week later, leading the Steelers to a convincing 33–7 victory over the Boston Yanks by running 23 yards for a touchdown after one of his teammates lateraled the ball to him and recording a career-long 80-yard TD reception.

Dudley followed that up with another strong outing, returning an interception 80 yards for a touchdown during a 14–7 win over the Washington Redskins on November 3, 1946.

Notable Achievements

- Returned one kickoff for a touchdown.
- Returned one interception for a touchdown.
- Surpassed 1,000 all-purpose yards twice.
- Recorded 10 interceptions in 1946.
- Amassed 242 interception-return yards in 1946.
- Led NFL in: rushing yards twice; punt-return yards twice; all-purpose yards twice; punt-return average once; interceptions once; interception-return yards once; and fumble recoveries once.
- Finished second in NFL in: yards from scrimmage once; kickoff-return yards once; punt-return average once; and punting yards once.
- Holds Steelers single-season record for most interception-return yards (242 in 1946).
- 1946 NFL MVP.
- Finished second in 1942 NFL MVP voting.
- 1942 Pro Bowl selection.
- 1942 First-Team All-Pro selection.
- 1946 Second-Team All-Pro selection.
- 1946 First-Team All-NFL/AAFC selection.
- Pro Football Hall of Fame All-1940s Team.
- Member of Pittsburgh Steelers Legends Team.
- #35 "unofficially" retired by Steelers.
- Elected to Pro Football Hall of Fame in 1966.

41

— JASON GILDON —

One of the more underrated players in Steelers history, Jason Gildon spent 10 seasons in Pittsburgh carrying on the rich tradition of exceptional linebacker play in the Steel City. Though often overlooked in favor of more flamboyant linebackers such as Greg Lloyd and Joey Porter, the extremely consistent Gildon did an outstanding job for the Steelers from his left-outside linebacker position, leading the team in sacks five times, en route to compiling the third most sacks in franchise history. A key member of Steeler teams that won six division titles and one AFC championship, Gildon earned three trips to the Pro Bowl, one All-Pro nomination, and one All-AFC selection during his time in Pittsburgh, missing just two games in his 10 years with the club.

Born in Altus, Oklahoma, on July 31, 1972, Jason Larue Gildon proved to be an anomaly of sorts while growing up in his home state, the only Steelers fan in a town littered with people that rooted for the Dallas Cowboys. Looking back at his early years, Gildon recalled, "Everybody was a Dallas fan. It was hard as a child when we'd go in the back yard to play football and everyone would pick a player he wanted to be. Sometimes we had 15 Cowboys, and I was the only Steeler."

After attending Altus High School, Gildon enrolled at Oklahoma State University, where he broke Leslie O'Neal's school record by registering a total of 39½ career sacks, earning along the way All–Big Eight Conference honors as a senior in 1993. Impressed with Gildon's outstanding play at OSU, the Steelers made him the 88th overall pick of the 1994 NFL Draft when they selected him in the third round. Gildon subsequently spent his first two seasons in Pittsburgh backing up Kevin Greene and Greg Lloyd at outside linebacker, recording just five sacks and 16 tackles on defense during that time. Expressing his desire to see more action on the defensive side of the ball, Gildon stated during the latter stages of the 1995 campaign, "At the beginning of the year, it was kind of frustrating, because, as a young player, you always want to play. But sometimes you have to realize that you are going to have to wait your turn. . . . So, once I got over that, everything fell into place, and I felt myself getting better and better every day at practice. Now, it's just a matter of time."

While Gildon waited for his opportunity, he established himself as one of the league's best special-team players, making an extremely favorable impression on Pittsburgh's coaching staff in the process. In discussing his primary role on the club, Gildon said, "You have to take advantage of every opportunity. On special teams, you don't get as much recognition as other guys on the field. I accept my role. I felt like, if I had to play special teams, then I'd play them well, but I feel like I'm ready to play as an every-down guy."

Commenting on Gildon's development over the course of his first two seasons, Steelers defensive coordinator Dick LeBeau stated, "Jason was a tremendous pass rusher in college, and that fits in with what we do with our outside linebackers. We've really been pleased with the way he has taken to dropping into pass coverage. He's a smart young man."

LeBeau then added, "Jason has stepped in and played quite a bit this year. We think his future is bright. He just needs to play and get experience. The limiting factor there, of course, is that he's behind Greg Lloyd and Kevin Greene."

With Greene scheduled to become a free agent following the conclusion of the 1995 campaign, the veteran linebacker suggested that the presence of Gildon likely signaled the end to his time in Pittsburgh, stating prior to the start of the season's final game, "I would love to be back, but I don't think I will be. I think Jason Gildon is ready to play. He's a great athlete, and he's ready to step in."

In response, Gildon said, "If Kevin was to leave the team, I would have no choice but to be ready. Whether he's here or not, I've got to prepare myself as though I'm going to play every day. Being with Greg Lloyd and Kevin Greene has helped me so

Jason Gildon recorded the third most sacks in franchise history.
Courtesy of the Pittsburgh Steelers

much and taught me so much. Eventually, I think I can become one of the league's premier pass rushers."

Living up to his own words, Gildon performed extremely well after he took over for Greene when the latter departed for Carolina at season's end, recording seven sacks and 59 tackles (47 solo) in his first year as a full-time starter. After another solid year in 1997, Gildon emerged as a true force on defense the following season, when he led the team with 11 sacks. Gildon also led the Steelers in sacks in each of the next four seasons, a period during which he combined with Joey Porter to give Pittsburgh one of the most dynamic outside linebacker tandems in the NFL.

While Porter drew attention to himself with his flashy on-field play and outspoken demeanor, the quiet and shy Gildon simply went about the business of making tackles and sacking quarterbacks, often causing him to be lost in the shuffle. Nevertheless, he remained an intimidating presence on defense, using his chiseled 6'4", 255-pound frame to frighten opposing quarterbacks and his tremendous quickness to outmaneuver offensive linemen and chase down opposing ball-carriers. One of the Steelers' most consistent players, Gildon recorded at least five sacks and 50 tackles in each of his eight seasons as a full-time starter, surpassing 10 sacks three times and 70 tackles once. Extremely durable as well, Gildon appeared in every game for the Steelers in nine of his 10 seasons with the club, starting all 16 contests in each of his last seven seasons.

Considered the leader of the Steelers defense by 2000, Gildon had arguably his finest all-around season, earning Pro Bowl honors for the first of three straight times by placing near the top of the league rankings with 13½ sacks and four fumble recoveries, while also recording 77 tackles (58 solo), forcing four fumbles, and scoring one touchdown. Gildon followed that up by gaining All-Pro recognition for the only time in his career in 2001, a season in which he recorded 12 sacks, 53 tackles (42 solo), three forced fumbles, one of his two career interceptions, and the last of his three career touchdowns.

Gildon remained with the Steelers for two more years, compiling another 15 sacks and 128 tackles, before the team elected to release him following the conclusion of the 2003 campaign. He left Pittsburgh with career totals of 77 sacks, 497 tackles (371 solo), 15 forced fumbles, 11 fumble recoveries, and two interceptions, with his 77 sacks representing the highest "official" total in franchise history at the time (although Joe Greene's "unofficial" total of 78½ sacks placed him just ahead of Gildon).

After leaving the Steelers, Gildon signed with the Buffalo Bills, who cut him during training camp. He then joined the Jacksonville Jaguars midway through the 2004 campaign, appearing in nine games with them and recording three sacks, before announcing his retirement at season's end. Choosing to pursue a career in coaching following his playing days, Gildon served as linebacker coach at both Seneca Valley High School and Peters Township, near Pittsburgh, before accepting the position of head football coach at Pittsburgh's Cardinal Wuerl North Catholic High School in 2015. Gildon remained in that post for two years, leading the school to an overall record of 17-6 during that time, before handing in his resignation.

Gildon led the Steelers in sacks five times.
Courtesy of the Pittsburgh Steelers

Looking back on his years with the Steelers, Gildon says, "To be a Pittsburgh Steeler linebacker, it adds a little more to it, it puts you in sort of a rarefied air. I think the guys that have been able to play it and be successful realize it."

Gildon added, "As far as not getting the glory some of those other guys got, I think it just depends on who you ask. I can honestly say I'm proud to have been a part of such a great legacy of Pittsburgh linebackers. I'm honored to be mentioned in the same sentence as they are. . . . When I look back on my career, I had a lot of fun. I can't complain. The Steelers organization is one of the best in the country. As for the glory, yeah, it depends on who you ask, really."

STEELERS CAREER HIGHLIGHTS

Best Season

Gildon earned his lone First-Team All-Pro nomination in 2001, when he helped the Steelers compile a record of 13-3 that represented their best mark in 23 years by recording 12 sacks, 53 tackles (42 solo), one interception, three forced fumbles, and two fumble recoveries, one of which he returned for a touchdown. However, even though the Steelers' mediocre 9-7 finish the previous season likely prevented Gildon from earning All-Pro recognition, he posted better overall numbers, concluding the 2000 campaign with one defensive touchdown and a career-high 13½ sacks, 77 tackles (58 solo), four forced fumbles, and four fumble recoveries.

Memorable Moments/Greatest Performances

Gildon recorded the first sack of his career when he brought down Dan Marino behind the line of scrimmage during a 16–13 overtime victory over the Miami Dolphins on November 20, 1994.

Gildon helped lead the Steelers to a 37–24 win over the Tennessee Oilers on September 28, 1997, by recording a sack and scoring the first of his three career touchdowns when he returned a fumble into the Tennessee end zone from 12 yards out.

Gildon made a huge play during the final minute of the Steelers' 7–6 victory over New England in the divisional round of the 1997 playoffs, when he prevented a possible Patriots game-winning field goal or touchdown by recovering a Drew Bledsoe fumble.

Gildon earned AFC Defensive Player of the Week honors for the first of three times by recording two sacks and returning a fumble 22 yards for a touchdown during a 48–28 win over the Cincinnati Bengals on November 26, 2000.

Gildon recorded three sacks for the first time in his career during a 15–12 overtime victory over the Cleveland Browns on November 11, 2001, earning in the process AFC Defensive Player of the Week honors for a second time.

Gildon contributed to a 47–14 win over the Detroit Lions on December 23, 2001, by recording two sacks and scoring the game's first points when he returned a fumble 27 yards for the last of his three career touchdowns.

Gildon earned AFC Defensive Player of the Week honors for the third and final time by recording three sacks and eight tackles during a 28–15 victory over the Arizona Cardinals on November 9, 2003, with his three sacks moving him past L. C. Greenwood into second place on the Steelers' all-time "unofficial" sack list (he has since slipped to third).

Notable Achievements

- Scored three defensive touchdowns during career.
- Recorded more than 10 sacks three times.
- Missed just two games in 10 seasons with Steelers.
- Led Steelers in sacks five times.
- Ranks among Steelers career leaders with 77 sacks (3rd) and 15 forced fumbles (tied—5th).
- Six-time division champion (1994, 1995, 1996, 1997, 2001, and 2002).
- 1995 AFC champion.
- Three-time AFC Defensive Player of the Week.
- Three-time Pro Bowl selection (2000, 2001, and 2002).
- 2001 First-Team All-Pro selection.
- 2001 First-Team All-Conference selection.

42

DALE DODRILL

An outstanding defensive player who excelled as both a lineman and a linebacker during his nine seasons in Pittsburgh, Dale Dodrill displayed a mental and physical toughness while wearing the Black and Gold that became synonymous with Steeler teams of the future. Starring for mostly losing Steeler squads during the 1950s, Dodrill played the game with an edge, never conceding anything to the opposition, even though the teams for which he played compiled a winning record just twice. Along the way, Dodrill earned four trips to the Pro Bowl, four All-Pro nominations, and a spot on the Steelers Legends Team, accomplishing all he did despite beginning his pro career at the rather advanced age of 25 due to time spent in the military during World War II.

Born in Stockton, Kansas, on February 27, 1926, Dale Fike Dodrill grew up on the family farm in Rooks County, Kansas, and spent his early years attending school in nearby Plainville. After moving with his family to Colorado in 1937, Dodrill lived in the towns of Fort Collins and Laporte, before finally settling in the city of Loveland, where he attended Loveland High School. Excelling on the gridiron as a two-way lineman in high school, Dodrill earned All-State honors twice, leading Loveland to the 1942 state championship. Drafted into the US Army following his graduation, Dodrill spent the better part of the next four years serving in the 30th Infantry Division during World War II, first in Germany and, then, in Japan, facing an enemy that earlier killed his brother Garrett at a prison camp in the Philippines.

Upon his return to the States following the war, Dodrill enrolled at Colorado A&M (now known as Colorado State University), after earlier rejecting scholarship offers from Denver University and the University of Colorado, neither of which would have allowed him to play as a freshman. In explaining his choice of schools, Dodrill stated, "After being in the service, I didn't want to wait—I wanted to play four years. I went up to Colorado A&M and (former coach) Bob Davis said I could play as a freshman as

Dale Dodrill starred for the Steelers on defense after serving his country during World War II.
Courtesy of the Pittsburgh Steelers

long as I was good enough. If I hadn't made the varsity, I really don't know where I would have ended up."

Dodrill proved to be worthy of a starting spot as a freshman, spending the next four years starring on both sides of the ball for the Aggies, in leading them to an overall record of 28-11-1 and earning All–Skyline Athletic Conference honors three times. Still, in spite of the success he experienced at the collegiate level, he never seriously considered turning pro until he received invitations to play in the East-West Shrine Game and the *Chicago Tribune* All-Star Game following his senior year. Recalling his thought process at the time, Dodrill revealed, "I never figured I was as good as those guys from the East Coast we read about all the time. But, when I played in those all-star games, I found that I was just as good as they were."

Subsequently selected by the Steelers in the sixth round of the 1951 NFL Draft, with the 67th overall pick, Dodrill joined a Pittsburgh team that had posted a winning record just three times since it entered the league 18 years earlier. Unfortunately, that trend continued following Dodrill's arrival, with the Steelers finishing above .500 in just two of his nine seasons with the club. Nevertheless, Dodrill, who served as defensive captain for three years, remained one of the few bright spots on mostly losing teams during his stay in Pittsburgh, excelling at middle guard (or defensive tackle) his first few years in the league, before moving to linebacker during the latter stages of his career. In discussing his varying responsibilities on defense, Dodrill explained: "In the early 50's, we ran the 5-1 defense, with five defensive linemen. I was called a guard then—I lined up over the center in the middle of the line. We later moved to a 4-3 and I played middle linebacker. So, I wasn't a defensive lineman, even though I've been called that and a guard."

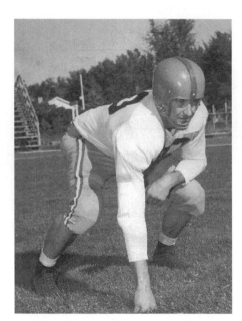

Doing an outstanding job at both posts despite being somewhat undersized for a lineman at 6'1" and only 215 pounds, Dodrill earned Second-Team All-Pro honors for the first of three times in 1952, before earning his lone First-Team nomination two years later, when his teammates named him the club's defensive MVP. Joining long-time teammate Ernie Stautner in bringing a toughness to the

Dodrill earned Pro Bowl and All-Pro honors four times each.
Courtesy of CSU Athletics

Pittsburgh defense, Dodrill played hard on every snap and never let up, serving as an early prototype of the tenacious players that comprised the "Steel Curtain" defense of the 1970s. An exceptionally well-conditioned athlete, Dodrill appeared in every game the Steelers played in each of his final eight seasons, attributing his good health to his offseason training regimen: "I had my own offseason camp. I'd go back to Colorado, and the first couple of years I worked at a lumber company. That was my conditioning. Then, the next few years, I worked at a brick company carrying the brick HOD. Now that was a real workout."

Dodrill, who intercepted 10 passes, recovered 11 fumbles, and scored two touchdowns during his career, remained a force on defense until he chose to announce his retirement following the conclusion of the 1959 campaign due to problems he encountered with third-year head coach Buddy Parker. In explaining his decision, Dodrill stated:

> I had lots of good times with the Steelers and Art Rooney. It all changed when he hired Buddy Parker to coach and run the team. Parker had control over the players when he was hired, and he lied to me. I didn't have much respect for him.

Dodrill continued:

> I wanted to be traded in my last year there. I told Buddy that I knew I didn't fit into his plans. I asked Art first, but he said he had no control over those things anymore. Buddy said he'd ask around to see if anyone wanted to trade for me, but he told me that no one had any interest. I knew that wasn't true because I knew at least one coach had told me he wanted me. So, I knew he lied. All coaches want their type of player I guess.
>
> If I had played another year in Pittsburgh, that would have been when the expansion draft happened and that was Dallas. I would have probably had to go to Dallas, and I couldn't tolerate that heat and humidity. So, it was a good time to hang them up. That's when the Broncos coach called me to coach their defense. At first, I said no, but, when he called me again, I decided to do it.

After retiring as an active player, Dodrill spent five years serving as an assistant on the coaching staff of the newly formed AFL's Denver Broncos, before leaving football to start his own insurance business in Denver, which he eventually sold to his sons. Honored by the Steelers during their 75th Season Celebration in 2007, Dodrill received the distinction of being named to the Steelers Legends Team as one of the franchise's best players to perform for the team prior to 1970.

Dodrill lived until January 18, 2019, when he passed away a little over five weeks shy of his 93rd birthday. Looking back on his life a few years earlier, Dodrill said, "I had a good life and family. I've been very fortunate. And the Pittsburgh fans are the best in the United States. They really are exceptional. Pittsburgh really is the number one place to play."

CAREER HIGHLIGHTS

Best Season

Although the Pittsburgh defense performed slightly better as a whole in 1953 and 1955, finishing second in the NFL in yards allowed in each of those campaigns, Dodrill's career-high three interceptions and 66 fumble-return yards earned him First-Team All-Pro honors for the only time in 1954, making that his finest all-around season.

Memorable Moments/Greatest Performances

Dodrill scored two touchdowns over the course of his career, with the first of those coming on November 2, 1952, when he returned a blocked field goal attempt 35 yards for a TD during a 24–23 win over the Washington Redskins.

Dodrill lit the scoreboard again on November 15, 1953, returning a fumble 16 yards for a touchdown during a 14–10 victory over the Giants.

Dodrill performed brilliantly during a 14–7 win over the Cardinals in the 1955 regular-season opener, anchoring a defense that surrendered only 86 yards of total offense to Chicago.

Notable Achievements

- Scored two touchdowns during career.
- Intercepted 10 passes during career.

- Played in 96 straight games over final eight seasons.
- 1954 Steelers Defensive MVP.
- Four-time Pro Bowl selection (1953, 1954, 1955, and 1957).
- 1954 First-Team All-Pro selection.
- Three-time Second-Team All-Pro selection (1952, 1955, and 1956).
- 1958 First-Team All-Conference selection.
- Pro Football Reference All-1950s Second-Team.
- Member of Pittsburgh Steelers Legends Team.

43

— ELBIE NICKEL —

The most impactful player the Steelers featured on offense during the first 25 years of their existence, Elbie Nickel made 329 pass receptions over the course of his career—a figure that remained a franchise record for nearly a quarter of a century. Starring at end for Pittsburgh for 11 seasons, Nickel also set a then-NFL record by appearing in 124 consecutive games during that time. Excelling as both a receiver and a blocker, Nickel served as the Steelers' offensive captain from 1949 to 1957, a period during which he led them in pass receptions twice and receiving yards four times. A three-time Pro Bowl selection, Nickel later earned the additional honor of being named to the Steelers' 75th Anniversary Team, with his exceptional play gaining him widespread recognition as the greatest tight end in franchise history prior to the arrival of Heath Miller.

Born in the rural town of Fullerton, Kentucky, on December 28, 1922, Elbert Everett Nickel grew up during the Great Depression, working hard on the family farm and pursuing an education, while also displaying a natural affinity for sports. After earning All-State honors in both basketball and football while attending local McKell High School, Nickel moved with his family to the state of Ohio, where he earned his degree from Chillicothe High School. Offered an athletic scholarship to attend the University of Cincinnati, Nickel spent his college days starring in baseball, basketball, and football, excelling as a pitcher-outfielder on the diamond, a top scorer on the hardwood, and an end on the gridiron.

Forced to put his education and athletic career on hold when he entered the US Army to serve his country during World War II, Nickel spent three years in the military, before returning to school after being discharged early in 1946. Picking up right where he left off on the football field, Nickel earned All-America honors as a senior in 1946, prompting the Steelers to select him in the 17th round of the 1947 NFL Draft, with the 149th overall pick. But, with Nickel also receiving a contract offer from the Cincinnati Reds, he seriously considered pursuing a career in baseball, before ultimately deciding to sign with the Steelers.

Arriving in Pittsburgh in 1947, the 6'1", 196-pound Nickel spent most of his rookie campaign playing on special teams, making just one reception for 10 yards. However, after bulking up to 220 pounds the following year, Nickel moved to tight end, where he spent the next four seasons serving mostly as a blocker in Pittsburgh's single-wing offense. Yet, even in that role, Nickel managed to establish himself as one of the Steelers' top offensive threats, finishing either first or second on the team in pass receiving yards in each of those years. Posting his most impressive numbers during that time in 1949, Nickel made 26 receptions for 633 yards and three touchdowns, with his average of 24.3 yards per reception leading the NFL.

Elbie Nickel's 329 receptions remained a franchise record for nearly a quarter of a century.
Courtesy of the Pittsburgh Steelers

Nickel didn't emerge as a truly elite offensive player, though, until the Steelers finally adapted to the T-formation in 1952, earning the first of his three Pro Bowl selections by placing near the top of the league rankings with 55 receptions, 884 receiving yards, and nine TD catches. He followed that up with another outstanding season, earning his second straight trip to the Pro Bowl in 1953 by finishing second in the league with 62 receptions, while also amassing 743 receiving yards and making four touchdown catches.

Blessed with excellent hands and outstanding speed, Nickel later drew praise from Steelers chairman Dan Rooney, who told Ed Bouchette of the *Pittsburgh Post-Gazette* in 2007, "Elbie was a great player, a better player than people really know. In those days, there wasn't a position called tight end, but he really was a tight end. He could block, and he caught the tough passes over the middle."

Nickel remained at tight end for two more years, making 40 receptions for 584 yards and five touchdowns in 1954, before catching 36 passes,

Nickel served as the Steelers' offensive captain for nine seasons.
Courtesy of the Pittsburgh Steelers

amassing 488 receiving yards, and making two TD grabs the following season. Moved to halfback in 1956, Nickel earned his final trip to the Pro Bowl by making 27 receptions for 376 yards and five touchdowns, with his solid play at a new position prompting his teammates to name him the club's Most Valuable Player. Assuming a backup role the following year, Nickel made just 10 receptions for 115 yards and one touchdown, before announcing his retirement at season's end with career totals of 329 receptions, 5,131 receiving yards, and 37 touchdowns. Nickel's 329 catches remained a Steelers record until Lynn Swann finally surpassed it in 1982.

Following his playing days, Nickel returned to Chillicothe, Ohio, where he worked alongside his father in the construction business for many years, before retiring to private life. After living in his home on McKell Road for nearly half a century, Nickel moved into a nursing home in Cincinnati, where he spent his final years suffering from Alzheimer's. He passed away at 84 years of age, on February 27, 2007, just eight months before Steeler fans named him to the franchise's 75th Anniversary Team. Years earlier, Nickel, who always held the city of Pittsburgh in high regard, stated, "I enjoyed my stay there. It was a good town. We didn't win too much. We were always a little short someplace."

CAREER HIGHLIGHTS

Best Season

Nickel had a big year for the Steelers in 1953, finishing second in the NFL with a career-high 62 receptions that remained a single-season franchise record until Roy Jefferson caught 67 passes in 1969. However, Nickel posted the best overall numbers of his career one year earlier, concluding the 1952 campaign with 55 receptions, 884 receiving yards, and nine touchdowns.

Memorable Moments/Greatest Performances

Nickel scored the first touchdown of his career on October 3, 1948, when he hauled in a 24-yard TD pass from Johnny Clement during a 24–14 win over the Boston Yanks.

Nickel recorded the Steelers' first points of the 1949 campaign in the regular-season opener, when he collaborated with Bob Gage on a 52-yard pass play during a 28–7 victory over the New York Giants.

Although the Steelers lost to the Chicago Bears by a score of 30–21 on December 4, 1949, Nickel had one of the most productive days of his career, making seven receptions for 192 yards and one touchdown, which came on a 48-yard pass from Joe Geri.

Nickel again starred in defeat on October 14, 1951, making five receptions for 149 yards and two touchdowns during a 28–24 loss to the San Francisco 49ers, with one of his TDs coming on a career-long 77-yard catch-and-run.

Nickel wasted another outstanding effort on November 16, 1952, when he made nine catches for 120 yards and one touchdown during a 29–28 loss to the Cleveland Browns.

Even though the Steelers suffered a 28–14 defeat at the hands of the Los Angeles Rams in the 1952 regular-season finale, Nickel once again excelled for the men in Black and Gold, making 10 receptions for a career-high 202 yards and one touchdown.

Nickel turned in another exceptional effort against Los Angeles on December 2, 1956, when, after being honored by the Steelers prior to the start of their final home game of the season, he led them to a 30–13 win over the Rams by collaborating with Jack Scarbath on a pair of scoring plays that covered 22 and 47 yards. With Nickel expected to announce his retirement at season's end, his teammates carried him off the field following the conclusion of the contest.

Yet, Nickel is remembered most in Pittsburgh for making what Steelers chairman Dan Rooney later called "the most famous play we had until the Immaculate Reception" during a 17–7 victory over the Philadelphia Eagles on October 23, 1954, that left the two teams tied for first place in the NFL's Eastern Division. Playing before a standing-room-only crowd at Forbes Field, Nickel hooked up with quarterback Jim Finks on a 52-yard play-action touchdown pass that sealed the win over the previously unde-feated Eagles. In placing Nickel's touchdown in its proper historical con-text, Rooney stated, "He was part of one of the most famous plays we ever had, probably the second most famous after the Immaculate Reception. We were playing the Eagles, and the Eagles had beaten us in a very controversial game earlier that season in Philadelphia, where they broke Jim Finks' jaw." Continuing to hold a prominent place in Steelers lore, the play was later depicted in a large X-and-O tapestry that has been hung at team offices for nearly half a century.

Notable Achievements

- Surpassed 50 receptions twice.
- Surpassed 700 receiving yards twice, topping 800 yards once (884 in 1952).
- Made nine touchdown receptions in 1952.

- Averaged more than 20 yards per reception twice.
- Led NFL with average of 24.3 yards per reception in 1949.
- Finished second in NFL with 62 receptions in 1953.
- Finished third in NFL with 55 receptions in 1952.
- Led Steelers in receptions twice and receiving yards four times.
- Ranks among Steelers career leaders with: 329 receptions (7th); 5,131 receiving yards (7th); and 37 touchdown receptions (8th).
- Missed just one game entire career, appearing in a then-NFL record 124 consecutive contests.
- 1956 Steelers MVP.
- Three-time Pro Bowl selection (1952, 1953, and 1956).
- Member of Pittsburgh Steelers Legends Team.
- Named to Steelers' 75th Anniversary Team in 2007.

44

GARY ANDERSON

Known to his teammates and Steelers fans as "Mr. Automatic" due to the level of consistency he displayed during his 13 seasons in Pittsburgh, Gary Anderson kicked more field goals and scored more points than anyone else in franchise history. Serving as the Steelers' placekicker from 1982 to 1994, Anderson scored more than 100 points eight times and successfully converted more than 85 percent of his field goal attempts twice, earning in the process three trips to the Pro Bowl, one All-Pro nomination, and four All-Conference selections. Along the way, Anderson helped the Steelers advance to the playoffs four times, with his outstanding kicking also earning him a spot on the franchise's 75th Anniversary Team. And, after leaving Pittsburgh, Anderson continued to perform at an extremely high level, eventually establishing himself as the leading scorer in NFL history at the time of his retirement.

Born in Parys, South Africa, on July 16, 1959, Gary Allan Anderson grew up in the Durban area of that country, where his father, a reverend who previously played soccer professionally in England, taught him how to kick a soccer ball from the time he could walk. Hoping to follow in his father's footsteps, Anderson played soccer and rugby while attending Brettonwood High School. But, shortly after he graduated from Brettonwood High, the 18-year-old Anderson had to alter his mindset when his father moved the family to the United States because of philosophical differences he had with the South African government over black suppression. Speaking of his father's decision years later, Anderson said, "My dad was very brave when he up and brought our family to America."

Presented with a few American footballs just days after he arrived in the United States, Anderson soon found himself drop-kicking them into the end zone from 50 yards out at a local high school football field in Downingtown, Pennsylvania. Discovered at his practice session by a group of college scouts, Anderson subsequently received scholarship offers from four different universities, one of which, Syracuse, promised him an opportunity to play for the school's soccer team as well. After accepting Syracuse's offer, Anderson spent his first two years in college playing both football and soccer, before devoting himself entirely to football his final two seasons.

Selected by the Buffalo Bills in the seventh round of the 1982 NFL Draft, with the 171st overall pick, Anderson failed to make much of an impression on Buffalo's coaching staff during training camp, prompting the team to cut him prior to the start of the regular season. However, he signed with the Steelers as a free agent just days later, beginning in the process his 13-year stint in the Steel City.

Gary Anderson kicked more field goals and scored more points than anyone else in franchise history.
Courtesy of the Pittsburgh Steelers

After earning a spot on the 1982 NFL All-Rookie Team by successfully converting 10 of his 12 field goal attempts and all 22 of his extra points, Anderson established himself as one of the league's elite placekickers the following season, earning team MVP, Pro Bowl, Second-Team All-Pro, and First-Team All-AFC honors by converting 27 of 31 field goal attempts and scoring 119 points. Performing well once again in 1984, Anderson connected on 75 percent of his field goal attempts, en route to placing among the league leaders with 24 field goals and 117 points. However, he had an even better year in 1985, earning First-Team All-AFC recognition and his second trip to the Pro Bowl by leading the NFL with 33 field goals and finishing second in the league with 139 points.

Despite playing for mediocre Steeler teams the next six seasons, Anderson remained one of the NFL's most consistent scorers and reliable placekickers, scoring more than 100 points and converting at least 80 percent of his field goal attempts two times each. Particularly effective in 1988, Anderson placed in the league's top three in field goals (28) and points scored (118). Known for his ability to focus on the task at hand, Anderson discussed what he considered to be his greatest asset, saying, "Probably the greatest ability a field-goal kicker has to have is the ability to concentrate. . . . When I'm out there kicking, I've got these big clowns standing seven yards from me, yelling at me, calling me names, calling my mom names, telling me, 'There's no way you're going to make this kick.' They try everything. You have to put that out of your mind and just concentrate on what you're doing."

Anderson remained with the Steelers through the end of 1994, having arguably his finest season for them in 1993, when he earned Pro Bowl and All-AFC honors for the last time as a member of the team by missing just two of his 30 field goal attempts and scoring 116 points. After failing to agree to terms on a new contract with the Steelers following the conclusion of the 1994 campaign, Anderson signed with the Philadelphia Eagles as a free agent. Expressing his dissatisfaction over having to leave Pittsburgh, Anderson said, "It's very disturbing to me that my career as a Pittsburgh Steeler seems to have come to an end over a contract. . . . It's the place I have my home. My wife is in Pittsburgh. My church is in Pittsburgh, and, as you know, thousands of loyal fans."

Anderson ended up spending two seasons in Philadelphia, before joining the San Francisco 49ers for one year and the Minnesota Vikings for five. Having the finest season of his career for the Vikings in 1998, Anderson successfully converted all 35 of his field goal attempts and all 59 of his extra points, becoming in the process the first placekicker in NFL history to finish the regular season with a 100 percent success rate in both categories. However, after being named First-Team All-Pro for the only time in his career, Anderson saw his season end on a sour note when his lone miss of the campaign led to an overtime loss to the Atlanta Falcons in the NFC championship game. After four more years in Minnesota, Anderson signed with the Tennessee

Anderson's consistency earned him the nickname "Mr. Automatic."
Courtesy of the Pittsburgh Steelers

Titans, with whom he spent his final two seasons, before announcing his retirement at 45 years of age following the conclusion of the 2004 campaign. Ending his career as the NFL's all-time leading scorer (he has since slipped to third), Anderson tallied 2,434 points over the course of 23 seasons, successfully converting 538 of his 672 field goal attempts and 820 of his 827 point-after attempts. During his time in Pittsburgh, he scored a total of 1,343 points, hitting on 309 of his 395 field goal attempts (78.2 percent), and missing only four of 420 extra-point attempts.

After retiring as an active player, Anderson moved his family to the Canadian Rocky Mountains in Canmore, Alberta, Canada, where he and his wife established an annual charity golf tournament that is aimed toward giving back to the community by making a positive difference in the lives of Bow Valley School athletes. Anderson also developed a passion for flyfishing, which has become his favorite hobby in retirement.

STEELERS CAREER HIGHLIGHTS

Best Season

Anderson earned his lone All-Pro nomination as a member of the Steelers in 1983, when he scored a total of 119 points, successfully converting 87.1 percent (27 of 31) of his field goal attempts and 97.4 percent (38 of 39) of his extra-point attempts. He also performed well in 1985, when, en route to finishing second in the NFL with 139 points scored, he led the league with 42 field goal attempts and 33 field goals made, successfully converting 78.6 percent of his field goal attempts in the process. However, Anderson had his best season for the Steelers in 1993, when he successfully converted 93.3 percent (28 of 30) of his field goal attempts and all 32 of his extra-point attempts, making him the league's second-most accurate kicker.

Memorable Moments/Greatest Performances

Anderson kicked four field goals in one game for the first time in his career during a 40–28 win over the Houston Oilers on September 18, 1983, splitting the uprights from 49, 35, 20, and 22 yards out.

Anderson accomplished the feat again on November 6, 1983, connecting from 45, 30, 49, and 42 yards out during a 26–3 win over the San Diego Chargers.

After converting a 48-yard field goal attempt earlier in the game, Anderson gave the Steelers a 20–17 victory over the eventual NFL champion San Francisco 49ers on October 14, 1984, by kicking a 21-yard field goal with just 1:42 left in regulation.

Anderson contributed to a 52–24 win over San Diego on November 25, 1984, by kicking a career-long 55-yard field goal.

Anderson proved to be the difference in a 36–28 victory over the Kansas City Chiefs on November 10, 1985, successfully converting all five of his field goal attempts, the longest of which came from 36 yards out.

Anderson once again thwarted the Chiefs on November 8, 1987, kicking a late-game 44-yard field goal that resulted in a 17–16 Steelers win.

Anderson kicked a career-high six field goals during a 39–21 victory over the Denver Broncos on October 23, 1988, with his longest kick coming from 37 yards out.

Anderson came up big for the Steelers in their 1989 AFC wild card matchup with the Houston Oilers, successfully converting all four of his field goal attempts, with his 50-yard kick in overtime giving them a 26–23 win that enabled them to advance to the divisional round of the postseason tournament.

Anderson accounted for all nine Steeler points during a 9–6 win over the New Orleans Saints on December 16, 1990, connecting from 29, 42, and 43 yards out.

Anderson once again scored every point the Steelers tallied during a 12–9 overtime win over the Houston Oilers on November 6, 1994, with his 40-yard field goal some four minutes into OT providing the margin of victory.

Anderson gave the Steelers another overtime win on November 20, 1994, when his 39-yard field goal with 4:41 left in OT enabled them to come away with a 16–13 victory over the Miami Dolphins.

Notable Achievements

- Scored more than 100 points eight times, surpassing 130 points once (139 in 1985).
- Converted more than 85 percent of field goal attempts twice, topping 90 percent once (93.3 in 1993).
- Led NFL with 33 field goals made in 1985.
- Finished second in NFL in: points scored once; field goals made once; and field goal percentage twice.
- Finished third in NFL in points scored twice.

- Holds Steelers career records for most points scored (1,343) and most field goals made (309).
- Ranks among NFL career leaders with: 2,434 points scored (3rd); 672 field goal attempts (2nd); 538 field goals made (3rd); 827 extra-point attempts (4th); 820 extra points made (3rd); and 353 games played (2nd).
- Four-time division champion (1983, 1984, 1992, and 1994).
- Member of 1982 NFL All-Rookie Team.
- 1983 Steelers MVP.
- Three-time Pro Bowl selection (1983, 1985, and 1993).
- 1983 Second-Team All-Pro selection.
- Three-time First-Team All-Conference selection (1983, 1985, and 1993).
- 1984 Second-Team All-Conference selection.
- Pro Football Hall of Fame All-1980s Second Team.
- Pro Football Hall of Fame All-1990s Second Team.
- Named to Steelers' 75th Anniversary Team in 2007.
- #1 "unofficially" retired by Steelers.

45

— ERNIE HOLMES —

The most feared member of Pittsburgh's "Steel Curtain" defense of the 1970s, Ernie Holmes played the game with an unmatched fury that revealed the inner demons he carried with him throughout much of his life. A powerful man who intimidated his own teammates, as well as the opposition, the massive Holmes once expressed his inner rage to *Time* magazine when he told that publication in 1975 that the violence of football attracted him, stating, "I don't mind knocking somebody out. If I hear a moan and a groan coming from a player I've hit, the adrenaline flows within me. I get more energy and play harder."

Yet, even though Holmes's volatile temperament sometimes made him nearly impossible to control, he proved to be a pillar of strength on the interior of Pittsburgh's defense for most of his six seasons with the Steelers, leading the team in sacks twice, while also enabling his fellow defenders to thrive by occupying multiple blockers on virtually every play. In all, Holmes contributed to five division championships, two AFC titles, and two Super Bowl victories during his time in Pittsburgh, earning in the process one All-Pro nomination and one All-AFC selection.

Born in Jamestown, Texas, on July 11, 1948, Ernest Lee Holmes acquired the nickname "Fats" due to his burly frame while growing up on his family's 45-acre farm located halfway between Dallas and the Louisiana border. After attending Wiergate High School, Holmes enrolled at Texas Southern University in Houston, where he spent three years starring on the gridiron at defensive tackle. Extremely busy off the field as well, Holmes married his girlfriend and started a family of his own, with his wife giving birth to two children before he graduated.

Selected by the Steelers in the eighth round of the 1971 NFL Draft, with the 203rd overall pick, Holmes arrived in Pittsburgh feeling as if he had the weight of the world on his shoulders. Believing that he needed to succeed at the pro level if he hoped to support his family, Holmes went all out on every play, both in practice and in games, using his helmet like a battering ram,

290

and butting his opponents under the chin as a way of knocking them off balance. With veteran Steelers offensive linemen forced to ask Holmes to ease up during practice so they didn't get hurt, former Oakland Raiders defensive tackle Tom Keating, who spent one season in Pittsburgh, later noted, "Nobody would line up against him in practice." Meanwhile, Steelers safety Mike Wagner commented, "He (Holmes) had a look that was really scary. I think he wanted to beat people to death—within the rules of the game."

After spending most of his rookie campaign of 1972 serving as a backup, Holmes assumed a far more prominent role the following year, laying claim to the starting right tackle job, which he held for most of the next five seasons. Stationed between left tackle "Mean" Joe Greene and right end Dwight White, Holmes proved to be as formidable as any member of Pittsburgh's defensive line, with Woody Widenhofer, who coached the team's linebackers, later saying that, on some days, he performed just as well as Greene. Greene, himself, said, "Oh, Ernie was definitely an enforcer. I suspect that a lot of guys were kind of afraid of him, not so much because of what he did on the field, but because of the things they read about him off the field. He'd probably do anything to win."

A fierce competitor who enjoyed the physicality of his sport, Holmes described the approach he took to his job when he said, "Once I hit the field, there's a feeling I get, a responsibility to get a job done, not to let down my teammates. . . . If I hurt someone, well, I hurt someone. That's a part of the job."

In discussing the ferocious nature of Holmes's play, former teammate Andy Russell stated, "He was devastating and would just destroy the opponent across from him. Sometimes I had to remind him to tackle the guy with the pigskin. He was a brilliant player. He played with all his heart."

Commenting on the difficulties that Holmes presented to opposing offensive linemen,

Ernie Holmes proved to be the most intimidating member of Pittsburgh's "Steel Curtain" defense.
Courtesy of the Pittsburgh Steelers

Steelers head coach Chuck Noll said, "You want to know how good he was, how tough? Take a look at the way the guy who had to play against him looks coming off the field after the game—if he was able to finish it."

Although listed at 6'3" and 260 pounds, Holmes spent most of his career playing at close to 300 pounds, making him extremely difficult for opposing linemen to budge, which Dan Rooney noted when he said, "He was one of those guys who really was important to the team and the Steel Curtain. He played in the middle and was really tough to get out of there, which gave Joe and the other guys a chance to get to the quarterback."

In addition to clogging up the middle, Holmes did an excellent job of rushing the passer himself, twice amassing more than 10 sacks in a season, en route to compiling a total of 40 over the course of his career.

Yet, as well as Holmes performed for the Steelers on the playing field, he developed a reputation during his time in Pittsburgh for being "stone crazy," as he explained to *Time* magazine in 1975, due to his eccentric behavior off the field. Acquiring the moniker "Arrowhead Holmes" after he shaved his head, leaving only an arrow-shaped pattern of hair on his skull, Holmes experienced his most bizarre moment as a member of the Steelers on March 16, 1973, when he had an emotional breakdown while driving on the Ohio Turnpike, firing a loaded handgun at passing trucks and a police helicopter that subsequently pursued him. Later found in a field near his abandoned car in Goshen Township, Mahoning County, Ohio, Holmes threw his gun away, put his hands up, and explained to the officers that apprehended him that traffic made him nervous. After pleading guilty to assault with a deadly weapon, Holmes had his initial sentence of five years' probation suspended when Chuck Noll and Dan Rooney spoke out on his behalf. However, he agreed to undergo psychiatric treatment, which revealed that he suffered from acute paranoid psychosis exacerbated by his recent marital woes.

Admitting that he sometimes did not understand his own behavior, Holmes once told *Time* magazine, "I don't know what my life is, except there's something pounding in the back of my head."

But longtime Steelers director of communications Joe Gordon suggested that Holmes had a much calmer side, stating, "He had a split personality. He was a maniac on the field and a teddy bear off it. But he was a terrific guy."

Joe Greene expressed similar sentiments when he called Holmes a "gentle soul," recalling a team Christmas party when he dressed up as Santa Claus and purchased gifts for all his teammates' children. Greene added that he found Holmes reading a Bible in a dorm room when he first met him at training camp, saying, "That's the Ernie Holmes I knew."

Holmes remained in Pittsburgh until the end of 1977, when the Steelers traded him to the Tampa Bay Buccaneers due to ongoing weight problems. After failing to make the Tampa Bay roster, Holmes signed with the New England Patriots, for whom he appeared in three games in 1978 before announcing his retirement.

Holmes initially experienced some problems following the conclusion of his playing career, being arrested for drunk driving in Phoenix, Arizona, in 1978, and being acquitted on drug charges in Amarillo, Texas, a year later. However, he eventually turned his life around, settling on a ranch on the southeast border of Texas, where he had a church and became an ordained minister.

Holmes led the Steelers in sacks twice.
Courtesy of the Pittsburgh Steelers

Holmes lived until January 17, 2008, when he perished in a one-car accident near Beaumont, Texas. Thrown from his vehicle after it left the road and rolled several times, Holmes was pronounced dead at the scene, with the Texas Department of Transportation reporting he had not been wearing a seat belt. Holmes was 59 years old at the time of his passing.

Upon learning of Holmes's death, Steelers chairman Dan Rooney said in a statement: "Ernie was one of the toughest players to ever wear a Steelers uniform. He was a key member of our famous 'Steel Curtain' defense, and many people who played against him considered Ernie almost impossible to block. At his best, he was an intimidating player who even the toughest of opponents did not want to play against."

Fellow "Steel Curtain" member Dwight White said of his longtime teammate, "Ernie was a very colorful person that you couldn't help but like off the football field. Ernie had gotten into the ministry, and he was a true inspiration to Joe, L.C., and myself when we were together. You know, it's all about where you end up, and Ernie blossomed into an individual that I respected, admired, and will miss."

White then added, "I just wish he could have gotten more recognition for the job he did. . . . Ernie was a tremendous football player. Not taking anything away from Joe—we know where *he* is—Ernie was as good, and, in some cases, even better."

Jack Ham expressed similar sentiments when he said, "Joe Greene got a lot of attention, and rightfully so, but Ernie was a great football player. We all knew it on the team. Our teammates knew how important he was to the team, and maybe he didn't get the recognition he deserved."

STEELERS CAREER HIGHLIGHTS

Best Season

Although the NFL did not keep an official record of quarterback sacks until the 1980s, the Steelers credit Holmes with a team-leading and career-high 11 sacks in 1974. Over the course of that campaign, Holmes tied a franchise record by recording at least one sack in six consecutive games, making that the most dominant season of his career.

Memorable Moments/Greatest Performances

Holmes's stellar play in the middle helped limit O. J. Simpson to just 49 yards on 15 carries during the Steelers' 32–14 victory over Buffalo in their 1974 divisional round playoff matchup.

Holmes continued his exceptional play against Oakland in that year's AFC championship game and Minnesota in Super Bowl IX, anchoring a defense that held the Raiders to only 29 yards rushing and the Vikings to just 17 yards on the ground and 119 yards of total offense. Looking back on Holmes's contributions to Pittsburgh's successful championship run, teammate Jack Ham recalled, "That run we had in '74 and through the playoffs and our first Super Bowl, he just had a dominating performance, especially against Gene Upshaw and the Raiders in Oakland in the AFC Championship Game. I think they rushed for 29 yards in that game. It was the most dominating performance against a great offensive line. He's a big reason why we ended up winning that game. . . . And what they did against Minnesota, the entire front four!" When asked how well Holmes played against Oakland, Dwight White replied, "Ask Gene Upshaw, and Gene was good. I had (Art) Shell, he had Upshaw, and he made a long afternoon for Gene, and that made it a much easier afternoon for me."

Notable Achievements

- Recorded more than 10 sacks in a season twice.
- Led Steelers in sacks twice.
- Ranks 12th in Steelers history with 40 sacks.
- Five-time division champion (1972, 1974, 1975, 1976, and 1977).
- Two-time AFC champion (1974 and 1975).
- Two-time Super Bowl champion (IX and X).
- 1974 NEA Second-Team All-Pro selection.
- 1975 Second-Team All-Conference selection.

46

— LOUIS LIPPS —

A victim of bad timing, Louis Lipps had the misfortune of joining the Steelers in 1984, five seasons after their NFL dynasty of the 1970s ended, and just one year after Terry Bradshaw announced his retirement. The fact that Lipps spent the next eight seasons playing for mostly mediocre Steeler squads that lacked an elite signal-caller has often prevented him from being recognized as one of the finest wide receivers in franchise history. Nevertheless, nearly three decades after he played his last game in Pittsburgh, Lipps, who led the Steelers in receptions four times and receiving yards six times, continues to rank high in team annals in every major pass-receiving category. Also excelling on special teams during the early stages of his career, Lipps returned three punts for touchdowns and led the NFL in punt-return yards once, with his outstanding all-around play earning him team MVP honors twice, two Pro Bowl selections, and a pair of All-Pro nominations.

Born in New Orleans, Louisiana, on August 9, 1962, Louis Adam Lipps Jr. grew up in the nearby town of Reserve, where he spent much of his youth dreaming of one day playing for the Cincinnati Reds. In discussing his early years, Lipps recalled, "I grew up in an itty-bitty country town. It's not much more than a grocery store, an auto-parts shop, and nothing but woods all around. You can pass through it without knowing it's there. I figured nobody would ever find me."

After starring in baseball and football while attending East St. John High School, Lipps enrolled at the University of Southern Mississippi, where, after accomplishing very little his first two seasons, he emerged as a top receiver and punt-returner his last two years. Performing especially well as a senior in 1983, Lipps led the nation with 460 punt-return yards and made 42 receptions for 800 yards and five touchdowns, prompting the Steelers to select him in the first round of the 1984 NFL Draft, with the 23rd overall pick.

Mentored by John Stallworth upon his arrival in Pittsburgh, Lipps made an immediate impact with the Steelers, scoring a pair of touchdowns in his first game as a pro. He then went on to make 45 receptions for 860 yards, lead the NFL with a rookie-record 656 punt-return yards, and score 11 touchdowns, earning in the process Pro Bowl, Second-Team All-Pro, First-Team All-AFC, and NFL Offensive Rookie of the Year honors. Lipps followed that up with an even more productive 1985 campaign in which he caught 59 passes, finished second in the NFL with 12 TD catches and 15 touchdowns, and ranked among the league leaders with 1,134 receiving yards, 437 punt-return yards, 1,827 all-purpose

Louis Lipps led the Steelers in receptions four times and receiving yards six times.
Courtesy of the Pittsburgh Steelers

yards, and an average of 12.1 yards per punt return, with his outstanding play earning him team MVP honors and Pro Bowl, All-Pro, and All-Conference recognition for the second straight year.

Unfortunately, after sneaking into the playoffs with a record of 9-7 in 1984, the Steelers posted their first losing record in 14 seasons the following year, concluding the 1985 campaign with a mark of 7-9. Sadly, that trend continued during Lipps's six remaining years in Pittsburgh, with the Steelers never finishing any better than 9-7 and advancing to the playoffs just once more during that time. Nevertheless, Lipps remained one of the NFL's better wide receivers throughout the period, catching at least 50 passes four more times and amassing more than 900 receiving yards twice, with his 50 receptions, 944 receiving yards, six touchdowns, and 180 rushing yards in 1989 earning him team MVP honors for the second time.

Blessed with outstanding speed, good moves, soft hands, and excellent route-running ability, Lipps proved to be one of the NFL's finest all-around receivers. Using his quickness to establish himself as a top deep threat, Lipps annually ranked among the league leaders in yards-per-catch, three times averaging more than 19 yards per reception, and making nine TD

Lipps earned NFL Offensive Rookie of the Year honors in 1984.
Courtesy of the Pittsburgh Steelers

catches of 60 yards or longer. Deceptively strong as well, the 5'10", 190-pound Lipps excelled at warding off his defender at the line of scrimmage and breaking into his route quickly. Seeking to make good use of Lipps's speed and sharp cutting ability, the Steelers used him in a variety of ways, employing him as a punt-returner his first two years in the league, before occasionally using him as a runner during the latter stages of his career.

Yet, despite Lipps's outstanding play the previous eight seasons, the Steelers chose to release him following a contract dispute that lasted into the opening weeks of the 1992 campaign. Subsequently signed by the New Orleans Saints, Lipps appeared in just two games for his hometown team, making only one reception, before suffering an injury that forced him to announce his retirement at season's end. Signing a one-day contract with the Steelers so that he might retire as a member of the team, Lipps ended his career with 359 receptions, 6,019 receiving yards, 388 rushing yards, 1,234 punt-return yards, 7,890 all-purpose yards, 39 touchdown catches, and 46 touchdowns, compiling virtually all those numbers during his time in Pittsburgh.

Choosing to remain in Pittsburgh following his retirement, Lipps has spent the last several years working for Steel City Mortgage Services and cohosting a weekly Steelers-themed radio program on ESPN. Looking back fondly on his years with the Steelers and the fans that frequented Three Rivers Stadium, Lipps says, "Here in Pittsburgh, you feel so attached to the fans because the fans are so attached to us. That's what makes it special. It makes you want to go out there and perform, not only for you and for your coaches and your teammates, but for the people that would do anything for you. Pittsburgh is just a special place to play."

STEELERS CAREER HIGHLIGHTS

Best Season

Lipps performed exceptionally well for the Steelers in his first NFL season, earning Second-Team All-Pro and 1984 NFL Offensive Rookie of the Year honors by making 45 receptions, amassing 860 receiving yards, 931 yards from scrimmage, and 1,587 all-purpose yards, scoring 11 touchdowns, and leading the league with 656 punt-return yards. However, he compiled even more impressive numbers the following year, concluding the 1985 campaign with a career-high 59 receptions, 1,134 receiving yards, 12 TD catches, 15 touchdowns, and 1,827 all-purpose yards, with his outstanding play once again earning him Second-Team All-Pro honors.

Memorable Moments/Greatest Performances

Although the Steelers lost the opening game of the 1984 regular season to Kansas City by a score of 37–27, Lipps began his pro career in style, making six receptions for 183 yards and two touchdowns, which came on an 80-yard connection with David Woodley and a 21-yard hookup with Mark Malone.

Lipps starred again during a 27–24 loss to the New Orleans Saints on November 19, 1984, catching four passes for 81 yards and scoring two touchdowns, one of which came on a 76-yard punt return.

Lipps contributed to a 45–3 blowout of the Indianapolis Colts in the 1985 regular-season opener by making nine receptions for 154 yards and three touchdowns, the longest of which covered 16 yards.

Although the Steelers lost to Cincinnati by a score of 26–21 on October 27, 1985, Lipps scored a pair of touchdowns, with one of those coming on a 49-yard reception and the other on a 62-yard punt return.

Lipps scored his final touchdown on special teams during a 36–28 win over the Kansas City Chiefs on November 10, 1985, when he returned a punt 71 yards for a TD.

Lipps torched Detroit's defensive secondary for eight catches, 150 receiving yards, and two touchdowns during a 27–17 win on December 7, 1986, with his scoring plays covering 12 and 39 yards.

Even though the Steelers suffered a 27–26 defeat at the hands of the Philadelphia Eagles on November 13, 1988, Lipps had a huge game, throwing a 13-yard TD pass to Merril Hoge and making six receptions for 171 yards and one touchdown, which came on a career-long 89-yard hookup with Bubby Brister.

Lipps helped the Steelers record a 37–34 victory over the Houston Oilers on December 4, 1988, by making four receptions for 166 yards and two touchdowns, with his scoring plays coming on 80- and 65-yard passes from Bubby Brister.

Lipps provided most of the offensive firepower during a 23–17 win over Kansas City on October 29, 1989, making seven catches for 130 yards and scoring both Steeler touchdowns on pass plays that covered 16 and 64 yards.

Lipps earned AFC Offensive Player of the Week honors for his performance during a 31–22 victory over the Tampa Bay Buccaneers in the final game of the 1989 regular season, when he made four receptions for 137 yards and two touchdowns, which came on collaborations of 79 and 12 yards with Bubby Brister.

Lipps helped the Steelers defeat the Denver Broncos by a score of 34–17 on October 14, 1990, by making nine receptions for 141 yards and one TD, which came on a 6-yard pass from Brister.

Yet, Lipps made perhaps the most memorable catch of his career during a 17–12 loss to Cincinnati on September 18, 1988, when he caught a pass from Bubby Brister in his facemask and was credited with a 9-yard TD reception that subsequently became known as the "Steel City Wonder."

Notable Achievements

- Surpassed 50 receptions five times.
- Surpassed 1,000 receiving yards once, topping 900 yards two other times.
- Amassed more than 1,000 yards from scrimmage three times.
- Amassed more than 1,000 all-purpose yards four times, topping 1,500 yards twice.
- Scored more than 10 touchdowns twice.
- Returned three punts for touchdowns.
- Led NFL with 656 punt-return yards in 1984.
- Finished second in NFL with 12 touchdown receptions and 15 touchdowns in 1985.
- Finished third in NFL in punt-return average twice.
- Led Steelers in receptions four times and receiving yards six times.
- Ranks among Steelers career leaders with: 358 receptions (5th); 6,018 receiving yards (5th); 39 touchdown receptions (7th); 46 touchdowns (7th); and 1,212 punt-return yards (5th).
- 1984 division champion.
- 1984 NFL Offensive Rookie of the Year.
- 1989 Week 16 AFC Offensive Player of the Week.
- Two-time Steelers MVP (1985 and 1989).
- Two-time Pro Bowl selection (1984 and 1985).
- Two-time Second-Team All-Pro selection (1984 and 1985).
- Two-time First-Team All-Conference selection (1984 and 1985).

47

— ROCKY BLEIER —

A study in courage and perseverance, Rocky Bleier overcame seemingly insurmountable odds to forge an extremely successful career for himself in Pittsburgh. Considered too small and too slow to make it as a running back in the NFL when he first entered the league, Bleier also had to contend with serious injuries that he suffered while serving his country in Vietnam—injuries that threatened to end his football career before it even began. But, through much hard work and dedication, Bleier eventually earned a spot on the Steelers roster, after which he went on to establish himself as an integral member of all four Super Bowl championship teams of the 1970s. One of the better all-around running backs in franchise history, Bleier ended his career as the fourth leading ground gainer in team annals. Meanwhile, his early struggles, underdog status, and friendly demeanor helped make him one of the most popular players ever to don a Steelers uniform.

Born in Appleton, Wisconsin, on March 5, 1946, Robert Patrick Bleier spent his youth living with his parents and four younger siblings in an apartment above his father's saloon. Acquiring the nickname "Rocky" as a baby, Bleier later explained how the moniker became affixed to him: "As the first born of the family, my dad was proud, as all parents are. And the guys would come into the bar and say, 'Bob, how's that new kid of yours?' And my dad would go, 'Aw, you should see him, guys, looks like a little rock sitting in that crib. He's got all these muscles.' So, they'd come back in the bar and they'd say, 'Hey Bob, how's that little rock of yours?' So, after that, that's how I got it. It stuck."

Bleier attended Xavier High School, where he starred in football, basketball, and track, serving as team captain in all three sports. Proving to be particularly proficient on the gridiron, Bleier earned All-State honors three times as a running back and made All-Conference at both linebacker and defensive back. After graduating from Xavier High, Bleier enrolled at the University of Notre Dame in South Bend, Indiana, where he spent

three seasons starting in the
offensive backfield, helping
the Fighting Irish capture the
National Championship as a
junior in 1966, before being
named a team captain the following year.

Subsequently selected by
the Steelers in the 16th round
of the 1968 NFL Draft, with
the 417th overall pick, Bleier
arrived at his first pro training
camp being given little chance
of making the team. Standing 5'10" tall, weighing just
over 200 pounds, and lacking
superior running speed, Bleier
possessed neither the size nor
the quickness of a prototypical
NFL running back. Nevertheless, he made enough of an

Rocky Bleier overcame tremendous odds
to star for the Steelers after serving his
country in Vietnam.
Courtesy of the Pittsburgh Steelers

impression on the coaching staff with his strong work ethic to make the
final cut, after which he spent most of his rookie season playing on special
teams.

Drafted into the US Army following the conclusion of that 1968 campaign, Bleier volunteered for combat duty in Vietnam, where, just a few
months later, on August 20, 1969, he sustained injuries to his legs and right
foot during an enemy ambush in a rice paddy near Chu Lai. Wounded in
the left thigh by an enemy bullet, Bleier fell to the ground, only to have
a grenade explode nearby, sending pieces of shrapnel into his lower right
leg and foot. Subsequently told by doctors that a return to the NFL did
not seem possible, Bleier, nonetheless, retained a glimmer of hope that
he might eventually resume his career in pro football, with a postcard he
received from Steelers owner Art Rooney while recovering from his wounds
in a Tokyo hospital giving him added incentive. The postcard, which read,
"Rock—the team's not doing well. We need you. Art Rooney," inspired the
injured soldier to do everything within his power to mount a comeback,
with Bleier later saying, "When you have somebody take the time and
interest to send you a postcard, something that they didn't have to do, you
have a special place for those kinds of people."

Despite being classified by the army as 40 percent disabled after undergoing multiple surgeries to remove the shrapnel from his leg and foot, Bleier returned to the Steelers following his discharge from the military in July 1970. Lacking stamina, unable to walk without pain, and weighing only 180 pounds, Bleier faced an uphill battle to regain a roster spot, failing to do so even though he put in a great deal of time and effort to get himself back into playing condition. Placed on injured reserve for the entire 1970 campaign, Bleier made just a few token appearances on special teams the following year, prompting various trainers, doctors, and coaches to advise him to quit. Bleier, though, refused to give up, stating years later that he continued to work as hard as he did so that "some time in the future you didn't have to ask yourself 'what if?'"

However, after playing almost exclusively on special teams in both 1972 and 1973, Bleier grew increasingly despondent, causing him to seriously consider leaving the game for the first time. Subsequently persuaded by teammate Andy Russell to return to the team in 1974, Bleier adopted an even more rigorous offseason training program that included weightlifting, yoga, and three running sessions per day, leaving him in tremendous physical condition by the time he reported to training camp that summer. Weighing 212 pounds and posting a personal-best time of 4.6 seconds in the 40-yard dash, Bleier received more significant playing time at running back during the early stages of the campaign, before starting the season's final seven games alongside Franco Harris in the offensive backfield. Proving to be a major contributor to a Pittsburgh team that captured the division title with a record of 10-3-1, Bleier did an exceptional job of blocking for Harris on running plays, while also rushing for 373 yards and two touchdowns himself during the regular season. He then gained another 208 yards in the playoffs, in helping the Steelers win their first NFL championship.

Bleier's strong running and superb blocking made him an invaluable member of four Super Bowl winning teams.
Courtesy of MEARSonlineauctions.com

Despite being limited by injuries to just 11 games the following year, Bleier put together another solid season, rushing for 528 yards and two touchdowns, before reaching the apex of his career in 1976, when he rushed for 1,036 yards, gained another 294 yards on 24 pass receptions, scored five touchdowns, and led the Steelers with 1,330 yards from scrimmage. With both Bleier and Harris gaining more than 1,000 yards on the ground, they became just the second running back tandem in league history to accomplish the feat.

Bleier's emergence as one of the NFL's better running backs, coupled with his superior blocking ability, helped make him a fan favorite in Pittsburgh. However, Steeler fans appreciated Bleier even more for the resolve he displayed that enabled him to overcome the many obstacles he faced during the early stages of his career. Bleier further ingratiated himself to the hometown fans with his ready smile, friendly demeanor, and willingness to give of himself whenever possible.

Although Bleier never again reached the heights he attained in 1976, he continued to contribute to the success the Steelers experienced throughout the remainder of the decade, performing especially well in 1978, when he rushed for 633 yards, gained 168 yards on 17 pass receptions, and scored a career-high six touchdowns. Choosing to announce his retirement following the conclusion of the 1980 campaign, Bleier ended his career with 3,865 yards rushing, which currently represents the ninth-highest figure in franchise history. He also caught 136 passes for 1,294 yards, amassed 5,467 all-purpose yards, scored 25 touchdowns, and compiled a rushing average of 4.2 yards per carry. A solid postseason performer, Bleier rushed for 480 yards, made 19 receptions for 202 yards, and scored six touchdowns in 18 career playoff games.

Bleier, whose book, *Fighting Back: The Rocky Bleier Story*, was made into a television movie in 1980, became an author and speaker on retirement and financial management after he left the game. Still considered one of Pittsburgh's foremost citizens, Bleier told writer Rick Telander in an article that appeared in a 1986 issue of *Sports Illustrated*, "I'm a breathing example of what you can do if you want to."

CAREER HIGHLIGHTS

Best Season

Bleier had easily his best season for the Steelers in 1976, when he established career-high marks in rushing yards (1,036), pass-receiving yards

(294), yards from scrimmage (1,330), and rushing average (4.7 yards per carry).

Memorable Moments/Greatest Performances

Bleier scored the first touchdown of his career on a 2-yard run during a 34–24 win over the Kansas City Chiefs on October 13, 1974.

Bleier had his breakout game two weeks later, rushing for 78 yards and one touchdown during a 24–17 win over the Atlanta Falcons on October 28, 1974.

Bleier proved to be a huge contributor to Pittsburgh's 32–14 victory over Buffalo in the divisional round of the 1974 playoffs, rushing for 45 yards and making three receptions for 54 yards and one touchdown, which came on a 27-yard pass from Terry Bradshaw.

Bleier followed that up with another strong performance against Oakland in the AFC championship game, carrying the ball 18 times for 98 yards, and gaining another 25 yards on two pass receptions during the Steelers' 24–13 win.

Bleier continued his outstanding postseason play against Minnesota in Super Bowl IX, rushing for 65 yards, in helping the Steelers defeat the Vikings by a score of 16–6.

Bleier had a huge day against Green Bay on October 26, 1975, leading the Steelers to a 16–13 victory by rushing for a career-high 163 yards.

Bleier saved many of his finest performances for his banner year of 1976, rushing for 102 yards during a 45–0 blowout of the Chiefs on November 7, before gaining another 110 yards on the ground during a 14–3 win over the Dolphins the following week. Bleier then contributed to a 42–0 romp over the Tampa Bay Buccaneers on December 5 by rushing for 118 yards and three touchdowns, before going over 1,000 yards for the only time in his career by gaining 107 yards on the ground during a 21–0 win over the Houston Oilers in the regular-season finale.

Bleier proved to be a major factor in Pittsburgh's 35–31 win over Dallas in Super Bowl XIII, catching a 7-yard touchdown pass from Terry Bradshaw that gave the Steelers a second-quarter lead they never surrendered, and recovering a Dallas onside kick in the closing seconds, thereby sealing the victory for the Steelers.

Bleier experienced one final moment of glory on October 7, 1979, when he recorded a career-long 70-yard touchdown run during a 51–35 victory over the Cleveland Browns.

Notable Achievements

- Rushed for more than 1,000 yards once (1,036 in 1976).
- Averaged more than 4.5 yards per carry twice.
- Led Steelers with 1,330 yards from scrimmage in 1976.
- Ranks ninth in Steelers history with 3,865 yards rushing.
- Seven-time division champion (1972, 1974, 1975, 1976, 1977, 1978, and 1979).
- Four-time AFC champion (1974, 1975, 1978, and 1979).
- Four-time Super Bowl champion (IX, X, XIII, and XIV).
- 1980 NFL Man of the Year.
- Named to Steelers' 75th Anniversary Team in 2007.

48

— DWAYNE WOODRUFF —

S ince Dwayne Woodruff did not join the Steelers until the final year of
their 1970s NFL dynasty, he often fails to receive the credit he deserves
for being one of the finest cornerbacks in franchise history. Woodruff is
also often overlooked because he spent most of his time in Pittsburgh playing on the opposite side of the field from Hall of Fame corners Mel Blount
and Rod Woodson. Nevertheless, Woodruff proved to be an extremely
consistent and reliable player for the Steelers, leading them in interceptions
five times, en route to recording the fifth-most picks in team annals. Also
ranking among the franchise's all-time leaders in interception-return yards
and defensive touchdowns scored, Woodruff earned team MVP honors
once and helped the Steelers capture three division titles. Yet, the contributions that Woodruff made to the Steelers over the course of his 11-year
NFL career pale in comparison to the things he has accomplished since
leaving the game.

Born in Bowling Green, Kentucky, on February 18, 1957, Dwayne
Donzell Woodruff grew up in Ohio after moving there with his mother
and father, a career Army infantryman who became a quadriplegic due to
the physical stress placed on his body during his military service, which
included fighting in the Vietnam War. After attending New Richmond
High School, Woodruff briefly considered pursuing a career as an Air Force
pilot, before his father's rapidly deteriorating physical condition prompted
him to go in a different direction. Choosing to enroll at the University of
Louisville, Woodruff spent the next four years excelling both academically
and athletically, with his outstanding play on the gridiron fostering in him
the notion of one day playing in the NFL. However, after he posted a poor
time in the 40-yard dash while battling a knee injury in his senior year,
Woodruff did not receive an invitation to the NFL combine. Nevertheless,
his on-field play made enough of an impression on the Steelers that they
ended up selecting him in the sixth round of the 1979 NFL Draft, with the
161st overall pick.

Dwayne Woodruff recorded the fifth most interceptions in franchise history.
Courtesy of the Pittsburgh Steelers

After arriving in Pittsburgh, Woodruff spent his first year in the league playing mostly on special teams and serving as a backup to starting cornerbacks Mel Blount and Ron Johnson. Still, he appeared in all 16 regular-season contests, recording the first interception of his career, which he returned for 31 yards. Assuming a more prominent role in the playoffs, Woodruff made huge contributions to the Steelers' successful run to their fourth NFL title in six years by picking off two passes, including one against

Miami in the divisional round of the postseason tournament and another against Houston in the AFC championship game. After continuing to function in a similar capacity in 1980, Woodruff broke into the starting lineup the following year, when, playing opposite Blount on the left side of Pittsburgh's defense, he intercepted one pass and recovered one fumble.

Woodruff subsequently emerged as one of the NFL's better corner-backs during the strike-shortened 1982 campaign, when he recorded five interceptions in just nine games, which tied him with five other players for the second-most picks in the league. Named the Steelers' Most Valuable Player for his outstanding performance, Woodruff went on to lead the team in interceptions in four of the next seven seasons as well, picking off five passes another three times and twice amassing more than 100 interception-return yards. Choosing to announce his retirement after he recorded three interceptions and 110 interception-return yards in a part-time role in 1990, Woodruff ended his career with 37 interceptions, 689 interception-return yards, three touchdown interceptions, and five defensive touchdowns scored, with his totals in all four categories placing him among the franchise's all-time leaders. Appearing in every game for the Steelers six times, Woodruff missed a significant number of contests just once, sitting out the entire 1986 campaign after undergoing reconstructive knee surgery during the preseason.

Only 33 years old at the time of his retirement, Woodruff decided to pursue a new career path for which he had set the foundation several years earlier. While still playing for the Steelers, he began studying law, later explaining his motivation by saying, "Being a lawyer would do two things: it was competitive, and I like the competitive side and the preparation. It's like a battle, like football."

Living with his wife in Louisville during the offseason at the time, Woodruff applied to two law schools, the University of Louisville and Pittsburgh's Duquesne University. Accepted by both, Woodruff ultimately elected to attend Duquesne since it had a night program. After relocating to Pittsburgh full-time, Woodruff adopted a new lifestyle during the football season that he described thusly: "I'd go to the stadium in the morning and leave early evening. Then, I'd go to class from 6:00 PM to 9:00 PM, then study, and then home by midnight."

After earning his degree in 1988, Woodruff spent three years practicing law at the Meyer Darragh law firm while still competing in the NFL. He remained at Meyer Darragh until 1997, when he became a founding part-ner of the law firm Woodruff, Flaherty and Fardo. Elected a judge in 2005, Woodruff left his private practice and has spent the last 14 years overseeing the Court of Common Pleas in Allegheny County, where he continues to use his position to educate and help others. Chairing many committees and commissions related to the betterment of family services and the Pennsylvania court system, Woodruff has received numerous accolades for his work. Woodruff is also the vice president of the NFL Alumni Players Association and a chairperson of the "Do the Write Thing" program in Pittsburgh, which is an initiative of the National Campaign to Stop Violence (NCSV). The program strives to empower middle school students to break the cycles of violence in their

Woodruff led the Steelers in picks five times.
Courtesy of the Pittsburgh Steelers

homes, schools, and neighborhoods by giving them an opportunity to examine the impact of violence on their lives through classroom discussions and written discourse.

CAREER HIGHLIGHTS

Best Season

An extremely consistent player, Woodruff did not have any one season that stood out above all others. But the fact that he earned team MVP honors in 1982 by finishing second in the NFL with five interceptions in only nine games would seem to indicate that Woodruff played the best ball of his career that year.

Memorable Moments/Greatest Performances

Woodruff recorded his first career interception during a 16–13 overtime victory over the Patriots in the 1979 regular-season opener.

Woodruff made the key play in a 26–20 overtime win over the Bengals on September 19, 1982, putting the Steelers in position to win the game on the very next play by picking off a Ken Anderson pass and returning the ball 30 yards to Cincinnati's 2-yard line during the overtime session. Terry Bradshaw subsequently gave the Steelers the victory with a short toss to John Stallworth.

Woodruff recorded two interceptions in one game for the first time in his career during a 44–17 win over the Cleveland Browns on October 16, 1983, returning his two picks a total of 79 yards.

Woodruff earned AFC Defensive Player of the Week honors for his performance during a 38–17 victory over Cincinnati on October 1, 1984, when he intercepted two passes, one of which he returned 42 yards for his first career touchdown.

Woodruff contributed to a 35–10 win over the Atlanta Falcons on October 28, 1984, by picking off a pass and returning a fumble 65 yards for a touchdown.

Although the Steelers lost to the New Orleans Saints by a score of 20–16 on November 29, 1987, Woodruff again crossed the opponent's goal line when he returned an interception 33 yards for a touchdown.

Woodruff provided much of the impetus for a 40–24 victory over the Miami Dolphins in the final game of the 1988 regular season when he scored the game's first points on a 78-yard interception return of a Dan Marino pass.

Woodruff scored the last of his five career touchdowns against the Dolphins as well, returning a fumble recovery that teammate Carnell Lake lateraled to him 21 yards for the tying score of a 34–14 win on November 26, 1989.

Notable Achievements

- Scored five defensive touchdowns during career.
- Recorded five interceptions four times.
- Surpassed 100 interception-return yards twice.
- Led NFL with two non-offensive touchdowns in 1984.
- Tied for second in NFL with five interceptions in 1982.
- Finished third in NFL with 65 fumble-return yards in 1984.
- Led Steelers in interceptions five times.
- Ranks among Steelers career leaders with: 37 interceptions (5th); 689 interception-return yards (4th); three touchdown interceptions (tied—5th); and five defensive touchdowns (tied—2nd).

- Three-time division champion (1979, 1983, and 1984).
- 1979 AFC champion.
- Super Bowl XIV champion.
- 1984 Week 5 AFC Defensive Player of the Week.
- 1982 Steelers MVP.

49

— LAMARR WOODLEY —

O ften criticized for being overweight and out of shape, LaMarr Woodley
failed to fulfill the enormous potential he displayed his first few seasons in Pittsburgh. Hampered by injuries likely brought on by poor
conditioning, Woodley missed a total of 14 games his last three years with
the Steelers, greatly diminishing his on-field production. However, prior to
that, he established himself as one of the NFL's top outside linebackers and
most feared pass-rushers, sacking opposing quarterbacks at least 10 times
in three straight seasons, en route to recording the seventh most sacks in
franchise history. Leading the team in that category twice, Woodley earned
Pro Bowl and All-Pro honors once each, helping the Steelers win three
division titles, two AFC championships, and one Super Bowl in the process.
Nevertheless, considering how well Woodley performed his first few years
in the league, most Steeler fans would likely view his time in the Steel City
as something of a disappointment.

Born in Saginaw, Michigan, on November 3, 1984, LaMarr Dewayne
Woodley attended Saginaw High School, where he teamed up with former
Detroit Lions wide receiver Charles Rogers and former Chicago Bulls point
guard Anthony Roberson to help lead the Trojans to the Michigan Division
II state championship in his sophomore campaign of 2000. Considered a
five-star recruit by Rivals.com, Woodley ultimately elected to enroll at the
University of Michigan, where he spent most of his college career playing
defensive end. Excelling at that post for the Wolverines, Woodley gained
the distinction of being named defensive captain prior to the start of his
senior year, when he finished eighth in the nation with 12 sacks, earning
in the process Big-Ten Defensive Player of the Year, Big-Ten Defensive
Lineman of the Year, and First-Team All-America honors. After also being
named the winner of the Lombardi Award as the nation's best lineman,
Woodley joined the Steelers when they selected him in the second round of
the 2007 NFL Draft, with the 46th overall pick.

Shifted to linebacker upon his arrival in Pittsburgh, Woodley spent his first year in the league playing mostly on special teams, while also serving as the primary backup to outside linebackers James Harrison and Clark Haggans. Yet, even though Woodley saw limited action on the defensive side of the ball as a rookie, he showed a great deal of promise, registering four sacks, 14 tackles, and one forced fumble. Promoted to starting left-outside linebacker following the free-agent departure of Haggans at season's end, Woodley had an excellent 2008 campaign, finishing sec-ond on the team with 11½

LaMarr Woodley's 57 career sacks rank as the seventh-highest total in franchise history.
Courtesy of the Pittsburgh Steelers

sacks and recording 60 tackles (41 solo), one interception, two forced fum-bles, a team-leading four fumble recoveries, and the first touchdown of his career. Continuing his outstanding play during the postseason, Woodley contributed to the Steelers' successful run to the NFL title by becoming the first player in league history to record at least two sacks in three straight playoff games. Performing extremely well once again in 2009, Woodley earned Pro Bowl and Second-Team All-Pro honors by recording 62 tackles (50 solo) and finishing third in the league with 13½ sacks. He followed that up with another solid season, registering 10 sacks and 50 tackles (35 solo) in 2010, while also forcing three fumbles, recovering two others, and picking off two passes, one of which he returned for a touchdown.

However, Woodley began to experience a precipitous decline in pro-duction shortly after he signed a lucrative long-term contract with the Steel-ers following the conclusion of the 2010 campaign. Despite tying James Harrison for the team lead with nine sacks in 2011, Woodley appeared in just 10 games, missing six contests with a hamstring injury. He then com-piled only nine sacks and 74 tackles over the course of the next two seasons, sitting out a total of eight contests during that time due to injury.

While Woodley's lackluster play could be attributed, at least in part, to the injuries he sustained between 2011 and 2013, at least some of the blame must be placed on Woodley himself, who others accused of becoming complacent after he inked his long-term deal with the Steelers. The massive 6'2" linebacker, who weighed close to 265 pounds when he first entered the league, became increasingly overweight during his time in Pittsburgh, exhibiting less passion for the game, while also displaying a poor attitude in the locker room. Criticized by the local media his last few years with the Steelers, Woodley found himself being called out by one of his own teammates prior to the start of the 2013 campaign, with the *Pittsburgh Post-Gazette* quoting an anonymous source as saying, "He was awful (last year). He tells us he works out, but we didn't see it. He wasn't in shape. That has to be a reason why he was always hurt."

Having grown dissatisfied with Woodley, the Steelers chose to release him in a salary cap–related move on March 11, 2014. Only 29 years old at the time, Woodley left Pittsburgh with career totals of 57 sacks, 299 tackles (213 solo), five interceptions, nine forced fumbles, 10 fumble recoveries, and three defensive touchdowns. Following his release by the Steelers, Woodley signed with the Oakland Raiders just two days later. He subsequently appeared in six games with the Raiders in 2014, before joining the Arizona Cardinals the following year. After starting seven of Arizona's first 10 contests in 2015, Woodley suffered a torn pectoral muscle in Week 11 that essentially ended his playing career. Although Woodley did not officially announce his retirement at season's end, he sat out the entire 2016 campaign, after which he told ESPN in February 2017, "I haven't put the (retirement) papers in. With the NFL thing, I tell people all the time, it's got to come to an end one day. Either you can walk away, they are

Woodley recorded at least 10 sacks in three straight seasons.
Courtesy of the Pittsburgh Steelers

going to throw you out, or you're going to get carried out. But you gotta get out, any way you go."

Woodley continued, "It's all about, 'Are you going to be prepared for when it's time to get out?' And I think I've been prepared my whole life for when that day comes. I'm 32 years old. I'm young in life, but they call it old in football. But I'm young in life . . . I'm prepared for it, and I'm excited for this next journey in life."

Woodley then added, "The thing is, when you come into the NFL, you have goals to accomplish. You want to win a Super Bowl. You want to be on a winning team. You want to go out there and set records. I've done all that. . . . So, I have nothing to look back on. I went to two Super Bowls, won one, lost one. Been to the Pro Bowl. I've set records. You know what I'm saying. I've done national things off the field, so I enjoyed it. I have nothing to look back on and say, 'I wish I would have done that.'"

STEELERS CAREER HIGHLIGHTS

Best Season

Woodley performed his best for the Steelers in 2009, when he earned Pro Bowl and All-Pro honors for the only time by scoring one touchdown and recording a career-high 13½ sacks and 62 tackles (50 solo).

Memorable Moments/Greatest Performances

Woodley recorded the first sack of his career in his second game as a pro when he tackled J. P. Losman for an 8-yard loss during a 26–3 win over the Buffalo Bills on September 16, 2007.

Woodley earned GMC Defensive Player of the Week honors in his first career start by recovering a fumble, intercepting a pass, recording a sack, and making three tackles during a 38–17 win over the Houston Texans in the 2008 regular-season opener.

Woodley helped lead the Steelers to a 23–20 overtime victory over the Baltimore Ravens on September 29, 2008, by recording 1½ sacks and eight tackles, forcing one fumble and recovering another, which he returned seven yards for his first career touchdown.

Woodley turned in another outstanding all-around effort on October 19, 2008, when he recorded two sacks, one forced fumble, and one fumble recovery during a 38–10 win over Cincinnati.

Woodley lit the scoreboard for the second time in his career during a 27–17 win over the Minnesota Vikings on October 25, 2009, when he returned a fumble 77 yards for a touchdown.

Woodley contributed to a 23–20 victory over the Baltimore Ravens on December 27, 2009, by recording two sacks, 10 tackles, and one forced fumble, earning in the process AFC Defensive Player of the Week honors.

In addition to sacking Carson Palmer twice during a 23–7 win over the Cincinnati Bengals on December 12, 2010, Woodley scored the last of his three career touchdowns when he returned his interception of a Palmer pass 14 yards for a TD.

Woodley played a key role in the Steelers' successful run to their sixth NFL championship in 2008, recording two sacks of San Diego's Philip Rivers in the divisional round of the playoffs, sacking Baltimore's Joe Flacco twice in the AFC championship game, and getting to Arizona's Kurt Warner twice in Super Bowl XLIII, with his second sack of Warner forcing the game-ending fumble that secured the victory for Pittsburgh.

Notable Achievements

- Scored three defensive touchdowns during career.
- Recorded at least 10 sacks three times.
- Finished third in NFL in: sacks once; fumbles recovered once; and fumble-return yards once.
- Led Steelers in sacks twice.
- Ranks seventh in Steelers history with 57 sacks.
- Three-time division champion (2007, 2008, and 2010).
- Two-time AFC champion (2008 and 2010).
- Super Bowl XLIII champion.
- 2009 Week 16 AFC Defensive Player of the Week.
- 2009 Pro Bowl selection.
- 2009 Second-Team All-Pro selection.

50

— WILLIE PARKER —

Perhaps the most explosive running back in franchise history, Willie Parker accomplished a great deal during his relatively brief stay in Pittsburgh, leading the Steelers in rushing in each of his four seasons as a full-time starter. The fourth-leading rusher in team annals, Parker gained more than 1,000 yards on the ground three straight times, with his outstanding play helping the Steelers win three division titles, two AFC championships, and two Super Bowls. Named team MVP in 2006, when he set a franchise record for the most touchdowns scored in a season, Parker also gained Pro Bowl recognition twice, reaching elite status among NFL running backs even though he entered the league as an undrafted free agent.

Born in Clinton, North Carolina, on November 11, 1980, Willie Everett Parker Jr. attended Clinton High School, where he lettered in football and track. A two-time All-Conference and All-Region honoree for his exceptional play on the gridiron, Parker rushed for 1,329 yards and 20 touchdowns as a junior, before gaining 1,801 yards and scoring another 18 touchdowns in his senior year. Excelling as a sprinter in track as well, Parker qualified for the state championships in both the 100-meter dash and the 4 × 100-meter relay, posting a personal-best time of 11.1 seconds in the first event.

Proving to be much less successful on the playing field after he enrolled at the University of North Carolina, Parker spent most of his college career serving as a backup, with the murder of his best friend during his sophomore campaign contributing to his inability to perform well enough to earn a starting job. Yet, even though Parker failed to distinguish himself during his time at UNC, the Steelers elected to sign him after all 32 teams bypassed him in the 2004 NFL Draft.

Impressing Pittsburgh's coaching staff with his speed and elusiveness during training camp, Parker earned a spot on the Steelers roster, after which he went on to gain 186 yards on only 32 carries while backing up Jerome Bettis and Duce Staley as a rookie in 2004. Promoted to the starting

319

Willie Parker led the Steelers in rushing in each of his four seasons as a full-time starter.
Courtesy of the Pittsburgh Steelers

unit the following year, Parker led the team in rushing for the first of four straight times, amassing 1,202 yards on the ground, while also making 18 receptions for 218 yards and scoring five touchdowns. Continuing his outstanding play in the postseason, Parker helped lead the Steelers to their first NFL title in 26 years by gaining 225 yards during the playoffs, with his 75-yard touchdown run in Super Bowl XL proving to be the pivotal play of a 21–10 victory over the Seattle Seahawks. Performing extremely well once again in 2006, Parker earned Pro Bowl honors by ranking among the league leaders with 1,494 yards rushing, 1,716 yards from scrimmage, 13 rushing touchdowns, and 16 touchdowns, with the last figure setting a new single-season franchise record.

The 5'10", 209-pound Parker, whose tremendous speed earned him the nickname "Fast Willie" during his time in Pittsburgh, had great quickness, excellent moves, and outstanding cutback ability that made him a threat to go the distance any time he touched the ball. A solid receiver as well, Parker amassed more than 200 receiving yards twice, with his 31 receptions and 222 receiving yards in 2006 both representing career-high marks.

Putting together another strong season in 2007, Parker earned his second consecutive trip to the Pro Bowl by finishing fourth in the league with 1,316 yards rushing. However, he suffered a broken right fibula during the first quarter of a 41–21 win over the St. Louis Rams in Week 16, bringing his season to a premature end, and all but ending his days as a dominant runner. Although Parker played well the following year, gaining 791 yards on the ground and scoring five touchdowns despite missing five games with a knee injury, he lacked the same burst he possessed earlier in his career, prompting the Steelers to turn to second-year running back Rashard Mendenhall the following season. Yet, even though Parker assumed a backup role in Pittsburgh in 2009, he remained a consummate professional, assisting in the development of Mendenhall into one of the league's better running backs. Released by the Steelers following the conclusion of the 2009 campaign, Parker ended his time in Pittsburgh with career totals of 5,378 yards rushing, 84 receptions, 697 receiving yards, 24 rushing touchdowns, and 29 total touchdowns scored.

Unable to land a roster spot in Washington following his release by the Steelers,

Parker's 16 touchdowns in 2006 set a new single-season franchise record.
Courtesy of the Pittsburgh Steelers

Parker sat out the 2010 campaign, before signing with the UFL's Virginia Destroyers in 2011. After one year in Virginia, Parker announced his retirement. He subsequently spent the next three seasons serving as an assistant coach for the West Virginia Wesleyan College football team, before becoming the running backs coach at Heritage High School in Wake Forest, North Carolina, in 2015.

CAREER HIGHLIGHTS

Best Season

Parker had easily his finest season for the Steelers in 2006, when he established career-high marks in rushing yards (1,494), receiving yards (222), yards from scrimmage (1,716), rushing touchdowns (13), and touchdowns scored (16), with the last figure representing a single-season franchise record.

Memorable Moments/Greatest Performances

Parker went over 100 yards rushing for the first time in his career in the 2004 regular-season finale, carrying the ball 19 times for 102 yards during a 29–24 win over the Buffalo Bills.

Picking up right where he left off the previous season, Parker earned AFC Offensive Player of the Week honors for his performance during the opening game of the 2005 regular season, when he helped lead the Steelers to a convincing 34–7 victory over the Tennessee Titans by gaining 161 yards on 22 carries and scoring his first career touchdown on an 11-yard run.

Parker contributed to a 27–13 win over the Cincinnati Bengals on October 23, 2005, by carrying the ball 18 times for 131 yards and one touchdown, which came on a 37-yard third-quarter run.

Parker starred during a 41–0 rout of the Cleveland Browns on December 24, 2005, rushing for 130 yards and one touchdown, which he scored on a career-long 80-yard run.

Parker closed out the 2005 campaign in style, gaining 135 yards on 26 carries during a 35–21 win over the Detroit Lions in the regular-season finale.

Parker continued his success in the postseason, helping the Steelers record a 21–10 victory over the Seattle Seahawks in Super Bowl XL by carrying the ball 10 times for 93 yards and one touchdown, which came on a 75-yard run that increased Pittsburgh's lead to 14–3 early in the second half. Looking back at his 75-yard scamper, which remains the longest in Super Bowl history, Parker says, "It is a play that defines me."

Parker earned AFC Offensive Player of the Week honors for his performance during a 38–31 win over the New Orleans Saints on November 12, 2006, when he carried the ball 22 times for 213 yards and two touchdowns, reeling off runs of 72 and 76 yards during the contest.

Parker turned in a similarly impressive performance a few weeks later, leading the Steelers to a 27–7 victory over the Cleveland Browns on December 7 by rushing for a career-high 223 yards and one touchdown.

Parker began the 2008 regular season by rushing for 138 yards and three touchdowns during a 38–17 win over the Houston Texans in Week 1, earning in the process AFC Offensive Player of the Week honors for the third and final time in his career.

Parker also excelled for the Steelers during their 35–24 victory over the San Diego Chargers in the divisional round of the 2008 playoffs, rushing for 146 yards and two touchdowns.

Notable Achievements

- Rushed for more than 1,000 yards three times.
- Surpassed 1,500 yards from scrimmage once (1,716 in 2006).
- Rushed for more than 10 touchdowns once (13 in 2006).
- Averaged more than 4.5 yards per carry twice, topping five yards per carry once (5.8 in 2004).
- Finished third in NFL with 16 touchdowns in 2006.
- Finished fourth in NFL in rushing yards once and rushing touchdowns once.
- Led Steelers in rushing four times.
- Holds Steelers single-season record for most touchdowns scored (16 in 2006).
- Ranks among Steelers career leaders with: 5,378 yards rushing (3rd); 6,075 yards from scrimmage (9th); and 24 rushing touchdowns (10th).
- Three-time division champion (2004, 2007, and 2008).
- Two-time AFC champion (2005 and 2008).
- Two-time Super Bowl champion (XL and XLIII).
- Three-time AFC Offensive Player of the Week.
- 2006 Steelers MVP.
- Two-time Pro Bowl selection (2006 and 2007).

SUMMARY
AND HONORABLE MENTIONS
(THE NEXT 50)

Having identified the 50 greatest players in Pittsburgh Steelers history, the time has come to select the best of the best. Based on the rankings contained in this book, the members of the Steelers' all-time offensive and defensive teams are listed below. Our squads include the top player at each position, with the offense featuring the three best wide receivers; top two running backs, tackles, and guards; and a third-down back. Dermontti Dawson has been inserted at right guard so that both he and Mike Webster may be included on the team. Meanwhile, the defense features two ends, two tackles, two outside linebackers, one middle linebacker, two cornerbacks, a pair of safeties, and a nickel back. Special teams have been accounted for as well, with a placekicker, punter, kickoff returner, and punt returner also being included. The punter and one of the offensive linemen were taken from the list of honorable mentions that will soon follow.

OFFENSE		DEFENSE	
Player	Position	Player	Position
Terry Bradshaw	QB	L. C. Greenwood	LE
Franco Harris	RB	Joe Greene	LT
Jerome Bettis	RB	Ernie Stautner	RT
Le'Veon Bell	3rd-Down RB	Dwight White	RE
Heath Miller	TE	Jack Ham	LOLB
Hines Ward	WR	Jack Lambert	MLB
Antonio Brown	WR	James Harrison	ROLB
Lynn Swann	WR	Rod Woodson	LCB
Jon Kolb	LT	Troy Polamalu	S
Alan Faneca	LG	Donnie Shell	S

OFFENSE		DEFENSE	
Player	Position	Player	Position
Mike Webster	C	Mel Blount	RCB
Dermontti Dawson	RG	Jack Butler	NB
Tunch Ilkin	RT	Bobby Walden	P
Gary Anderson	PK	Rod Woodson	PR
Rod Woodson	KR		

Although I limited my earlier rankings to the top 50 players in Steelers history, many other fine players have worn a Pittsburgh uniform over the years, some of whom narrowly missed making the final cut. Following is a list of those players deserving of an honorable mention. These are the men I deemed worthy of being slotted into positions 51 to 100 in the overall rankings. Where applicable and available, the statistics they compiled during their time in Pittsburgh are included, along with their most Notable Achievements while playing for the Steelers.

51—ROBIN COLE (LB; 1977–1987)

Courtesy of the Pittsburgh Steelers

Steeler Numbers

16½ Sacks, 5 Interceptions, 79 Interception-Return Yards, 14 Fumble Recoveries.

Notable Achievements

- Tied for 10th place in Steelers history with 14 fumble recoveries.
- Five-time division champion (1977, 1978, 1979, 1983, and 1984).
- Two-time AFC champion (1978 and 1979).
- Two-time Super Bowl champion (XIII and XIV).
- 1984 Pro Bowl selection.
- 1984 Second-Team All-Conference selection.

52—KEVIN GREENE (LB; 1993–1995)

Courtesy of George Kitrinos

Steeler Numbers

35½ Sacks, 184 Tackles, 1 Interception, 6 Forced Fumbles, 6 Fumble Recoveries.

Notable Achievements

- Recorded more than 10 sacks twice.
- Led NFL with 14 sacks in 1994.
- Led Steelers in sacks three times.
- Two-time division champion (1994 and 1995).
- 1995 AFC champion.
- 1994 Week 5 AFC Defensive Player of the Week.
- Two-time Pro Bowl selection (1994 and 1995).
- 1994 First-Team All-Pro selection.
- 1994 First-Team All-Conference selection.

53—TUNCH ILKIN (OT; 1980–1992)

Courtesy of the Pittsburgh Steelers

Notable Achievements

- Three-time division champion (1983, 1984, and 1992).
- Two-time Pro Bowl selection (1988 and 1989).
- 1988 First-Team All-Conference selection.
- Named to Steelers' 75th Anniversary Team in 2007.

54—GLEN EDWARDS (DB; 1971–1977)

Courtesy of the Pittsburgh Steelers

Steeler Numbers

25 Interceptions, 652 Interception-Return Yards, 8 Fumble Recoveries, 2 TDs, 941 Punt-Return Yards, 257 Kickoff-Return Yards.

Notable Achievements

- Recorded at least five interceptions three times.
- Surpassed 100 interception-return yards three times.
- Finished second in NFL with 186 interception-return yards in 1973.
- Led Steelers in interceptions twice.
- Ranks fifth in Steelers history in interception-return yards.
- Five-time division champion (1972, 1974, 1975, 1976, and 1977).
- Two-time AFC champion (1974 and 1975).
- Two-time Super Bowl champion (IX and X).
- 1974 Steelers MVP.
- Two-time Pro Bowl selection (1975 and 1976).
- 1976 Second-Team All-Pro selection.
- 1976 First-Team All-Conference selection.
- Two-time Second-Team All-Conference selection (1973 and 1975).

55—SAM DAVIS (G; 1967–1979)

Courtesy of the Pittsburgh Steelers

Notable Achievements

- Seven-time division champion (1972, 1974, 1975, 1976, 1977, 1978, and 1979).
- Four-time AFC champion (1974, 1975, 1978, and 1979).
- Four-time Super Bowl champion (IX, X, XIII, and XIV).
- Named to Steelers' 50th Anniversary Team in 1982.

56—FRANK VARRICHIONE (OT; 1955–1960)

Courtesy of the Pittsburgh Steelers

Notable Achievements

- Four-time Pro Bowl selection (1955, 1957, 1958, and 1960).
- Member of Pittsburgh Steelers Legends Team.

57—KEITH WILLIS (DE; 1982–1991)

Courtesy of the Pittsburgh Steelers

Notable Achievements

- Recorded more than 10 sacks twice.
- Led Steelers in sacks three times.
- Ranks sixth in Steelers history with 59 sacks.
- Two-time division champion (1983 and 1984).

58—DICK HOAK (RB; 1961–1970)

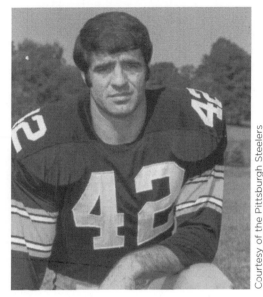

Courtesy of the Pittsburgh Steelers

Career Numbers

3,965 Yards Rushing, 146 Receptions, 1,452 Receiving Yards, 25 Rushing Touchdowns, 33 Touchdowns, 3.5 Rushing Average, 4 Touchdown Passes.

Notable Achievements

- Surpassed 1,000 yards from scrimmage once (1,111 in 1968).
- Finished fourth in NFL with 858 yards rushing in 1968.
- Finished third in NFL with average of 4.9 yards per carry in 1968.
- Ranks among Steelers career leaders in: rushing yardage (7th); rushing touchdowns (9th); and rushing attempts (5th).
- 1968 Pro Bowl selection.
- 1968 First-Team All-Conference selection.
- Member of Pittsburgh Steelers Legends Team.

59—BOBBY LAYNE (QB; 1958–1962)

Courtesy of RMYAuctions.com

Steeler Numbers

9,030 Yards Passing, 66 Touchdown Passes, 81 Interceptions, 49.2 Completion Percentage, 65.5 QBR, 382 Yards Rushing, 8 Rushing Touchdowns.

Notable Achievements

- Passed for more than 2,000 yards once.
- Threw 20 touchdown passes in 1959.
- Finished second in NFL in passing yards once and TD passes once.
- Finished third in NFL in pass completions once and passer rating once.
- Ranks among Steelers career leaders in passing yards (6th) and touchdown passes (5th).
- Two-time Pro Bowl selection (1958 and 1959).
- Two-time Second-Team All-Pro selection (1958 and 1959).
- 1958 First-Team All-Conference selection.
- Member of Pittsburgh Steelers Legends Team.

60—DAVID DECASTRO (G; 2012–2018)

Courtesy of Jeffrey Beall

Notable Achievements

- Three-time division champion (2014, 2016 and 2017).
- Four-time Pro Bowl selection (2015, 2016, 2017, and 2018).
- Two-time First-Team All-Pro selection (2015 and 2017).
- 2016 Second-Team All-Pro selection.

61—LYNN CHANDNOIS (RB/PR/KR: 1950–1956)

Courtesy of the Pittsburgh Steelers

Career Numbers

1,934 Yards Rushing, 162 Receptions, 2,012 Receiving Yards, 16 Rushing Touchdowns, 7 TD Receptions, 3.3 Rushing Average, 312 Punt-Return Yards, 2,720 Kickoff-Return Yards, 6,978 All-Purpose Yards, 3 Kickoff-Return TDs.

Notable Achievements

- Surpassed 700 yards from scrimmage three times.
- Surpassed 1,000 all-purpose yards three times.
- Led NFL with 1,593 all-purpose yards in 1953.
- Led NFL with average of 35.2 yards per kickoff return in 1952.
- Finished third in NFL in: all-purpose yards once; kickoff-return yards twice; and kickoff- and punt-return yards once.
- Ranks fourth in Steelers history in total return yardage.
- Two-time Pro Bowl selection (1952 and 1953).

62—BOBBY WALDEN (P; 1968–1977)

Courtesy of the Pittsburgh Steelers

Steeler Numbers

Averaged 41.1 yards per punt; Career long: 72 yards.

Notable Achievements

- Averaged better than 42 yards per punt four times.
- Recorded longest punt in NFL in 1972 (72 yards).
- Finished second in NFL with 45.2 punting average in 1970.
- Finished third in NFL in punting average three times.
- Holds Steelers career record for most yards punting (29,462).
- Five-time division champion (1972, 1974, 1975, 1976, and 1977).
- Two-time AFC champion (1974 and 1975).
- Two-time Super Bowl champion (IX and X).
- 1969 Pro Bowl selection.
- 1975 Second-Team All-Conference selection.
- Named to Steelers' 75th Anniversary Team in 2007.

63—ROY JEFFERSON (WR/PR; 1965–1969)

Courtesy of SportsMemorabilia.com

Steeler Numbers

199 Receptions, 3,671 Receiving Yards, 29 Touchdown Receptions, 436 Punt-Return Yards, 1 Punt-Return TD, 4,314 All-Purpose Yards.

Notable Achievements

- Surpassed 50 receptions twice.
- Surpassed 1,000 receiving yards twice.
- Scored more than 10 touchdowns once.
- Averaged more than 20 yards per reception twice.
- Led NFL with 1,074 receiving yards in 1968.
- Finished second in NFL in: receptions once; receiving yards once; and TD receptions once.
- 1969 Steelers MVP.
- Two-time Pro Bowl selection (1968 and 1969).
- 1969 First-Team All-Pro selection.
- 1968 Second-Team All-Pro selection.
- Two-time First-Team All-Conference selection (1968 and 1969).
- Member of Pittsburgh Steelers Legends Team.

64—LARRY BROWN (OT/TE; 1971–1984)

Courtesy of the Pittsburgh Steelers

Career Numbers

48 Receptions, 636 Receiving Yards, 5 Touchdown Receptions.

Notable Achievements

- Nine-time division champion (1972, 1974, 1975, 1976, 1977, 1978, 1979, 1983, and 1984).
- Four-time AFC champion (1974, 1975, 1978, and 1979).
- Four-time Super Bowl champion (IX, X, XIII, and XIV).
- 1982 Pro Bowl selection.
- Named to Steelers' 75th Anniversary Team in 2007.

65—SANTONIO HOLMES (WR/PR; 2006–2009)

Courtesy of the Pittsburgh Steelers

Steeler Numbers

235 Receptions, 3,835 Receiving Yards, 20 Touchdown Receptions, 496 Punt-Return Yards, 1 Punt-Return TD, 4,812 All-Purpose Yards.

Notable Achievements

- Surpassed 50 receptions three times, topping 70 catches once.
- Surpassed 1,000 receiving yards once (1,248 in 2009).
- Surpassed 1,000 all-purpose yards three times.
- Led NFL with average of 18.1 yards per reception in 2007.
- Led Steelers in receiving yards twice.
- Two-time division champion (2007 and 2008).
- 2008 AFC champion.
- Super Bowl XLIII champion.
- Super Bowl XLIII MVP.

66—BARRY FOSTER (RB: 1990–1994)

Courtesy of the Pittsburgh Steelers

Career Numbers

3,943 Yards Rushing, 93 Receptions, 804 Receiving Yards, 26 Rushing Touchdowns, 28 Touchdowns, 4.3 Rushing Average.

Notable Achievements

- Rushed for more than 1,000 yards once.
- Surpassed 2,000 yards from scrimmage once.
- Rushed for more than 10 touchdowns once (11 in 1992).
- Averaged more than five yards per carry twice.
- Finished second in NFL with 1,690 yards rushing in 1992.
- Finished third in NFL with 2,034 yards from scrimmage in 1992.
- Holds Steelers single-season rushing record (1,690 yards in 1992).
- Ranks among Steelers career leaders in: rushing yardage (8th); rushing touchdowns (tied—7th); and rushing attempts (9th).
- Two-time division champion (1992 and 1994).
- Two-time AFC Offensive Player of the Week.
- 1992 Steelers MVP.
- Two-time Pro Bowl selection (1992 and 1993).
- 1992 First-Team All-Pro selection.
- 1992 First-Team All-Conference selection.

67—ROY GERELA (PK; 1971–1978)

Courtesy of Steel City Collectibles

Steeler Numbers

146 Field Goals Made, 227 Field Goal Attempts, 64.3 Field Goal Percentage, 731 Points Scored.

Notable Achievements

- Scored more than 100 points twice.
- Successfully converted more than 80 percent of field goal attempts once.
- Finished second in NFL in: points scored twice; field goals made twice; and field goal percentage once.
- Ranks third in Steelers history in field goals made and points scored.
- Six-time division champion (1972, 1974, 1975, 1976, 1977, and 1978).
- Three-time AFC champion (1974, 1975, and 1978).
- Three-time Super Bowl champion (IX, X, and XIII).
- Two-time Pro Bowl selection (1972 and 1974).
- Three-time Second-Team All-Pro selection (1972, 1973, and 1974).
- Two-time First-Team All-Conference selection (1972 and 1974).
- 1975 Second-Team All-Conference selection.
- Named to Steelers' 50th Anniversary Team in 1982.

68—BEN MCGEE (DE; 1964–1972)

Courtesy of the Pittsburgh Steelers

Notable Achievements

- Scored one defensive touchdown.
- 1972 division champion.
- Two-time Pro Bowl selection (1966 and 1968).
- 1966 First-Team All-Conference selection.
- Member of Pittsburgh Steelers Legends Team.

69—LARRY FOOTE (LB; 2002–2008, 2010–2013)

Courtesy of the Pittsburgh Steelers

Steeler Numbers

21 Sacks, 620 Tackles, 3 Interceptions, 7 Fumble Recoveries, 1 Safety.

Notable Achievements

- Recorded more than 100 tackles twice.
- Led Steelers in tackles once.
- Ranks 12th in Steelers history in tackles.
- Five-time division champion (2002, 2004, 2007, 2008, and 2010).
- Three-time AFC champion (2005, 2008, and 2010).
- Two-time Super Bowl champion (XL and XLIII).

70—KORDELL STEWART (QB; 1995–2002)

Courtesy of the Pittsburgh Steelers

Steeler Numbers

13,328 Yards Passing, 70 Touchdown Passes, 72 Interceptions, 56.5 Completion Percentage, 72.3 QBR, 2,561 Yards Rushing, 35 Rushing Touchdowns, 41 Receptions, 658 Receiving Yards, 5 TD Catches.

Notable Achievements

- Passed for more than 3,000 yards twice.
- Threw 21 touchdown passes in 1997.
- Completed more than 60 percent of passes twice.
- Ran for 537 yards in 2001.
- Led NFL quarterbacks with five game-winning drives in 1997.
- Finished third in NFL with 11 rushing touchdowns in 1997.
- Ranks among Steelers career leaders in: passing yards (3rd); touchdown passes (3rd); and rushing touchdowns (tied—3rd).
- Five-time division champion (1995, 1996, 1997, 2001, and 2002).
- 1995 AFC champion.
- 2001 Steelers Co-MVP.
- 2001 Pro Bowl selection.

71—BILL MCPEAK (DE; 1949–1957)

Courtesy of the Pittsburgh Steelers

Notable Achievements

- Recorded three safeties.
- Three-time Pro Bowl selection (1952, 1953, and 1956).
- 1953 Second-Team All-Pro selection.
- Member of Pittsburgh Steelers Legends Team.

72—PLAXICO BURRESS (WR; 2000–2004, 2012)

Courtesy of the Pittsburgh Steelers

Steeler Numbers

264 Receptions, 4,206 Receiving Yards, 23 Touchdown Receptions.

Notable Achievements

- Surpassed 60 receptions three times, topping 70 catches once.
- Surpassed 1,000 receiving yards twice.
- Finished second in NFL with average of 19.9 yards per catch in 2004.
- Finished fifth in NFL with 1,325 receiving yards in 2002.
- Led Steelers in receiving yards once.
- Three-time division champion (2001, 2002, and 2004).

73—MIKE MERRIWEATHER (LB; 1982–1987)

Courtesy of the Pittsburgh Steelers

Steeler Numbers

31 Sacks, 11 Interceptions, 140 Interception-Return Yards, 9 Fumble Recoveries, 2 Touchdowns.

Notable Achievements

- Finished fifth in NFL with 15 sacks in 1984.
- Led Steelers in sacks twice.
- Two-time division champion (1983 and 1984).
- Three-time AFC Defensive Player of the Week.
- 1987 Steelers MVP.
- Three-time Pro Bowl selection (1984, 1985, and 1986).
- 1984 First-Team All-Conference selection.
- Two-time Second-Team All-Conference selection (1985 and 1987).

74—YANCEY THIGPEN (WR; 1992–1997)

Courtesy of the Pittsburgh Steelers

Steeler Numbers

222 Receptions, 3,651 Receiving Yards, 21 Touchdown Receptions.

Notable Achievements

- Surpassed 75 receptions twice.
- Surpassed 1,000 receiving yards twice.
- Finished second in NFL with average of 17.7 yards per catch in 1997.
- Finished third in NFL with 1,398 receiving yards in 1997.
- Led Steelers in receptions and receiving yards twice each.
- Five-time division champion (1992, 1994, 1995, 1996, and 1997).
- 1995 AFC champion.
- Two-time Pro Bowl selection (1995 and 1997).
- 1997 Second-Team All-Pro selection.
- 1997 First-Team All-Conference selection.
- 1995 Second-Team All-Conference selection.

75—CAMERON HEYWARD (DE/DT; 2011–2018)

Courtesy of Jeffrey Beall

Career Numbers

45 Sacks, 317 Tackles (209 solo).

Notable Achievements

- Has surpassed 10 sacks once (12 in 2017).
- Has led Steelers in sacks three times.
- Ranks 10th in Steelers history in sacks.
- Three-time division champion (2014, 2016, and 2017).
- Two-time AFC Defensive Player of the Week.
- Two-time Pro Bowl selection (2017 and 2018).
- 2017 First-Team All-Pro selection.

76—JERRY SHIPKEY (LB/FB; 1948–1952)

Courtesy of the Pittsburgh Steelers

Steeler Numbers

310 Yards Rushing, 16 Rushing Touchdowns, 2.8 Rushing Average, 12 Receptions, 138 Receiving Yards, 13 Interceptions, 238 Interception-Return Yards, 1 TD Interception, 9 Fumble Recoveries.

Notable Achievements

- Finished second in NFL with eight rushing touchdowns in 1948.
- Recorded six interceptions and 113 interception-return yards in 1951.
- Three-time Pro Bowl selection (1950, 1951, and 1952).
- Two-time First-Team All-Pro selection (1951 and 1952).
- Member of Pittsburgh Steelers Legends Team.

77—BILL WALSH (C; 1949–1954)

Courtesy of SportsMemorabilia.com

Notable Achievements

- Two-time Pro Bowl selection (1950 and 1951).
- 1954 First-Team All-Pro selection.

78—MARVEL SMITH (OT; 2000–2008)

Courtesy of Michael Rooney

Notable Achievements

- Five-time division champion (2001, 2002, 2004, 2007, and 2008).
- Two-time AFC champion (2005 and 2008).
- Two-time Super Bowl champion (XL and XLIII).
- 2004 Pro Bowl selection.

79—MIKE SANDUSKY (G; 1957–1965)

Courtesy of SportsMemorabilia.com

Notable Achievements

- 1960 Pro Bowl selection.
- 1962 Second-Team All-Pro selection.
- Member of Pittsburgh Steelers Legends Team.

80—DARREN PERRY (DB; 1992–1998)

Courtesy of the Pittsburgh Steelers

Steeler Numbers

32 Interceptions, 574 Interception-Return Yards, 515 Tackles, 2½ Sacks, 8 Fumble Recoveries, 1 Touchdown.

Notable Achievements

- Recorded at least five interceptions three times.
- Surpassed 100 interception-return yards twice.
- Finished fourth in NFL with seven interceptions in 1994.
- Led Steelers in interceptions three times.
- Ranks among Steelers career leaders in interceptions (tied—7th) and interception-return yards (6th).
- Five-time division champion (1992, 1994, 1995, 1996, and 1997).
- 1995 AFC champion.
- Member of 1992 NFL All-Rookie Team.
- 1994 Second-Team All-Conference selection.

81—GEORGE TARASOVIC
(DE/LB; 1952–1953, 1956–1963)

Courtesy of the Pittsburgh Steelers

Steeler Numbers

11 Interceptions, 160 Interception-Return Yards, 14 Fumble Recoveries.

Notable Achievements

- Scored one defensive touchdown.
- Recorded four interceptions in 1962.
- Led NFL with five fumble recoveries and 57 fumble-return yards in 1959.
- Ranks among Steelers career leaders in fumble recoveries (tied—10th).
- 1959 Second-Team All-Pro selection.

82—JOHN REGER (LB; 1955–1963)

Courtesy of the Pittsburgh Steelers

Steeler Numbers

9 Interceptions, 98 Interception-Return Yards, 17 Fumble Recoveries.

Notable Achievements

- Scored one defensive touchdown.
- Recovered five fumbles twice.
- Finished third in NFL in fumble recoveries twice.
- Ranks among Steelers career leaders in fumble recoveries (tied—5th).
- Three-time Pro Bowl selection (1959, 1960, and 1961).
- 1959 Second-Team All-Pro selection.
- Three-time First-Team All-Conference selection (1959, 1960, and 1961).

83—BENNIE CUNNINGHAM (TE; 1976–1985)

Courtesy of the Pittsburgh Steelers

Career Numbers

202 Receptions, 2,879 Receiving Yards, 20 Touchdown Receptions.

Notable Achievements

- Surpassed 500 receiving yards twice.
- Six-time division champion (1976, 1977, 1978, 1979, 1983, and 1984).
- Two-time AFC champion (1978 and 1979).
- Two-time Super Bowl champion (XIII and XIV).
- Named to Steelers' 75th Anniversary Team in 2007.

84—GARY BALLMAN (WR/KR; 1962–1966)

Courtesy of the Pittsburgh Steelers

Steeler Numbers

154 Receptions, 2,949 Receiving Yards, 22 TD Receptions, 155 Rushing Yards, 3 Rushing Touchdowns, 1,711 Kickoff-Return Yards, 4,815 All-Purpose Yards, 1 Kickoff-Return TD.

Notable Achievements

- Surpassed 800 receiving yards twice, topping 900 yards once.
- Surpassed 1,000 all-purpose yards four times.
- Averaged more than 20 yards per reception once (21.5 in 1965).
- Finished second in NFL in average yards per reception once and average yards per kickoff return once.
- Ranks eighth in Steelers history in kickoff-return yardage.
- Two-time Pro Bowl selection (1964 and 1965).
- 1964 First-Team All-Conference selection.

85—BRYAN HINKLE (LB; 1982–1993)

Courtesy of the Pittsburgh Steelers

Career Numbers

15 Interceptions, 205 Interception-Return Yards, 22½ Sacks, 11 Fumble Recoveries, 3 Touchdowns.

Notable Achievements

- Recorded at least five sacks in a season twice.
- Three-time division champion (1983, 1984, and 1992).
- 1986 Steelers MVP.
- 1986 Second-Team All-Conference selection.

86—JOHN NISBY (G; 1957–1961)

Courtesy of the Pittsburgh Steelers

Notable Achievements

- Two-time Pro Bowl selection (1959 and 1961).
- 1961 NEA Second-Team All-Pro selection.
- Two-time First-Team All-Conference selection (1959 and 1961).

87—JEFF HARTINGS (C; 2001–2006)

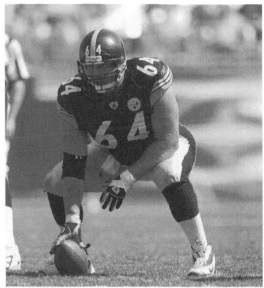

Courtesy of the Pittsburgh Steelers

Notable Achievements

- Three-time division champion (2001, 2002, and 2004).
- 2005 AFC champion.
- Super Bowl XL champion.
- Two-time Pro Bowl selection (2004 and 2005).
- 2004 First-Team All-Pro selection.
- 2001 Second-Team All-Pro selection.

88—AARON SMITH (DE; 1999–2011)

Courtesy of the Pittsburgh Steelers

Career Numbers

44 Sacks, 452 Tackles, 1 Interception, 7 Forced Fumbles, 9 Fumble Recoveries.

Notable Achievements

- Recorded eight sacks in a season twice.
- Recorded 70 tackles in 2002.
- Led Steelers with eight sacks in 2004.
- Ranks 11th in Steelers history in sacks.
- Six-time division champion (2001, 2002, 2004, 2007, 2008, and 2010).
- Three-time AFC champion (2005, 2008, and 2010).
- Two-time Super Bowl champion (XL and XLIII).
- 2008 Week 15 AFC Defensive Player of the Week.
- 2004 Pro Bowl selection.
- *Sports Illustrated* 2000s All-Decade Team.

89—RASHARD MENDENHALL (RB; 2008–2012)

Courtesy of the Pittsburgh Steelers

Steeler Numbers

3,549 Yards Rushing, 77 Receptions, 661 Receiving Yards, 29 Rushing Touchdowns, 31 Touchdowns, 4.1 Rushing Average.

Notable Achievements

- Rushed for more than 1,000 yards twice.
- Surpassed 1,000 yards from scrimmage three times.
- Finished second in NFL with 13 rushing touchdowns in 2010.
- Ranks among Steelers career leaders in: rushing yardage (10th); rushing touchdowns (6th); and rushing attempts (11th).
- Two-time division champion (2008 and 2010).
- Two-time AFC champion (2008 and 2010).
- Super Bowl XLIII champion.
- Two-time AFC Offensive Player of the Week.

90—BRUCE VAN DYKE (G; 1967–1973)

Courtesy of the Pittsburgh Steelers

Notable Achievements

- 1972 division champion.
- 1972 Week 8 Offensive Player of the Week.
- 1973 Pro Bowl selection.
- Two-time Second-Team All-Conference selection (1972 and 1973).

91—RON SHANKLIN (WR; 1970–1974)

Courtesy of the Pittsburgh Steelers

Steeler Numbers

166 Receptions, 3,047 Receiving Yards, 24 TD Receptions.

Notable Achievements

- Averaged more than 20 yards per reception twice.
- Led NFL with average of 23.7 yards per reception in 1973.
- Finished third in NFL with 10 touchdown receptions in 1973.
- Finished sixth in NFL with 49 receptions in 1971.
- Two-time division champion (1972 and 1974).
- 1974 AFC champion.
- Super Bowl IX champion.
- 1973 Steelers MVP.
- 1973 Pro Bowl selection.
- 1973 First-Team All-Conference selection.

92—RYAN SHAZIER (LB; 2014–2017)

Courtesy of the Pittsburgh Steelers

Career Numbers

303 Tackles (205 solo), 7 Interceptions, 7 Sacks, 7 Forced Fumbles.

Notable Achievements

- Surpassed 80 tackles three times.
- Three-time division champion (2014, 2016, and 2017).
- Two-time Pro Bowl selection (2016 and 2017).

93—GERRY MULLINS (G/OT; 1971–1979)

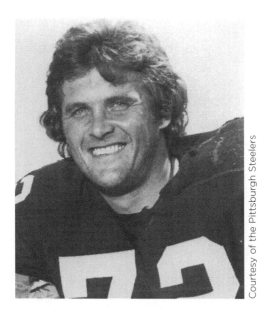

Courtesy of the Pittsburgh Steelers

Notable Achievements

- Scored three touchdowns.
- Seven-time division champion (1972, 1974, 1975, 1976, 1977, 1978, and 1979).
- Four-time AFC champion (1974, 1975, 1978, and 1979).
- Four-time Super Bowl champion (IX, X, XIII, and XIV).
- Named to Steelers' 50th Anniversary Team in 1982.

94—MIKE WALLACE (WR; 2009–2012)

Courtesy of the Pittsburgh Steelers

Steeler Numbers

235 Receptions, 4,042 Receiving Yards, 32 Touchdown Receptions, 151 Rushing Yards, 4,193 Yards from scrimmage.

Notable Achievements

- Surpassed 60 receptions three times, topping 70 catches once.
- Surpassed 1,000 receiving yards twice.
- Made 10 touchdown receptions in 2010.
- Led NFL with average of 19.4 yards per reception in 2009.
- Finished second in NFL with average of 21 yards per reception in 2010.
- Led Steelers in receptions twice and receiving yards three times.
- Holds Steelers record for longest TD reception (95 yards vs. Arizona on October 23, 2011).
- 2010 division champion.
- 2010 AFC champion.
- 2011 Pro Bowl selection.

95—MYRON POTTIOS (LB; 1961–1965)

Courtesy of the Pittsburgh Steelers

Steeler Numbers

7 Interceptions, 126 Interception-Return Yards.

Notable Achievements

- Three-time Pro Bowl selection (1961, 1963, and 1964).
- 1963 Second-Team All-Pro selection.
- 1963 First-Team All-Conference selection.
- Member of Pittsburgh Steelers Legends Team.

96—MAX STARKS (OT; 2004–2012)

Courtesy of Keith Allison

Notable Achievements

- Four-time division champion (2004, 2007, 2008, and 2010).
- Three-time AFC champion (2005, 2008, and 2010).
- Two-time Super Bowl champion (XL and XLIII).

97—STEVE FURNESS (DT; 1972–1980)

Courtesy of PristineAuction.com

Steeler Numbers

32 Sacks.

Notable Achievements

- Led Steelers with 8½ sacks in 1977.
- Seven-time division champion (1972, 1974, 1975, 1976, 1977, 1978, and 1979).
- Four-time AFC champion (1974, 1975, 1978, and 1979).
- Four-time Super Bowl champion (IX, X, XIII, and XIV).

98—DAVID LITTLE (LB; 1981–1992)

Courtesy of the Pittsburgh Steelers

Career Numbers

10 Interceptions, 69 Interception-Return Yards, 9 Sacks, 11 Fumble Recoveries.

Notable Achievements

- Three-time division champion (1983, 1984, and 1992).
- 1992 Week 13 AFC Defensive Player of the Week.
- 1988 Steelers Co-MVP.
- 1990 Pro Bowl selection.
- 1990 First-Team All-Conference selection.

99—IKE TAYLOR (DB/KR; 2003–2014)

Courtesy of Jeffrey Beall

Career Numbers

14 Interceptions, 151 Interception-Return Yards, 636 Tackles, 3 Sacks, 5 Fumble Recoveries, 1 Touchdown, 1,146 Kickoff-Return Yards.

Notable Achievements

- Recorded more than 80 tackles twice.
- Ranks 11th in Steelers history in tackles.
- Five-time division champion (2004, 2007, 2008, 2010, and 2014).
- Three-time AFC champion (2005, 2008, and 2010).
- Two-time Super Bowl champion (XL and XLIII).
- Two-time AFC Defensive Player of the Week.

100—JOHN "FRENCHY" FUQUA (RB; 1970–1976)

Courtesy of the Pittsburgh Steelers

Steeler Numbers

2,942 Yards Rushing, 132 Receptions, 1,236 Receiving Yards, 21 Rushing Touchdowns, 24 Touchdowns, 4.2 Rushing Average.

Notable Achievements

- Surpassed 1,000 yards from scrimmage once.
- Finished second in NFL with average of five yards per carry in 1970.
- Finished fifth in NFL with seven rushing touchdowns in 1970.
- Finished sixth in NFL with 49 receptions in 1971.
- Led Steelers in rushing twice.
- Four-time division champion (1972, 1974, 1975, and 1976).
- Two-time AFC champion (1974 and 1975).
- Two-time Super Bowl champion (IX and X).

— GLOSSARY —

ABBREVIATIONS AND STATISTICAL TERMS

C: Center.

COMP %: Completion percentage. The number of successfully completed passes divided by the number of passes attempted.

FS: Free Safety.

INTS: Interceptions. Passes thrown by the quarterback that are caught by a member of the opposing team's defense.

KR: Kickoff returner.

LCB: Left cornerback.

LE: Left end.

LG: Left guard.

LOLB: Left-outside linebacker.

LT: Left tackle.

MLB: Middle linebacker.

NB: Nickel back.

NT: Nose tackle.

P: Punter.

PK: Placekicker.

PR: Punt returner.

QB: Quarterback.

QBR: Quarterback Rating.

RB: Running back.

RCB: Right cornerback.

RE: Right end.

REC: Receptions.

REC YD: Receiving yards.

RG: Right guard.

ROLB: Right-outside linebacker.

RT: Right tackle.

RUSH TD: Rushing touchdowns.

RUSH YD: Rushing yards.

S: Safety.

SS: Strong Safety.

ST: Special teams.

TD: Touchdowns.

TD PASSES: Touchdown passes.

TD RECS: Touchdown receptions.

TE: Tight end.

WR: Wide receiver.

— BIBLIOGRAPHY —

BOOKS

Jones, Danny. *More Distant Memories: Pro Football's Best Ever Players of the 50's, 60's, and 70's*. Bloomington, IN: AuthorHouse, 2006.

Loede, Matt. *100 Things Steelers Fans Should Know & Do Before They Die*. New York: Triumph Books, 2013.

Mendelson, Abby, and David Aretha. *The Steelers Experience: A Year-By-Year Chronicle of the Pittsburgh Steelers*. Minneapolis, MN: MVP Books, 2014.

Wexell, Jim, *Pittsburgh Steelers: Men of Steel*. Champaign, IL: Sports Publishing LLC, 2006.

VIDEOS

Greatest Ever: NFL Dream Team. Polygram Video, 1996.

WEBSITES

Biographies, online at Hickoksports.com
(hickoksports.com/hickoksports/biograph)

Biography from Answers.com
(answers.com)

Biography from Jockbio.com
(jockbio.com)

CapitalNewYork.com
(capitalnewyork.com)

CBSNews.com
(cbsnews.com)

ESPN.com
(sports.espn.go.com)

Hall of Famers, online at profootballhof.com
(profootballhof.com/hof/member)

Inductees from LASportsHall.com
(lasportshall.com)

LATimes.com
(articles.latimes.com)

Newsday.com
(newsday.com)

NYDailyNews.com
(nydailynews.com/new-york)

NYTimes.com
(nytimes.com)

Pro Football Talk from nbcsports.com
(profootballtalk.nbcsports.com)

SpTimes.com
(sptimes.com)

StarLedger.com
(starledger.com)

Steelers.com
(steelers.com)

SunSentinel.com
(articles.sun-sentinel.com)

The Players, online at Profootballreference.com
(pro-football-reference.com/players)

YouTube.com
(youtube.com)